NEW INTERNATIONAL BIBLICAL COMMENTARY

Old Testament Editors,
Robert L. Hubbard Jr.
Robert K. Johnston

EXODUS

Old Testament Series

NEW INTERNATIONAL BIBLICAL COMMENTARY

EXODUS

JAMES K. BRUCKNER

Based on the New International Version

Exodus
New International Biblical Commentary
© 2008 by Hendrickson Publishers, Inc.
P. O. Box 3473
Peabody, Massachusetts 01961-3473

First published jointly, 2008, in the United States by Hendrickson
Publishers and in the United Kingdom by the Paternoster Press.

Paternoster is an imprint of Authentic Media,
9 Holdom Avenue, Bletchley, Milton Keynes, MK1 1QR, UK
1820 Jet Stream Drive, Colorado Springs, CO 80921, USA
OM Authentic Media, Medchal Road, Jeedimetla Village,
Secunderabad 500 055, A.P., India
www.authenticmedia.co.uk
Authentic Media is a division of IBS-STL UK, a company limited by
guarantee (registered charity no. 270162).

Printed in the United States of America

First printing — March 2008

Library of Congress Cataloging-in-Publication Data

Bruckner, James K.
    Exodus / James K. Bruckner.
        p. cm.—(New International biblical commentary.
  Old Testament series ; 2)
    Includes bibliographical references and indexes.
    ISBN-13: 978-1-56563-212-7 (alk. paper)
    1. Bible. O.T. Exodus—Commentaries. I. Title.
  BS1245.53.B78 2008
  222'.1207—dc22
                     2007037388

ISBN 978-1-56563-212-7 (U.S. softcover)

British Library Cataloguing in Publication Data
A catalogue record for this book is available
from the British Library.

ISBN 978-1-85364-723-9 (U.K. softcover)

For Rolland and Janis
So that the Lord's "name might be proclaimed in all the earth."
(Exodus 9:16)

Table of Contents

Foreword xi

Preface xiii

Abbreviations... xv

Introduction 1
§1   The Need for Deliverance (Exod. 1:1–22) 19
§2   Moses' Beginnings (Exod. 2:1–10)........................ 26
§3   Moses Encounters Violence (Exod. 2:11–25) 31
§4   Yahweh Calls Moses (Exod. 3:1–22) 39
§5   God Prepares Moses (Exod. 4:1–31) 49
§6   Oppression Increases (Exod. 5:1–6:1).................... 57
§7   Yahweh's Promises (Exod. 6:2–30) 64
§8   The Plagues Begin (Exod. 7:1–25) 70
§9   Frogs, Gnats, and Flies (Exod. 8:1–32) 79
§10 Dead Livestock, Boils, and a Storm of Hail with
     Lightning (Exod. 9:1–35)............................... 86
§11 God Hardens Pharaoh's Heart: Locusts and Darkness
     (Exod. 10:1–29) 95
§12 Final Warning (Exod. 11:1–10) 104
§13 Passed Over or Destroyed? (Exod. 12:1–27) 108
§14 The Devastating Blow and the Beginning of the Exit
     (Exod. 12:28–51) 117
§15 Unleavened Bread and Firstborn Redemption,
     Revisited (Exod. 13:1–22) 122
§16 Crossing the Sea (Exod. 14:1–31)...................... 128
§17 Singing at the Sea (Exod. 15:1–21)..................... 137
§18 Journey from the Sea into the Wilderness
     (Exod. 15:22–27) 144
§19 Leadership, Learning, Manna, Meat, and the First
     Sabbath Rest (Exod. 16:1–36) 148
§20 Quarreling, Water from a Rock, Amalekite Attack, and
     a Banner (Exod. 17:1–16)............................. 156
§21 Father Jethro and God's Just Justice (Exod. 18:1–27)....... 163

§22 Meeting God at Sinai (Exod. 19:1–25)....................170

§23 Ten Commandments: First through Fifth (Exod. 20:1–12)..180

§24 Ten Commandments: Sixth through Tenth
     (Exod. 20:13–26) 188

§25 Covenant Laws I: Debt Slaves and Capital Offenses
     (Exod. 21:1–17) 197

§26 Covenant Laws II: Personal Injury, Bulls, and Oxen
     (Exod. 21:18–36) 203

§27 Covenant Laws III: Property Rights, Capital Offenses,
     Using Power, Relationship to God (Exod. 22:1–31) 209

§28 Covenant Laws IV: Corruption, Poverty, Three
     Festivals, God's Promises (Exod. 23:1–33) 216

§29 The Covenant Is Received and Sealed (Exod. 24:1–18).....224

§30 Introduction to the Tabernacle (Exod. 25–40)............230

§31 I Will Dwell Among Them: Materials, Ark, Table, and
     Lampstand (Exod. 25:1–40) 236

§32 Instructions for Making the Tent of Meeting
     (Exod. 26:1–37) 245

§33 Instructions: Altar, Courtyard, Lamp Oil (Exod. 27:1–21)..251

§34 Instructions: Priestly Garments (Exod. 28:1–43) 255

§35 Instructions: Aaron's Consecration, the Altar
     Consecration, and Daily Sacrifices (Exod. 29:1–46).......262

§36 Instructions: Incense Altar, Money, Water,
     Anointing Oil, and Incense (Exod. 30:1–38) 269

§37 Instructions: Bezalel and Sabbath (Exod. 31:1–18)........273

§38 Crisis at Sinai: The Golden Calf (Exod. 32–34) 277

§39 The Golden Calf (Exod. 32:1–35)........................281

§40 Crisis: Will Yahweh Go with Them? (Exod. 33:1–23).......293

§41 Crisis Resolved: The Name of the Lord (Exod. 34:1–9).....300

§42 Crisis Resolved: Yahweh Renews the Covenant
     (Exod. 34:10–35) 309

§43 Building Yahweh's Dwelling Place: Willing Hearts
     (Exod. 35:1–35) 314

§44 Creating a Space for God: Overabundant Donations
     and Making the Tabernacle Tent (Exod. 36:1–38) 318

§45 Building: Ark, Table, Lampstand, Incense Altar, and
     Anointing Oil (Exod. 37:1–29) 320

§46 Building: Altar, Basin, and Courtyard (Exod. 38:1–31) 322

§47 Making Priestly Garments (Exod. 39:1–43) 325

§48 The Presence of the Lord in the Midst of the Camp
     (Exod. 40:1–38) 327

For Further Reading 333

Subject Index 339

Scripture Index 343

Foreword
New International Biblical Commentary

As an ancient document, the Old Testament often seems something quite foreign to modern men and women. Opening its pages may feel, to the modern reader, like traversing a kind of literary time warp into a whole other world. In that world sisters and brothers marry, long hair mysteriously makes men super-human, and temple altars daily smell of savory burning flesh and sweet incense. There, desert bushes burn but leave no ashes, water gushes from rocks, and cities fall because people march around them. A different world, indeed!

Even God, the Old Testament's main character, seems a stranger compared to his more familiar New Testament counter-part. Sometimes the divine is portrayed as a loving father and faithful friend, someone who rescues people from their greatest dangers or generously rewards them for heroic deeds. At other times, however, God resembles more a cruel despot, one furious at human failures, raving against enemies, and bloodthirsty for re-venge. Thus, skittish about the Old Testament's diverse portrayal of God, some readers carefully select which portions of the text to study, or they avoid the Old Testament altogether.

The purpose of this commentary series is to help readers navigate this strange and sometimes forbidding literary and spiritual terrain. Its goal is to break down the barriers between the ancient and modern worlds so that the power and meaning of these biblical texts become transparent to contemporary readers. How is this to be done? And what sets this series apart from others currently on the market?

This commentary series will bypass several popular ap-proaches to biblical interpretation. It will not follow a *precritical* approach that interprets the text without reference to recent scholarly conversations. Such a commentary contents itself with offering little more than a paraphrase of the text with occasional supplements from archaeology, word studies, and classical theol-ogy. It mistakenly believes that there have been few insights into the Bible since Calvin or Luther. Nor will this series pursue an *anticritical* approach whose preoccupation is to defend the Bible against its detractors, especially scholarly ones. Such a commentary has little space left to move beyond showing why the Bible's critics are wrong to explaining what the biblical text means. The result is a paucity of vibrant biblical theology. Again, this series finds inadequate a *critical* approach that seeks to understand the text apart from belief in the meaning it conveys. Though modern readers have been taught to be discerning, they do not want to live in the "desert of criticism" either.

Instead, as its editors, we have sought to align this series with what has been labeled *believing criticism*. This approach marries probing, reflective interpretation of the text to loyal biblical devotion and warm Christian affection. Our contributors tackle the task of interpretation using the full range of critical methodologies and practices. Yet they do so as people of faith who hold the text in the highest regard. The commentators in this series use criticism to bring the message of the biblical texts vividly to life so the minds of modern readers may be illumined and their faith deepened.

The authors in this series combine a firm commitment to modern scholarship with a similar commitment to the Bible's full authority for Christians. They bring to the task the highest technical skills, warm theological commitment, and rich insight from their various communities. In so doing, they hope to enrich the life of the academy as well as the life of the church.

Part of the richness of this commentary series derives from its authors' breadth of experience and ecclesial background. As editors, we have consciously brought together a diverse group of scholars in terms of age, gender, denominational affiliation, and race. We make no claim that they represent the full expression of the people of God, but they do bring fresh, broad perspectives to the interpretive task. But though this series has sought out diversity among its contributors, they also reflect a commitment to a common center. These commentators write as "believing critics"—scholars who desire to speak for church and academy, for academy and church. As editors, we offer this series in devotion to God and for the enrichment of God's people.

ROBERT L. HUBBARD JR.
ROBERT K. JOHNSTON
Editors

Preface

God's creating and redeeming work in the book of Exodus, based on promises made to the family of Jacob, has established hope for the world. For over two thousand years, this ancient document has declared God's intention to be known by all the cultures of the world. Any emerging and growing people of God may find joy, knowledge, and guidance in its pages. Exodus challenges us to learn to live as the Lord's delivered people. My purpose is to explain the text so that readers will more fully understand the depth and breadth of that hope.

The bush "did not burn up" (3:2). My hope is that readers will hear the living voice of the Lord in the book of Exodus and see in it the foundations and pillars of the gospel of Jesus Christ. In Exodus, God saves the people, instructs them for daily living, forgives their rebellion, and promises to dwell visibly in the midst of their community through the glory of the cloud and the tabernacle. God delivers the people from bondage and they grow to know and trust God daily in the wilderness. God forgives their rebellion and they create a new society based on God's justice and presence.

This commentary is designed to be read beside an open Bible. It is my prayer that anyone reading a few verses at a time with the respective commentary paragraphs will understand the background and meaning of Exodus in a new and deeper way. References to the original Hebrew language throughout this commentary do not require a background in the language.

I have been surrounded by a host of witnesses and scholars in the last year and am indebted to those who have commented on Exodus over the last two millennia. I am also thankful for my students, many of whom are pastors and teachers. Their love of Scripture, passion for its questions, and discoveries of its revelations have motivated me to work. I am grateful to the teachers who first showed me the value of slow and close readings of the Bible, Fredrick Carlson Holmgren and Terence E. Fretheim, for their friendship, and for demonstrating their care for and delight in the biblical text. Thanks also to all the people at Hendrickson for the opportunity to deepen my appreciation for Exodus and write about it. Special thanks to Allan Emery III, associate editor, who read the manuscript and made it a better book.

I am also thankful to those who gave me opportunity and support during the labor of writing. North Park University and the Seminary administration provided a sabbatical for my research. Thanks also to Andrew Freeman for his labor on the indexes. While I was in Prague, the International Baptist Theological Seminary provided kind hospitality during much of the writing, especially Petra, Tomaš, and Petra, who provided valuable logistical help. My three sons also deserve credit, as they have influenced this volume: Ben, for his courage and wit in complex circumstances; Nick, for his patient victory in the Lord; and Luke, for his clear reading. Each was a sustaining force during my writing. Special thanks are due to Karin and Paul Lundstedt who graciously provided a place for me to finish writing when I needed it most.

I owe an enduring debt to the one who shared every aspect of this book: my wife, Kris. This volume is a tribute to her endurance with me and with the manuscript, and to her delight in the text. It would not be a book without her. Finally, thanks to Rolland and Janis Carlson for their constant love and support. To Rolland, for embracing the double *lamed* in his name (as in "hallelujah"); and to Janis, for her profligate love of the old, new, and living Lord of Exodus. This volume is dedicated to them (Exod. 9:16).

James K. Bruckner
North Park Theological Seminary

Abbreviations

AB	Anchor Bible
ABD	*Anchor Bible Dictionary*
ANET	J. B. Pritchard, ed. *Ancient Near Eastern Texts*
BA	*Biblical Archaeologist*
BDB	Brown, F., S. R. Driver, and C. A. Briggs. *A Hebrew and English Lexicon of the Old Testament*
BSac	*Bibliotheca sacra*
CBC	Cambridge Bible Commentary
CBQ	*Catholic Biblical Quarterly*
ExAud	*Ex auditu*
HBC	*Harper's Bible Commentary*
IBC	Interpretation: A Bible Commentary for Preaching and Teaching
Int	*Interpretation*
JBL	*Journal of Biblical Literature*
JSOTSup	Journal for the Study of the Old Testament: Supplement Series
JSS	*Journal of Semitic Studies*
LXX	Septuagint (Greek translation of the Hebrew Old Testament)
NCB	New Century Bible
NIBC	New International Biblical Commentary
NIV	New International Version
NT	New Testament
NTS	*New Testament Studies*
OBT	Overtures to Biblical Theology.
OT	Old Testament
OTL	Old Testament Library
PSB	*Princeton Seminary Bulletin*
Them	*Themelios*
TynBul	*Tyndale Bulletin*
VT	*Vetus Testamentum*
VTSup	Vetus Testamentum Supplements

WBC	Word Biblical Commentary
WTJ	*Westminster Theological Journal*
ZAW	*Zeitschrift für die alttestamentliche Wissenschaft*

Introduction

Why Read Exodus?

The witness of Exodus has changed the course of human history. Its claims are essential pillars of the Jewish and Christian faiths. This ancient book declares that more than three thousand years ago the Creator of the universe descended and delivered an oppressed people from Egyptian slavery. The ongoing remembrance of this meeting formed and reformed Israel's identity during its thousand-year history as a nation. This venerable text introduces many theological themes basic to Israel's relationship with God. That relationship with God required Israel's trust in the earlier promises God made to Abraham—promises of protection, provision, progeny, land, and blessing. Israel also had to learn to trust new promises concerning their redemption from slavery, their freedom to serve and worship the Creator, and the abiding presence of the Lord in their gathered, and often resistant, midst.

The action of Exodus unfolds dramatically. A new king rose to power in Egypt who did not remember Joseph. He oppressed the Hebrew people with hard labor and killed their infant boys. The people resisted and cried out to the Lord, who responded by sending them Moses and by revealing his name. Exodus 1–14 recount many demonstrations of God's identity as Creator in graphic detail. When God called the people to exit Egypt so they might worship at Sinai, God also protected and delivered them from Pharaoh's army. After the Lord's victory at the Red Sea, God guided the people and provided for them in their vulnerability in the wilderness.

Chapters 15–18 describe the people's slowly growing trust in God's provision for their daily needs: manna, meat, water, and protection from attack. At Sinai, they agreed to worship God and received the Ten Commandments and the book of the covenant. Chapters 19–24 combine the story of their sojourn with laws that provided a new kind of sociality based on God's justice and mercy. The Ten Commandments were to be placed in the holiest place, at the center of the community. God's blessing would come by means of a just society, rule by laws, and reliable judges. Maintaining their newfound freedom would not be easy.

A dramatic movement of the plot follows the giving of the Sinai law. God vowed to *descend from the heavens* and from Mt. Sinai and *dwell in the midst of their encampment.* Chapters 25–31 provide specific instructions for the creation of the tabernacle, the location of God's visible presence in the camp. In the lengthy, descriptive details, the Lord promised to be present on a daily basis and to travel with them. While Moses was on the mountain receiving these life-changing instructions, Aaron and the people were building the golden calf, crediting it with their deliverance from Egypt.

The events surrounding and following the worship of the calf in chapters 32–34 are a watershed for Exodus and, more broadly, for Scripture. The Lord's deliberations over *how* to dwell in the midst of this sinful and rebellious people resulted in an expanded declaration of God's name (34:6–7). God forgave Israel and provided a second exodus for them, an exodus from the bondage of their own sinful inclinations. These critical verses are some of the most theologically significant in the OT (see commentary at 34:6–7).

Chapters 35–40 describe the heartfelt response of the people, who willingly brought generous offerings and built the tabernacle. At this juncture the emerging community was honest about the source of their salvation. They worked and celebrated as the Lord's redeemed people. The book ends with the visible descent of the Lord into the midst of their encampment. This *descent to dwell on earth* had implications that reached into the NT (see "Tabernacle and Incarnation" at Exod. 25).

The contents of Exodus may be outlined as follows:

I. 1–14   Exit from Egypt

II. 15–18   Journey to Sinai

III. 19–24   Ten Commandments and the Book of the Covenant

IV. 25–31   Tabernacle Instructions

V. 32–34   Golden Calf Crisis and God's Forgiveness

VI. 35–40   Tabernacle Built and God's Dwelling Presence

In summary, Exodus presents God's *formation of* and *relationship with* a redeemed, yet willful, people. The first major portion of the book (I) tells of God's intervention in delivering the people from forces of evil, oppression, and bondage. The second portion (sections II, III, V) concerns equipping the people to live in free relation with God. In these chapters God gives wilderness provision, builds trust for daily troubles, orders their lives by laws, and begins to teach them to live as forgiven sinners. The laws, given by God as the Creator of the earth, would be critical in their future role as a blessing to all the nations. These laws created a new set of social responsibilities and standards. They revealed God's concern for: pure relationships; lifting the burdens of the oppressed; just courts; healthy standards of living; truth-telling in one's allegiances; and worship.

The last portion of Exodus (sections IV, VI) concerns God's presence and the challenging practice of incorporating the daily presence of the Lord in the midst of their lives. The people would build the tabernacle as a creative joint venture, creating space for God as well as a place to belong, to give with generous hearts, and to experience the glory of the Lord.

Literary Elements. Diverse classical literary forms abound in the book of Exodus. It weaves compelling narrative and legal texts together in what may be the richest combination of theologically based literature known in the ancient Near East. The narrative is full of first-person dialogue between the Lord and Moses, revealing the heart and mind of the Lord. The text artfully describes the resilient resistance of the midwives against Pharaoh. The litany of the plagues develops the battle of wills between Pharaoh and the Lord, who collide like converging seas. The narrative also contains genealogies, historiography, and the ancient Song of the Sea.

The legal texts present the Ten Commandments and the book of the covenant. The book of the covenant includes a variety of legal material including case law, prohibitions, and commands. Exodus ends with long descriptions of fabrics, wood, and metals used in creating the tabernacle. The book weaves these literary elements together in a theological narrative of God's will and Israel's will. Together, they function rhetorically to engage the will of the reader.

Exodus as Scripture

Theological Themes. Exodus establishes the foundational biblical perspective of God's relationship with the people of Israel.

The commentary on the text in this volume discusses many aspects of the Lord's relationship with the created world and with Israel. What follows here is a summary of several fine theological treatments of the text.

T. Fretheim notes six themes in Exodus.[1] 1) Creation is the basic foundation (ontologically and theologically) and the Lord's motivation for redeeming the people in Exodus. The redeeming God is first of all the Creator, who is fulfilling his creational mission in restoring Israel to relationship with their Creator, with cosmic consequences. This is the motivation behind hardening Pharaoh's heart during the plagues. God demonstrated to Pharaoh, the people, and to everyone who reads the story, that he was the Lord of all creation. 2) The knowledge of Yahweh as God is a central concern of the text. The narrative returns to who "knows" and who "does not know" repeatedly (7:17; 8:10, 22; 9:14, 29; 10:2; 11:7; 14:4, 18; 29:46). The Lord's purpose is that God's "name might be proclaimed in all the earth" (9:16). 3) Exodus presents images of God as Lord, judge, king, warrior, and ruler over creation. This sovereignty includes the remarkable self-portrayal of the Lord as long-suffering and compassionate (3:7–10; 34:6–7). 4) The paradigm of liberation in Exodus rests in God's initiative and for the purpose of serving the Lord. 5) Worship themes resound in the Passover celebration, the Song of the Sea, instructions for proper worship, and the building of the tabernacle. 6) The narrator establishes Israel's identity in God's promises and Israel's obedience in witness to the world.

For J. Durham, the theological centerpiece of Exodus is the *presence of Yahweh* in the midst of the people Israel.[2] The Lord is present with Moses; the plagues prove God's presence to Pharaoh and Israel; God's visible presence at the sea protects the people; God provides for their wilderness needs; and God establishes a presence in their midst at Sinai. The Lord provides his presence as the basis of Israel's existence after the golden calf crisis. Finally, the building of the tabernacle creates a place for the Lord's permanent and movable presence in Israel's midst.

Walter Brueggemann highlights four themes in the book of Exodus. 1) Exodus is fundamentally a narrative of sociopolitical liberation from a situation of oppression to freedom. 2) God's first-person declaration of the Sinai law is the "announcement of God's will for all aspects of Israel's personal and public life." 3) The covenant made at Sinai is binding. Israel and the Lord are "intimately, profoundly, and nonnegotiably committed to each other." 4) God establishes an enduring presence in Israel's midst through the structure of the tabernacle.[3]

Interpretive Perspectives. Certainly all of the themes noted above are significant in Exodus. This commentary benefits from the many excellent perspectives of these and other commentators. My interpretation of Exodus texts in this volume is based on the following six perspectives. First, the purpose of the exit from Egypt is not freedom for freedom's sake, but freedom to serve the Lord. This means that the exodus itself is missional (see commentary at 3:18; 5:1; 6:6–8; also 13:21–22; 19:4; 20:2), as demonstrated, in part, in the worship that culminates their exit from Egypt (15:1–18, 20–21; 19:10–19). Fully one half of the book of Exodus focuses on worship of the creating and redeeming God (chs. 20 to 40).

Second, Exodus highlights God's fulfillment of the promises made in Genesis, to bless all the cultures of the world through the descendents of Abraham. God's declaration in 4:22–23 regarding "my *firstborn* son, Israel," helps readers to understand the plagues better. These were the people through whom the Lord promised to change and bless the world. On this basis, God told Pharaoh through Moses, "They are my people. Let them go."

Third, the exit from Egypt and God's victory at the Red Sea were the *delivering grace* upon which the law at Sinai was based. God gave the law in order to constitute a good and healthy community life for those God had already chosen, blessed, delivered, redeemed, and saved, and with whom God had entered into a personal relationship. The law was never the means of that salvation (despite first-century interpretations). God continually reminded the people that prevenient grace and saving action in bringing them "up, out of the land of Egypt" preceded the law.

Fourth, Exodus concerns the formation of an *emerging* people of God. God did not accomplish everything for all God's people all at once. Neither did God let the revealed promise to bring blessing fall to the ground when they resisted it. Exodus records the first crises of their grumbling and rebellion against God *after* their deliverance. The book also describes the consequences. The upshot was that the Lord redeemed them, even from the self-destructive worship of the golden calf. God was revealed for the first time as a redeemer who delivers them not just from an oppressor, but from their own sin as well. The *emerging people of God* learned that even their rejection of the Lord would not drive God away. The people learned that God's presence would positively affect every aspect of their lives.

Fifth, the Lord invited the people into a cooperative venture for the first time, in the creation of the tabernacle. God's glory was first manifest in the beauty of the original creation, and then in the cloud, fire, manna, and mountain. God's glory would now be accessible daily, since God would dwell in their midst as they moved, in the tabernacle through the clouds of presence.

Finally, the purpose of Exodus was to create hope. Remembering the Lord's acts of deliverance in history would give God's people hope for the future. In the book of Deuteronomy, Moses continually looks back to the events of Exodus as a source of inspiration and hope.

The book of Exodus is part of a larger story in the biblical canon. The name "Exodus," from the Greek Old Testament (Septuagint or LXX), is a reference to the "exit" from Egypt. The Hebrew title, *ve'elleh shemot,* is from the first verse of the text, meaning "and these are the names" (of the sons of Israel who went to Egypt with Jacob). These names indicate that the book is a continuation of the story that precedes it.[4]

Genesis ends with Joseph's dying words, "God will surely come to your aid, and then you must carry my bones up from this place" (Gen. 50:25). Exodus begins at a critical juncture. The people who went to Egypt with Joseph had become enslaved in the approximately four hundred intervening years (Gen. 15:13; Exod. 12:40). How then could they fulfill the promises made to Abraham that his descendents would bring blessing to all the nations of the earth? They were enslaved, and yet Joseph had asked them to believe the promises.

J. Fokkelman has demonstrated many other ways that Exodus links with Genesis. For example, beginning with Joseph's genealogy (1:1–5); the announcement of Joseph's death and a new pharaoh (1:6–8); God's remembering the promises to Abraham (2:24; 6:4–5, 8); the fruitful multiplication of the Israelites (Gen. 1:28; Exod. 1:7, 12, 20); the "divisions" God made between waters (Gen. 1; Exod. 14), between darkness and light (Gen. 1; Exod. 10:21–23), and between the Egyptians and the Israelites (8:23; 13:21–22; 14:19–20); the covenant of circumcision (Gen. 17; Exod. 4:24–26; 12:43–48); and the Sabbath (Gen. 2:1–3; Exod. 20:8–11; 31:12–17; 35:1–3).[5]

The book of Exodus is not the whole story, as it abruptly ends with the people at Mt. Sinai. God has only partially delivered the law of Sinai. Leviticus and Numbers 1–10 continue to elucidate the law. The overarching narrative of the journey from Mt.

Sinai resumes in Numbers 10:11. That narrative carries them some forty years to the plains of Moab, ready to enter the land of promise. Moses pointed out to them that remembering God's deliverance and provision in the past exodus was the means of trusting God for the future (Deut. 5:15; 15:15; 16:12; 24:18, 22; 26:5–9; Josh. 24:5–8, 14).

Exodus is a foundational document of the Torah (Pentateuch, or first five books of the Hebrew Bible), of the OT, and of the entire canon of Scripture. These forty chapters chronicle the formation of the core identity of the people of God. The exodus tradition appears repeatedly and at length in liturgical form in the Psalms. The retelling of the exodus reminds readers of the human tendency to resist God and also engenders hope in God's deliverance (e.g., Pss. 77:16–20; 78:9–16; 81:1–16; 95:1–11; 105:23–45; 106:6–33; 114:1–8; 136:10–16). The prophets, including Ezekiel and especially Isaiah, expand the exodus theme for the exiles in Babylon, describing a *new exit* from bondage (e.g., Ezek. 20:33–42; Isa. 43:1–3, 9–10, 16–21; 52:7–12). At the time of the rebuilding of the temple, Ezra remembered the exodus in a prayer to create hope among the people (Neh. 9:9–21). The single most widely heard echo from Exodus is the expanded name of the Lord given in 34:6–7 (Pss. 86:5, 15; 103:8, 12; 111:4; 145:8–13; 2 Chr. 30:8–9; Joel 2:13; Neh. 9:17, 31; Jonah 4:2; Lam. 3:18; Hos. 2:19–20; Num. 14:18; Mic. 7:18; Nah. 1:3). The NT draws on the *name* and other themes of Exodus to explain the person and work of Christ after the resurrection (see "Exodus and God" below).

Exodus and History

The book of Exodus is a seminal testimony to God's direct and indirect acts of deliverance in human history. This canonical witness claims that God delivered and dwelt with the people of Israel during a fairly specific time (15th c. to 13th c. BC) in the ancient land of Egypt. God did not remain aloof, but "came down" to see the suffering of the people, to bring judgment upon the arrogant, to deliver those who cried out to God out of slavery, to meet them on the mountain of God, and to dwell in their midst in the tabernacle. The Lord created this people by delivering them and the term "the children of Israel" further demonstrates the intimacy between God and these people. Moreover, God established a reputation in the wider created world by this intervention. God uses the formula of self-identification "I am the LORD your God, who brought you out of the land of Egypt" more than one hundred times. This unmistakable historical claim is essential to the biblical view of reality (Sarna, "Exodus," p. 316).[6] It also prepares the way for the even more shocking physical claims of the NT.

N. Sarna has noted many correlations between descriptions in Exodus and situations described in other documents of the ancient Near East.[7] An Egyptian frontier official reported bedouin tribes moving into Egypt's delta to "keep them and their cattle alive" (*ANET*, p. 259). Egyptian texts praise the beautiful cities of Pithom (House of Atum) and Rameses (House of Rameses) named in Exodus 1:11 and built by Rameses II in the eastern Nile delta (*ANET*, pp. 470–71; see also Gen. 47:5–6, 11). "Satire on the Trades" describes the harsh conditions of agricultural laborers and brick makers from an Egyptian perspective (*ANET*, p. 433; 1:14). Records note that a two thousand brick quota per day was expected from a gang of forty men and was rarely achieved (5:7–8, 13–14).[8] "The Admonitions of an Egyptian Sage" mentions turning water into blood (the first plague), copied by the Egyptian magicians (*ANET*, p. 441; 7:19–22). These examples from Egyptian texts do not prove the events of the exodus, but they demonstrate some corroboration of the claims of the Exodus testimony in ancient Egyptian literature.

The history of the composition of the Exodus text has disproportionately occupied the efforts of scholars in the last two centuries. Tradition has assumed Mosaic authorship. Referring to Exodus as "the second book of Moses" (as is done in many pre-critical commentaries) calls upon Moses' authority for its content. The book itself never claims that Moses was the sole writer. The Lord asked Moses to "write" parts of the book, including the description of the battle with the Amalekites (17:14), the laws of the book of the covenant (24:4), and the Ten Commandments (34:27–8; see the comments on Moses' "writing" at 24:4). This is consistent with the NT reference to Moses' writing of the "law" in accordance with the claims of Exodus (Mark 1:5; 12:19; Luke 20:28).

The reconstructed history (formally called "source criticism") of the Pentateuch, of which Exodus is the second book, has centered on the Documentary Hypothesis of (mostly nineteenth-century) European scholarship. It continues to hold sway for scholarship in the interpretation of Exodus into the beginning of the twenty-first century. This hypothesis proposed an elaborate compositional history behind the present Exodus text as the best way to understand its import. It described three edited prior sources: the Jahwist (J), for its use of the name Yahweh; the Elohist (E), for its use of "Elohim" (God); and the Priestly (P) for its attention to the Levitical issues of worship and tabernacle. None of these assumed documents had external validation, but they were derived from the biblical text based on the content and style of each verse. The book of the covenant ("Covenant Code") and the Decalogue of 20:1–17 were assumed to be older, independent sources.

The J source was assumed to be written during the time of David and Solomon. It represented older oral tradition and written sources. Its two primary characteristics were narrative skill and a focus on Yahweh's work in salvation history. The E source was considered to run parallel to J, but it was marked by a "pre-literary" character. Texts that did not fit the profiles of J or P were attributed to E. The Elohist document was considered a version of the exodus from a northern (ten tribes) perspective. J was considered a southern source (Jerusalem, Judah). P was considered to be a much later source as well as the editor (or redactor) of the combined JE document. P's perspective concerned the exile and post-exilic period, written between 571 and 515 BC.[9] It sustained a focused interest on the foundations for Levitical authority and the rebuilding of the temple, and it added legal ordinances and cultic instructions (e.g., Passover, sacrifice, feasts, tabernacle details) to the combined JE document. Past critics have routinely considered these priestly (P) additions a less vital and living form of faith.[10]

The Documentary Hypothesis has often resulted in fragmented interpretations of the text. Rather than commenting on the text as a theological whole, scholars often drew attention to the competing perspectives of JE and P. Commentators' insights were diffused, and they (ironically) ignored the unified text with its literary complexity. Fortunately, as Brueggemann notes, "current scholarship finds the hypothesis in its classical form less and less useful."[11] This commentary, though aware of the diverse interests and styles within the text, works to interpret the theological meanings of their juxtaposition rather than drawing attention to the differences. The final form was likely redacted from diverse sources in the crisis of the sixth century, in view of deliverance from Babylon. In that context, an authoritative account of the deliverance from Egypt, some seven hundred years earlier, took on a new and truly critical importance. A scholarly consensus on details beyond these basic tenets is not likely.[12]

The exact date of the exit from Egypt is a matter of long debate, and there is a lack of definitive evidence.[13] The best deduction of the biblical and extrabiblical data is between 1299 and 1250 BC, during the reigns of Seti I and Rameses II. The most likely time for Jacob's immigration to Egypt was 430 years earlier, during the "foreign rule" of the *Hyksos* (Exod. 12:40; Gen. 15:13). The exit from Egypt was complete by the time of Merneptah (who followed Rameses II), with the people of Israel in *Canaan*, according to the Merneptah stele. Egyptian texts from the time of Rameses II and Merneptah also describe using Semite slaves (*hapiru*) for massive building projects. The city Pi-Rameses, mentioned in Exodus 1:11, was built by Rameses II after the beginning of his reign around 1290 BC (see commentary at 1:11). Finally, the archaeological evidence of the conquest of Canaan provides as many questions as answers, but it makes a thirteenth-century conquest most likely.[14]

The exact route of the exit from Egypt and the site of Mt. Sinai/ Horeb have also been difficult to locate. The text attempts to be very specific, naming places that were known in ancient times but that are now lost to us.[15] In Egypt, Rameses and Succoth, the locations mentioned before the crossing of the Red Sea, are the most certain (12:37). After that point in the narrative, Etham, Pi Hahiroth, and Migdol are unknown (13:20–14:2). The scholarly discussion proceeds largely with a shortage of data (see commentary at 13:18–20). Two proposals, a northern route and a southern route, garner the most support among scholars. The southern route to Mt. Musa is the option traditionally accepted and is the site of St. Catherine's monastery (see the commentary at 15:23 and 19:2).

Interpreting Exodus in History

God's liberation of the slaves from Egypt has been a source of hope for oppressed followers of the Lord for over three thousand years. Preachers in freedom movements have used the exodus as a paradigm for the Lord's presence in their own struggles. These have included Protestant reformers fighting for independence from the power of the bishop of Rome and the Habsburg (Holy Roman) Empire in Europe; Puritans escaping persecution in "new England"; African slaves in the Americas; and American colonists seeking freedom from England's domination. Many other Bible readers experiencing oppression have found hope and sometimes the courage to resist "empires" by reading Exodus.[16]

The tradition of reading Exodus as *a source of hope for freedom from oppression* has its beginning in the OT itself. The prophet Isaiah used themes of the exodus in preaching to the exiles more than seven hundred years after the exit from Egypt. Like their forebears, the Babylonian captives were separated from Canaan by an inhospitable wilderness. Through Isaiah, the Lord declared a *new exodus* from captivity. In the wilderness, God would create a highway (Isa. 40:3) and take them from slavery to freedom (Isa. 42:10–11; 43:9–10; 52:7–12; 55:12–13). God would provide food and water in the wilderness (Isa. 40:11; 41:17–20; 48:20–21; 49:7–12). The captives would pass through water and the Lord would bring victory over chaos (Isa. 11:15–16; 43:1–3, 16–21; 51:9–10). The second exodus would be greater than the first as people came to Mt. Zion, the new Sinai (Isa. 2:1–5; 35:1–10; Jer. 23:7–8; Mic. 4:1–5). The new covenant was understood by means of, and in the language of, the first exodus (Jer. 31:31–34). At the end of Isaiah, in the context of initial disappointments in returning to Zion, the prophet prayed, recounting before God the guidance and compassion of the first exodus (Isa. 63:11–16). Remembering the Lord's past deliverance created hope for the future.

In more recent times, the book of Exodus has been *a source of hope and action for the poor* in Latin America. They have identified with the people of Israel, who also suffered economic and social oppression under corrupt rulers. G. Gutierrez and J. Croatto use the exodus paradigm and the text of Exodus to interpret and guide the oppressed communities they represent.[17] This paradigm includes the following affirmations: God acts in history; God listens to the cry of the oppressed; God acts with a preferential option for the poor (22:21). Moses was called to confront the rulers; and the people were called, as a people, to participate in their emancipation.

In North America, Exodus has been *a resource of hope for those daily oppressed* by racism. The violent racial conflict of the 1960's brought a renewed interest in Exodus. As God delivered the slaves in Egypt, so God also delivered slaves in America. This interpretation shares many of the hermeneutical affirmations of Latin American readings of Exodus, applying them in a new context. Black theology, as preached by M. L. King and written by J. Cone and J. D. Roberts, is based on the premise that God will also bring the delivered slaves to freedom from enduring racial oppression.[18]

Challenges to those twenty-first-century people identifying with oppressed Israel in Egypt have come from within liberation theology itself. L. Dykstra summarizes three perspectives of people groups trapped by socioeconomic structures.[19] M. Guider writes from the perspective of Brazilian prostitutes trapped in sexual servitude. She objects that the exodus paradigm of liberation centers on "men, liberation, and conquest" (Dykstra, *Set Them Free*, p. 39). D. Williams writes from the perspective of a black woman, saying that the exodus paradigm of liberation does not deal with the "awful reality of victims making victims."[20] R. Warrior writes from the perspective of a dispossessed Native American. He observes that the Hebrews are liberated, but then they conquer the indigenous Canaanites. Is *liberation* indeed the theme if the liberated become the oppressors (see commentary at Exod. 23:23)?

The upshot of all of this is that modern applications of the liberation themes in Exodus require an honest appraisal of one's social group as oppressor and/or oppressed. Many evangelical Christians may thus end up in the unflattering position of identifying with the silent Egyptian populace. Honesty does not allow many of us the hermeneutical luxury of identifying ourselves as oppressed slaves. Moreover, most of us are Gentiles, like the Egyptians. Critical scholars often assert that the exodus from slavery should not be used as a paradigm at all, since it was a one-time event initiated by God to liberate Israel and create it as a people. Whatever the scholarly realities, socially oppressed people with faith in the Lord continue to derive hope from reading and rereading Exodus. The witness of the text remains a living voice for freedom in covenant with God.

Exodus and God

God revealed himself and his intention to the world in Exodus. Emancipation from slavery was not the end of the story. The stated purpose, "Let my people go," was "so that they may *worship/serve* me" (*ʿebed*; the root of the word means "work"; 5:1; 7:16; 8:1, 20; 9:1, 13; 10:3). B. Childs has noted that the continual resistance of the people to *this kind* of emancipation (grumbling before and rebelling after receiving the commandments) is an indication that God *had* to reveal the divine will. "Israel could not discover it for herself."[21]

God's initiatives in creating a new and enduring people constitute the constant theme. (e.g., Exod. 6:2–9). *God appeared* to Moses in a fiery bush that was not consumed. *God called* Moses to participate in bringing Jacob's family out of Egypt, in order to form them into a new people at Mt. Sinai. *God revealed* that, having seen their misery, heard their cry, and been concerned about their suffering, God's purpose was to come down to rescue them. The Lord was thus revealed for the first time as a delivering God. Human initiative was also blessed when it sought to preserve life (e.g., Jochebed, Shiphrah and Puah, Zipporah) or improve it (e.g., Jethro).

In Egypt, the Lord prolonged the plagues, hardening Pharaoh's heart that the whole earth might know God's name (Exod. 9:16). The Lord's reputation as ruler of all creation and all peoples was thereby extended. *In the Passover,* God protected them from death, demonstrating the efficacy of blood applied in faith. *At the Red Sea,* God pushed the people forward toward a new life, dramatically delivering them from Pharaoh's chariots. *In the wilderness,* God built the daily trust of these children by testing and then providing every need. In difficult circumstances God gave them water, manna, and victory when attacked. *At the mountain,* God's presence and will were revealed most fully. God descended on the mountain—that way the people could see and hear God coming. The Lord declared grace to be the foundation of the laws and covenant (19:4). God gave commandments, specifying a life based on the rule of law and justice for the most vulnerable in society.

In the tabernacle instructions, the Lord revealed these intentions more fully. In the daily tabernacle service God gave the people their food, sacrificed cleanly on the altar according to the law. In the tabernacle's tent of meeting God dwelt *in a tent* like the people, in their midst. In the building of the tabernacle, the people offered their wealth and artistic gifts for God's service. This ideal vision established a new possibility on earth. The God of the heavens saturated their very earthly existence. After the golden calf, God forgave their dishonest worship and rebellion. Rather than withdrawing, God more fully revealed the meaning of the divine name, taking on more responsibility for the people's weaknesses. In this self-limitation, the Lord began the road to the cross.

In the midst of all these initiatives, God demonstrated a desire for a personal relationship with this emerging people at the revelation of God's name. On three occasions at Sinai/Horeb God's name, Yahweh (usually translated the "Lord," though closer in meaning to "the One who is/the One who will be"), was revealed. Each instance expanded God's reputation. When the Lord called Moses into service, God declared "I am" (3:14–15). In the first three commandments, God expanded the import of this divine name

("I am 'the One who is' "; 20:1–7). In the fullest expression of God's name, the Lord promises to forgive sinful people (34:6–7; see the commentary on each of these texts).

The Lord of Exodus was the same Lord inflected in the person Jesus Christ. Jesus claimed the name (Yahweh; the "Lord") revealed to Moses in the three Exodus texts (3:14–15; 20:1–7; 34:6–7; and in John 8:58 Jesus used the same expression, "I am," Gk. *egō eimi*). For Christians, Jesus' claim to this *name* makes these texts central to understanding the person and work of Christ. The central hymn of the incarnation draws on the Exodus revelations of God "tabernacling" (dwelling) in the midst of the people, on the visible glory of God, and on the Lord's "grace and truth" (see the comments on John 1:14 in "Tabernacle and Incarnation" on Exod. 25).[22]

In the book of Exodus God kills and makes alive. Many readers have struggled with God's violent actions toward the Egyptians and toward God's own people in Exodus. The Lord acts as a giver of life and death, shaping creation and these people. God kills and makes alive, destroys and creates, takes away human life and sustains it. These actions cause us to pause, wonder, and sometimes to discredit the One who would act as no human being ever ought to act. Indeed, God acts in ways *no one else* has the right to act.

Discomfort with this side of the God of Scripture leads some readers to reject the Lord. Even Jesus speaks more words of ultimate judgment than most Bible readers want to acknowledge. This discomfort leads some interpreters to pursue explanations that lessen God's role in the killing, explaining it as a necessary catastrophe ("evil"). Even when it is a response to human sin, Scripture itself leaves little room for these theological maneuvers. The Bible assumes a categorical difference between the Lord God and us and between God's actions and human action. It assumes *a difference* between human motivations and the motivation of the Creator and redeemer of all the earth.

God is sometimes *against Israel*, implying that sometimes God is *against me*, even when motivations are "righteously" reasoned. To recognize that the Lord is God, and we are not, means to cease judging God's actions by human motivations. In the biblical narrative this recognition *does not exclude* prayers of protest, struggle, or lament in conversation with God. It *does mean* that we do not judge God's motivations or actions *as if we were* God. Genesis 3 demonstrates this tendency as the originating cause of our alienation from God, others, and life itself. To recognize the *difference* means to trust God and God's motivations—not simply because God is God and we are not, but because God's ultimate motivations have been revealed as *good*.

In Exodus, as in all Scripture, God fought the struggle against oppression of all kinds for the good of the people. Some innocents, including infants, died in that struggle. Their memory was honored, especially in the narratives of the midwives' defiance, of Jochebed and Miriam's strategies to save the baby Moses, and of children and slaves living under Pharaoh's lordship. Others died, however, in defiance of the Creator who longed to redeem and bless them.

Notes

1. T. Fretheim, *Exodus* (IBC; Louisville: John Knox, 1991), pp. 12–22.

2. J. Durham, *Exodus* (WBC; Waco: Word, 1987), pp. xxi– xxiii.

3. W. Brueggemann, "Exodus," in *The New Interpreter's Bible* (ed. L. Keck et al.; Nashville: Abingdon, 1994), pp. 678–80.

4. The book of Exodus has also been called the "Second Book of Moses," the "Second Book of the Pentateuch," and the "Second Book of the Torah." These latter names point to the foundational authority of the books as Scripture.

5. J. Fokkelman, "Exodus," in *Literary Guide to the Bible* (ed. R. Alter and F. Kermode; Cambridge, Mass.: Harvard University Press, 1987), pp. 56–65.

6. "I am the Lord, who brought you out" is constitutive of a people who have a specific ethic of care for the most vulnerable members of society, as Sarna notes. The description is often used as a preface to commands for justice. See my commentary on Exodus 22:21–22 and N. Sarna, "Exodus," in *Etz Hayim: Torah and Commentary* (ed. D. Lieber; New York: Jewish Publication Society, 2001), pp. 316–572.

7. In all, Sarna notes 17 correlations with *ANET* texts. N. Sarna, "Book of Exodus," in *ABD* 2 (ed. D. N. Freedman; New York: Doubleday, 1992), pp. 697–98. For the *ANET* documents, see J. B. Pritchard, ed., *Ancient Near Eastern Texts Relating to the Old Testament* (3d ed.; Princeton: Princeton University Press, 1992).

8. K. Kitchen, "From the Brickfields of Egypt," *TynBul* 27 (1976), pp. 136–47.

9. M. Noth, *Exodus: A Commentary* (OTL; Philadelphia: Westminster, 1962), p. 17.

10. Noth, *Exodus*, p. 17.

11. Brueggemann, "Exodus," p. 678.

12. For a full discussion of the critical issues see R. Rendtorff, *The Problem of the Process of the Transmission of the Pentateuch* (trans. J. Scullion; JSOTSup 89; Sheffield: Sheffield Academic Press, 1990). For a shorter overview of the debate see R. Whybray, *Introduction to the Pentateuch* (Grand Rapids: Eerdmans, 1995), pp. 12–28; and G. Wenham, "Pentateuchal Studies Today," *Them* 22 (1996), pp. 3–13. The Holy Spirit is the author and guarantor of the final form of Scripture that has been written, edited, and copied by many faithful people over thousands of years.

13. On archaeological evidence see K. Kitchen, "The Exodus," in *ABD* 2 (ed. D. N. Freedman; New York: Doubleday, 1992), pp. 700–708. The main objection to a 13th-century date is the period of 480 years mentioned in 1 Kgs. 6:1. This is generally interpreted as a symbolic number (12 x 40), with "40" representing a "generation" which could be much shorter. Most conservative scholars now also support the 13th-century date. For a defense of a 15th-century exit from Egypt, see K. Waltke, "Palestinian Artifactual Evidence Supporting the Early Date of the Exodus," *BSac* 129 (1972), pp. 33–47. For a presentation of all the literary and archaeological variables see J. Walton, "Date of Exodus," in *Dictionary of the Old Testament Pentateuch* (ed. T. Alexander and D. Baker; Downers Grove: InterVarsity, 2003), pp. 258–72.

14. Many critical scholars (and archaeologists) now think that the exit from Egypt and Joshua's conquest were literary constructs. In order to come to terms with the absence of complete archaeological data for the conquest, scholars have proposed that Israel originated through a "peasant revolt" (see Mendenhall, Gottwald) from within the land of Canaan or "infiltrated" the land over a longer period of time (Alt). See a survey of the various proposals for historical reconstruction in K. L. Younger Jr., "Early Israel in Recent Biblical Scholarship," in *The Face of Old Testament Studies: A Survey of Contemporary Approaches* (ed. D. Baker and B. Arnold; Grand Rapids: Baker, 1999), pp. 176–206.

15. For a discussion of the proposals for the locations of the crossing of the Red Sea and of Mt. Sinai see G. I. Davies, *The Way of the Wilderness: A Geographical Study of the Wilderness Itineraries in the Old Testament* (Cambridge: Cambridge University Press, 1979). For a shorter discussion see P. Enns, "Exodus Route and Wilderness Wandering," in *Dictionary of the Old Testament Pentateuch* (ed. T. Alexander and D. Baker; Downers Grove: InterVarsity, 2003), pp. 272–80.

16. For a survey of the wide variety of peoples using Exodus as a paradigm of hope and resistance, see M. Walzer, *Exodus and Revolution* (New York: Basic, 1985), pp. 3–17; L. Dykstra, *Set Them Free: The Other Side of Exodus* (Maryknoll, N.Y.: Orbis, 2002), pp. 27–31. For Korean, Palestinian, Asian feminist, and Black African perspectives on Exodus see

R. Sugirtharajah, ed. *Voices from the Margins: Interpreting the Bible in the Third World* (Maryknoll, N.Y.: Orbis, 1991).

17. For an introduction to Latin American readings of Exodus see G. Gutierrez, *A Theology of Liberation: History, Politics and Salvation* (Maryknoll, N.Y.: Orbis, 1973); J. Croatto, *Exodus: A Hermeneutics of Freedom* (Maryknoll, N.Y.: Orbis, 1981). For a wider review of the use of exodus as a paradigm for historically and socially located liberation, see B. van Iersel and A. Weiler, eds. *Exodus: A Lasting Paradigm* (Edinburgh: T&T Clark, 1987).

18. For an introduction to Black Theology in North America, see J. Cone, *God of the Oppressed* (Maryknoll, N.Y.: Orbis, 1997); J. D. Roberts, *A Black Political Theology* (Philadelphia: Westminster, 1974); also C. H. Felder, ed. *Stony the Road We Trod: African American Biblical Interpretation* (Minneapolis: Fortress, 1991).

19. For recent challenges to using the dominant paradigm in reading Exodus see L. Dykstra, *Set Them Free*, pp. 31–50.

20. D. Williams, *Sisters in the Wilderness: The Challenge of Womanist God-Talk.* (Maryknoll, N.Y.: Orbis, 1993), p. 149.

21. B. Childs, *Introduction to the Old Testament as Scripture* (Philadelphia: Fortress, 1979), p. 174.

22. The christological correlation of Exodus themes is developed in T. Fretheim, "Book of Exodus," in *Dictionary of the Old Testament Pentateuch* (ed. T. Alexander and D. Baker; Downers Grove: InterVarsity, 2003), pp. 257–58. Brueggemann notes that Stephen's sermon in Acts 7:17–44 recounts much of the Exodus narrative as the work of God's Spirit in the world. He also points to Jesus' priestly work in heaven, described in Heb. 7–11, which is based on Aaron's priesthood (Exod. 25–40). See Brueggemann, "Exodus," pp. 686–87.

§1 The Need for Deliverance (Exod. 1:1–22)

The beginning of Exodus is closely linked with the ending of Genesis. In Joseph's dying words he beseeched his brothers to believe that God would one day bring them out of Egypt:

> "I am about to die. But God will surely come to your aid and take you up out of this land to the land he promised on oath to Abraham, Isaac and Jacob." (Gen. 50:24)

The first chapter of Exodus sets the context and quickly establishes the crisis of the narrative: Jacob's descendants prospered and multiplied in Egypt, which created a threat to a pharaoh who no longer remembered the legacy of Joseph. In order to limit their numbers, Pharaoh oppressed them with forced labor and ultimately with a policy of male infanticide. God provided even in these difficult circumstances by continuing to multiply the population and through the midwives' passive resistance to Pharaoh's orders.

1:1–7 / Jacob's family prospered and grew. **These are the names of the sons of Israel who went to Egypt with Jacob, each with his family** (lit., "household"). The first words of Exodus look back to Genesis 46:8 by repeating these exact words (NIV wording differs, but the Hebrew is the same). Exodus is the second "chapter" in the ongoing narrative of God's work, creating a people who will bring blessings to all the nations. As in Genesis, God's work with the family of Abraham, Isaac, and Jacob continued in Exodus. We are reminded that they "went to Egypt" and remained as "sojourners," though they lived there for many generations.

The names Israel and Jacob, both mentioned in these verses, referred to the same person. Why use both names? The emerging nation would be commonly referred to as the "sons of Israel" (lit., "children of Israel;" sometimes translated "Israelites" in the NIV). The name "Jacob," here and elsewhere in Scripture, recalls his struggle in becoming "Israel" (lit., "God rules"). The name reflects

Jacob's striving "with God and with humans" and his prevailing (Gen. 32:28). The use of both names indicates the ongoing nature of the struggle of a people to become the family in which *God rules*: through the exodus, in the wilderness, and at Sinai.

Jacob's sons are listed not by birth order, but as follows: Leah's sons (**Reuben, Simeon, Levi and Judah; Issachar, Zebulun**), Rachel's son (**Benjamin**), Rachel's maid Bilhah's sons (**Dan and Naphtali**), and Leah's maid Zilpah's sons (**Gad and Asher**). The order of these names reinforces the sequence in Genesis 35:23–26, where Jacob accepted God's final promises to him (Gen. 35:9–15). Especially significant for understanding Exodus 1:1–7 is God's command to "be fruitful and multiply" and the promise that kings would come from his family in the land of promise.

The descendants of Jacob numbered seventy in all. This is a quotation from Genesis 46:27. (Gen. 46:8–27 lists the sons and grandsons by name.) Seventy is a number that symbolizes completeness. The text notes that **Joseph was already in Egypt**, as a reminder of the Joseph cycle in Genesis 37–50. The God of the exodus had already demonstrated faithfulness by appearing, guiding, protecting, and redeeming the family to whom God had repeated these promises.

The **Israelites were fruitful and multiplied greatly and became exceedingly numerous, so that the land was filled with them**. This verse is intentionally redundant and in the Hebrew has five verbs that repeat the words of blessing and promise to the patriarchs (Gen. 1:28; 9:1, 7; 17:2; 18:18; 28:14; 48:4). The rabbinic commentators suggest that this repetition functions to interpret the verbs in terms of the sequence of a child's growth. It can mean, "The Israelites were fertile (they conceived easily), they crawled, they grew (childhood), became very, very strong (adolescence), and the land was filled with them." This kind of translation communicates a double meaning. The Israelites grew in number, as well as raising large and strong families. Their families were "everywhere" as they fulfilled the promises God made to Abraham, Isaac, and Jacob that they would be as the stars and as the sands of the sea. The amazing fecundity of the people, despite continued and increasing oppression (1:12), introduces the central theme of the power of God's creation in Exodus.

1:8–14 / The Egyptians forced Israel's people to labor. A **new king, who did not know about Joseph, came to power in Egypt**. This is an ominous phrase. The memory of Joseph's good reputation in Egypt, described in Genesis, was forgotten. The entire time of the sojourn in Egypt is reported as 430 years (Exod. 12:40; see also Gen. 15:13). Joseph lived to be 110 years old (Gen. 50:26). The time of the beginning of the oppression is uncertain. Most interpreters place it in the nineteenth dynasty of Egypt under Rameses II (ca. 1290–1224 B.C.) and his successor Merneptah (ca. 1224–1211 B.C.). Rameses II moved Egypt's administration to the Nile's eastern delta (see the discussion in the Introduction). The text does not name this pharaoh (king). Whoever he was, he created obstacles to the fulfillment of the promises God made to Abraham.

This pharaoh "did not know" Joseph. He did not remember or care about what Joseph had done for Egypt. The verb *yada*^c "know" is an important concept in Exodus 1–14, especially concerning what Pharaoh knew or didn't know in relation to the Lord (1:8; 2:25; 3:7; 5:2; 6:3, 7; 7:5, 17; 8:10, 22; 9:14, 29–30; 10:2, 7, 26; 11:7; 14:4, 18; 16:6, 12; 18:11; 23:9; 29:46; 31:13; 33:12, 13, 16–17).

"Look," he said to his people, "the Israelites have become much too numerous for us. Come, we must deal shrewdly with them or they will become even more numerous and, if war breaks out, will join our enemies, fight against us and leave the country." The pharaoh's main concern was that they would leave the country. His response might be understood as an administrative strategy, as "shrewdly" also can mean "wisely." He did not try to eliminate them directly.

Egypt had a problem with mobile populations. The problem was not that they would take over the country, but that they would join forces with Egypt's enemies and leave. Before the children of Israel were victims of forced labor, they were subject to forced residency in a totalitarian state. Even Joseph had to ask the pharaoh's permission to go to Canaan to bury his father Jacob (Gen. 50:4–14). The words "with them" can also mean "with it," in which case it would refer to the problem of the immigrant population explosion. The pharaoh didn't want the Israelites to grow too strong or to leave, since they formed an important part of his economic base. His comment that they were much too numerous "*for* us" is otherwise translated "more numerous *than* us," which could be a political spin on the actual situation.

Pharaoh's two concerns as an administrator (that they are "too numerous" and might "leave the country") set him in direct opposition to God's two promises to Jacob: that "a company of nations" would come from him and that God would give him the land of Canaan (Gen. 35:11–12). This sets the stage for the battle between the God of creation ("be fruitful and multiply") and of history ("I will give you the land") and the great and powerful Pharaoh.

The **slave masters** were Egyptian (Exod. 5:6, 14). Literally, they were "captains of labor gangs," so "taskmasters" is a better translation here. They oversaw the building of the northern and northeastern border towns, Pithom and Rameses, that served as military supply cities for protection and campaigns.

The word root translated "oppressed" (*'anah*) means "violently afflicted," or "cruelly crushed." It includes the graphic nature of dispiriting violence. Yet the population continued to multiply, fulfilling God's command to fill the earth. This frightened the Egyptians and caused them to loathe (**dread**) the Israelites. They responded with even more vigorous brutality. The fact that the Israelites continued to thrive even under extreme duress was like a plague to the Egyptians. They could not explain it except that God helped them (Houtman, *Exodus*, vol. 1, p. 223). The agents of life and death in creation were the Lord's to command, yet Pharaoh believed that they were under his personal control.

They made their lives bitter with hard labor in brick and mortar and with all kinds of work in the fields; in all their hard labor the Egyptians used them ruthlessly. The literary key here (vv. 12–14) is the five occurrences of the Hebrew word root (*'abad*), translated "hard labor," "work," and "used." "Used them ruthlessly" expresses the corruption of the goodness of work (Gen. 2:15). It is likely that this indicates an intensification to a full and crushing slavery. The Hebrew word for "ruthlessly" means "with violent hate."

1:15–22 / The midwives' courage and fear of the Lord contrast with a powerful, yet paranoid, pharaoh. Although the chapter begins with the patriarchal list, the hope of the Israelites was in the daily life of the Hebrew home and childbirth. Here we see the beginning of the key role women played in God's deliverance of Israel from crisis in Exodus 1–4 (see also Exod. 2:1–10; 4:24–26).

The "power" of **the Hebrew midwives, whose names were Shiphrah and Puah,** was at once real and tenuous—completely opposite to the power of Pharaoh's violence. Their existence and their fear of the Lord empowered the midwives. It was enough.

The text communicates this by repeating the word "midwives" seven times in seven verses.

These two women and their sassy courage dominate the narrative. The NIV has abbreviated the deliberately high-profile rhetoric of their introduction (lit., "the name of the first was Shiphrah and the name of the second was Puah"). The contrast to the *nameless* "Pharaoh" is stark.

Because of the extreme difference in political power, the conversation between them is ironically humorous. It is odd that Pharaoh himself spoke to these women and that the ruler of Egypt would say, **"When you . . . observe them on the delivery stool."** The command **"if it is a boy, kill him"** is also ironic, because it reveals that Pharaoh thought *men* were the threat. In fact, it was the women who continued to outfox him. His fear of the Hebrews' ever-increasing numbers caused him to escalate his policy to infanticide.

The midwives feared God (vv. 17, 21). They believed that the murder of infants was wrong in God's eyes. The phrase **feared God** announces an important theme for the book of Exodus. The "fear of God" (*yir'at 'elohim*) was the belief that certain things were wrong simply because they were contrary to the order of the life God had woven into the fabric of the created world (see 9:30; 14:31; 18:31; 20:20; also Gen. 20:11).

When Pharaoh asked, **"Why have you done this?"** the women responded, **"Hebrew women are not like Egyptian women; they are vigorous and give birth before the midwives arrive."** The women removed suspicion from themselves by stating what was partly true. They spared the boys through a form of "civil disobedience," since it is unlikely they arrived too late for *every* birth. Pharaoh follows their impudent and courageous response with a weak one, perhaps because they had confirmed his superstitious fears. When he oppressed them, they became more numerous (v. 12). When he enlisted Shiphrah and Puah to kill baby boys, the **people increased and became even more numerous** (v. 20; see also v. 7). The women outmaneuvered him by reinforcing his fear with their comments about the vigor of the Hebrew women.

God **gave them families** (lit., "households") **of their own**. God made households for them. They may have been childless previously and God gave them fertility as a reward for their courage.

Pharaoh then gave a more general command, **"Every boy that is born you must throw into the Nile."** The word "Nile" is an

Egyptian loan word that simply means "water" or "canal." In Egypt, that usually meant the Nile River and its tributaries. What had begun as forced residency escalated to forced labor, then to increased brutality, to a policy of forced infanticide, and finally to a general order to **all his people** to kill Hebrew babies.

The drowning of babies, albeit cruel, seems like an ineffective method for a pharaoh who could have killed them by the sword to employ. The command sets up several deep ironies for the continuing narrative. Is the Nile a source of life or of death? Who is ruler of the great river, if not the one who would turn it to blood? Who would God drown in the Reed Sea, but the Egyptians (14:28)? God repeats the pattern of using creational means that "match the crime" to resolve injustice throughout the Pentateuch and the Prophets.

A second irony prevails, for Pharaoh repeated the command to **let every girl live.** As we will see in Exodus 2, females were *more than capable* of thwarting the machinations of the mighty pharaoh. In spite of their resistance, it is clear that the Hebrew people need salvation. Pharaoh's command sets up a narrative tension for the birth of Moses in Exodus 2:1.

Additional Notes §1

1:1 / "Jacob" can be translated "he grabs," and "Israel" means "God rules." Gen. 32:28 indicates a wordplay between *srr* ("rule") and *srh* ("strive"). Even after God changed his name, Israel is called "Jacob" in order to reinforce the ongoing process of God's rule in his life and the difficulty of becoming Israel.

1:7 / The NIV treats the Hebrew verbs (*sharats*) "crawled" and (*rabah*) "to become great" as a verb-adverb pair, a hendiadys, translated into English as "multiplied greatly." "Crawl" or "swarm" is a word used in Genesis (1:21; 8:17) to describe the action of reptiles upon the ground. Here it has the meaning of "fecund" or "prolific reproduction" (see Greenberg, *Understanding Exodus*, p. 19). The word translated "numerous" can mean "strong" or "strong-boned."

1:8 / See Stephen's sermon in Acts 7:18.

1:11 / Pithom and Rameses were situated at the entrance to Egypt from the Sinai Peninsula. Pithom (Pir-Atum, or "house of Atum," the creator and sun god) has been excavated as tell er-Retabeh, 60 mi. northeast of Cairo. Rameses was capital of the delta region. Seti I (1294–

1279 B.C.) built a summer palace there that was enlarged by his son Rameses II. The city (Pir-Ramesse-Meri-Amon, or "house of Rameses, beloved of Amon") is very likely tell ed-Dabᶜa, 80 mi. northeast of Cairo. This delta region is known in Exodus as the "land of Goshen."

1:15 / Rabbinic commentary has noted the wordplay between the Hebrew words *toledot* (generations) and *meyalledot* (midwives). The LXX and some interpreters translate the phrase "midwives to the Hebrews," meaning that these were righteous Gentile Egyptian women. The name Shiphrah comes from a word that means "to be beautiful, to be bright, and to shine." The name Puah is more obscure, possibly from a Ugaritic word meaning "fragrant blossom" that came to mean, more generally, "girl" (a cognate of *pᶜy*).

1:16 / The Samaritan Pentateuch, LXX, and Targumim add to "Every boy that is born" the expression "to the Hebrews"—as is implied from the context.

§2 Moses' Beginnings (Exod. 2:1–10)

Exodus 2 begins with the story of Moses, through whom God delivered and shaped the people of Israel. This part of Exodus (chs. 2–15) describes how God used a Levite family and the forces of creation to bring these people out of Egypt into the Sinai wilderness. Exodus 2 includes Moses' birth, his amazing deliverance and adoption (2:1–10), his identification with "his" Hebrew people, the killing of an Egyptian, his escape to the land of Midian, his marriage to Zipporah, and the birth of their son, Gershom (vv. 11–22). The chapter concludes with a reminder of the groaning of the people in Egypt and God's attentive ear (vv. 23–25).

2:1–10 / *The women and baby Moses.* Exodus 1 ends with the king's phrase, "let every girl live." Now it is the daughters who will thwart Pharaoh. The women of this text play all the decisive roles. Jochebed ("the baby's mother"), Miriam ("his sister," see Num. 26:59), the daughter of Pharaoh, and her maidens surrounded the baby Moses. The suspenseful and poignant story is full of literary tensions and human emotions. In ten short verses the human risk is set up and resolved again and again. By the end of the story, the pharaoh (who never shows up in this narrative) is thwarted by the women, even as he was by the midwives in Exodus 1.

The narrative explains how Moses ended up in Pharaoh's court, where he received training essential to being the future deliverer of Israel. The story creates the possibility of Moses' education through the dramatic events of his rescue from the water. It is the story of the *salvation of a savior.* The saving of Moses from the edict of Pharaoh is paradigmatic. It foreshadows God saving Israel from the violence of Pharaoh at the crossing of the Red Sea. Matthew 2 echoes this salvation story—a son who would be the savior of the world is born, laid in a rough bassinet by a lowly mother, and survives the senseless murder of children by a violent king.

Exodus 2:1 tells us that **a man of the house of Levi married a Levite woman.** At this point God has not yet established the Levites as a "religious" tribe. Exodus 6:14–27 again emphasizes Moses' Levitical lineage. The narrative moves directly to the announcement that the Levite woman **became pregnant and gave birth to a son.** Moses was the third child born to Jochebed and Amram (after Miriam and Aaron; see Exod. 7:7; 15:20; Num. 26:59). The story presses forward quickly, leaping over several years between Moses' birth and his salvation, in which his sister played a key role.

The translation **When she saw that he was a fine child, she hid him** raises unnecessary questions about what she would have done if he wasn't "fine." The combination of the Hebrew words *tob* and *tsapan* (NIV "fine" and "hid") communicates that she saw he was "precious" and she "treasured" or "hid him as a treasure" for three months. The expression "saw that he was precious" echoes the repeated declaration in Genesis that the Lord saw that the creation was "good." The expression is the same here, literally, "she saw that he was good" (*tob*). In verse 6, the daughter of Pharaoh would also "see him" and be moved to preserve his life.

A host of wordplays resound in the Hebrew words behind **she got a papyrus basket** (*tebah*) **and coated it with tar** (*khemar*) **and pitch** and put it **among the reeds** (*sup*). "Sup" is the name of the Sea of Reeds (or Papyrus Sea) that the people would cross in Exodus 14 (see the discussion of the name of the "Red Sea" at note 13:18). Moses' deliverance is paradigmatic for the salvation of the people. Both were saved where the water and the papyrus reeds (*sup*) meet.

Her coating the "basket" (*tebah*) or "ark" with "pitch" fulfills the instruction given to Noah for the "ark" (*tebah*; Gen. 6:14; 7:7). In both cases the word means "a chest" or "container in which something precious is stored." The baby's basket was an ark of salvation for the boy. As with Noah, the salvation of humanity depended on this little ark. A fine irony is that the word sounds like the word for "coffin" in Egyptian. The "tar" (*khemar*) or "plaster" that sealed the basket ark also carries literary weight, as the "mortar" (1:14) with which the laborers toiled is the same word. The same substance Pharaoh used as a means of oppression, a mother's hands spread as an agent of salvation.

She **put it among the reeds along the bank of the Nile.** Some interpreters suggest that exposure in a basket on the water was the means used *to kill* the babies without the trauma of directly drowning them. Such exposure without feeding or protection from crocodiles would indeed lead to death. Yet here, his sister's watchful eye and the many echoes of Noah's ark suggest that this was intended as a means of saving, not exposing, the baby. The irony, of course, is that he was put into the river as an act of literal obedience to Pharaoh's death order with the intention of preserving his life.

The narrative style is masterful in describing the daughter of Pharaoh and her young women finding the basket. The NIV does not express fully the detail of the discovery present in the original language. Verse 6 could instead be translated, "She opened it and saw him. The little boy! Oh look, the boy is crying! And she was moved to compassion. 'This is one of the Hebrew babies,' she said." The fact that she adopts the child as her own, in spite of her father's command, reveals the depth of her "compassion" (Heb. *khamal* is not simply pity or being sorry).

Miriam came out of nowhere. No longer at a distance (v. 4), she was among the women as "coconspirator" (Fretheim). For the next three verses (vv. 7–9) the talk is of lactating (four times in three verses; the NIV leaves out "nursing woman" in v. 7a as redundant). The women had this young life under their protection and care.

The reader may laugh out loud with wonder that the daughter of Pharaoh agreed to accept the baby's mother as his nurse and also agreed to pay her. This arrangement not only saved the child from death and ensured his protection and continued life, but it also reunited him with his mother. She would actually be paid to nurse her own son by the one who had ordered his death. When she adopted him as her son, the daughter of Pharaoh also insured Moses' education in the ways of Egypt. God's deliverer grew up in the very court from which he would deliver his people. Only this environment could sufficiently equip him to speak to the next pharaoh (v. 23).

When the child grew older, Moses' mother took him to Pharaoh's daughter and **he became her son.** The narrative does not even raise the question of Pharaoh's approval of his daughter's adopting this boy. Perhaps the reader can assume that Pharaoh's daughter got whatever she wanted. Regardless of his response, this action of Pharaoh's daughter seems to have ended the decree to kill Hebrew baby boys. There is no biblical or extrabiblical evidence to indicate that it persisted. When Moses led the people out of Egypt, he certainly had male contemporaries with him. Her action was a public display against her father's genocidal policy. A member of Pharaoh's own family saved the savior of the Hebrews. God used a non-Hebrew to accomplish his saving work, as later in Moses' life God would use the Midianite Jethro/Reuel (2:16–22; 18:1–27).

The daughter of Pharaoh **named him Moses, saying, "I drew him out of the water."** The name Moses likely came from an Egyptian verb that sounds like "Moses" (Egyptian root *ms'i*) and means "to give birth." The noun from this root means "son of" or "boy." It is part of Egyptian names like Ahmose. It *sounds like* the participle of a Hebrew verb (*mashah*) that means "one who pulls out" or "one who draws from." Pharaoh's daughter makes this connection when she uses that verb to say "I drew him out." A double meaning is at work here, since Moses will later be the "one who draws" the people out from Egypt.

This narrative does not mention God at all. God is working behind the scenes through the actions of ordinary and extraordinary people.

Additional Notes §2

2:1 / Fretheim titles this section "Daughters Save Moses." For a close reading of the ironies of this text see Fretheim, *Exodus*, pp. 36–40. Exum ("You Shall Let Every Daughter Live," pp. 74–82) best describes the women's decisive roles.

2:1b / Levi (lit. "be joined") was Jacob and Leah's third son. He was the great grandfather of Jochebed's husband, whose name (not given in this verse) was Amram (lit. "exalted people"). Moses' mother (also not named here) was Jochebed (lit. "the Lord is honored"). In fact, this narrative does not name anyone until the very end, when Pharaoh's daughter names the baby Moses. The blessing Levi received from his father Jacob was not gracious. Jacob "blessed" Levi together with his brother and partner in crime, Simeon. Together they had overavenged the rape of their sister Dinah by their mass murder of the Shechemites (Gen. 34:25–31). Their actions did not please Jacob and he prophesied that they would be "scattered" and "divided" in Israel. Levi's fate was redeemed in Exodus and his "scattering" among the other tribes became a means to religious service in Israel.

2:3 / Scholars compare this narrative with several ancient Near Eastern stories of the exposure and subsequent rescue of a child who would later become a great leader (e.g., Sargon, king of Akkad). For an analytic discussion and bibliography of the comparisons see Enns, *Exodus*, pp. 58–60.

2:6   /   See the discussion of resisting Pharaoh's killing of infants in Houtman, *Exodus*, vol. 1, p. 269 and in Fretheim, *Exodus*, p. 37. See also Fretheim's discussion of how Pharaoh's daughter parallels God's actions in saving Israel in general: she comes down, sees, has compassion, and draws him out.

§3 Moses Encounters Violence (Exod. 2:11–25)

The second half of Exodus 2 (vv. 11–25) begins with Moses walking among the Hebrew laborers. Three times in these verses he intercedes on behalf of weak persons who had been wronged, thereby showing himself to be God's friend. Nevertheless, in addition to demonstrating the gifts God had given him, these three short scenes also reveal what was lacking in Moses' character and education. Each encounter shows who he was and also changed him in significant ways. In striking down the Egyptian Moses encountered the violent culture of his upbringing, and through this incident he learned that violence would not be the way into the future. When he confronted his "brothers" who were fighting he found that he had no credibility with them, no influence over them, nor any call from a higher authority to lead them. His rescue of the seven daughters of Reuel (Jethro) confirmed his identity as a man of justice because he rose up with appropriate force to deliver them from the violence of the herdsmen. As a result, he received their father's invitation to join the daily life of a new community.

2:11–15a / Moses experiences an identity crisis. **One day, after Moses had grown up, he went out to where his own people were and watched them at their hard labor.** This scene demonstrates a disjuncture in Moses' identity. Although he went "out to where his own people" (lit., "his relatives") were, he was watching them. He was not forced to labor with them. He was already forty years old (Acts 7:23) and an outsider. He would be compelled to choose the Hebrew culture over the Egyptian and the transition would not be easy.

He saw an Egyptian beating a Hebrew, one of his own people. Glancing this way and that and seeing no one, he killed the Egyptian and hid him in the sand. The NIV translation here creates a false impression. The verse has a long history of being misunderstood and even of anti-Semitic interpretation. It stems from the impression that Moses' action was a premeditated murder, as he glanced around to be sure he would not "be caught," and then did it. The choice of the word "glance" subtly impugns his motivation. The meaning, which is clear in the Hebrew, is rather this:

> He saw an Egyptian striking down (*nakah*) a Hebrew, one of his kinsmen. He looked this way and that and saw that there was no one *to intervene*, so he struck down (*nakah*) the Egyptian and hid him in the sand.

Three grammatical points lead to this translation. First, the verb for the Egyptian's and Moses' "striking" is the same word root and stem (Hiphil). This sort of blow might or might not lead to death, but it was equal in force and meaning (see below). Secondly, "the Egyptian" (lit., "a man of Egypt") is not identified as a taskmaster but was an ordinary man. He had no "authority" to carry out the beating, which was why Moses looked around for someone to intercede. Thirdly, the expression that Moses "saw that there was no one" is exactly the phrase used in Isaiah 55 (*ki ʾen ʾish*). The rabbis note that the phrase is not used in any other way in Scripture (Leibowitz, *Shemot*, p. 44).

> The LORD looked and was displeased that there was no justice. He *saw that there was no one*, he was appalled that *there was no one to intervene*. (Isa. 59:15b–16a)

In the NT, Stephen interprets Moses' motivation. "Moses thought that his own people would realize that God was using him to rescue them" (Acts 7:25). The Exodus text, however, does not tell us what Moses was thinking. The death of the Egyptian (whether Moses intended it or not) was certainly illegal in Egypt. The laws that follow in Exodus allow a variety of verdicts for the crime of "striking" (*nakah*; see the comments on Exod. 21:12–27). Exodus 21:12–13 best fits Moses' action and describes the outcome.

> Anyone who *strikes* (*nakah*) a man and kills (*mut*) him shall surely be put to death. However, if he does not do it intentionally, but God lets it happen, he is to flee to a place I will designate.

No moral law allows for the killing of a man who simply beats or strikes another. Our narrative in its context leaves open the possibility that Moses did not intend to kill, but that he was guilty of unintentional manslaughter in his zealousness for justice in a violent land.

Many interpreters point out how Moses' action "anticipates" God's action in striking down (*nakah*) the Egyptians. God
struck them with "wonders" (3:20): water to blood (7:17; 20:25);
lice (8:12–13); hail (9:25, 31–32); and the death of the firstborn
(12:12–13, 29). Nevertheless Moses struck back first against the
Egyptians who had struck the Israelites. If it was not Moses' intention to kill, his action can be interpreted as a sign of his anticipation of the intervening hand of God. If it was his intention to kill
the Egyptian, the narrative itself stands against the action as a *premature* anticipation (see v. 14). In the exodus from Egypt God, and
only God, had the right to give or take life.

Moses showed in this encounter that he had the courage
and desire to deliver the oppressed. He was filled with the passion
necessary for leadership. He was not yet tempered enough, however, to lead his people from a culture of violence—as the repetition of words in verses 11–15 emphasizes ("beating," "killed,"
"fighting," "hitting," "killing," "killed"). His own killing of the
Egyptian, intentional or not, would not be the means of deliverance. It would take forty years and much convincing by God before Moses would work to help his people again.

The next scene, where Moses **saw two Hebrews fighting,**
reveals a gap in his credibility as a leader. The Hebrews had no
reason to accept his authority as one of them, as he did not share
their experience. But even if he had been "one of them," he was not
their leader. His idealized solidarity with them assumed too much
and the disjuncture in his identity is evident. His violent method
of resolving conflict, which they had apparently either observed
or heard of, carried no special hope for them. They knew all about
that. When Moses **asked the one in the wrong,** **"Why are you hitting your fellow Hebrew?"** he used the same word *nakah* ("strike,"
or "hit"). The one in the wrong had no respect for Moses, given
Moses' fatal "hitting" of the previous day. Presumably Moses could
have "hit" and killed him as well! From the Hebrews' perspective,
Moses would have to do better than striking down those who
struck others.

The man asked, **"Who made you ruler and judge over us?"**
Moses had no answer for him. Later, he would be able to respond
without hesitation (3:11–18). For now, Moses' attempt to recon-
cile his brothers is pushed aside in anticipation of the need for a
revealed law from God. The people would trust Moses to adjudi-
cate disputes after his experience at Sinai and Israel, and would

receive a legacy of rule by law, not by might, in the Sinaitic laws given by God.

These incidents, then, briefly foreshadow Moses' need for authority from God and God's law in the wilderness. Moses' kinsmen would be impulsive and reactionary. They would refuse to listen to him, have disputes among themselves, accuse Moses of trying to kill them, and question Moses about his abilities to lead (see also Num. 14, 16). The time was ripe for God's intervention.

Then Moses was afraid. It was clear that Moses' way of human violence would not be God's way of deliverance. God had not called him to violence and his fellow Hebrews would not support violent resistance. In fact, Moses' own people were hostile toward him. This encounter with his kinsmen moves Moses out of Egypt to the land of Midian, where he will prepare in the ways of the Lord in the wilderness.

2:15b–22 / Reuel (Jethro) and his daughters received and welcomed Moses as a stranger **in Midian.** Moses' third test on his quest for identity and purpose began as an anticlimax: **he sat down by a well.** The serenity of a rural well and seven sisters drawing water contrasts with the tumult of Egypt. Unruly shepherds who "bully" the daughters of Reuel briefly interrupt this pastoral peace. Moses defends the sisters, demonstrating that his sense of justice was still intact but that he had learned a more measured use of force.

Midian and the Midianites were located in the desert regions in the vicinity of the Dead Sea, in the Sinai wilderness, and in the northwest region of the Arabian Peninsula. They were a nomadic people sometimes associated with the Ishmaelites. In Genesis 25:2–4 Midian is identified as a descendant of Abraham and Keturah (Abraham's wife after Sarah's death). Jethro/**Reuel** was a priest there, of an undisclosed religion, who would declare faith in Yahweh (the Lord) after the exodus (Exod. 18:10–12). Jethro (lit., "his abundance") was his name throughout the rest of Exodus. He is called "Reuel" (lit., "God's friend") here and in Numbers 10:29 and "Hobab" (lit., "embracing one" in Num. 10:29; Judg. 4:11). These various names reflect different ancient traditions. Jethro/ Reuel had the perfect number of **seven daughters,** and he was in need of a son-in-law. The daughters were capable, but dominating shepherds **drove them away** from **the troughs** that they filled **to water their father's flock.**

Moses got up and came to their rescue. When their father asked, they said, **"An Egyptian rescued us."** Two different and significant words are translated "rescue" in these sentences. Both usually have God as their subject. The first, *yasha͏ᶜ*, means "he saved" and is the root for Yeshua (Jesus) and Joshua. It reflects the metaphor of liberation, freedom from, victory over forces of bondage, and being placed in a wide and free place. The second is the synonym *natsal*, meaning "he delivered" or "snatch away," as from the jaws of an animal. It has the sense of recovering and restoring life. The English text cannot easily convey that richness of meaning, but the words are strong indications of the women's response to, and the text's opinion of, Moses' actions. The daughters had been living under the domination of pushy men. They appreciated his "rescue," and Moses came home to a place he had never been.

A strong rhetorical style communicates the warm excitement of the father's three questions. The tone moves from suspicion to hospitality, salvation, and welcome. **"Why have you returned so early today?"** ... **"And where is he?"** ... **"Why did you leave him? Invite him to have something to eat."** He imagined "the Egyptian," very far from home, having confronted the local muscle and still sitting alone at the well. It is not surprising that **Moses agreed to stay with the man.** "Agreed" (*ya͏ʾal*) can be translated more strongly: "he was pleased" or "he was content." The text does not mention God, who was nonetheless working behind the scenes through strangers to provide for this chosen man. When Jethro **gave his daughter Zipporah** (lit., "Birdie") **to Moses in marriage,** they sealed the long-term apprenticeship.

The last four verses of the chapter are rich with meaning and significance for understanding Exodus. They announce, for the first time, major themes of Scripture. Verse 21 presents the theme of *living as a resident alien.* **Zipporah gave birth to a son, and Moses named him Gershom, saying, "I have become an alien in a foreign land."** In the OT and beyond, God's people see again and again that their identity is as "aliens" or sojourners wherever they live. In this verse, we have a wordplay on two Hebrew words and their meanings (a common occurrence in Hebrew that can rarely find its way into an English translation). "Alien" (the "ger" in "Gershom") in the OT means "resident alien" or "landed immigrant." Moses says that he has been an alien, meaning *in Egypt.* Now he is content. It could also imply the irony that he is at home as a stranger in Midian (only the NIV translates the phrase "I have

become"). This theme will echo, especially in God's laws concerning resident aliens (e.g., "Do not mistreat an *alien* or oppress him,
for you were aliens in Egypt," 22:21).

"Ger" is also a play on the sound of the actual root of
"Gershom," *garash* that means "driven out." Gershom is a pun anticipating the creation of Israel as a nation. This verb repeats the
theme that the Hebrews would be *driven out* of Egypt (otherwise
they never would have made it out; see 6:1; 11:1; 12:39). In a similar way, Moses himself was forced to leave. Moses learned the hospitality of God's wilderness even as Israel later would.

2:23–25 / *Israel groaned and God heard.* Here, at the first
mention of God (*'elohim*) since giving families to the midwives, is
the announcement of a second key theme and an important turning point. God will now increasingly take center stage and dramatically intervene in history, using the nonhuman creation in an
unprecedented way and communicating directly with Moses.
These verses summarize for the first time the dynamic of that
intervention.

The oppression had not abated after forty years and the
death of the old pharaoh. (If the old pharaoh was Rameses II, the
new one would be Merneptah.) The **Israelites groaned in their
slavery and cried out, and their cry for help because of their slavery went up to God. God heard their groaning.** The pattern
groan-cry-cry-groan rhetorically emphasizes the situation of the
people. They "groaned" (*'anakh*) because of the *physical distress* of
their forced labor. They "cried out" (*za'aq*) as a *legal appeal* to God
for how they were being wronged. Their "cry for help" was *a cry
for liberation* from their bondage. Their "groaning" (*ne'aqah*) was
that of a *wounded person* (see Ezek. 30:24).

"God" is the subject of the last four verbs. God "heard." God
remembered. God looked. God knew (NIV **was concerned about
them**). These four verbs answer the four kinds of cries and groans
of the people. "God heard" their groaning, and therefore was
about to intervene. God "remembered" the covenant with Abraham, with Isaac, and with Jacob. God's own integrity and faithfulness to these promises formed the basis of this intervention.
Repeatedly God insisted to the patriarchs that they would "fill the
earth" *and* receive Canaan as an inheritance. With God, "remembering" was not the opposite of "forgetting," but indicated that
God was about to intervene specifically on the matter of their location in Canaan. "God looked" is what Hagar said when God pro-

vided for her and Ishmael in the wilderness (Gen. 16:13) and she gave God the name *"Roi"* or "the one who sees me" (*roʾi*). The implication is that God was moving toward them to provide. The last of the four verbs is brief in the original, with the sense simply that God knew. God understood their situation and their suffering. This divine knowledge stands opposite the statement in 1:8 that the pharaoh "did not know . . . Joseph." God was on the move to enter into their experience, a move that would eventually cost God something (see chs. 32–34).

By the end of Exodus 2, the text has established Moses' identity as a Hebrew and as a person who desired to rescue those who were victimized. The cataclysmic experience of killing the Egyptian radically shaped his character. Moses did not repeat this behavior and did not fight against the bondage of Egypt for another forty years. He "stood up" to injustice against the seven daughters in Midian in a more measured way and with results.

At this point in the narrative, we see that the fullness of time for God's intervention in history had come. Although God was working through people and events up to this point, this work was behind the scenes through the channels and tributaries of creation: Jochebed's love for her child; Miriam's attentiveness to her little brother; Moses' courage to stand against domination; Jethro's and Zipporah's hospitality; the death of the pharaoh; the cry of the people; and Moses' shepherding of sheep near a familiar mountain. The stage was set for a new word from God.

Additional Notes §3

2:12 / Numbers 20:11 echoes Moses' tendency to "strike" on his own—there he strikes (*nakah*) the rock twice instead of speaking to it and waiting on the Lord to strike it. It is for this action that the Lord keeps him from entering the promised land. For a discussion of the history of interpretation of this text see Jacob, *Exodus*, pp. 36–38; Leibowitz, *Shemot*, pp. 40–46. For another opinion of Moses' right to "kill" the Egyptian, see Enns, *Exodus*, pp. 78–84; see also Durham, *Exodus*, pp. 18–19.

2:14 / See a close reading of these anticipatory relationships between Moses and the Israelites in Fretheim, *Exodus*, p. 44.

2:18 / I am treating Reuel and Jethro as the same person. It is also possible that Reuel is Jethro's father and Hobab is Jethro's son (Num. 10:29). The relational terms in Hebrew are ambiguous. My best judgment is that the two names represent the same person from two different traditions, merged in Exodus.

2:22 / The word for "resident alien" (*ger*) refers to Abraham (e.g., Gen. 23:4; 35:27) and occurs many times in the law (e.g., Exod. 12:48; 23:9; Lev. 19:33; 25:35; Num. 9:14; Deut. 24:17). Since "God loves the alien," so we should too (Deut. 10:18). The NT reminds Christians that they were aliens to God before Christ (Eph. 2:19), that those that live by faith are aliens in this world (Heb. 11:13), and that we are aliens until Christ returns (1 Pet. 2:11–12).

2:23 / Their cry for help begins a pattern that persists through the judges and prophets. The pattern usually is this: (1) the people turn away from God; (2) God sends someone to oppress them; (3) they turn toward God and cry for help; (4) God sends a deliverer to help them. Moses is the first deliverer.

§4 Yahweh Calls Moses (Exod. 3:1–22)

The third chapter of Exodus is filled with revelation and interaction. It includes a theophany (the appearing of God) and the story of Moses' call. Moses meets God for the first time in the burning bush, where God calls him to go back to Egypt. We are reminded of the oppression there and hear the first two of Moses' five objections to God's call. Exodus 3 gives the name of the Lord, repeats the promise of land to Abraham's family, and predicts Pharaoh's resistance. Finally, God promises to do "wonders" until the Egyptians let the people go and send them away with silver, gold, and clothing. The complete interaction continues through 4:17 and ideally should be read as one conversation.

3:1–6 / The Lord God introduces himself to Moses. **Moses was tending the flock of Jethro his father-in-law, the priest of Midian** (see comment at 2:18). According to tradition, Moses had forty years left in his life, since he died at the age of one hundred and twenty (Deut 34:7). **Horeb, the mountain of God,** was on **the far side** of the *wilderness.* (NIV has **desert,** but the Hebrew *midbar* means semiarable land where flocks graze in season, as in this text.) "Horeb" (lit., "dry place") is the name used for Sinai in Deuteronomy. Exodus uses both names. The word Sinai sounds like the word "bush" (*seneh*). Scholars have identified the bush as *rubus sanctus,* a thorny desert plant that grows near wadis, or stream beds.

The messenger **of the LORD appeared to him in flames of fire.** This was not an "angel" in the traditional sense, but a "flame of fire" that served as a "messenger," which is the literal meaning of the word. God was present here and spoke directly to Moses. The flame was not God, but was rather the visual part of the message. It created heat and light, but it did not consume the bush. Speculation about the physical phenomenon of the fire (whether it was natural gasses, the sun setting behind a red-leafed or berried bush, etc.) is beside the point. Rather, this miracle hints at the pillar of fire of God's presence in the exodus and the fire of the "dwelling" (Shekinah) glory that would later descend on the tent of meeting and the tabernacle.

Moses turned in verse 3 to **see.** The rabbis said that God's presence was lowly to make possible a personal encounter with Moses. (This theophanic move foreshadows incarnation.) **When the LORD saw** that he turned to look, **God called to him from within the bush.** This is the first mention of "the Lord" (Yahweh, see the discussion on this name at 3:11–15) in the book of Exodus. To this point the word "God" (*ʾelohim*) has been used, without reference to the Lord (Yahweh). It is significant that the two words occur together here, since the identity of the "Lord God" is a primary subject of this text. The double designation of the God of the Judeo-Christian tradition appears first in Genesis 2–3, throughout the Abraham narrative and, after its appearance here, regularly throughout Exodus.

In verses 3–6 God speaks three times. First, God knew Moses' name and called him. **"Moses! Moses!" And Moses said, "Here I am."** God called to Abraham (Gen. 22:11) and Samuel (1 Sam. 3:10) twice as well, perhaps so they would be certain their ears were not deceiving them. This is the typical form of a divine call, and "here I am" is the formal response.

Then God said, **"Take off your sandals"** because the ground was **holy.** This is a call to respect and reverence, in part (as the rabbis said) because of the dirt shoes carried into the sanctuary. Shoeless feet also symbolized poverty and humility before God and solidarity with the oppressed. Moses had entered the natural "temple" of worship.

For the third time, God disclosed Moses' relationship to his past and to God. **"I am the God of your father, the God of Abraham, the God of Isaac and the God of Jacob."** Knowing *who* was present, **Moses hid his face, because he was afraid to look.** Moses' reaction reflects the ancient tradition that one cannot see the face of the Lord God and live. In Exodus 24:11 God was "seen" without death. Even though Moses did not "see" God, this was a "face to face" conversation (see comment about this paradox at Exod. 33:11). The phrase "look at God" is literally "at *the* God," shorthand in Hebrew for "*the God* of Abraham, Isaac, and Jacob." It means "*the true God* of all the earth," since the promise from the beginning is that all the earth will be blessed through the patriarchs.

The theophany (appearing of God) text is full of words of sight: "appearing" and "seeing" and "looking." The words demonstrate that the word of the Lord is external and embodied very early in biblical tradition. In verses 2–6 Moses does most of the seeing and looking, until he is "afraid to look." In verses 7–9, God does all the *seeing* and invites Moses *to look* into the Egypt problem again. The original verb root is the same in each case, except when Moses is afraid to look (*nabat*, lit., "stare" or "gaze"):

Moses

the [messenger] of the Lord *appeared* to him...Moses *saw* . . . it did not burn up (v. 2)

"I will go over and *see* this strange *sight*" (v. 3)

The LORD saw that he had gone over *to look* (v. 4)

he was afraid *to look* (v. 6)

The Lord God

"*I have indeed seen* the misery" (lit., "seeing I have seen") (v. 7)

"*I have seen* the way the Egyptians are oppressing" (v. 9)

3:7–10 / The Lord called Moses to work with God **to bring them up out of that land.** God would not act alone and did not ask Moses to do it himself. It would be a cooperative effort. The text demonstrates this with its structure as well as with its words. The structure of this passage can be illustrated as follows:

3:7–8

A "I have indeed seen the misery of my people in Egypt.

  B I have heard them crying out because of their slave drivers,

    C and I am concerned about their suffering. So I have come down

      D to rescue them from the hand of the Egyptians and to bring them up out of that land"

3:9–10

  B' "And now the cry of the Israelites has reached me,

A' and I have seen the way the Egyptians are oppressing them.

    C' So now, go. I am sending you to Pharaoh

      D' to bring my people the Israelites out of Egypt."

Several relationships are evident. First, in A–D (vv. 7–8) God was not distant, but very close. We hear God's direct, first-person speech: (A) I have indeed seen, I have heard, I am concerned, I have come down to rescue, to bring them. Secondly, in A'–D' (vv. 9–10) God continued by restating the situation (B', A' as in A, B) so that we might expect God to continue to be the sole actor in C' and D'. But although God echoed the themes of C and D, God called *Moses* to carry out this work: God was concerned and had "come down" (C), but Moses was asked to go, sent to Pharaoh (C'). Their work would be related. Thirdly, in D God would rescue them, but God and Moses would bring them out (D, D'). While God would take responsibility for the rescue, Moses would lead alongside God.

At the center of this structure is the *promise of land* God made to Abraham's descendants, restated for the first time in an expanded form. God intended to bring them into a good and spacious land, a land flowing with milk and honey. This description of the land of Canaan occurs twenty times in the OT (in Exod. at 3:8, 17; 13:5; 33:3). Milk and honey are sweet to taste and result from a land with good grassland and flowers, or honey from dates. God's goal in intervening in history was to accomplish a new creation and a new people in a new place. History and creation were dynamically linked in God's purview.

God directly acknowledged that the land was the home of the **Canaanites, Hittites, Amorites, Perizzites, Hivites and Jebusites.** This expression has posed, and continues to pose, problems for Bible readers. Exodus repeatedly uses refrains listing the people to be dispossessed (3:8, 17; 13:5, 11; 23:23, 28; 33:2; 34:11). Scripture is not embarrassed to say that the Lord gives and takes away, both life and land. The possession of the land would come with strict guidelines for keeping it. Later God, through the preaching of the prophets, would *dispossess God's own people* in order to draw them back to the Lord. The promise of land is always conditional in Scripture. The land belongs to God, who made it.

The Canaanites were the largest group on the list and lived in fortified cities. The Hittites were a people originally from Asia Minor who moved into Canaan about 1400 B.C. "Amorite" was a generic term for western Semites, probably originating from the area of modern-day Syria. The Jebusites were specifically the inhabitants of Jerusalem. Extrabiblical sources do not mention the Perizzites, the Jebusites (to whom they may be related), or the Hivites.

God acted in history to dispossess Egypt of its slaves and the peoples of Canaan of their land. God took the initiative but chose not to act alone. Gifted human leadership was crucial to God's work in the world from the very beginning. Moses had a strong sense of justice and was not indifferent to evil, no matter who the oppressor or victim. Moses was deeply concerned for the lives of weaker people and was intolerant of abuse by the strong. These concerns were integral to his call.

3:11–15 / In these verses, Moses raises the first two of his five objections. He was realistic about the dangers of this assignment. He had, after all, experienced some hostility in Egypt. Following are the essence of his five objections and God's responses.

(1) "Who am I?" God responded, "I will be with you; You will worship me." (3:11–12)

(2) "Who are You?" God responded with his name. (3:13–16)

(3) "Suppose they don't believe me?" God gave him three "demonstration" signs (staff, leprosy, blood; 4:1–9).

(4) "I am not eloquent." God said, "I will teach you." (4:10–12)

(5) "Send someone else." God, who had already sent Aaron to help, became angry. (4:11–17)

Moses' *first* objection concerned his identity. **"Who am I, that I should go to Pharaoh and bring the Israelites out of Egypt?"** These words echo the question he heard when he left Egypt many years before: "Who made you ruler and judge over us?" (2:14). God did not answer his question of identity directly, but gave the only answer that would satisfy Moses. Moses would be restless until he rested in God's presence with him. The response, **"I will be with you,"** emphasized that Moses' true identity was not self-referring, but would be found in the God who made him. Its true referent was the presence of the Creator *with* him. God would be doing the "rescuing," not Moses (v. 8). The Hebrew for "I will be" (*'ehyeh*) is tied to verse 14, which describes God's identity in exactly the same form. The promise of the Lord to be *with Moses* was enough to satisfy his self-identity crisis. His singular "who am I" has become God's "I-You." His previous experiences in Egypt and in the ways of the wilderness, although vital to his identity, were not enough. God's presence added to them *was* enough.

God gave a further answer to his question about identity in revealing a sign. **"When you have brought the people out of**

Egypt, you (all) **will worship God on this mountain.**" Moses' personhood and the identity of Israel would be grounded *in their worship of God*. Even bringing the people out of Egypt would not be conclusive proof that God was with him. The proof of their success would be whether or not they worshiped God on this mountain. (The Hebrew highlights this by switching to the plural "you all.") As we shall see in Exodus 32, the people almost did not make it. Escape from slavery was, in God's eyes, neither the primary measure of success nor the limit of God's involvement. Only a people who worshiped God could truly claim deliverance by God. This text announces the theme of worship (serving) that will be repeated throughout Exodus (*ʿabad*, sometimes translated "worship," includes the meaning "serve": 3:12, 18; 4:23; 7:16; 8:1, 20; 9:1, 13; 10:3, 7–8, 11, 24–26; 12:31; 20:5; 23:24–25, 33; 24:1; 34:14). The worship of, or serving, the Lord is the culmination of the exodus event (ch. 15) and the subject of the second half of the book (chs. 20–40). It is no surprise that it was part of the answer to Moses' first and most basic objection.

The Lord's response to Moses' second question was to give him the name of God. "**Suppose I go ... and they ask me, 'What is his name?' Then what shall I tell them?" God said to Moses, "I AM WHO I AM** (*ʾehyeh ʾasher ʾehyeh*). **This is what you are to say to the Israelites: 'I AM** (*ʾehyeh*) **has sent me to you.'" God also said ... "The LORD** (Yahweh) **... This is my name forever.**" The word behind the designation "the LORD" is the name, Yahweh. It is sometimes referred to as the tetragrammaton ("four consonants") for the four Hebrew consonants יהוה (YHWH) that are used in the Hebrew Bible for the personal name of Israel's God. Note that, since it contains no vowels, the pronunciation of this name is not certain, although we know from indirect evidence that "Yahweh" is likely close to how it was originally spoken. The tradition of the Jewish people from centuries before the Christian era says that this name should not be pronounced because it may be spoken or taken in vain (Exod. 20:7). Scripture refers to this name simply as "the name" (Heb. *hashem*, Pss. 20:1, 5; 44:20). English language Bible publishers maintain this "fencing" tradition by using capital letters for "Lord" wherever "the name" appears. Some scholars write out and pronounce the name "Yahweh" for clarity, rather than using the word "Lord." Readers should remember that "LORD" has an actual name behind it.

The name Yahweh, given in verse 15, is preceded in verse 14 by the statement "WHO I AM" (*ʾeyeh*), from the verb "to be" (*hayah*).

This indirect wordplay communicates the nature of the continual active being of God (Durham). There have been many suggestions for translating it, including: "I am that I am," "I will be who I will be" (see Exod. 33:19), and "I will be whatever I will be." The Greek tradition (LXX) translated it, "I am who I am." The important point is that God's name is first revealed as an active verb, not a noun. Yahweh (the Lord) is not an abstraction, but a living, acting being. God's name "Yahweh" lacks much specificity at the beginning of Exodus. In the narrative that follows, it gradually gains meaning in relation to what transpires between God and the people.

God continued to tell Moses what specific words he should speak to the Israelites in verse 15: **"Say to the Israelites, 'The LORD (Yahweh), the God of your fathers—the God of Abraham, the God of Isaac and the God of Jacob—has sent me to you.'"** This whole sentence was God's title, God's very specific answer to Moses' original question, "What is his name?" In verse 16 and following, God shortened the name to **the God of Abraham, Isaac and Jacob.** Verse 15, however, reminds us that God is the God of each individual journey and story. The transcendent and elusive "I AM" was rooted in an immanent historical and revealed God. Yahweh is both hidden and revealed; beyond us and near us.

The early chapters of Exodus often use this patriarchal title, and we also see it at the crisis at Sinai (chs. 32–34). It serves as a reminder that God is present now as well as faithful over a long period of time (Exod. 2:24; 3:6, 15–16; 4:5; 6:3, 8; 32:13; 33:1). God says, **"This is my name forever."** This is the title by which God was to be remembered. The "remembrance" of the name, including the reputation that God would earn *with this name* in the exodus, was an important inheritance. Remembering God's name meant remembering the mighty acts of salvation and deliverance God had performed (see Ps. 111:2–9).

3:16–22 / God's response for the sake of all the Israelites was to give them the name Yahweh. Having answered Moses' question (v. 13), God did not wait for him to agree to go to Egypt. Instead, God simply continued with the next steps of instruction and direction for the assembled elders. The elders were, literally, the older people of Israel. One became an "elder" by living long enough. The elders are sometimes overlooked, yet they were a vital part of the leadership (3:16, 18; 4:29; 12:21; 17:5–6; 18:12; 19:7; 24:1, 9, 14). Among other things, the elders believed (in God), were the leadership for the Passover feast, stood with Moses when he struck the rock for water, ate two meals with Moses in the Lord's presence, and agreed to the covenant at Sinai. The elders were with Moses in support from the beginning. God told him here in verse 18, **the elders of Israel will listen to you.**

God gave Moses seven points for the elders. (1) **Go, assemble the elders of Israel** and tell them that the Lord appeared to you. Moses "saw" as well as heard the Lord. (2) Tell them that God has witnessed their affliction. (3) God has **promised to bring** them up out of Egypt. (4) God promises to bring them to an occupied **land flowing with milk and honey.** (5) The elders are to ask the pharaoh to let them go **into the desert to offer sacrifices to the LORD.** (6) They could expect a threefold result of asking: (a) the pharaoh will refuse; (b) God will strike the Egyptians with mighty deeds; and (c) the pharaoh will let them go. (7) Finally, **Every woman is to ask her neighbor and any woman living in her house for articles of silver and gold and for clothing** (v. 22) so that they **will not go empty-handed** (v. 21).

God did not ask the elders to participate in this plan until they had believed that Moses had spoken with the Lord and that the Lord had, indeed, witnessed their trouble. God had made irrevocable promises. Only after the elders believed these things were they asked to join Moses in seeking a religious holiday. The plan included the inevitable "No" from the pharaoh. God promised to take responsibility for accomplishing the persuasion. It was a plan with some risk, but it came with divine guarantees, if they would but act with Moses.

God told Moses exactly what to say to the elders and to the pharaoh. When he said, **The LORD, the God of the Hebrews, has met with us,** he spoke the name of their God. This would seem like a natural ethnic religious request to the pharaoh. Egyptian records of forced-labor administration mention such religious pilgrimages. Pharaoh recognized the ethnic designation "God of the Hebrews" though he claimed not to know Yahweh (the Lord; 5:2–3; 7:16; 9:1, 13; 10:3). The request for a **three-day journey into the desert** was more of a problem for the pharaoh. Not only would they miss work, but they also wanted three days to walk into the desert. After the worship, it would take three days to walk back. They were not instructed to say, however, that they would come back. (Others interpret this as a three-day round trip.) The request ended as it began, repeating the name, **the LORD our God.** If the elders were to do this, they would have thus confessed their faith in the God of Abraham.

God spoke emphatically, **I know** that he will not let you go. Pharaoh did not (5:1–4; 8:21–24; 10:8–11). Verse 20 is the first mention of the **wonders** (alternatively, "extraordinary deeds," "mighty acts," or even "miracles;" Exod. 34:10; Judg. 6:13; Pss. 78:4, 11; 106:22; Mic. 7:15) that the "hand" of God would perform. This word refers to God's direct intervention and well-timed involvement in human affairs, usually through the nonhuman creation. It comes with the verb "I will **strike**." This is the word (Heb. *nakah*) used for the beating of the Hebrew foremen (5:14, 16). The word would be used again when Yahweh "struck" the Nile to blood (7:17, 20, 25); the dust to gnats (8:12, 13); sent hail to beat down the grain (9:25, 31, 32); and when the firstborn were struck down (12:12–13, 29). It was a case of God's striking in response to the Egyptians' striking the people. **After that,** God says of Pharaoh, **"he will let you go."**

God's instructions for the elders concluded with a promise that they would not leave Egypt impoverished or "empty-handed" (Gen. 15:14; Deut. 15:13; the Sinaitic law states that Israel must not release debt slaves empty-handed). The people had been oppressed as slaves. Their material goods were very limited. The text uses a word root repletion (vv. 19, 21) to make the point that although the king of Egypt "will not *grant* (*natan*) you leave" (NIV "will not let you go"), the Lord "will *grant* (*natan*) this people favor with the Egyptians" (NIV "I will make the Egyptians favorably disposed"). Where Pharaoh would not give, the Lord would make sure that the pharaoh's people give generously. This may have been a token of compensation for the years of forced labor (see further comment on the plundering of the Egyptians at 11:2–3).

God's final word for the elders was that every woman was to "ask her neighbor" for "silver and gold and for clothing." The word for "neighbor" here usually refers to a "neighboring nation." The proximity of actual "neighborhoods" in Egypt is not known. The expression **any woman living in her house** is ambiguous, but the most likely meaning is "any woman living as a tenant in an Egyptian household."

The wordplay in this final verse hints at the theme of building the tabernacle for the first time. The phrase "from her neighbor" (*mishkentah*) sounds like, and is from the same root as, the word for tabernacle (*mishkan*). The Israelites would use this very silver and gold from the Egyptians in building the tabernacle in the wilderness—but not before Aaron would use some of it to smelt the golden calf.

Additional Notes §4

3:8 / See a Native American perspective on the historical problems of using the exodus as a paradigm for liberation in Warrior, "Native American Perspective," pp. 287–95. See also my discussion of liberation theologies in the Introduction.

3:14 / For a fuller discussion of suggested meanings for "the name," see Fretheim, *Exodus*, pp. 63–65; Enns, *Exodus*, pp. 102–4; Houtman, *Exodus*, vol. 1, pp. 94–100, 367.

3:15 / Here and hereafter the text uses the expression, "the God of your fathers" as the title for God used by all Israel. The more general term "your fathers" is now placed before the personal names of the patriarchs.

3:18 / The elders did listen and responded by worshiping God when they heard from Moses (4:31). They did not go with him to Pharaoh—probably because Aaron's presence was sufficient (see commentary on 5:1).

§5 God Prepares Moses (Exod. 4:1–31)

The first half of Exodus 4 continues with Moses' last three protests. Having responded to Moses' first two excuses by Exodus 3:15, God pressed on with instructions for Moses' leadership without giving him a chance to speak. As soon as another another opportunity arose, Moses voiced his third objection: "What if they don't believe me?"; his fourth, "I am slow of speech;" and, lastly, his simple plea: "Send someone else."

In the second half of Exodus 4 Moses has five short encounters: with Jethro; with the Lord for instruction; with the Lord's assault against him; with Aaron; and with the Israelite elders. Each encounter prepared him for, and moved him significantly closer to, his first meeting with Pharaoh.

4:1–9 / Would the *elders* believe Moses had seen God? The third objection completed the third part of the relationship between Moses, God, and the elders. The first question, "Who am I . . . ?" concerned Moses. The second question, "Who are you?" concerned God. His next, a "What if" question, concerned the elders. God had answered this question before he asked it, in 3:18, where God assured Moses that they would listen to him. Moses wasn't sure that providing the elders with notice of the name would be enough to convince them. We see here Moses' growing anxiety about leading the people. The key word in this section is **believe,** which occurs five times (4:1, 5, 9 and twice in v. 8). The issue is **"What if they do not believe** (or "trust") **me"** and say, **" 'The LORD did not appear to you'?"** The Lord took Moses' concern seriously and was ready to provide three signs. These signs were as much for Moses' benefit as they were for the people.

In reply to Moses' theoretical conjecture, God reveals the first sign by asking a concrete question, **"What is that in your hand?"** The **staff** was a shepherd's tool, the means of his control and power to guide and protect the flock. God told Moses to throw it down. It **became a snake, and he ran from it.** The physical humor highlights the irony, as Moses' means of *control* (the staff) was lost and had instead become a *threat*. He took it **by the tail** only because he trusted God (as herpetologists advise, the fangs are controlled only if you take it by the head). God said, **"take it"** (ʾ*akhaz,* "catch it"), but Moses **took hold** (*khazaq,* "snatched it"). This wordplay hints at Moses' legitimate nervousness. He "snatched" the snake quickly.

The purpose of the staff-to-snake sign was **so that they may believe that the** Lord **(Yahweh), the God of their fathers—the God of Abraham, the God of Isaac and the God of Jacob—has appeared to you.** This verse is at the center of the section, reminding us of the issue of the elders' belief. God corroborated his appearance and message to Moses with *visual signs.* Moses had heard and he had also *seen*—so would the elders. This was not, however, just any local god. It was the God of their fathers who they knew as the Creator, the God who sojourns, and the God who redeems. This was the God who had appeared; the one who could create a new reality for them. "Believe" is from the root ʾ*aman,* from which the modern word "amen" comes. It refers, therefore, to something being "true," "trustworthy," "believable."

The second sign of Moses' *believability* was not the staff in his hand, but the **hand** itself. The sign touched Moses' flesh. It was a sign of power because he would appear to control, with God, his own health and illness. The phrase **inside your cloak** is, literally, "on your chest," meaning "on the skin of your chest." The rhetoric follows an oral storytelling style, using extreme repetition to heighten the suspense. Verses 6–7 repeat "on your chest" five times. The word **leprous** refers to skin diseases described in Leviticus 13–14, significantly different from what we think of as leprosy today (Hansen's disease). The phrase is, literally, "encrusted like snow."

The Lord's third response to Moses' concern about the elders' possible disbelief emphasizes the word "believe." **"If they do not** *believe* **you or pay attention to the first miraculous sign, they may** *believe* **the second. But if they do not** *believe* **these two signs . . ."** God instructed Moses in this instance to pour water from the Nile on the ground, at which point it would become blood. This anticipated the first plague in which the whole Nile turned to blood (7:14–25). Moses showed this authenticating sign, along with the other two, to the people (including the elders). They "believed" (4:30–31) or "trusted" Moses. Moses' initial credibility was not, therefore, a problem.

Each of the three signs was a symbol of Egypt's lack of power before the Lord. The staff and serpent were both symbols of authority. The serpent appeared on the front of the pharaoh's headdress, symbolizing his cobra-goddess protection and his power over the lives of his subjects. Leprosy in Scripture was considered a punishment for arrogance before God (Num. 12; 2 Kgs. 5:22–27; 2 Chr. 26:16–21). The Nile was a primary source and symbol of Egypt's prosperity, the source of its export grain harvest. The use of the staff, the skin disease, and the blood were primers for Moses. They also demonstrated the thin line between visible miraculous signs that engendered belief (as with the Israelites) and miraculous signs that hardened hearts, as the plagues would. Later, Israel would respond with "stiff necks" after they had become too accustomed to miraculous signs.

4:10–17 / *Moses' mouth* was the subject of his fourth objection, and this theme would spill into the fifth. His first sentence was appropriately awkward. He addressed the Lord as "Lord," meaning simply "master" (ʾ*adonay*). **"O Lord, I have never been eloquent** (lit., "a man of words"), **neither in the past nor since you have spoken to your servant."** The key word "mouth" occurs seven times in verses 10–17. Moses referred to himself as **slow,** meaning "heavy" of mouth and tongue. It may be overinterpretation to conclude that he had a speech impediment. He may have done poorly in Egyptian rhetoric, or he may simply have been a man of few words in the wilderness.

When Moses complains, "Heavy of *mouth* I am," God's response is poetic: **"Who gave man his mouth? Who makes him deaf or mute? Who gives him sight or makes him blind? Is it not I, the LORD?"** God promised to **help** Moses speak and **teach** him what to say. God says, literally, "I am (ʾ*eyeh*) with your mouth." Surely Moses should be out of excuses at this point. The Lord spoke as though the conversation were over when he said, **"Now go"** (v. 12). But Moses had one more comment.

Moses' final excuse undid his former mouth problem. He speaks with ironic eloquence (at least in Hebrew). **"O Lord, please send someone else to do it"** is much more subtle in the original: "Pardon me, Lord. Please send by hand whomever you send" (meaning "handpick" whomever *else* you send). It may be subtle, but it is nonetheless a refusal. Moses *refused* to do it, *even with* the Lord's help. The Lord responded directly. He would send someone else—not in Moses' place, but to go with him. Aaron was "handpicked" and **already on his way.** God compensated for Moses' weakness.

Then the LORD's **anger burned against Moses.** God showed little sign of this anger in the responses that follow. If the narrator had not told us, we would not know of God's anger. All God did in response was to mention Aaron, who was already on the way. God told Moses that Aaron's **heart will be glad when he sees** him. The joy of their reunion was not compromised. The Lord repeated the promise to **help both** of them **speak** (lit., "I am with your mouth and with his mouth"). This does not sound like anger. God continued to make promises to undergird Moses' reluctance. **"I . . . will teach you what to do . . . it will be as if he were your mouth and as if you were God to him."** God responded positively and with grace to Moses' resistance, even in his anger. God provided everything Moses needed to complete this difficult task.

As this conversation drew to a close, Moses still had not agreed. God drew his attention back to the first sign, the staff in his hand. In saying, **"But take this staff in your hand"** God focused Moses on the simple task of walking with his staff. If he went, God would be with his mouth, and Moses would speak to Aaron. Aaron would speak for him, at least until Moses grew into God's original plan for him to speak himself.

In the second half of Exodus 4 Moses moves closer to his first meeting with Pharaoh through five brief, but significant, encounters.

4:18–20 / The *first* of the five encounters, with Jethro, serves to move the narrative forward. It looks back to Moses' experience in Midian, forward to Egypt, and settles in the present with Zipporah and the boys. After forty years with his generous father-in-law, Moses sought Jethro's blessing and received it with his words, **"Go, and I wish you well"** (*shalom*). Jethro had welcomed him, given him his daughter, a home, and constant employment (2:20–21; 3:1). He would later continue in a supporting role, taking Zipporah and the children out of harm's way during the exodus, returning her, and giving administrative advice (18:1–27). Looking forward, the Lord spoke to Moses again in Midian. God will never be far from Moses throughout the rest of his life. As Moses contemplated his return to Egypt, the memory of killing the Egyptian was still vivid. God's reassurance that **"all the men who wanted to kill you are dead"** is therefore timely. It was now safe for him to return to Egypt.

Verse 20 mentions the family together for the first time. **So Moses took his wife and sons . . . and started back to Egypt.** It was a vulnerable beginning. Zipporah, Gershom, and their second son, Eliezer (18:4), and a donkey were walking with Moses through the wilderness. It is no wonder that we are told that **he took the staff of God in his hand** as God had reminded him to do (4:17). By taking the staff, Moses had accepted his commission.

4:21–23 / Moses' *second* encounter in Midian was with the Lord, who gave him additional instructions for his imminent meeting with Pharaoh. This short conversation gives a preview of conversations and important themes to come. It anticipates this meeting and the **wonders** to come, the "hardening" of Pharaoh's heart (7:3, 13, 22), as well as the threat (11:4–8) and killing of the firstborn sons of Egypt (12:29–30). In these words God claims control of the whole sequence of events about to unfold.

Here for the first time we hear the Lord say, **"I will harden his heart so that he will not let the people go."** (See the discussion of the hardening of Pharaoh's heart at the commentary on 7:1–7; 10:1–2.) Here the word for "harden" means "toughen" or "strengthen" (*khazaq*). The hardening of Pharaoh's heart is sometimes a red herring for interpreters. Pharaoh's heart was already "hard" enough—he had harshly enslaved a whole people. The theological problem is not that Pharaoh was compassionate and the Lord made him "hard." The more difficult issues arise from the fact that the hardening prolongs the enslavement of the children of Israel and eventually requires that the Lord kill the firstborn of Egypt.

These verses also mention the Lord's killing of the **firstborn** for the first time (4:22–23; 6:14; 11:5; 12:12, 29; 13:2, 12–15; 22:29; 34:19–20). Verse 23 is set apart and highlighted in the narrative by its verb change in the words, **"I told you."** This introduction to the importance of the firstborn son makes several important claims. The text itself illustrate this by its structure:

I told you,

A "Israel is my **firstborn son,**

B **Let my son go,** so *he may worship me.*

B' But *you refused* **to let him go;**

A' So I will kill your **firstborn son."**

The repetitions (in bold) form the structure of the key themes of Exodus 1–18. "Israel is my firstborn. Let my son go." This structure holds the crucial relationship (in italics) and makes the point: *worship* of the Lord is the goal; the *refusal* of the pharaoh is the obstacle. This was a cultural battle for the freedom and life of the firstborn. The Lord's firstborn (Israel) was held captive and dying. Only a similar measure against Egypt's firstborn would purchase Israel's freedom. For the first time here, Scripture portrays God as *a parent defending a child.* The word "worship" (*ʿabad*), which also means to serve as a servant, provides a more subtle contrast. Israel was the Lord's servant, not Pharaoh's.

4:24–26 / A description of an assault by the Lord and Zipporah's response comprises the *third* encounter. The interruption of the narrative with the words **the LORD met Moses and was about to kill him** is abrupt. The many ambiguities in the words that follow have led to hundreds of pages of scholarly conjecture about their original meaning. The primary theological question concerns what would have motivated the Lord to kill Moses—for God had worked so hard to convince and prepare him to go back to Egypt. The extremity of the phrase "about to kill" signifies something nonnegotiable. The text tells us that circumcision is the *sine qua non.* Moses cannot lead the people without a circumcised family. This extreme enforcement only applied to Moses, who was to help *birth* the Lord's firstborn nation through the waters of the sea. It is certain in this text that uncircumcision was not an option. It is also certain that **Zipporah** understood the situation, acted to save her family, and satisfied the Lord's concern. In doing so, this Midianite woman proved her commitment to the God of Abraham who commanded circumcision as an "everlasting covenant" (Gen. 17:1–14). Her action resolved the ambiguity of Moses' identity as a Hebrew who was raised in Pharaoh's house and married to a Midianite woman. Her closing comment could be paraphrased, "Our marriage is marked by the Yahwistic covenant of circumcision given to Abram." *God allowed time for Zipporah's mediation* in the words "about to kill" by hesitating before carrying out the action.

The rhetorical effect of the text is to unsettle the reader. Just when Moses was finally on his way to Egypt (because God told him it was safe), we encounter God's complete freedom to act in what seems to us a crazy way. If we could edit this account today we would no doubt leave this story out (perhaps also as we might like to omit Acts 5:1–11). The text does not apologize, however, nor does it give rationalizations for the Creator's willingness to take back the life God gives. Even Moses cannot presume upon God.

The placement of this account has a moral-theological function against arrogance. It follows the first mention of God's killing Egypt's sons. Moses is about to speak to Pharaoh about his sons and their deaths. Anyone about to say such things should consider his own death and the deaths of his own sons.

4:27–31 / Moses, Zipporah, and the boys traveled back to the **mountain of God** to meet Aaron. Moses' *fourth* encounter on the way to meeting the pharaoh was this reunion with Aaron. Here the contrast is between the conflict of the "meeting" with God and the anticlimax of the glad "meeting" with Aaron that God had promised (4:14). For the first time we are told that the Lord spoke to Aaron. **So he met Moses** at the "mountain of God" **and kissed him. Then Moses told Aaron everything.** Aaron began, as Moses did, at the mountain to which they would return for worship and transformation with the people.

Back in Egypt, the fifth and final encounter is between **Moses, Aaron, all the elders,** and **the people**. It begins with a wordplay on "Joseph": Moses and Aaron **brought together** "all the elders." In the Hebrew, he "josephed" or "gathered" them. A more important translation issue in the NIV involves **the Israelites**—literally, "children of Israel." While translators often reduce the designation "children of Israel" to "Israelites," it serves an important function. God was creating a *new sociality* among a new people by taking them on a *journey into the wilderness* for *worship*, for *formation as a people in the laws of Sinai*, and to *teach them trust* in the Lord's providing and protecting hand. They began and continued on this journey as "children." Too much is lost when this word is replaced with a more abstract word.

The narrative concludes after **Aaron told them everything.** Aaron did the talking to the elders. Moses performed the signs (staff-to-snake, hand like snow, water to blood) for all **the people, and they believed.** Moses' worries faded. **And when they heard that the LORD was concerned . . . and had seen their misery, they bowed down and worshiped.** The people would respond by bowing and worshiping twice more: once when they heard of the Passover protection from death (12:27) and once for the apostasy of the golden calf (see also further inconsistency of behavior in 32:8 and 34:8). They were now ready for Moses to go to the pharaoh.

Additional Notes §5

4:1 / On the Lord's willingness to develop new strategies in relation to Moses' concerns and the real openness of the future because of the uncertainty of human behavior, see Fretheim, *Exodus*, pp. 68–69.

4:5 / The "appearing" of the Lord to Moses at Sinai (and throughout Exodus) and later to the elders (24:9–11) is an important theme for the book (see comment on 33:11). For Christians it is an anticipation of the incarnation.

4:13 / Some interpreters take this fifth excuse as a continuation of the fourth, since God's response presses the issue of finding Aaron, who can speak well. Moses, however, is concerned about going alone. The text here speaks of Aaron, who is prominent in Exodus, for the first time. God mentions that Aaron is a Levite, as is Moses. This may be the one indication of God's tone of anger, if it is read, "Aaron is a *true* Levite."

4:19 / The NIV translates several different Hebrew verbs as "kill" in 4:19–24 (v. 19: *baqash* with *nepesh*, "sought your life;" v. 23: *harag*, "slay;" and v. 24: *baqash* with *mut*, "sought to cause death").

4:21 / The miracles given to Moses and the so-called plagues are sometimes called "signs" (from *ʾot* in 3:12; 4:8, 9, 17, 28, 30; 7:3; 8:19; 10:1–2; 12:13), "wonders" (*mopet*, meaning "display of power," sometimes as a sign of a future event, in 4:21; 7:3, 9; 11:9–10), and "extraordinary deeds" (*nipleʾot* from *palaʾ* meaning "surprisingly wonderful," in 3:20; 15:11; 34:10). The NIV uses "wonders" for both *mopet* and *nipleʾot*.

4:22 / The "firstborn" is an important paradigm for Christians and their understanding of who Jesus is. When the people of Israel are called *firstborn* in relation to God, the promise to Abraham to bless all the nations of the world through them moves toward fulfillment. The NT calls attention to this parallel between the promise and the first fulfillment when it calls Jesus the "only begotten" of the Father.

4:24 / One ambiguity concerns who exactly was attacked. *Moses* is italicized in the NIV text, since the original only has "him." The text could be referring to Moses' son. A second ambiguity is whether touching Moses is a sign that he was not circumcised and needed this vicarious sign. None of these ambiguities change the central point of the Lord's attack and Zipporah's response. "Feet" is sometimes a euphemism for genitals. For a survey of the many conjectures about the original meaning of this text, see Houtman, *Exodus*, vol. 1, pp. 433–49 and Durham, *Exodus*, pp. 56–58.

§6 Oppression Increases (Exod. 5:1–6:1)

The major theme of Exodus 5 focuses on the question, "Who will serve *whom*?" The players and their commitments are center stage: Aaron and Moses, the pharaoh and his servants, and the Israelite foremen caught in between. The conflict that begins here will not be resolved until Exodus 12:31–33.

This chapter echoes some of the material in Exodus 1, reminding readers of the situation in Egypt: heavy work, servitude, making bricks, and numerous Hebrews. The difference here is that Moses and Aaron, as called by the Lord, have had an effect on this situation. The initial negative effect was an intensification of the pharaoh's demands for making straw into bricks (5:7, 8, 10–14, 16, 18–19). While Moses and Aaron mention God for the first time in Pharaoh's presence, the Lord, like the laboring people, does not speak directly in this chapter.

5:1–9 / Aaron and Moses' first request from the Lord to Pharaoh results in a resounding "No" (vv. 1–5) and a new policy of intensified work (vv. 6–9).

The first exchange with Pharaoh takes the form of a direct demand. **"This is what the LORD, the God of Israel, says: 'Let my people go, so that they may hold a festival to me in the desert.'"** Here is the first, but not the last, demand from Yahweh (the Lord) to "Let my people go" (5:1; 7:16; 8:1, 20; 9:1, 13; 10:3; see also 4:22). In this way, Moses and Aaron introduce "Yahweh" to Pharaoh. The use of the *name* was necessary in the polytheistic Egyptian context. Pharaoh, however, did **not know** who Yahweh was and, as King of Egypt, would certainly not obey him. What Pharaoh and others know and do not know dictates their decisions in Exodus. They, and the reader of Exodus, will know much more about Yahweh before the end of the book. "Knowing the Lord" is a main theme fleshed out in the book's rhetorical shape (1:8; 5:2; 6:3, 7; 7:5, 17; 8:10, 22; 9:14; 10:2, 7, 26; 11:7; 14:4, 18; 16:6, 12; 18:11; 23:9; 29:46; 31:13; 33:12, 13, 16–17).

Moses explains the Lord in terms Pharaoh might understand: **"The God of the Hebrews has met with us."** Moses' second statement (v. 3) is also more specific about the "festival": **"Now let us take a three-day journey into the desert to offer sacrifices to the LORD our God."** This six-day round-trip would have involved taking livestock for sacrifices. Moses added his concern (which the attack in 4:24 proved was legitimate) that God might assail them **with plagues or with the sword** if they didn't go. (The word "strike" in the NIV is not from *nakah*, but *paga^c*, "assail"; see the comments at 5:14.) The foremen raise a competing concern about the threat of *Pharaoh's* sword in verse 21. Whom would they serve? Whom would they revere ("fear")?

The king's second response focuses on his labor projects and lost man-hours. He mentions how **numerous** they are because they constituted a significant percentage of his workforce. Egyptian labor logs show that workers were given religious holidays, but the Hebrew workers were too numerous to let go for so long. When the king says, **"Get back to your work! . . . you are stopping them from working"** he uses the word for "work" that means "burden" (*siblah*), a reference to "forced labor" (1:11; 2:11; 5:4–5; 6:6–7). As a competent administrator, he did not want this "ruse" to interrupt production. Ironically, he also used the word "stop" (*shabat*), which is the root for "Sabbath." The LORD would command them to "stop" working every seventh day (see 16:23–29; 20:8–11; 31:14–16; 35:2–3).

In verses 6–9 the pharaoh issues a new **order** to the Egyptian **slave drivers** (who had a job description similar to modern-day project managers) and the **foremen in charge of the people.** The foremen are identified later, in good narrative style, as *Israelite* foremen, when they are beaten and bring their complaint to Pharaoh (vv. 14–15). The taskmasters (translated in the NIV as "slave drivers") are identified as *Pharaoh's* (v. 14). They drove or enforced the work while the foremen organized the workers. This system is corroborated by Egyptian work records.

The order was an administrative decision that created a new policy (vv. 7–8). The new law, or declaration, from the mouth of Pharaoh had three parts, each of them repeated in verses 17–18. (1) **You are no longer to supply the people with straw for making bricks; let them go and gather their own straw. (2) . . . require them to make the same number of bricks as before. (3) They are lazy; that is why they are crying out, "Let us go and sacrifice to our God."**

The official declaration of "laziness" (*rapah*, idleness or relaxation) was a propaganda tool that reinforced the law. After the foremen complain to the pharaoh, it is the first thing he mentions (v. 17)—for it gives the "logic" for his new policy. Pharaoh claims that Aaron and Moses' request for the religious pilgrimage to the desert is based on **lies** (v. 9), motivated by laziness. The reader knows that the logic is fallacious, but Pharaoh was impervious. The so-called lies in this case are the words of Moses from verse 1 that the LORD, the God of Israel indeed said, "Let my people go, so that they may hold a festival to me in the desert." Pharaoh believed that Moses was a fake and his god was false.

5:10–14 / The labor intensification policy ("no straw, same quota") was put into effect by the Egyptian taskmasters and the Hebrew "foremen." The kind of language they used to communicate the policy reveals the legal nature of this order. They declared, **"This is what Pharaoh says."** The more formal "Thus says (*koh ʾamar*) the pharaoh" communicates the original more completely. It is sometimes called a "transmission formula" and is primarily used in Scripture as "Thus says the LORD" with prophetic words from Yahweh. The words are exactly the same when they refer to Pharaoh here and to the Lord in verse 1. The words **your work will not be reduced at all** end with the older "it is spoken" (*dabar*, NIV "at all"). This, too, is jurisprudence language, echoed in the translation **required of you for each day** (*dabar*, lit., "spoken of," vv. 13, 19). In verse 14, the phrase **quota of bricks** uses the word meaning "statute" (*khoq*) or "ordinance" (as it is translated in 12:24 and throughout Exodus). The Pharaoh's word was law. Whose law would they serve?

In Egypt bricks were made in rectangular blocks of mud, clay, and chopped wheat or barley stalks. They were as large as twelve inches long, six inches tall and six inches deep. The stalks or decaying **straw** provided humic acid, which increased its effectiveness as a binder. The labor was intensified when **the people scattered all over Egypt to gather stubble to use for straw.** "Stubble" generally refers to the dried-out remains in the fields after the harvest, less suitable for bricks because it was dry (and thus contained no humic acid). The doubled task proved to be impossible, as the pharaoh knew it would be. The purpose of the law was to quell the desire for a religious holiday by driving out the "lie" of Yahweh's request. Concomitant with this objective, the **Israelite foremen . . . were beaten** and taunted.

5:15–18 / The foremen's dilemma serves to focus the primary theme, "Who will serve whom?" When the Israelite foremen went to Pharaoh, they encountered the red tape of the new policy. Pharaoh simply repeated his policy from verses 7–8. The ordinary workers had no voice and no opportunity to register complaint. They could only groan under their daily labor. The foremen, however, seemed to be positioned to make some choices. Their conversation with Pharaoh revealed their now-critical position. They had relatively better situations than the laboring slaves but they were, nonetheless, servants of a pharaoh who had no regard for them. He had established a "statute" (*khoq*) or **quota** that was impossible to meet and he beat those who did not meet it.

When they went to speak to the pharaoh, they may have supposed that their special status as foremen would give them a platform for negotiation. They were granted a conversation and had enough status to make the appeal, **"Why have you treated your servants this way?"** They were also able to say, **"Your servants are being beaten, but the fault is with your own people."** They were certainly his "servants" (*'ebed*), a term that is also translated "officials" (*'ebed*) in reference to the Egyptians. They were all his servants, who served him. The same word is used in the command that follows: "Now go *serve*!" (NIV **Now get to *work*,** *'abad*). The theological weight of the word *'abad* is that it also means "worship" and is used that way extensively in Exodus. Whom you *serve* is whom you *worship*. The word is the same root used in 3:12, "You will *worship* God on this mountain" (also, e.g., 4:23; 9:1, 13; 12:31; see also 14:12). The foremen's loyalties become the focus in their declaration that Pharaoh's people were at "fault" (lit., "sinning," or "wrong").

The Hebrew also subtly marks the crisis of service by using the expression ***appealed* to Pharaoh** (lit., "cried out," from *tsa'aq*). This word only appears elsewhere in Exodus when it refers to a desperate appeal to Yahweh (2:23; 8:8; 14:10, 15; 15:25; 17:4; 22:22, 26). Only in this chapter is the "crying out" to Pharaoh (vv. 8, 15), once in this appeal and also in the telling sentence, "They are lazy; that is why they are *crying out*, 'Let us go and sacrifice to our God.'" The one to whom they cry out is the one they serve. The Lord's poetic response to the beating (*nakah*) of the foremen will be to strike (*nakah*) Egypt with wonders (3:20), with blood (7:17, 25), with gnats (8:12–13), and with hail (9:25, 31–32).

5:19–21 / Moses and Aaron were waiting for the foremen when they left Pharaoh. The foremen complained to them

bitterly and say, ironically, "leave it in the LORD's hands to judge."
This expression usually means that they believed God would
punish Moses and Aaron for what they had done. They also complained, **"You have made us a stench to Pharaoh and his officials**
(lit., "made our odor offensive") **and have put a sword in their
hand to kill us."** The sword of Pharaoh was a fitting contrast to
the sword of the Lord mentioned at the beginning of the chapter
(v. 3), so a battle had clearly begun. It would not be fought with
swords, but with the might of the Creator who called Moses to
lead the people out of Egypt. In addition to Pharaoh and his servants, the foremen would also need to be convinced that Moses
was not lying.

5:22–6:1 / At the end of this first round, Pharaoh has
clearly won. Everyone is discouraged, including Moses, who complained to God. Yahweh responded as though everything was
going according to plan. The Lord had told Moses that Pharaoh
would refuse (3:19; 4:21).

The key word in Moses' complaint is "trouble" (ra^ca^c, "evil
plight," or "catastrophic situation"). The foremen also **realized
they were in *trouble*** (v. 19). In verse 22 Moses asks, **"why have you
brought *trouble* upon this people?"** and complains that **"Pharaoh
. . . has brought *trouble* upon this people."** Moses and the foremen
were correct about the seriousness of the situation. They would either capitulate to Pharaoh or the Lord would have to do something. Moses knew that the problem pivoted on the *name* of the
Lord. Moses began one of his complaints to the Lord, **"Ever since I
went to Pharaoh to speak in your name."** Pharaoh had accused
him of lying when he asked, "Who is Yahweh? . . . I don't know
Yahweh" (v. 2). It was time, Moses intimates, to prove Yahweh's
existence and power. He placed the burden on the Lord by saying
"you" or "your" to the Lord four times.

Moses said, **"you have not *rescued* your people at all."**
Moses had *rescued* Zipporah and her sisters at the well (2:19) and
God had promised to *rescue* the people when calling Moses (3:8),
so Moses knew a rescue when he saw one. God did not blame
Moses for his honest appraisal in a difficult moment. God knew
this would be a prolonged conflict with *trouble*. God responded to
Moses' complaint in parallel verse:

> "Because of my *mighty hand* he will let them go;
> because of my *mighty hand* he will drive them out of his country."

Exodus 5 sees the full engagement of the conflict concerning who was in control and who would be served. The Egyptian perspective was that the hierarchy of service went as follows: Pharaoh → other gods → Egyptians → other peoples including the Hebrews. The book of Exodus has another perspective: Yahweh → Moses, Aaron, and the Hebrews → Pharaoh. The conflict between these two political models will not be resolved until 12:31–33, when Pharaoh says, "Leave . . . Go, worship the LORD." Here in Exodus 5, however, the pharaoh wins the first round. Moses is in the midst of the fray when God renews his call in Exodus 6. God does not leave him without guidance when Moses seeks the face of the Lord.

Additional Notes §6

5:1 / Throughout the book of Exodus God is genuinely interactive in dialogue with the community and with Moses. God makes three major kinds of adjustments in Exodus. First, God takes Moses' objections seriously (3:1–4:17), as well as his later intervention to save the people (chs. 33–34). Secondly, God and Moses were not locked into the exact strategy against Pharaoh stated in 3:16–22. Although the plan originally stated by God had predictive elements, it was not unchangeably predictive. The plan was contingent on God's interaction with human anxiety, fear, and even resistance. God's stated plan changed with events on the ground. The elders did not go to the pharaoh after Aaron was included (v. 1; the rabbis said they dropped out one by one because of fear, *Exodus Rabbah* 5:14). The foremen did go (God said nothing about them) and Moses and Aaron prudently waited to speak with them after the meeting (vv. 15–20). Thirdly, the plan could be effectively resisted. God gave humanity that power. Sin, doubt, and rebellion caused God to alter his strategy. At Sinai, the good that God set out to do almost ended in disaster. God adjusted to this freedom to rebel, using a combination of force and forgiveness. These interactive changes in strategy account for most of what may seem to be inconsistencies in the narrative. (For a fuller discussion of this theme, see Fretheim, *Exodus*, pp. 66–68.)

5:3 / The alternating use of "God of the Hebrews" and "God of Israel" is significant in Exodus (vv. 1, 3). God is forming the nation *Israel* from the ethnic group known as the *Hebrews*. This group may be related, but it is not identical to a larger social group designation found in ancient Near Eastern texts known as *ḥapiru*. They were the socially displaced persons of the ancient world. Before and during the exodus, Abraham's descendents were known as "Hebrews." During and after the exodus, they were known as "Israel" or the "children of Israel" (NIV "Israelites"). Israel was formed as a unique cultural group and nation under the Lord's instruction at Sinai. Later, after the Babylonian exile (587–538 B.C.), they would begin to refer to themselves as *Jews* (deriving from "Judah," see Esth. 2:5).

5:23 / This commentary section ends with Exodus 6:1 instead of 5:23 because God and Moses are in the middle of an important conversation. Exodus 6:2 begins a new conversation. The chapter divisions we commonly use were not part of the ancient manuscripts. Chapter divisions were first accepted and used in the Paris Bible, added by Stephen Langton (d. 1228), the archbishop of Canterbury.

§7 Yahweh's Promises (Exod. 6:2–30)

This "pause" in Moses' interaction with Pharaoh continues until 7:8, and the section from 6:2 to 7:7 contains more dialogue between Moses and the Lord and Aaron's genealogy. All of this material is significant to the narrative as it expands the revelation of the Lord's identity and promises; renews Moses' call after the conflict and discouragement of Exodus 5; and establishes Aaron's call, credentials, and legitimacy as a leader. Structurally, Moses' two comments about his "faltering lips" (vv. 12, 30) serve to hold the diverse conversations and lists together in a chiasmus (a common rhetorical device found in the Old Testament, frequently referred to in the field of biblical studies as a "chiasm," where the syntactic elements of parallel phrases are inverted) as follows:

A Moses' **renewed call** (vv. 2–9)

  B *"Faltering lips"* (vv. 10–12)

    C **Aaron's call and genealogy** (vv. 13–27)

  B' *"Faltering lips"* (vv. 28–30)

A' Aaron's and Moses' **united call** (7:1–7)

6:2–9 / The Lord's fuller self-identification, expanded details of the promises to the children of Israel, and a renewal of Moses' call are found in these verses. The refrain **"I am the LORD"** (*'ani yhwh*, vv. 2, 6, 7, 8) resounds in these verses as it did in Moses' initial call in Exodus 3. The contrast between "God Almighty" (*'el shadday*; Gen. 17:1; 28:3; 35:11) and "the LORD" was meant to announce something *new* in God's self-revelation in history. Of course Abraham, Isaac, and Jacob also knew God as "the LORD" (Gen. 15:2; 18:1; 25:21; 28:16).

The text itself explains the distinction between the two names. The earlier name was associated with the promise **to give them the land of Canaan, where they lived as aliens.** The *new* name contrasts with the earlier name by means of the Lord's "I" statements and the promises listed in verses 6–8.

> **"I am the LORD, and *I will bring you out* from under the yoke of the Egyptians. *I will free you* from being slaves to them, and *I will redeem you* with an outstretched arm and with mighty acts of judgment. *I will take you* as my own people, and *I will be* your God . . . And *I will bring you* to the land . . . *I will give it to you* as a possession. I am the LORD."**

These seven first-person promises constitute a new revelation of the Lord's reputation in the world. This revelation is connected to the older promises of land but adds the unconditional promises of freedom, deliverance, redemption, and election as a people by God. These new promises—identified with his name—define the reputation of the Lord, not only in Exodus, but throughout Scripture. Redemption (*ge᾽ullah*) refers to the right of receiving back one who had previously belonged to God's chosen family (Lev. 25:47–49).

The use of the verb "know" (*yada῾*) indicates the essential "newness" of the revelation. **I did not make myself *known* to them** (v. 3) and **you will know that I am the LORD your God, who brought you out from under the yoke of the Egyptians** (v. 7). What the people know or don't know about the Lord is a critical theme (vv. 3, 7; 7:5; 10:2, 26; 16:6, 12; 29:46; 31:13). The Lord "*who brought you out*" will be the key definition of the Lord, used as a refrain in Israel's Scriptures (e.g., 16:6; 20:2; 32:4).

It was important to renew these promises to Moses at this point in the narrative. The crisis had heightened in three ways: the labor and oppression of Pharaoh had intensified; the Hebrew taskmasters had called upon the Lord to judge Moses (5:21); and Moses himself had cried out to God in distress (5:22–23). Moses was isolated—Aaron was nowhere to be seen at this juncture. Moses needs to hear that God's reputation is intact and to be reminded of God's intentions. God took responsibility for the situation with a new word—Moses' task was simply to preach this reputation to the people.

The people's response indicates the depth of the crisis. **Moses reported this to the Israelites, but they did not listen to him because of their discouragement and cruel bondage.** The people were so broken they could not even listen to God's promises, although these promises and God's faithfulness to act on them was their only hope. Physical deliverance was necessary before they could hear or understand. Only the Lord's gracious intervention would be able to carry the people beyond their broken spirit (lit., "short breath," NIV "discouragement"). Their own strength or action could not accomplish their redemption. The text does not mention the people again until the Passover, and then only to describe how they eat a meal and are saved from death. This is the "gospel" of the exodus: God has to intervene with a mighty hand (vv. 1, 6) and needs Moses (and Aaron) simply *to declare* the Lord's judgment to the oppressors and *to claim deliverance* of the people (see Fretheim, *Exodus,* pp. 91–96).

6:10–30 / The remainder of this chapter establishes Aaron's call and credentials. The genealogy functions mainly to demonstrate his legitimacy as a leader with Moses. The narrative structure ingeniously serves this purpose, as it begins and ends with Moses' concern about his **faltering lips** (vv. 12, 30)—which makes Aaron's presence necessary. The Lord's instructions to Moses to speak to **Pharaoh king of Egypt** also frame this section (vv. 10–11 and 28–29). This *inclusio* (found within the chiastic framework above), or matching thematic beginning and ending, to the genealogy can be further diagrammed as follows:

   B   "Faltering lips," speak to the king of Egypt (vv. 10–12)

      C   Formal introduction: Moses and Aaron (v. 13)

         D   Genealogy of Aaron (vv. 14–25)

      C′ Formal conclusion: Aaron and Moses, Moses and Aaron (vv. 26–27)

   B′ "Faltering lips," speak to the king of Egypt (vv. 28–30)

The formal introduction and conclusion subtly reinforce the emphasis on Aaron. The conclusion, in verse 26, reverses the names, with Aaron first. The genealogy describes Aaron's family (vv. 23, 25) but only mentions Moses as Aaron's brother (v. 20). While Aaron is the focus here, Moses is ultimately first (v. 13) and last (v. 27).

The significance of the genealogy in verses 14–25 lies in who it includes and who it ignores. Its primary purpose within this narrative is to explain the importance of the clans of Levites and especially Aaron and his descendents.

The motivations behind the shaping of the text in this way are obvious. First, it mentions only the first three of the twelve sons of Jacob/Israel: Reuben, Simeon, and Levi. The fourth son,

Judah, will be very important as the family of the Davidic kingship, but he is conspicuous by his absence here. **Reuben** and **Simeon** were the first- and second-born of Jacob and Leah. The text mentions them and their sons simply to get to the third-born, **Levi.**

Levi is significant because of Moses, Aaron, and the Levitical priestly tradition is introduced here for the first time. Levi's personal reputation was poor because he had murdered the Shechemites (Gen. 34:30; 49:5). Two of his three sons (**Gershon** and **Merari**) are relevant here because of their general role as ancestors of the *clans of the Levites* (vv. 19b and 25b). His second son **Kohath,** however, had three sons, two of whom were very important (**Amram** and **Izhar**) because of *their* sons (**Moses, Aaron,** and **Korah**).

The second clue in this text to the motivation behind it is that it lists ages for *only* Levi, Kohath, and Amram. This is the most important lineage, since it leads us to Aaron. The third marker of the genealogy's purpose is that it fully develops two linear branches:

> Levi → Kohath → Amram → Aaron → Eleazar → Phinehas
> (six generations)

> Aaron, Eleazar, and Phinehas each served as high priest.

> The other full branch has a less celebrated function:

> Levi → Kohath → Izhar → Korah → three sons
> (five generations)

Korah was known for his rebellion against Aaron and Moses (see Additional Notes for 6:2–9).

What is critical to glean from these verses is the legitimacy of the lineage of Aaron and his sons and grandsons; the Levite clan names for their tabernacle service; and the fact that Korah is Moses' and Aaron's cousin.

The narrative that concludes the genealogy returns to the introductory themes, listing Aaron first. **It was this same *Aaron and Moses* to whom the LORD said, "Bring the Israelites out of Egypt by their divisions"** (or "in an orderly way"). A similar sentence, which names Moses first, follows (v. 27). These two verses match verse 13, providing a conclusion that matches the introduction (*inclusio*).

God responds in part to Moses' concern about his faltering lips by the renewed call and by listing Aaron's credentials. God will answer it further in 7:1: "I will make you like God to Pharaoh." In 4:16 the Lord had promised to make him like God to Aaron. The brothers were now fully prepared to stand in the gap as representatives while God administered mighty deeds. It would not be Moses' or Aaron's speech that would convince Pharaoh, nor the participation of the disheartened and silent people. They would be brought out "by their divisions," an ironical military designation (12:17, 41, 51; 13:18; 18:21). God would do the fighting, and the people would march out in victorious formation.

Additional Notes §7

6:2–9 / The **heads of the Levite families, clan by clan** listed here surface again in Numbers 3, a text that delineates their special duties and camping places around the tabernacle. Levi's son Gershon and his sons' clans camped behind the tabernacle on the west. They were responsible for the fabric of all the tent coverings and screens (Num. 3:21–26). Levi's son Kohath and his sons camped on the south side. All the furniture, including the ark, table, lampstand, and vessels were their responsibility. Levi's son Merari and his clans were responsible for the tent frames, bases, ropes, and pegs. They camped on the north side. Aaron and his sons and Moses (Kohath's grandsons) camped on the east.

A few of Levi's descendants are memorable for their arrogance before the Lord. Aaron's cousin Korah and others rose against Aaron's privilege as high priest and were swallowed by the earth with 250 men and their families (Num. 16). Two of Aaron's four sons with Elisheba, **Nadab** and **Abihu**, offered unauthorized fire before the Lord and were consumed by the fire (Lev. 10:1–2). **Eleazar** became high priest and succeeded Aaron in service (Exod. 28; Num. 3:32). Aaron's son **Phinehas** received special commendation for dramatically ending the sexual rebellion and its attendant plague at Baal-Peor that had already killed 24,000 people (Num. 25; Ps. 106:30–31). Later, in Canaan, Phinehas intervened with Reuben, Gad, and Manasseh to prevent unnecessary war (Josh. 22:1–34).

6:3 / Scholars sometimes explain the claim that Abraham did not know the name Yahweh by varying source traditions, but since it was not smoothed out by the redactor, the contextual interpretation offered above in the commentary is more helpful.

6:6–8 / The Passover Seder service still marks the promises of these verses with five cups of wine symbolizing five stages of redemption. The first four cups represent: physical freedom; psychological deliverance; redemption of the relationship with God; and being taken securely as the people of the Lord. The fifth cup is reserved for the coming of Elijah and the messianic promise of the land (see Sarna, "Exodus," p. 352).

6:8 / **I swore with uplifted hand** is a Hebrew expression that refers to lifting one's hand to take an oath.

6:12 / "Faltering lips" is, lit., "uncircumcised lips." This probably means "undisciplined" or "untrained."

6:14 / Establishing Aaron's legitimacy in the genealogy is important for his role in Exodus. It is also necessary in light of the golden calf incident in Exod. 32–24. His lineage and call by God established his role as priest in perpetuity, in spite of his inability to lead the people in Moses' absence (see the discussion on Exod. 32). For further discussion of genealogies see Rendsburg, "The Internal Consistency," pp. 185–206.

6:24 / In Num. 16, Korah and others rebelled against Moses' and Aaron's leadership. The Lord consumed 250 men with fire as they attempted to offer the incense reserved for the Aaronic priests. God also opened the earth and swallowed the tents of their families. Korah's clans, however, did not all participate in the rebellion, for "the line of Korah . . . did not die out" (Num. 26:11). Many of the Psalms (42, 44–49, 84–85, 87–88) are attributed to the sons of Korah, an honored guild of musicians or poets whose clans and genealogies are listed in 1 Chr. 6:1–48.

§8 The Plagues Begin (Exod. 7:1–25)

Exodus 7–12 describes the Lord's dramatic intervention in the lives of the Israelites. God accomplishes two main objectives through the plagues and the eventual exit from Egypt in the crossing of the sea. We see these in the refrains, "Let my people go so that they might *worship* me," and "so you may *know* that I am the LORD." These events reveal that God is the Creator of all things and the redeemer of this people. The Lord is not simply the one who redeems Israel, but also the Creator who draws near in a terrifying deliverance. Conversely, the Lord is not simply an awesome Creator, but a personal force of deliverance, seeking an exclusive and intimate relationship with the people of Israel in history.

The Lord's use of plagues against Egypt creates dissonance for many readers. There are other instances in the OT where God uses plagues as a weapon against injustice and rebellion. In some cases, such as in the ten plagues of Egypt, they were used to fight *for* Israel and their deliverance (against their enemies). In others, such as at Baal-Peor (Num. 25:1–8) and with the fiery serpents (Num. 21:4–9), God used plagues *against Israel* to stop their rebellion and cause them to return to the Lord.

The theological function of these catastrophic events is to establish the identity of Yahweh as the Creator of all creation. The text gives the reason for the use of the plagues and the trouble they caused: "that I might show you my power and that my name might be proclaimed in all the earth" (Exod. 9:16; see the discussion at 9:14–16). Water, weather, insects, animal health, and the light of the sun are all in God's control. The plagues demonstrate that the God who seeks the people's deliverance is also the God of the whole creation, even the Lord of Egypt.

There are three parts to the basic macro structure of the plague narrative:

> (1) Plagues 1–3: Blood, frogs, gnats; by Aaron stretching out his hand/
> staff (7:14–8:19)

(2) Plagues 4–6: Flies, livestock, boils; by God acting *without* the use of
any staff (8:20–9:12)

(3) Plagues 7–9: hail, locusts, darkness; by Moses' hand/staff.
(9:13–10:29)

Each set of three begins with Moses confronting the pharaoh "in the morning" (7:15; 8:20; 9:13). The death of the firstborn
stands alone, set apart by instructions for the Passover.
In general, the plagues became more intense and destructive as they unfold. They begin as serious nuisances with water
becoming blood, and frogs, gnats, and flies everywhere. They escalate with the destruction of property and animal life and culminate in the taking of human life.
The plague cycles develop two major themes of Exodus in
the form of refrains. The first is "Let my people go that they may
worship me." This refrain, or a variation thereof, is a common
thread that runs through Exodus 4–12 (see 4:23; 5:1, 8, 17; 7:16;
8:1, 20; 9:1, 13; 10:3, 7–8, 11, 24, 26; 12:31). The shortened form,
"Let my people go" and its variations, occurs another twenty-
eight times. The centrality of this theme of release from servitude
under a tyrant in order to worship (or "serve," another meaning
of ʿabad) the Lord cannot be overestimated. The trajectory of Exodus 1–12 leads to the *worship of* and *service to* Yahweh in a new way
of living (Exod. 20–23) and to gathering a new community around
a new place of worship (Exod. 24–31; 35–40). The crisis at Sinai
also puts the same theme of whom Israel would *worship* in bold
relief (Exod. 32–34).
The refrain "So you may know that I am the LORD" develops the second major theme of Exodus in the plague cycles. God's
revelation had the whole earth in mind. When Exodus begins, no
one knows much about the Lord God. The Lord's purpose in the
plagues was "that my name might be proclaimed in all the earth"
(9:16b).
Pharaoh will know the Lord. Many times the text informs us of
what Pharaoh, the king of Egypt, knows, doesn't know, or will
know about the Lord (5:2; 7:17; 8:10, 22; 9:14, 29; 10:7; 11:7). At
the beginning he declared that he did not know the Lord (5:2).
This set up the sequence of revelation to him in the form of the
plagues. Pharaoh acknowledged Yahweh in a limited way when
he asked Moses to pray for the removal of the frogs. When God removed the plague of frogs from the land, Moses let Pharaoh
choose the time, "It will be as you say, so that you may know there

is no one like the LORD our God" (8:10). The removal of the flies
served the same function (8:22). In 8:28 Pharaoh said, "I will let
you go to offer sacrifices to the LORD your God." God also stopped
the thunder and hail "so you may know that the earth is the
LORD's" (9:29). The closest Pharaoh came to *knowing* the Lord was
after the death of the firstborn, when he sent the children of Israel
away to "worship the LORD" (12:31).

The Egyptians will know the Lord. Exodus 7 is the first place
that expresses concern for what the *Egyptians* know. "And the
Egyptians will know that I am the LORD when I stretch out my
hand against Egypt and bring the Israelites out of it" (7:5). The
knowledge of these Gentiles depended on the Lord's rescue of the
children of Israel. The Egyptians would only know the Lord when
they were no longer benefiting from the oppression of the people
of God. The Lord's action against them was necessary for their en-
lightenment. "I will send the full force of my plagues against you
and against your officials and your people, so you may know that
there is no one like me in all the earth" (9:14). They knew for sure
only after God's mighty acts had set the people free (14:4, 18).

Israel will know the Lord. The original audience of the book of
Exodus was Israel. As such, what the children of Israel knew as a
result of God's action may be the most important contextual
theme.

> "I will take you as my own people, and I will be your God. Then
> *you will know that I am the* LORD *your God, who brought you out
> from under the yoke of the Egyptians."* (6:7)

> ". . . that you may tell your children and grandchildren how I dealt
> harshly with the Egyptians and how I performed my signs among
> them, and *that you may know that I am the* LORD." (10:2)

The struggle to know the Lord was not over for Israel after
the exit from Egypt. In the wilderness they also needed to learn to
trust the Lord, this newly revealed redeemer (16:6, 8, 12; 29:46;
31:13).

7:1–7 / After the genealogy of Exodus 6, these verses rein-
troduce the action of the plagues that are about to commence. The
Lord told Moses, **"I have made you like God to Pharaoh"** even as
he has been to Aaron (4:16). This might have been a response to the
Egyptian belief that the pharaoh was divine. In any case, Moses'
faltering lips (6:12, 30) would be inconsequential, since it was not by
Moses' or Aaron's strength, magic, or authority that God would act.

God had established Aaron as Moses' prophet, and Aaron acted as the agent of the first three plagues (vv. 9–10, 12, 19). They repeated the Lord's command to **"let the Israelites go."**

God told Moses and Aaron again, **"I will harden Pharaoh's heart and . . . he will not listen to you."** How much harder could the pharaoh's heart become? This expression of God's involvement seems odd at first. Pharaoh's decisions not to let the people go are not surprising given the great economic loss of slaves. God's claim to be involved at all in his hardness of heart *is* surprising, since it does not seem necessary to the story. It is included because the prolongation of the plagues *demonstrated God's control over the elements of nature.* The Lord is God over life and death, even in a country where the pharaoh, emissary of the gods of Egypt, believed that he controlled life and death. God lengthened the cycle of plagues to demonstrate the range of life under the Lord's own control, from cattle to insects and from water to the light of day.

Throughout the plague cycles Pharaoh expresses his hardness of heart in three different ways: *Pharaoh hardened his own heart* (8:15, 32; 9:34), Pharaoh's heart *was hardened* or *became hard* (7:13–14, 22–23; 8:19; 9:7, 35) and God *hardened it* (9:12; 11:10; 14:8). God had also *promised* to harden it (4:21; 7:3; 14:4, 17). There are no special distinctions between these expressions. It may be concluded that God calcified Pharaoh's own stubbornness and cruelty to accomplish divine purposes. (For in-depth discussion see the comments on Exod. 10:1–2.)

God also told Moses that the pharaoh "will not listen to you." This is what Moses was afraid of, because of his faltering lips (6:12, 30). The Lord reminded him that his speaking ability was not a problem, since it was not Moses or his words that would accomplish the deliverance. Here we see the first instance of the refrain that occurs throughout these chapters: Pharaoh **would not listen to them, just as the LORD had said** (7:13, 22; 8:15, 19; 9:12, 35; 11:9). The pharaoh's hard heart creates a pause during which the Lord demonstrates who is the Creator of the earth and redeemer of the people. It was the Lord's strategy so that the Egyptians would see and know Yahweh (9:14–16) and Israel would trust and fear their God (10:1–2; 14:31).

The plagues demonstrate the Lord's identity to the world in a specific way (to the Egyptians and Israelites in the text as well as to readers of the text). It is important to understand the function of the plagues in the text since our common response to plagues and destruction by God is generally disapproving. Judgment is rarely welcome in the world, even from the Creator. This resistance to judgment is a part of the problem of interpretation that we must address.

God said, "**I multiply my** *miraculous signs* **and** *wonders* **in Egypt . . . Then I will lay my hand on Egypt and with** *mighty acts of judgment* **I will bring out . . . my people the Israelites.**" The three words God uses to describe the plagues are generally synonymous, but they have different referents. "Miraculous signs" (ʾot, lit. "signs") is the most general term and does not necessarily imply the sense of "miraculous" as the NIV adds. In Exodus this word refers to the blood of the Passover lamb (12:13); eating unleavened bread as a *sign* of remembering God's law (13:9); the sacrifice of firstborn animals as a *sign* to remind the people that the Lord brought them out of Egypt (13:16); and to resting on the Sabbath to remind them that their holiness is a gift from God (31:13, 17). The plagues function in a similar way, as a sign that they come from *God*. These signs are not ordinary catastrophes, and it is in this sense that they were "miraculous."

The word "wonders" (*mopet*) refers to a *portent* or *symbol*, often of a future event. In Exodus the term describes the staff-to-snake, the snow-white hand, and the plagues (4:21; 7:3, 9; 11:9, 10). The word indicates that these unusual sights are not the main event, but point to something in the future. Indeed they function in the narrative to point the people toward the crossing of the sea, the wilderness formation, the new sociality at Sinai, and worship in the tabernacle as God's fledgling people. They are *portents* of things to come. The phrase "mighty acts of judgment" describes the necessary forceful hammer on Egypt's political and social shackles. The purpose of God's *judgment* here, as in Scripture in general, was to free the people to live in righteous relationship with others and with the Lord (6:6; 7:4). This meant judgment on whatever powers or gods controlled the shackles. The phrase is most fully explained in Exodus 12, "I will bring judgment on all the gods of Egypt. I am the LORD" (12:12).

The exclusivity of the expression "my people the Israelites" is necessary in the context of the biblical canon. The children of Israel are God's people. The Lord makes a distinction between Egyptians and the people of Israel. All people are God's, but the reference to "my people" has its basis in their relation to Abraham, Isaac, and Jacob (Exod. 2:24; 3:6, 15–16; 4:5; 6:3, 8; 32:13; 33:1). God consistently repeated two promises to them. The first was that they would eventually possess the land of Canaan. The second was that they would be a blessing to all the cultures of the world. These two promises balanced their election as both privileged and responsible before the Lord. As the Egyptians stood in the way of these promises, they made themselves enemies of God (as applied to Israel in Hos. 1:10; 2:23). They were, in any case, not the recipients of the privilege or responsibility to be a blessing. We hear only a whisper of their relation to their Creator when God says, "I have raised you up . . . that I might show you my power and that my name might be proclaimed in all the earth" (9:16).

7:8–13 / The conflict between the pharaoh and the Lord commences with a prefatory symbolic wonder. While Moses' staff is sometimes called the "staff of the Lord" (4:20; 17:9), God uses the staffs of Aaron and Moses interchangeably to perform the wonders in Egypt. In the first encounter with the pharaoh, Aaron's staff becomes a reptile. In the first two wonders God tells Moses to take his staff (v. 15; the Lord speaks of "the staff that is in *my* hand," v. 17), but the agency of the wonders is Aaron's staff (vv. 9–10, 12, 17, 19–20). This shifting of staff references demonstrates that the power lay not in any of the staffs, but in the Lord. The most ambiguous reference is at the end of the chapter when *someone* ("he") "raised his staff in the presence of Pharaoh" (v. 20). The verse probably refers to the Lord, who was the initiator and the authority behind raising a staff in the presence of the authority of the great Pharaoh of Egypt.

The **LORD** spoke to both **Moses and Aaron,** who formed a united front representing Yahweh. Pharaoh would ask them to **"Perform a miracle."** The request could also be paraphrased, "Show me your credentials in a wondrous act." They respond to this request in consummate fashion. In this first sign, Aaron's staff becomes a fearsome reptile.

Translations usually miss God's improvisation and the highly symbolic significance of this text. (The NIV unfortunately has "snake.") The word is not the same one used to refer to Moses' staff becoming **a snake** (*nakhash*) in 4:3. Aaron's staff became a "monstrous snake" (so Durham, from *tannin*) or perhaps a "crocodile" (the Egyptian crocodile god was Sobek). In other biblical texts the NIV translates this word as "monster of the deep" (Job 7:12) or as "monster" (Isa. 27:1), associated with Leviathan, the symbol of the chaos of the sea (see also Pss. 74:13; 148:7; Isa. 51:9; Jer. 51:34; Gen. 1:21). The word occurs in parallel verse with "cobra" in

Deuteronomy 32:33 and Psalm 91:13. In Ezekiel it is a symbol of the pharaoh (Ezek. 29:3; 32:2). The point is that it was a large and *terrifying reptile* that was a symbol of Pharaoh's power and the chaos he had brought upon the children of Israel. The emphasis stands in contrast to verse 15, where Moses' staff "that was changed into a *snake*" once again uses the common word for snake (*nakhash*).

The **Egyptian magicians also did the same things by their secret arts.** Their staffs also became fearsome reptiles (*tannin*). Yahweh easily won this competition for the control of chaos, as **Aaron's staff swallowed up their staffs.** The triumph was a wonder (portent) that pointed forward to the battle of chaos at the crossing of the sea (see discussion on Exod. 15). The consumption of the magicians' staff-to-reptiles by Aaron's portends the *swallowing* of the chariots of Egypt at the sea. The incident was also a practical and somewhat humorous defeat of the magicians. Their staffs of power had disappeared for good.

This marks the beginning of the brief competition between the Egyptian magicians and Aaron and the Lord. In 8:18–19 they recognize the difference between their magic and the miraculous intervention of God (see the discussion at 8:18). "Magicians" is usually understood to include both the **wise men** and their assistants, the **sorcerers.** At the end of this first encounter and display of power, **Pharaoh's heart** was hard. While the NIV translates **became hard,** however, the plain meaning is that it was hard before the event and was hard after it.

7:14–25 / *First Blood.* The account of the first plague begins with the notice that **Pharaoh's heart is unyielding.** The Hebrew word here is *kabed,* meaning a "fat" heart or "heavy and sluggish" heart. In this context it could be paraphrased "self-fulfilled" or "self-satisfied." The word describes Pharaoh's "hard heart" in 7:14; 8:14, 28; 9:7, 34; 10:1; 14:4, 17. The synonym used elsewhere for "hard heart" is *khazaq,* which means "tough" or "strong." Pharaoh will not change much in the conflict that follows. He remains tough and self-satisfied.

The Lord told Moses to wait for the pharaoh on the banks of the Nile with his staff. The next twelve verses mention the Nile's waters seven times. The river was the source of Egypt's economic power. Its irrigation canals and reservoirs made Egypt the breadbasket of the Mediterranean world. By turning the Nile to blood, God symbolically demonstrated that the Lord, and not

Pharaoh, controlled Egypt's economic might. The Prophets refer to Pharaoh's attitude: "The Nile is mine; I made it for myself" (Ezek. 29:3).

The Lord's message for Pharaoh begins in verse 16 with the refrain **"Let my people go, so that they may worship** (or "serve") **me in the desert."** God's direct speech continues, describing what will happen. **"With the staff that is in my hand I will strike the water of the Nile."** The result of this action was threefold. First, **all the water was changed into blood** (v. 20). The Hebrew for "changed" is a strong word that means "transformed" (*hapak*, vv. 17, 20). There is no doubt that this was a change of substance and not simply a change in appearance (v. 19, lit., "it will *be* blood"). By transforming the water, the Creator touched the foundation of life (Gen. 1:2). Amazingly, the Lord was willing to bring ecological disaster to the life-giving Nile to free his people. The Lord also demonstrated control over the Egyptian god Osiris, embodied in the flow of the Nile especially at red-flood stage.

Next, the fish died, which caused it to stink. Later in the narrative, the frogs and spoiled manna will also stink, as a physical reminder of rebellion (8:14; 16:20, 24).

The **Egyptians could not drink its water** (v. 21). They had no voice in Pharaoh's realm. Their only response was thirst. They **dug along the Nile to get drinking water,** to find water that had filtered through sand. The magicians would have had to use this water to perform their imitative magic, since all the surface water was already blood.

Blood was everywhere in Egypt, even in the **wooden buckets and stone jars.** The mention of these containers for water is a translator's interpretation. The Hebrew simply says, "in the trees and in the stones." This may mean in the tree sap and in the rock springs. Whatever the case, the blood, like the swallowed "snakes," was a portent of a greater bloodletting to come in the killing of the Passover lamb and the firstborn of Egypt.

Scientific explanations for the plagues interest some interpreters. For example, some have suggested that the "blood" of the Nile was red algae or red mud flooded from the upper Nile from which the frogs fled. Subsequently the gnats and flies bred in dead frogs and spread disease (cattle, blight, and boils). Then seasonal wind blew in hail, locusts, and sand that caused the darkness in some parts of the land. The bubonic plague then accounted for the deaths of the firstborn. These events of natural history were present in the ancient world. Attempts to prove or explain the plagues only in this way, however, miss the point of the text. The narrative claims that the Lord was the initiator and power behind the plagues. The Lord did use "nature," but the biblical claim is that God used it in a way that demonstrated a specific divine intervention (miraculous). The nature of these ancient historical events cannot be proven. They are, in the text, a matter to be rejected or believed. Their purpose is so *you might know* that the Lord is God, that is, in control of the timing *and* substance of the creation (Hort, "The Plagues of Egypt," pp. 84–103).

The first plague ended as it began: **Pharaoh's heart** was **hard** (vv. 14, 22). Responding, **he turned and went into his palace** (lit., "faced and went into his house"). The picture of his facing his own house stands in sharp relief to the people, who had to dig along the Nile to find water. Pharaoh's lack of power to provide water for his people is juxtaposed to the Lord's control of the water, and later provision of water for the thirsty people in the wilderness. The Lord would provide water in a very dry place, but Pharaoh could only go into a house on the banks of an unpotable Nile. Pharaoh is an imposter Lord.

Additional Notes §8

7:3 / A concise review of the prevailing theory of the history of composition of the plague narrative may be found in McCarter, "Exodus," pp. 128–29.

7:9 / Aaron's staff is used in the first three plagues. In the central three plagues no staff is used. The staff in Moses' hand is used for the third three plagues. After these events, Moses alone takes center stage as God's spokesman and staffbearer. Aaron reemerges as the chief priest later in the book. His staff blossoms and bears almonds in the tabernacle and is thereafter kept with the ark (Num. 17:8–10; Heb. 9:4).

7:21 / Durham quotes an older Egyptian text that describes a bloody river in an earlier era (ca. 2300 B.C., "Admonitions of Ipuwer," see Durham, *Exodus*, p. 98). "WHY REALLY, the River is blood. If one drinks of it, one rejects (it) *as human* and thirsts for water" (*ANET*, p. 441, ii.10, italics mine). Perhaps this poem reflects a time when the slaughter of war upstream on the Nile resulted in blood and dead bodies in the Nile. Certainly it records a time of upheaval and trouble for Egyptian life. Durham also notes that this may be a rhetorical form of judgment on Egypt, since the Nile is its source of life. Any disruption of the Nile would have been a symbol of serious societal and economic trouble.

§9 Frogs, Gnats, and Flies (Exod. 8:1–32)

8:1–15 / The second plague was an army of hopping and noisy frogs. While the first plague brought death to the fish of the Nile and to the waters of the Nile itself, the second brought an overabundance of amphibious life from the waters. *Frogs* (*tsepardeʿim*) invaded the land. The Hebrew word is considered an onomatopoeia, as it sounds like the noise made by new frogs. Creation seemed out of control, with the Egyptian frog goddess *Heqet* (whose purpose was to assist in childbirth) running amok. Moses and Aaron presented the competing claim, which was that the Creator (Yahweh) was controlling the creation for a specific purpose.

The text recounts this plague in an abbreviated form, without a description of the actual conversation with Pharaoh or his response to the threat of the plague. The shortened form picks up the pace of the narrative.

The Lord instructed Moses to go again to Pharaoh and say, **"This is what the LORD says."** Moses functions as a prophet here, using the prophetic transmission formula for the third time (5:1; 7:17; 8:1, 20; 9:1, 13; 10:3; 11:4). Again he said, **"Let my people go, so that they may worship me."** As we have seen above, the word translated "worship" (*ʿabad*) usually means "serve." The Lord's primary purpose in liberating the people from slavery was so that they might serve God.

What followed was a strong warning. **If you refuse to let them go** (here the NIV unfortunately leaves out the word *hinneh,* or "Look out!"), **I will plague your whole country with frogs.** The English word "plague" is not strong enough for the Hebrew word which appears here for the first time in Exodus. A fuller expression is, "I will *deliver a punishing blow* to your whole country with frogs." God was delivering a challenging warning. This plague would conclude with heaps of frogs, anticipating the heaps of bodies from the Egyptian army on the shore of the Red Sea (Fretheim, *Exodus,* p. 117).

Aaron stretched out his hand over the waters of Egypt for
the second of three times (7:19–20; 8:5–6, 16–17). The result was
not humorous for Pharaoh or Egypt, but the picture is amusing.
Frogs are leaping and peeping everywhere. These verses name ten
personal places where the frogs will appear: **your palace, your bed-
room, your bed, into the houses of your officials, on your people,
into your ovens, kneading troughs, on you, on your people and
all your officials.** Eating, sleeping, sitting, or cooking, the pharaoh, official servants, and commoners all experienced the invasive, undignified nuisance of frogs. The mention of the kneading
troughs may be a jab at Egypt's status as the ancient world's abundant grain source and breadbasket. That **the magicians . . . also
made frogs come up on the land of Egypt** did not help the situation (see the discussion of the magicians in vv. 18– 19). They used
magic foolishly to mimic the plague, exacerbating the problem
rather than solving it.

Pharaoh was not impressed with his magicians' work and
called on **Moses and Aaron** to **"Pray to the LORD to take the frogs
away from me and my people."** The unusual Hebrew word for
"pray" here is specifically a word for supplication. Its Hebrew
homonym, meaning "abundant," may be a wordplay referring to
the frogs. Pharaoh sought their help in dealing with the Lord.
Pharaoh's use of the name Yahweh was not a conversion but a co-
gent administrative attempt to find relief from the problem.

Pharaoh begins the first of his many deceitful negotiations
here. Readers should not assume that Pharaoh became alternately
soft and hard as the plagues progressed (see the discussion on
10:2). He began with a hard heart and negotiated with skill as the
head of the most powerful country in the ancient world at that
time. The rhetoric of the text points to this reading in the first negotiation. Pharaoh suggests that he might allow the people to go
offer sacrifices if the frogs were taken away. He doesn't say how
far, how long, or who might go. He will play those cards later. He
said, "I may let you go" (NIV "I will let you go"). Neither did he indicate *where* they might go (a move he would try to manipulate
in v. 25).

Moses' response indicates that he understood the game (see
also Moses' comment at v. 29, "be sure that Pharaoh does not act
deceitfully again"). He promises to pray for the removal of the
frogs—not so the people would be freed, but **"so that you may
know there is no one like the LORD our God."** Moses knew that
the removal of the frogs would not result in the release of the

people but would function, rather, just like the onslaught of the frogs. It would increase everyone's knowledge of the Lord. The text mentions Pharaoh's knowledge of the Lord for the first time (8:10, 22; 9:14, 29).

Moses also demonstrates his increased confidence in the ways of the Lord when he says, **"I leave to you the honor of setting the time."** Literally, the Hebraism is, "Glorify yourself over me." The truth of the matter was that Pharaoh's setting a specific time and keeping it would be a sure sign that Moses and the Lord were glorified. Another ironic twist piles up when the so-called *removal* of the frogs was occasioned by their *dying* **in the houses, in the courtyards and in the fields . . . and the land reeked of them.** Even the relief left a stinking mess.

Pharaoh was relieved (he saw **there was relief,** *rewakhah,* "break, clearing") nonetheless, since dead frogs were easier to remove from one's bed and kitchen. He **hardened his heart and would not listen to Moses and Aaron, just as the LORD had said.** The narrator announces Pharaoh's *hard heart* for the third time, followed by the fulfillment formula: Pharaoh "would not listen to Moses and Aaron, just as the LORD had said" (7:13, 22; 8:15, 19; 9:12, 35). The stage is set for the third plague.

8:16–19 / The third plague was gnats, that came from the dust. "Gnats" is the traditional interpretation, but the word can mean "mosquitoes." The word *kinnam* (translated "gnats") is used only in reference to this plague. Other suggestions are "ticks" and "lice" or, generally, "vermin." Both gnats and mosquitoes were indigenous to Egypt, but the latter were much more personally invasive. This third plague, like the sixth (boils), is in a short form concluding its cycle of three. Although the account is short, the rhetorical effect is striking. The word "gnats" occurs five times in three verses.

The Lord told Moses to tell Aaron, **"Stretch out your staff"** for the third and final time. The chords of the theme of creation are struck again, for **when Aaron stretched out his hand with the staff and struck the dust of the ground, gnats came upon men and animals.** The phrase "dust of the ground" reminds the reader that God created Adam "from the *dust of the ground*" (Gen. 2:7), and also resonates with the words, "for *dust you are* and to dust you will return" (Gen. 3:19). The first plague touched the waters and the second touched the amphibious creation from the waters.

The third employs the dust from which God created. God is in the process of creating something new.

The magicians had reached their limit. They **could not** produce gnats from the dust. There was no one like the Lord "in all the earth" (9:14, 16). Their competition with Aaron and with the Lord was over. In 7:12, Aaron's staff swallowed up their staffs. In 7:22 they mimicked turning water to blood, exacerbating Egypt's drinking water crisis. In verse 7 they also called forth frogs, so that Pharaoh had to ask Moses to pray for him to the Lord. They could not copy the gnats and never tried to match Aaron again. After a brief note about their suffering from boils (9:11), they disappear from the narrative as insignificant.

When the magicians said to Pharaoh, **"This is the finger of God"** they did not necessarily acknowledge Yahweh. It is even possible to translate this phrase, "This is the finger of *a* god." At most, they had been forced to admit that some divine power was at work. This was the beginning of the escalation of power in the plagues, yet they said "finger" rather than referring to the more powerful hand or arm. It is no surprise that the narrator announces for the fourth time that **Pharaoh's heart was hard** (7:13, 22; 8:15, 19, 32; 9:7, 12, 34–35; 10:20, 27; 11:10; 14:8), followed by the fulfillment formula: Pharaoh **would not listen, just as the LORD had said** (7:13, 22; 8:15, 19; 9:12, 35). The text does not describe the removal of the pesky insects. The natural cleansing cycles of creation and the weather would clear them away, as with the blood in the Nile. As elsewhere, here God uses creation to deliver judgment as well as to remove it and renew the earth.

8:20–32 / The fourth plague consisted of **dense swarms of flies,** but only in Egyptian houses. This central cycle of plagues (flies, dying livestock, and boils) begins just as the first and last three began, following a confrontation with Pharaoh **early in the morning** (7:15; 8:20; 9:13). Moses declares the transmission formula, **This is what the LORD** (Yahweh) **says,** together with the refrains that state, for the fourth time, the main purpose for the exodus: **Let my people go, so that they may worship** ("serve") **me** (5:1, 7:16; 8:1, 20; 9:1, 13; 10:3; 11:4). The new threat was **swarms of flies** on every Egyptian, *inside* and *outside* the houses (NIV, awkwardly: "even the ground"). These infestations affect Pharaoh in particular, since he was ostensibly the power that controlled death and life in Egypt. The generic term used for flies here may refer to biting stable flies, common flies, gadflies, or horseflies.

Yahweh offered a new sign with the advent of the flies. For the first time the Lord made **a distinction between my people and your people.** The swarms of flies did not appear in the NE delta region of Goshen, where Yahweh's people lived (Gen. 46:28–34; 47:6).

This announcement that the Lord would **deal differently** (lit. "cause a separation") with the people anticipates the division between the peoples on the night of death passing over Egypt. It also points toward the pillar of fire/cloud that saved them by dividing them from the chariots, and the ultimate separation and redemption at the sea (14:19–31). The *distinction* between "my people" and the pharaoh's people (that the pharaoh initiated through the forced labor) demonstrated the Lord's power to offer special protection from catastrophe. This distinction began with the flies and continued in the fifth, seventh, ninth, and tenth plagues (9:4, 26; 10:23; 11:7; 12:23).

Verse 22 mentions Pharaoh's knowledge of the Lord for the second time (8:10, 22; 9:14, 29). This reference to his knowledge has an important rhetorical function as well as a theological purpose. The rhetoric of mentioning Pharaoh's knowledge is for the reader who does not know the Lord of the exodus. By talking about what he knows and doesn't know, the text allows the reader to know more than Pharaoh does. Theologically speaking, if the pharaoh could be shown that Yahweh is God of all the earth, then the exodus is more than a story of some Hebrew slaves escaping from Egypt. The text points to this with the words **so that you will know that I, the LORD, am in this land.** The Hebrew touches a more universal theme. A better translation would be "that you will know that I am Yahweh, in the midst of the earth." The word for earth here (*'erets*) is the same word used in Genesis 1:1. This is the first time knowing God "in the earth" is mentioned, but not the last (9:14, 29). It is a creational theme concerning knowledge of the creating Lord in the whole world, beginning in Egypt.

Negotiations began in earnest. When he and Aaron were summoned, Moses took the initiative in exit negotiations with the pharaoh, who was ready to strike a deal. Yahweh had made Moses *as God* to the pharaoh (7:1) and he bargained for the second time with confidence (vv. 8–9, 25–29). Pharaoh's opening offer was not exactly what Moses had requested. **"Go, sacrifice to your God here in the land."**

Moses' initial request was to "take a three-day journey into the desert to offer sacrifices" (5:3). After Pharaoh increased the workload and oppression, Moses repeatedly stated the Lord's message more directly: "Let my people go, that they might worship/serve me in the wilderness" (7:16; 8:1, 20). Pharaoh was toying with words when he said "offer sacrifices" instead of "worship/serve." God's own repeated request in the midst of each plague was that the people worship or "serve" the Lord, rather than "serving" Pharaoh (7:16; 8:1, 20; 9:1, 13; 10:3; 11:4).

Moses responded with two objections to Pharaoh's counteroffer. First, he said, it wouldn't work. **"That would not be right"** means that the plan was "not stable." It is unclear why Hebrew sacrifices **would be detestable to the Egyptians.** Perhaps the sacrifice of cattle would be offensive because of local Egyptian gods (the sacred bull, Apis, or the the cow or love goddess, Hathor). It could also have had to do with a general detestation of Hebrew culture or the specific abomination of sheep (Gen. 43:32; 46:34). Moses' second reason was more to the point. It was not what the Lord had asked. Moses improvised and returned to the former request: **We must take a three-day journey** into the wilderness **to offer sacrifices.** If "sacrifices" were Pharaoh's focus, Moses would negotiate for "time." A full week would be necessary for the round-trip ("three days into the desert"). Pharaoh agreed because of the swarms of flies and asked for prayer again. He was not, however, ready to let them go to perform the fuller worship and service to Yahweh. He insisted **you must not go very far.** The pharaoh's controlling expression **"I will let you go"** is, more emphatically, "I myself will allow you to go."

Moses continued to find his way within God's direction and the resistant concessions of the king. If he could get the people out of Egypt, he trusted that Yahweh would see to the rest. He agreed to pray for the removal of the flies, careful to name the time once again, so that the Lord would receive credit. He said, **"As soon as I leave."** The demonstration of Yahweh's power to immediately clear the land of flies would be the point. Moses' confidence and savvy are evident in his parting words, **"Only be sure that Pharaoh does not act deceitfully again by not letting the people go to offer sacrifices to the LORD."** Moses continued to be the initiator with God as well, **and the LORD did what Moses asked.** The narrator concludes by announcing the pharaoh's hard heart for the third time in this chapter.

Additional Notes §9

8:8 / The translation "I may let you go" rather than "I will let you go" is indicated by the use of the Hebrew cohortative *he* with the imperfect. This Hebrew may be translated, "I may" or "I might" or "I could let you go."

8:21 / A common identification of the flies has been *stomoxys calcitrans* (stable fly), since they are carriers of skin anthrax (cattle plague), and may have laid their eggs in the rotting frogs and fish (Walton, "Exodus," p. 83).

8:22 / Goshen's exact location has not been identified but evidence points to the area of Wadi Tumilat. Egyptian records describe the residence of "Asian people," including Semites, there during the New Kingdom (1500–1000 B.C.) (Sarna, "Exodus," p. 363).

8:25 / The repetition of "the land" (*'erets*) may indicate Pharaoh's belief that sacrificing to a troublesome deity in **the land** would appease God and put an end to the plagues.

Exodus 9 presents the fifth, sixth, and seventh plagues. The livestock pestilence (fifth) and the plague of boils (sixth) conclude the second cycle of three (flies-livestock-boils) and the text presents them in abbreviated form. Pharaoh responds very briefly to the fifth plague and not at all to the sixth. The Lord simply informs Moses of the pestilence on the livestock (vv. 1–5) and the pestilence of boils (vv. 8–9); they broke out (vv. 6, 10–11); and the text reports Pharaoh's hard heart (vv. 7, 12). The chapter describes the storm of thunder, hail, and lightning, the seventh plague, in fuller form because it begins the third and final cycle (hail-locusts-darkness). This last cycle intensifies the struggle for control between Yahweh and Pharaoh for the service (worship) of the children of Israel. In this chapter we also see the transition from Pharaoh's hardening of his (own) heart, to the Lord as the one who hardened Pharaoh's heart as the exit from Egypt approaches (vv. 7, 12).

9:1–7 / The fifth plague brought the deaths of Egyptian domestic animals: horses, donkeys, camels, cows, sheep, and goats. The narrative drama begins with three rhetorical devices. The same narrative marker begins the second, fifth and eighth plagues (the second of each cycle): **Then the LORD said to Moses, "Go to Pharaoh"** (8:1 frogs; 9:1 livestock; 10:1 locusts). This marker continues with the familiar words, **"This is what the LORD . . . says."** The verse concludes with the freedom to worship formula: **"Let my people go, so that they may worship me."** This is the fifth statement of the main reason for the exodus (5:1, 7:16; 8:1, 20; 9:1, 13; 10:3).

The description of this plague begins with a threat. **If you refuse to let them go** is the same challenge that was made in the second plague (frogs) and that will be made in the eighth plague (locusts), but a new phrase here directly challenges the pharaoh's power: if you **continue to hold them back** (using the word for "muscle"). It could be paraphrased, "If you continue to muscle them (or "use power over them") . . . look out!" The NIV omits the emphatic *hinneh* (KJV "behold"). The threat was quite clear: **the LORD will bring a terrible plague on your livestock in the field.**

The sensitive target was Pharaoh's personal property. Moses refers to "your" (in the personal singular form) three times. The word translated "livestock" comes from the root that means "purchasable property" (*miqneh,* from the verbal root *qanah*). The "terrible plague" (lit., "a very heavy epidemic") would take his source of income from work animals (horses, donkeys, and camels) and his sources of food (cows, sheep, and goats).

The Lord made **a distinction** for the second time: **"no animal belonging to the Israelites will die."** This foreshadows the final distinction between the death of the Egyptians under Pharaoh's rule and the life of the children of Israel under Yahweh's protection. As the plagues worsen, the stakes become greater. The **LORD set a time,** as Pharaoh's visible control diminishes and Yahweh's increases. In the plague of frogs, Pharaoh set the time (8:9). With the flies, Moses set the times of their infestation and removal (8:23, 29). Hereafter, the Lord would establish the timing (9:18 hail; 10:4 locusts).

For the reader of the entire plague cycle, the report that **All the livestock of the Egyptians died** creates later confusion, since additional animals (livestock) are afflicted by later plagues (see the additional notes). The discussion around this point may detract from the intent of the biblical declaration here, which contrasts the death of Egyptian animals with the protected animal life among the children of Israel: "Look!" (which NIV again omits) **not one animal belonging to the Israelites died.** As in the plague of flies, the key discovery in the text is that the Israelites have again experienced the miracle of *protection.* This was also the proleptic sign of their deliverance during the Passover. The biblical claim is that the Lord set the limits (v. 4) and "Behold!" Yahweh fulfilled the promise of protection from the epidemic.

Pharaoh did continue to have power over his subjects and **sent men.** The irony of his "sending" is hidden in the verb root that is the same as the root in "Let my people go" (*shalakh*). This time the pharaoh's "heart was hard" (NIV "was unyielding"), indicating his customary intransigence. In the next plague, the Lord would begin to take an active role in the hardening, becoming the subject of the verb (v. 12).

9:8–12 / The sixth plague was an outbreak of boils, directly striking (for the first time) the bodies of the Egyptians. Yahweh was the God of the health of the body, in Israel and in Egypt. Israel had believed the sign of Moses' hand, and now it was the pharaoh's turn.

Up to this point the plagues have generally followed the pattern of the creation of life described in Genesis 1. The Lord had mirrored creation, *undoing its goodness* as a sign of the sin of Pharaoh's oppressive dynastic rule. Egypt's lordship over the children of Israel also would be undone. Like the first creation account, the undoing of the creation in Egypt began with water (turned to blood). It continued with life *from the water* (frogs, out of control). Then, from the *dust of the ground* came the gnats, followed by flies for good measure. Livestock, also *created from the earth* (Gen. 1:24) were decimated next. Finally, the bodies of God's created human beings were touched by inflamed and erupting sores.

The outbreak of boils begins with **handfuls of soot** (fine powdery ashes) **from a furnace,** literally a kiln for firing pottery or bricks, perhaps used by the Hebrews in their labor (although most bricks were dried in the sun). The image of Moses tossing it **into the air in the presence of Pharaoh** may be more dramatic in a more literal rendering: "Have Moses scatter it abundantly toward the heavens before the eyes of Pharaoh." Soot filled the air in Pharaoh's court. Moses must have seemed mad, throwing ashes up by the handful, but no one was laughing.

Then **festering boils broke out on men and animals.** Three Hebrew words are behind the translation "festering boils broke out": *shekhin,* meaning "inflamed" or "hot," *parakh,* meaning "breaking out" or "sprouting," and *ʾabaʿbuʿot,* meaning "boil" or "blistering." The purpose of all of these words is to convey the pain. Speculative interpretation has identified this plague as an epidemic of skin anthrax because of the ulceration (see Hort, "The Plagues of Egypt"). Whatever the transformed soot caused, the animals were not exempt. The Hebrew word for "animals" (*behemah*) in verses 9–10 is different from the word for "animal" (*miqneh*) in verse 6. *Behemah* refers to all kinds of animals, not just domestic livestock. The **magicians** suffered as well. Their power in relation to Moses and Aaron had been broken with their inability to replicate the gnats. Now their solidarity with Pharaoh was also broken. They **could not stand before Moses because of the boils.**

The narrator announces for the first time here that **the
LORD hardened Pharaoh's heart.** Previously (six times) the narrator announced that the pharaoh hardened his heart or had a hard
heart (7:13, 22; 8:15, 19, 32; 9:7; see additional note). The Lord increasingly took control to demonstrate who the true Creator is.
God's intention was to bring the enslaved people from an oppressive regime into God's own protection and service.

9:13–35 / A thunderstorm with hail and ground-striking
lightning killed the first Egyptians in the seventh plague. As the
risks grew, *the Lord provided warning.* Anyone who would seek life
under God's rule would survive. God cautioned Pharaoh's officials to bring their servants in from the storm. Some of them re-
spected the warning and saved human and animal life. The Lord
explained the purpose of all the plagues in this text, "that you
might know that the earth belongs to Yahweh" (v. 29, author's
translation).

Moses begins here, as always, with the imperative *freedom to
worship* formula, **"Let my people go, so that they may worship
me."** Again, this third cycle of three plagues begins in the same
way as the first two cycles of three, confronting the pharaoh **early
in the morning** (7:15; 8:20; 9:13).

Verses 14–21 present two purposes for the Lord's actions.
The Lord states the first explicitly (vv. 14–17) and the situation
with the officials demonstrates the second—some of them "feared
the word of the Lord" and some did not. These verses (as well as
10:1–2) most clearly explain the point of the ten plagues. They are
to proclaim Yahweh's name and reputation as God of all the earth.
We see this in two purpose clauses:

> "so you may know that there is no one like me in *all the earth*"
> (v. 14b)

> "that my name might be proclaimed in *all the earth*" (v. 16b)

Verse 15 also emphasizes the Lord's relation to the earth as
Creator with an explanation of how restrained he had been: **"For
by now I could have . . . wiped you off the earth."** In good
compositional style, the chapter ends with a restatement of this
primary theme to the pharaoh: **The thunder will stop . . . so you
may know that the earth is the LORD's** (v. 29b).

Yahweh is Lord of all humanity, all the nonhuman creation,
and the entire cosmos. Water, storms, insects, animals, health, disease, the light of the sun, life and death are his creations. Jethro

will speak similar words when the Israelites complete their exit from Egypt. "Praise be to the LORD, who rescued you from the hand of the Egyptians and of Pharaoh, and who rescued the people from the hand of the Egyptians. Now I know that the LORD *is greater than all other gods*, for he did this to those who had treated Israel arrogantly" (18:10–11).

In the greater context of Exodus the whole point is to recognize who the Lord is. Pharaoh had said, "Who is the LORD . . . I do not know the LORD" (5:2). By now, the reader is beginning to know. As Creator of the universe, this God, the Lord, was continuing to create. *God was creating a specific people with a unique sociality to whom God would give the law at Sinai.* The creation of the people of Israel was the means by which God's name would *be made known in all the earth.*

Pharaoh was *still standing* (**I have raised you up**) so that the name of the Lord **might be proclaimed** in all the earth. The world was educated about the reputation of God, who stooped down into history (3:8; 19:11) to rescue and to create a people who might live congruently with the Creator's intention. Pharaoh, however, *exalted himself over* the people. The Hebrew uses a word that expresses Pharaoh's *lordship* over the people (*salal*). It is used generally in the expression "exalt the name of the Lord." Pharaoh *exalted himself* over the people when it was the Lord who should have been exalted. This concisely expresses the conflict between them.

Yahweh's actions in carefully providing shelter for anyone who **feared** (or trusted) **the word of the LORD** demonstrates *the second purpose* of the plague. God's goal was that all would come to fear and trust the Lord (14:31). To that end God sent the hail, but with it the provisional warning to avoid its effects. God provided this one last opportunity for Pharaoh and his officials to participate in saving life. The Lord did not harden his heart in this case (vv. 34–35), but Pharaoh did not respond to save his people. Here was a small opportunity for Pharaoh to show his concern for *any life at all*. The emphasis throughout this text is on *human* life, especially the non-Israelite slaves working in the fields (vv. 19–22).

Pharaoh's officials were divided. Some acted and **hurried to bring their slaves** and their property inside. Some **ignored the word of the LORD** and abandoned **their slaves** and property in the fields. The Hebraism behind "those who ignored" is, literally, "the one who did not set his heart on" the word of the Lord. This division over the word of Yahweh functions as a warning parable for the reader and for the children of Israel. Who will fear the word of the Lord? Who will take it to heart? The one who fears God's word will find **shelter** from the storm (Nah. 1:7; Ps. 27:1). The plague itself began when **Moses stretched out his staff toward the sky.** From here forward, Moses and his hand or staff would lead the people (9:23; 10:13, 21; 14:16; 17:9). The description of the storm and its effect is the longest written description of any plague.

> . . . the LORD sent thunder and hail, and lightning flashed down to the ground. So the LORD rained hail on the land of Egypt; hail fell and lightning flashed back and forth. It was the worst storm in all the land of Egypt since it had become a nation. (vv. 23–24)

The description, with its repetition, simulates the storm itself. "The worst storm" means "the very heaviest hail." The unprotected human beings and animals suffered the same beating as the plant life. They were exposed to the power of an electrical storm that surpassed any in the illustrious thousand-year history of this civilization. This uncanny storm marked the beginning of something new in the world and in history.

Briefly, the narrator points to a previously unannounced distinction: **The only place it did not hail was the land of Goshen, where the Israelites were.** The plants and animals under the care of the Lord's people fared better than those under the oppressive regime. Having Yahweh as one's God was significant for all living things. Even the Egyptian officials' temporarily believing the word of the Lord benefited their animals (as well as their slaves).

The storm was persistent as well as destructive. In the midst of the continuous lightning and pounding thunder **Pharaoh summoned Moses and Aaron.** Pharaoh's response was unprecedented, and the reader knows that everything he says is true. **"I have sinned . . . The LORD is in the right, and I and my people are in the wrong . . . I will let you go; you don't have to stay any longer."** He sounds like he is convinced and convicted, and yet the words "in the right" (*tsaddiq*) and "in the wrong" (*rasha*ᶜ) are legal admissions, not moral confessions. In spite of the penitent words, his admission of guilt was under the duress of booming thunder, pounding hail, pouring rain, and ground-strike lightning that would not quit. This was the third time he had said that he would let them go (8:8, 28; 9:28).

We hear the pharaoh's motivation when he says, **Pray to the LORD, for we have had enough thunder and hail** (lit. "God's thunder"). Durham translates it, "Enough of God's thunderclaps and hail!" Pharaoh simply wanted the cacophonous storm to stop. Moses interpreted the pharaoh's response when he said, **I know that you and your officials still do not fear the LORD God.** The king used his rhetoric to make an admission of convenience. He addressed the presenting problem quite practically. Moses' God, Yahweh, had brought a terrible storm, so Moses must see to its removal, as he had in the past.

Moses was willing to ask the Lord to remove the storm, in spite of the pharaoh's unchanging heart. Moses explained God's perspective. Removing the storm was also a witness to God's lordship over the creation. Repeating the first of the two major themes of the chapter, Moses said, **"The thunder will stop . . . so you may know that the earth is the LORD's."** This theme recurs later in the Sinaitic law (see also Ps. 24; 1 Cor 10:26).

Moses also reiterated the second theme, *the fear of the Lord.* Some of the officials did fear the word of the Lord and warn their servants (v. 20). Trusting the word may have been preliminary to the fear of the Lord, but it was not equivalent. Moses was very specific, using the rare combination of "Lord God" (*yhwh ʾelohim*). In Exodus, these words occur together only here—they appear almost exclusively in Genesis 3 and in worship texts (e.g., Psalms and Chronicles). "Lord God" is a specific reference to the combination of God's *creating* and *redeeming* work.

Exodus 9 concludes with a notice that some grains were not destroyed, to assure the reader that the locusts would have something to consume in Exodus 10. Moses' prayer for the hail to stop follows almost anticlimatically, since it was predictable. The narrator then announces the pharaoh's hard heart for the eighth and ninth times. Here both the Hebrew words translated "hard" (*kabed*, v. 34 and *khazaq*, v. 35) occur together. Pharaoh is the subject of both hardenings. The text mentions the hard hearts of his officials for the first and last time. Pharaoh had also exercised his prerogative to harden his own heart for the last time. The Lord would do all the hardening in the last three plagues.

Additional Notes §10

9:3 / The mention of "camels" is thought to be anachronistic since they were introduced to Egypt under Persian rule in the 6th century B.C.

9:6 / "All the livestock of the Egyptians died." The phrase "all the cattle of the Egyptians" (v. 6, *kol miqneh*) has been problematic for understanding what animals remained to suffer the plagues of boils on "the animals" (v. 10, *behemah*), and the death of the "livestock" and "animals" by hail (v. 19, *miqneh* and *behemah*). The common solution is to call it an intentional exaggeration (like the expression "all the dust" in 8:17) since some animals clearly survived the livestock pestilence. Several solutions for limiting the expression "all" are possible. It could be only those "in the field" that died (v. 3). It could be only the flocks of Pharaoh, meaning the animals that were officially property of dynastic Egypt (see the repetition of the singular "your" in v. 3). In this case "of the Egyptians" could be translated "of Egypt." It is also possible to translate the general term *miqneh* as "possessions," referring to the livestock that are named in v. 3 (horses, donkeys, camels, cattle, sheep, and goats) and as "possessions," referring to other kinds of animals later in v. 19. The focus in v. 19, however, is on the servants, who are also possessions at risk in the hail.

9:7 / The NIV uses the translation "was unyielding" twice (7:14; 9:7) for the verb *kabed* ("fattened" or "self-assured"). It uses "hardened" for *kabed* everywhere else (4 times) as well as for its synonym *khazaq* ("toughened" or "strengthened"). See further discussion of "hardened" at 7:3, 14; 10:1–2.

9:14 / The importance of vv. 14–16 should not be underestimated as a source for interpreting the plagues. This explanation is given for all readers of the text, but especially for non-Jewish readers, who ought to identify with the Gentile Egyptians (Rom. 11:17–20).

9:16 / The word for "proclaimed," *sapar*, is found again in 10:2. This instruction is kept by means of the Passover service described in 12:27–28 and in the Feast of Unleavened Bread described in 13:8.

9:20 / The expression "fear" of the Lord is sometimes translated "reverence" or "respect." It is certainly not the same as "being afraid" in 20:20. The midwives were the first to "fear the Lord" (1:17, 21). "Capable men" are defined as those who are trustworthy and "fear the Lord" (18:21). This "fear" has an element of awe as well as trust in the One who inspires the awe. Trust and "fear of the Lord" are used in parallel in the summary statement: "when the Israelites saw the great power the LORD displayed against the Egyptians, the people feared the LORD and put their trust in him" (14:31).

9:23 / The thunder and fire fall (lightning) point forward to a similar experience at Mount Sinai (19:16, 18). The fire fall and the later reference to "right and wrong" (v. 27) are reminiscent of the words used to describe the destruction of Sodom (Gen. 18:23–24). Hail is frequently a sign of God's presence and judgment (Isa. 28:2, 17; 30:30–31; Ezek. 13:11–13; 38:22–23; Hag. 2:17). The people stand between judgment and the possibility of a new way of life.

§11 God Hardens Pharaoh's Heart: Locusts and Darkness (Exod. 10:1–29)

The Lord begins actively to harden Pharaoh's heart late in the plague cycles, and more frequently in the last three plagues. God's hardening functions alongside the choices Pharaoh himself made to "self-harden" his heart. The Hebrew has two different words, both generally translated "hardened," that the narrative uses interchangeably (without pattern). *Khazaq* refers to physical or political strengthening, as in "making tough" or uncompassionate. *Kabed* refers to being stubborn, self-satisfied ("fat"), or self-fulfilled ("honored"). Together these words convey Pharaoh's calcified will, encrusted stubbornness, and the rigor mortis of his reason.

Four times God actively hardens Pharaoh's heart ("the Lord hardened"): after the plague of boils (9:12), after the locusts (v. 20), after the darkness (v. 27), and before the death of the firstborn (11:10). Additionally, before the plague of the locusts (v. 1), God claims to have hardened Pharaoh's heart immediately after the narrator twice states that Pharaoh and his officials hardened their own hearts. Later in the narrative, after Pharaoh had begun preparations to pursue the people to the sea (14:8), the text states that the Lord again hardened his heart.

The Lord promised to harden Pharaoh's or the Egyptians' hearts in the future ("I will harden," 4:21; 7:3; 14:4, 17). The balance of the references to his hard heart remind us that Pharaoh himself was responsible for his hard heart (7:13–14, 22–23; 8:15, 19, 32; 9:7, 34–35). He enslaved and oppressed the people of his own volition long before the Lord began this hardening.

God claimed to harden the pharaoh's heart (thereby prolonging the slavery of the Israelites and the plagues) in order to "perform these miraculous signs of mine among them." These signs further revealed to the Israelites who God is ("these signs of mine"). As we see in both Genesis and Exodus, the Lord's identity is complex. By means of the plagues we see that Yahweh controls the creation, using natural phenomena in supernatural ways. Yahweh worked among them and with individuals (e.g., Moses and Aaron) to accomplish these purposes. Yahweh distinguished between those who were under the pharaoh's protection and those who were under the Lord's protection. God did not liberate them quickly, but used strategies that worked with the creation and the political structures that were in place.

10:1–2 / "Go to Pharaoh, for I have hardened his heart and the hearts of his officials." The first two verses of Exodus 10 give reasons ("so that") for the Lord's actions. The explanations are brief, but they are critical to understanding who the Lord is. The focus is on the Israelites and their progeny: **so that I may perform these miraculous signs of mine among them that you may tell your children and grandchildren.**

The Lord wanted their "children and grandchildren" to know about the hardening of Pharaoh's heart and the signs of Egypt. What exactly did God want them to know? Three things: the Lord is the dangerous and powerful redeemer of the oppressed; the Lord is the Creator of the entire creation; you are the people who must tell the world the story of how God redeemed and recreated you.

The Lord is the dangerous and powerful redeemer of oppressed people. The Lord's statement, **"how I dealt harshly with the Egyptians,"** is an anathema for Christians who struggle with the harsh actions of God in the OT. The narrative context of the pharaoh's crimes is essential here. The Lord wants to be known as one who responds with strength when God's children cry out for relief from violent oppression. God is a restorer of justice (23:2, 6). God redeems and delivers the helpless (6:6). In the plagues, for the first time, God acted to deliver a people from slavery. God's restrained and measured power—that is, nonetheless, by its calculated nature and its effect, "harsh"—met Egypt's power, which was no match.

The RSV translation represents the "harsh" treatment communicated in verses 1–2 as "I have made sport of." The NRSV has "I have made fools of," and the NASB translates the phrase "I have made a mockery of." The word may simply mean that God had personally "occupied himself" with the arrogance of the Egyptians. God actually used this limitless power with measured control, as earlier the Lord had said, "I could have . . . wiped you off the earth" (9:15).

In the NT, this sort of harshness does not disappear. In the incarnation and cross God sought out and suffered the harshness of oppression to overthrow it with love. The combination of the protection of love and the harshness of judgment against rebellion is also a NT theme (Matt. 25:33–34, 41; 2 Cor. 5:10). This refrain has its beginning in the protection of the children of Israel and the story of God's harshness against the oppressors in Egypt.

The second part of the explanation in verses 1–2 is that you may know **"how I performed my signs among them."** The creation-based signs themselves hold the theological interpretive key. The Lord is the Creator of the whole creation. God used creation and its symbolic undoing to communicate the sins and false gods of Egypt. God used the signs of the creation in a negative way to show that God is the Creator as well as to intervene for Israel. The Lord could have intervened with a delivering army, as in Babylon with Cyrus the Persian. Rather, God "performed signs," demonstrating for all future generations that human sin and creation run amok are related. God's performance of signs links ecological disaster with the pharaoh's theological and moral failures (see Fretheim, "The Plagues as Ecological Signs"). Later, in the wilderness, the Lord would teach the children of Israel the relationship between the glory of the Lord and the fullness of the created order (Num. 14:21; Exod. 16:7).

The final reason for the hardening of Pharaoh's heart (and the extended plagues) is **"that you may know that I am the LORD."** In this context the phrase "that you may know" indicates an active and continual knowing, generation after generation. Scripture provides two illuminating Psalms (105, 78) that retell the story of the plagues for future generations in worship settings.

10:3–20 / The eighth plague was **locusts** that blackened the face of the ground. It begins with the same narrative markers as the second (frogs) and fifth (death of livestock) plagues: Then the LORD said to Moses, "Go to Pharaoh," continues with the familiar words, **"This is what the LORD . . . says,"** and concludes with the freedom to serve Yahweh formula, **"Let my people go, so that they may worship me."** This is the final statement of the main reason for the exodus (as in 5:1; 7:16; 8:1, 20; 9:1, 13; 10:3). God would not ask Pharaoh again.

The complications resulting from the Lord's active role in hardening Pharaoh's heart began to appear in his erratic behavior and conversation. With the threat of locusts on the horizon, his officials convinced Pharaoh to let the people go (v. 7). He said they could go (v. 8) and then used the Lord's name sarcastically (v. 10), driving Moses and Aaron away (v. 11). This was all before the locusts arrived. Afterward he begged for their personal forgiveness (vv. 16–17), yet the Lord "strengthened" (*khazaq*) his heart once again.

The text here only implies that God gave Moses instructions for speaking to Pharaoh. Verse 3 begins with the actual message from the Lord. These descriptions of the threat of locusts (vv. 4–6) and the actual onslaught of locusts (vv.12–15) are part of a chiasm:

A Pharaoh asked to humble himself (v. 3)

   B threat of locusts described (vv. 4–6)

      C Negotiations between officials, the pharaoh, and Moses (vv. 7–11)

   B' onslaught of locusts described (vv. 12–15)

A' Pharaoh humbles himself (v. 16)

The second description (vv. 12–15) seems redundant in a linear reading, because many of its phrases echo the threat (less precisely in the NIV than in Hebrew). For example, **cover the face of the ground . . . devour what little you have left after the hail . . . every tree that is growing in your fields** (v. 5, see also v. 15); **something neither your fathers nor your forefathers have ever seen from the day they settled in this land till now** (v. 6, see also v. 14). The content of the repetition emphasizes both the extent of the ecological devastation as well as the historic uniqueness of the event.

The expressions translated "cover the face of the ground so that it cannot be seen" (v. 5) and **covered all the ground until it was black** (v. 15) convey a second meaning in Hebrew. Literally they could be translated, "cover the eye of the earth so that no one will be able to see the earth" and "covered the eye of the whole earth so that the earth was darkened." The basic meaning is that the locusts were very dense. The secondary allusion is to the beginning of a total blackout in Egypt. In the next plague, total darkness would cover Egypt's sky. With the locusts, the earth became "black" (*khashak*). Further, the world of Egypt was figuratively returning to the beginning of creation, where darkness (*khoshek*) covered everything. Egypt had become blind.

The other practical consideration was that, after the locusts, Egypt returned to the situation of starvation it faced in Joseph's day. Ironically, it was wisdom and knowledge from God, given to the Hebrew ancestor Joseph, that had saved Egypt from the famine (Gen. 41:53–57). The pharaoh's policies and the Lord's poetic justice now reversed that salvation.

The negotiations among the officials, the pharaoh, and Moses (vv. 7–11) are at the center of the narrative chiasm. Pharaoh's officials made an initially successful attempt to offer wise counsel. The NIV translates their counsel as very wise. Their question, however, **"How long will this man be a snare to us?"** could also be translated, "How long will this situation be a problem?" since the word "man" is missing from the text (Durham, *Exodus*, p. 133). The absence of the word could also lead to a derogatory reading of tone, "How long will this *nobody* be a problem for us?"

There is a second issue, found in their suggestion, **"Let the people go."** The Hebrew word for "people" in Exodus is almost always ʿ*am*. Here, however, the word is ʾ*anashim,* which usually means "men." It could mean, "Let the men go." When the pharaoh tells Moses, **"Have only the men go,"** he uses still another word (*gebarim*), meaning "able-bodied men." The word the officials use could refer (and probably does) to the people who can travel easily, including men and women without children. They probably thought that this would appease Moses. Just exactly who would go is ambiguous, not just for our translation, but likely because it was the main issue at stake in the negotiation. Therefore the variety in the vocabulary may be intentional. The officials were not yet as blind as the pharaoh. They said, **"Do you not yet realize that Egypt is ruined?"**

Nowhere is the effect of the hardening of the heart more succinctly expressed than in Pharaoh's words, **"Go, worship the LORD your God . . . But just who will be going?"** The idea that he might let them go before the plague strikes creates a new, however brief, possibility. But it was a false hope. He was still exercising his administrative lordship over the Lord's people. He said, "Go," but he could not help asking the further logistical question. In his acknowledgment of "the LORD your God," it is likely that "God" should not be capitalized.

Moses responds with a full description of who and what would make the journey to **"celebrate a festival to the LORD."**

Everyone and everything would go. Pharaoh begins his response with quiet, harsh sarcasm and ends with an emphatic **"No!"** The sarcastic use of the name of the Lord may be heard better by reading, **"The LORD be with you** *when* **I let you go, along with your** *toddlers!"* "Women" (NIV) is only implied in the text by the presence of children. The Hebrew word really means "toddlers" (*tap*), and its usage here adds to the sarcasm. The power that holds a people's toddlers hostage also holds their parents hostage.

"Clearly you are bent on evil." This is the conflict in brief. For Pharaoh, losing his slaves to another "lord" would be an unbearable evil. Moses and the people certainly were "bent" on obeying the Lord. Achieving freedom to serve or worship another lord would mean the end of Pharaoh's lordship over them. Literally, the expression is, "evil is before your faces," meaning "on your minds." It could also be a threat, suggesting that they might encounter evil if they were to proceed.

The narrative ends as it began, with dialogue about Pharaoh's humility. He had refused to be "humble" (lit., "to bend down from my face"). Not lowering one's eyes in the presence of the king was a sign of arrogance. This might also mean that he did not acknowledge either his need or his difficulty before the Lord. The plague of locusts forced him to acknowledge what he hitherto could not face about himself. He said, **"I have sinned against the LORD your God and against you."** This statement is stronger than his previous admission to have generally made a mistake (9:27). Here he admits his moral fault in relation to Moses' God. He has finally been humbled by a superior power. He says nothing about letting the people go but is simply a supplicant. Not capable of giving mercy, still he seeks it. God gives him the mercy he sought (removal of the locusts), but Pharaoh remains locked in his pattern of self-serving. His confession of humility is primarily for the benefit of the reader of the text. It was too late for the pharaoh in any case. The narrative begins and ends with the Lord hardening his heart (vv. 1, 20).

The narrative concludes when the Lord transforms (*hapak*) the wind into **a very strong west wind** (*ruakh yam khazaq me³od*), a wind **which caught up the locusts.** The verb for "caught up" is the same verb Pharaoh used to say "forgive" my sin (*nasa³*). He received the "lifting" he requested, that the "deadly plague" be removed. God lifted it by the west wind. The text mentions the sea for the first time in verse 19. The NIV translates the reference as **Red Sea.** This follows the LXX and NT Greek references rather than

the Hebrew text. The Hebrew text has "Reed Sea" (*yam sup*), referring to the papyrus reeds that grow in the margins of bodies of
water in that region. God drove the locusts into this sea so that
"Not a locust was left anywhere in Egypt."

10:21–29 / Thick darkness covered Egypt for three days.
In presenting the ninth plague in abbreviated form, the text continues a pattern—shortening the accounts of the third plague in
each of the cycles of three (gnats [third] and boils [sixth]). It begins
without warning. **Moses stretched out his hand toward the sky,
and total darkness covered all Egypt.** As the Lord said, it was
"darkness that can be felt."

The text does not describe the cause except to say that it was
from the Lord. The phrase for unnatural "gloom of darkness" (NIV
"total darkness") employs the same word the prophets use to describe the eerie darkness of the Day of the Yahweh when the Lord
comes in judgment of the nations (Isa. 8:22; Zeph. 1:15; Joel 2:2).
Rabbinic commentators call this "the darkness of Hell" (*Exodus
Rabbah*, 14:2). In the undoing of creation, Egypt was symbolically
returned to the primordial darkness before light was created (Gen.
1:2). The darkness language returns in the sea crossing (Exod.
14:20–21).

The effect was total. The statement that no one could **leave
his place for three days** is also metaphorical in Hebrew. "No one
could rise from under it" implies that a kind of depression set in.
The darkness immobilized everyone psychologically and physically. Yet the Lord again made a distinction, communicated in the
odd phrase, **all the Israelites had light in the places where they
lived.** Scholars have given a variety of interpretations for this exception (e.g., the sun shone in Goshen or unnaturally on their
dwellings). The Hebrew says that they had light "in their dwellings," meaning in their homes. The darkness was over "all Egypt."
The Hebrew's lamps worked in their homes while, by implication,
the unnatural darkness kept Egyptian lamps from functioning.
Light during unnatural darkness is a miracle, which the Creator
gave them through ordinary lamps.

This plague of darkness may not appear to be as bad as the
previous calamities, but in terms of the Egyptian cosmology it was
by far the worst. It was the death of their worldview. The sun god
Amon-Re was greatest among their gods and the national god of
Egypt. Pharaoh was his divine son and representative. In this
plague, the Lord blotted out Egypt's supreme god. The blackout

of the ground by the locusts brought death to Egypt's economy. It was matched by a blow to their cosmology in the blackout of the light of the sky. Houtman calls the horror of this plague the night when the Egyptians were the "living dead" (Houtman, *Exodus*, II, p. 116). As a result, the pharaoh made his greatest concession up to this point: **Even your women and children may go with you** (lit., "those who toddle," "women" are implied).

Pharaoh wanted to hold the animals hostage to guarantee the return of the people, who could not survive long in the wilderness without them. The negotiation for the animals focused on **worshiping the LORD.** It is fitting that the last argument between the pharaoh and Moses repeats a combination of the words for "worship" and "Lord" three times in three verses (vv. 24–26). Moses' powers of negotiation were finely tuned and his words precise: **not a hoof is to be left behind.** They were to be prepared to present to the Lord everything they had.

We expect the conversation between them to end when we read the familiar refrain that **the LORD hardened Pharaoh's heart.** It is the eleventh announcement of the hard heart of the pharaoh, but the dialogue is not over. Pharaoh had some parting words: **"Get out of my sight!"** (lit., "Get away from me"). He also had a personal threat for Moses: **"The day you see my face you will die."** Moses knew he would never see him again. The artificial chapter break causes many readers to think that now the conversation is over, but it is not. Moses, who knew he would not speak to Pharaoh again, still had to deliver the warning of the last plague, the death of the firstborn. He did this immediately following (11:4–8), leaving the pharaoh "hot with anger."

Additional Notes §11

10:1 / For further discussion of the issues attendant to the hardening of the pharaoh's heart see the following: Childs, *Exodus*, pp. 170–75; Fretheim, *Exodus*, pp. 96–103; Wilson, "The Hardening of Pharaoh's Heart."

10:2 / For a comparison of the content and order of the plagues in Pss. 78 and 105 see McCarter, "Exodus," pp. 128–29. Psalms 78 and 105 are a formal literary means of "telling your children and grandchildren" to pass on knowledge of the Lord, as is the book of Exodus. The plagues against the pharaoh and the exodus are also forever remembered in the

Jewish Passover service and the Feast of Unleavened Bread. The Lord commanded these remembrances so that all their descendants might know God as Creator and redeemer. Reinterpreted in light of the Christ, Christians observe them (with no reference to the plagues) in the Lord's Supper, or Eucharist. There the defeated and harassed enemies are the forces of darkness, the oppression of individual sin, and death itself.

10:9 / The expression translated by the NIV as "festival *to* the Lord" (*khag yhwh*, better translated "festival *of* the Lord") is unique in pilgrimages to a specific location for worship. It occurs exactly in this form only 4 times in the OT (Exod. 10:9; Lev. 23:39; Judg. 21:19; Hos. 9:5). See Durham, *Exodus*, p. 133. "Festival to the Lord" (*khag layhwh*) is used later in Exodus to refer especially to the Passover feast (12:14) and the Feast of Unleavened Bread (13:6; 23:15–17).

10:11 / The statements that Moses "left" Pharaoh ("exited," *yatsa²*, v. 6) and that Moses and Aaron **were driven out** (*garash*, v. 11) are a premonition of the children of Israel *exiting* Egypt (*yatsa²*; 12:41; 19:1) and being *driven out* by Pharaoh (6:1; 11:1; 12:39).

10:12 / The Lord asked Moses to "Stretch out your hand" in v. 12, but he "stretched out his staff" in v. 13. The two are equivalent in meaning in the context of the plague cycle. The difference is sometimes attributed to different source traditions.

10:21 / "Darkness that can be felt" or "darkness that caused groping" is from the *hip²il* stem of *mashash* (see Durham, *Exodus*, p. 141). Scientific explanations describe the sirocco, a hot dust storm from the Sahara, as a possible cause of the dust being "felt."

§12 Final Warning (Exod. 11:1–10)

Exodus 11 is a transitional chapter in several ways. Moses' final conversation with Pharaoh continues from Exodus 10. Having been warned by Pharaoh never to appear before him again, Moses delivers the warning of the tenth plague, the death of the firstborn (vv. 4–8). Verses 1–3, however, contain God's instructions for asking for silver and gold articles from the Egyptians. The chapter as a whole marks the ending of the first nine plagues (chs. 7–10), provides the announcement of the final plague to Pharaoh, and introduces the beginning of the exit from Egypt (chs. 11–15).

11:1–3 / Exodus 11 begins with a remarkable aside between Moses and the Lord. The Lord delivers the long-awaited announcement that, after **one more plague,** the pharaoh **will let you go from here, and when he does, he will drive you out completely.** This time the word translated "plague" (*nega*ᶜ) is new. When God is the initiator, this word means his "touch" of judgment (Gen. 12:17; 2 Sam. 7:14). This word is more personal than the typical word used for plague (*deber*). Indeed, the Lord is the one who brings the death (v. 4) that leads not only to their exit, but also to being driven out (6:1; 11:1; 12:39). The Egyptians would want them out.

God adds a public service announcement for the people to the announcement of the momentous exit. **Tell the people that men and women alike are to ask their neighbors for articles of silver and gold.** The seemingly abrupt placement of this instruction prepares the people and the reader for the dramatic changes about to take place in the narrative's events. The people would make a *hurried* exit. Two interpretations of this command are possible in the biblical context, neither of which supports the so-called *"plundering* of the Egyptians." First, asking for silver and gold was consistent with the Lord's requirements, given later at Sinai, for the respectful release of a debt slave. The Lord insisted that a person bound by debt as a servant should be released after six years of labor (Deut. 15:12–15). At the time of release, the owner must generously shower the person with material goods, giving them a good material start for their new life after slavery. God was requiring the same generosity from the Egyptians.

The second possible context for interpreting the so-called "plundering" of the Egyptians is found in the three Exodus texts that describe the giving of the silver and gold. Exodus 3:21–22 and 12:35–36 use similar language. They say that the Egyptians will give graciously (*khen*), being "favorably disposed" toward the Hebrews. "Plunder" is a possible translation of *natsal*, but not if they were *favorably disposed* toward them. The preferable translation is the more innocuous "deliver" that has the double meaning of "deliver them of their goods" and "deliver them of their duty, or debt, toward you." The word is used in a play between "strip off" the jewelry and "put it on" your children (3:22).

In any case, verses 2–3 repeat the gracious language that **The LORD made the Egyptians favorably disposed toward the people.** Fretheim calls this the Lord's "softening of their hearts" in contrast to the Lord's hardening of Pharaoh's heart (Fretheim, *Exodus*, p. 131). Using the strong word "plunder" may miss the point of the text. The new respect and graciousness of the ordinary Egyptians is an ironic miracle, demonstrating the lordship of Yahweh over all people.

11:4–10 / Verse 4 continues Moses' conversation with the pharaoh and the description of the tenth plague. Moses' last comment had been, "Just as you say . . . I will never appear before you again" (10:29). Here he delivers his eighth and last, **"This is what the LORD says"** (5:1; 7:17; 8:1, 20; 9:1, 13; 10:3; 11:4), but this time he does *not* follow these words with the release formula ("Let my people go, that they may serve me"). Judgment had come and the pharaoh would not "let them go," but would, rather, "drive them out."

The Lord speaks in the first person: **"About midnight I will go throughout Egypt. Every firstborn son in Egypt will die."** Yahweh would be directly responsible for death—as well as for life. God would "go" (*yatsaʾ*) not *out* of Egypt, but *throughout* Egypt. God went throughout, so the people could *go out* (*yatsaʾ*, v. 8). Without God no slave would be released. Moreover, God did not say, "I will kill." The text stops short of that.

God would come and the firstborn would "die" (*mut*). From a broad perspective, God, the giver of all life, has already ordained the giving and taking of every life. This incident is considered a *plague* because of the *timing of all the deaths at once*—one son in each home. Life would go out like the light went out in the plague of darkness. The Creator, who gave life, would remove the gift of living. Even **the slave girl, who is at her hand mill** (at midnight, probably because it was the only time she had to grind meal for herself) would lose her son. Even the firstborn of the cattle that remained would die. The **loud wailing** (*tseʿaqah*) would be **worse than there has ever been**, even worse than the cries (*zaʿaq*) of the Hebrew slaves to God (2:23). The unanswered cry contrasts with the answered cry in the words of the psalmist (Ps. 22:1–5) echoed on the cross. Scripture does not back away from the difficult reality that God takes life to redeem life. Innocent life was taken, by the one who created it.

The deaths of firstborn sons may also be understood in light of Exodus 13:1–2, 11–16. The firstborn of Israel, man or animal, particularly belonged to the Lord (13:2). From this time forward this symbol reminded Israel that life itself belongs to the Creator, who "goes" (*yatsaʾ*) to Egypt in order to redeem Israel from slavery. If God had not gone "throughout Egypt," no Israelite would ever have left the country. The Creator purchased redemption with the innocent life of the firstborn of animals, slave girls, the freeman, and the nobility. It costs God the very creation itself to do this.

In the midst of this terrible redemption, Moses told Pharaoh that God would protect the children of Israel. Protection was not possible under the pharaoh's lordship. No one could respond to the Egyptians' cries. But God would protect those under the Lord's rule. The Israelites would not have to kill anyone or give their lives to buy their freedom. The LORD **makes a distinction** once again (9:4, 26; 10:23; 11:7; 12:23; 14:28). Israelite lives were secure, for their redeemer was present. The note that **among the Israelites not a dog will bark at any man or animal** expresses their complete security. Dogs, beloved by the Egyptians, would not even bark at an animal belonging to the Hebrews. God even protected their animals. On the Passover of death, in the middle of the night, there would be no disturbance in Hebrew homes sleeping under the blood of the lamb (12:13–14, 23).

Moses' parting words rhetorically pound the meanings of "Go out" (*yatsaʾ*, it is lost in the NIV English). The officials will say, "Go out!" A better translation, then, for **"I will leave"** would be, "I will go out." At the end of the conversation, **Moses, hot with anger,** *went out* from **Pharaoh.** Yet the exit from Egypt had not begun. All human agency and effort with Pharaoh were finished. No one could do anything else to negotiate or leverage the release of the Hebrews. The people were not free and the path to the pharaoh had been severed (10:29; 11:8). God alone could act. God's next move was to institute a meal of lamb and bread and to give them the blood of protection from death, signaling the first elements of serving the Lord rather than the pharaoh. The chapter ends by reiterating that Pharaoh **would not let the Israelites go out of his country**—"his" country.

The plague cycle formally ends here with the concluding report in verses 9–10. Its words refer to and match the announcement that began the plagues in 7:3–4. The narrator announces the pharaoh's hard heart for the twelfth and last time in the plague cycle (7:13, 22; 8:15, 19, 32; 9:7, 12, 34–35; 10:20, 27; 11:10). The narrative of the exit from Egypt includes a brief report on the dying of the firstborn (12:29–30) but focuses mainly on the protected Passover feast and preparations for their journey out of Egypt.

Additional Notes §12

11:2 / The motive given for the release of the debt slave and gift giving in Deut. 15:15 is "that you were slaves in Egypt and the LORD your God redeemed you." For the full interpretive rationale for interpreting Exod. 11:2–3 in this context, see Daube, *The Exodus Pattern,* pp. 55–72. A discussion of its merit may be found in Brueggemann, "Exodus," p. 770.

11:5 / In the book of Exodus the Lord speaks and acts as the Creator of life and death and, therefore, the one who rightly takes and gives life. In calling Moses, the Lord said, "Israel is my firstborn son . . . Let my son go . . . but you refused . . . so I will kill your firstborn son." In the next verse, the Lord sought to cause Moses' death, presumably because he had not dedicated *his* firstborn son through circumcision (4:22–24). See comments in the Introduction.

§13 Passed Over or Destroyed? (Exod. 12:1–27)

Exodus 12 and 13 stand together as a single literary unit, describing the Passover (*pesakh*; lit., pass over). If we read this lengthy portion (12:1–13:16) in a simple linear fashion, it may seem oddly organized and redundant. The most we could say is that *the length itself* was part of what served to establish the exodus event and its perpetual observance in Israel's memory and liturgical practice. It was indeed a primary formational event. We can understand the themes of this vital material even better, however, when we notice the internal structure and the relationships between the paragraphs. The text structurally braids together the three themes of protecting the precious firstborn, the Passover lamb, and the Feast of Unleavened Bread in 12:1–13:16. The chiastic structure below reveals this pattern. The whole pericope includes a description of the first Passover as well as the institution of the legacy of Passover observance for generations to come.

A First Passover instruction *to Moses* for the protection of firstborn (12:1–13)

   B First instruction regarding Feast of Unleavened Bread to Moses (12:14–20)

      C First Passover instruction *to the people* for protection of firstborn (12:21–27)

         D First historical Passover-unleavened event: The exodus (12:28–42)

      C′ Perpetual Passover ordinance *to Moses* (12:43–51)

   B′ Perpetual Feast of Unleavened Bread ordinance to Moses (13:3–10)

A′ Perpetual firstborn ordinance *to the people* (13:11–16)

The central panel, often the most important in a chiastic structure, presents the historical action of Exodus. Everything else is a dialogue between God and Moses or Moses and the people.

This structure is also helpful for seeing the narrative logic in providing details concerning the Passover lamb in three separate places (A, C, C'). Each section adds small amounts of new material. We can best understand these differences by considering the subtly changing conversations and contexts. The three related themes of protection of the firstborn, the Passover lamb, and the Feast of Unleavened Bread form the structure. The following commentary on these chapters is organized according to this internal biblical structure.

12:1–13 / The Lord gave instructions for surviving the tenth plague during the first Passover **to Moses and Aaron in Egypt.** The instructions for celebrating the Passover *in Egypt* included a description of family groups, when and how to select the lamb, the blood of protection on the doorframes, the cooking of the lamb, the side dishes, disposal of the leftover food, and the symbols of hurriedness. Each of these details was significant for the first Passover in Egypt. Some parts of this instruction, but not all, would also be relevant for the perpetual observance of Passover. The people would never again, for example, need to place blood on the doorposts. This was the culmination of the Lord's judgment of the "gods of Egypt" (v. 12).

The fundamental experience of God's creation of Israel as a people in the Passover-exodus experience affected the reckoning of the months of the year. **This month is to be for you . . . the first month of your year.** The name of this month is found later (13:4) and is associated with Abib/Nisan (earlier/Second Temple names of the month; Exod. 23:15; 34:18; Neh. 2:1; Esth 3:7). Abib is the seventh month of the Jewish calendar, in the spring (Exod. 23:16; 34:22). Chronologically, the first month is Tishri, beginning with Rosh Hashanah ("the first of the year") and the Day of Atonement (Yom Kippur) during autumn. These verses call this month first in importance, or prominence, since it was the beginning of the Lord's establishing Israel as a people.

Moses was to address **the whole community** and detail the instructions for organizing and planning the meal. "No waste" was a central concern, and the meal was organized with neighbors eating together. The larger groups were to organize themselves by proximity to the **nearest neighbor** rather than by extended families. Even how much **each person will eat** was of consequence to the Lord.

Verse 5 describes the small flock animals. The Hebrew reads like a list of requirements: "lamb, sound, male, one year." They were to be sound **year-old males, sheep** or goat kids. The word "lamb" (*seh*, vv. 3–4) is a generic word that could refer to either one.

The instruction to **Take care of them until the fourteenth day of the month** after selecting them on the **tenth day** (v. 3) provided for three days of care before the day of slaughter. Commentators offer several explanations. It may be as simple as providing time to control the animal's diet, since it would be cooked with its entrails (v. 9). Benno Jacob suggests that the narrative implies that the three days of darkness were the same days (10:22). They therefore selected the animal in the light of the tenth day, before the darkness, and kept it, perhaps inside, during the darkness. The light returned on the fourteenth day, when they slaughtered the animal (Jacob, *Exodus*, p. 301). The book of Joshua provides another possibility—that three days allowed for the healing of the newly circumcised adults (Josh. 4:19; 5:8–11). After the wilderness journey, the men submitted to circumcision on exactly the same day (tenth day of Abib/Nisan) and celebrated the Passover on the fourteenth. The entry to and exit from the wilderness, then, began with the Passover celebration on the fourteenth of Abib/Nissan.

All the people of the community of Israel were to **slaughter** the animals **at twilight,** thereby preparing their meal and the blood of the animal just in time for the night of the tenth plague. We learn later that they applied the blood with hyssop branches to the doorframes (v. 22; see comment on the use and meaning of the blood at vv. 13, 22–23). The imperative phrase **Eat it in haste** sums up the specific instructions for eating the meal.

Many of the details here are necessities of haste or symbols of haste. The **same night** that they slaughtered at twilight, they were **to eat the meat roasted over the fire.** This cooking method was a symbol of traveling, when large pots were not available for boiling. Neither was the animal eviscerated, but cooked whole, with **head, legs and inner parts** intact. Evisceration does not take very long, but this was a symbolic action of haste. The **bread made without yeast** was certainly a quicker method, since it did not need to rise. Eating while fully dressed for travel was both practical and symbolic. Eating with **your staff in your hand** must have been intentionally awkward. Because they would be traveling the next morning, they had no means to care for leftover meat. The command was, **if some is left till morning, you must burn it.** This may also reflect care not to profane it.

The first Passover meal, like subsequent remembrances of it, was eaten **along with bitter herbs.** The rabbinic tradition identified varieties of bitter herbs including lettuce, dandelion, and chicory. People today often use horseradish. Eating these herbs was a reminder that their lives had been "bitter with hard labor" (1:14).

The expression "Eat it in haste" has a secondary meaning in Hebrew: Eat it with trepidation. The word for "haste" (*khippazon*) means "trepidation," "hurry," or "alarm." Why would the people tremble in trepidation as they ate? Because **it is the LORD's Passover** (*pesakh*). The Lord would literally "pass over" (*pesakh*) the houses as they ate and as young men and animals died in Egypt. The rabbinic interpreters note that all the marks of "haste" were symbolic. It would take only half an hour to eat, although they would have had all night. The important issue was the attitude in which they ate. This was not a celebratory feast. The people were not to be indifferent to the suffering outside the walls of their homes, even the suffering of their enslavers (Prov. 24:17). They should eat with the haste of alarm, since their deliverance was purchased at such a cost of human and animal life. **I will pass through Egypt and strike down every firstborn—both men and animals—and I will bring judgment on all the gods of Egypt. I am the LORD.** The Lord's judgment of the gods of Egypt brought suffering to every home outside the protection God gave to Israel. God did the work while they ate in safety. God made a distinction between those whose God was the Lord and those who worshiped/served other gods, though they were all God's creatures.

The final verse of this section may be the most theologically overinterpreted. The language is very direct. **The blood will be a sign for you on the houses where you are.** The blood was a sign for the people. The Hebrew word for "sign" is the same used for the other plagues. This culminating sign was not for the pharaoh, however, but for the people ("for you"). The people received the miracle when they accepted the Lord's offer of grace, protection, and lordship by placing the blood on their doorposts. This was not a blood ritual that fended off an angry God. God's grace had provided them with a sign of the Lord's prevenient provision of protection in the midst of general judgment in the land. The provision was part of the Lord's identity and the whole exodus pattern. God had come down to deliver the people. The miracle was that anyone responded by seeking God's shelter and lordship.

The text continues with the promise that **when I see the blood, I will pass over you.** If God had provided the blood, and had previously "made a distinction" between the children of Israel and the Egyptians, why did God need to "see" the blood? The people could not protect themselves with the blood that the Lord had provided in this revelation, as though it were magical and designed to avert evil (apotropaic). It was God who protected them. The word "pass over" (*pesakh*) carries the meaning of "protect" or "shield" (Isa. 31:5). Verses 23 and 27 also explain this nuance. The Lord protected and saved them. The people could, however, reject the protection God offered. The absence of blood on a doorframe would constitute a rejection of God's offer of grace, protection, and lordship. The Lord offered three promises, better translated, "I will see the blood and I will pass over you; no destructive plague will touch you when I strike Egypt." This was the very purpose for which God had come down.

12:14–20 / The Lord continues in these verses to give Moses instructions for traveling light and for remembering his deeds. The people were to use no yeast (*seʾor*) for one week after the Passover meal. They were to eat unleavened bread (*matsah*). Verse 14 links the two observances (Passover/Feast of Unleavened Bread) by referring to the day of the Passover: **This is a day you are to commemorate.** It continues by describing the seven days of eating bread without yeast that follow it. They celebrated these observances together. It was a day to remember with a week-long feast in **generations to come.** The Lord protected them in the Passover and they traveled fast, eating only matzo bread. In this way the people participated in the Lord's deliverance.

These verses describe the **lasting ordinance** of "no yeast" in the bread in three similar ways using different vocabulary. Verses 18–19, at the end of the passage, repeat these three instructions. (1) **Eat bread made without yeast.** (2) **On the first day remove the yeast** (*seʾor*) **from your houses.** This refers to the sourdough starter used to leaven dough. (3) **Whoever eats anything with yeast** (*khamets*) **in it . . . must be cut off from Israel.** *Khamets* was any food that had the yeast in sourdough added to it. The concluding verse (v. 20) also emphasizes "no yeast." Anyone who did not keep this feast cut themselves off (*karat*) from the community by not participating in this formational event and remembrance. "Cutting off" was not enforced legally in Judaism, but was left to God, with the expectation of no descendents and an early death.

The central verse of this section gives the reason for the celebration: **because it was on this very day that I brought your divisions out of Egypt.** Verse 17b and verse 14 frame this centerpiece of the Lord's instruction to Moses. **Celebrate this day as a lasting ordinance for the generations to come.** The people were to hold **a sacred assembly,** working only to **prepare food** on the first and last days of the week of "no yeast" (v. 16). Even the **alien** (*ger,* better translated "immigrant" or "resident alien") must observe the feast.

The striking repetition of phrases in this passage is not accidental. The Passover and Feast of Unleavened Bread event and observance as a feast has constitutional force for God's people. Anyone who does not participate cannot be part of Israel. They are **cut off** (vv. 15, 19). It is comparable to someone who will not be baptized as a Christian or share in the Lord's Supper. Participation is stated as nonnegotiable. The participation in, and remembrance of, the Lord's deliverance is a primary theme of the book of Exodus. It is emphasized throughout (13:6–7; 16:4–15, 29–32; 23:5; 25:30; 29:2, 23, 32–34; 34:18, 28; 35:13; 39:36; 40:23). God's work on this day *and* the remembrance of that work are the constitutive event and practice of the Lord's continually renewed people, effective for "generations to come." Participation in this shapes the life of the people.

12:21–27 / **"Go at once . . ."** here Moses speaks to the Israelites for the first time since they refused to listen to him in 6:9. (We last heard from the elders in 4:29.) They had experienced God's protection during the plagues in the meantime. **Moses summoned all the elders** and gave them imperative directions for the protection of their firstborn (vv. 21–23) and instructions for future remembrance of the event (vv. 24–27). He directed them to **select the animals** for their families, **slaughter the Passover lamb,** and mark blood **on the top and on both sides of the doorframe.** He told them to use **hyssop,** probably a kind of marjoram with bunches of small white flowers on the end, to **put some of the blood** on the house. The word "put" is a weak translation of the root *naga*^{c}, better translated "touch." The same word was translated "plague" in 11:1, "I will bring one more *plague* (touch) on Pharaoh." The wordplay substitutes the blood "touching" the doorframe for the "plague" that was coming.

Moses assured the people of the Lord's intention to protect them. The Lord came **"to strike down the Egyptians."** He would protect them with his passing over (*pasakh*, "protect"; see v. 12 above). The presence of the Lord would **"not permit the destroyer to . . . strike you down."** The Lord would do this when he saw that the family had accepted his lordship by applying the blood to their house. The blood of the lamb, through the protection of the Lord, provided them with victory over certain death and over the evils of Egyptian enslavement.

The NT uses the theme of the Passover lamb in relation to Jesus' death. The Synoptic Gospels describe the Passover Feast that became the Last Supper (Mark 14:12–16; Matt. 26:17–19; Luke 22:7–13). John alludes clearly to the death of Jesus as the Passover lamb (19:14, 31–33, 42). Paul tells the Corinthians that they have been delivered from the "yeast" (= bondage) of malice and evil by the sacrifice of Christ, the Passover lamb. The theme at work in these texts is the protection from bondage to sin, death, and evil.

Moses continues pointing to future remembrances of the Passover event by giving instructions to the elders (vv. 24–27). **"Obey these instructions as a lasting ordinance for you and your descendants."** In the midst of the narrative, the text looks forward to verses 43–51, where God will give further instructions to Moses. The remarkable thing to note here is that God gives the people liturgical instructions for the future *before* their deliverance or exit from Egypt. Hope was created as plans were laid. The text emphasizes the meaning of the **ceremony** (or "service," *ᶜabodah*) given to the **children.**

Moses said to tell the children that **"It is the Passover sacrifice to the LORD, who passed over the houses of the Israelites in Egypt and spared our homes when he struck down the Egyptians."** The translation "Passover sacrifice" perpetuates a wide misunderstanding in Christian circles, that this was a sin-offering. Sin offerings were called *khattaʾt,* and were not eaten by the one who offered them. The word used here is *zebakh,* and means "slaughter for eating." The meat was cooked and eaten like a thank-offering for deliverance from danger or like a fellowship offering (Lev. 7:11–17). Nothing was said about forgiveness or being made clean. The instructions for later Passovers never again mention the blood of the lamb (e.g., Num. 9), since this was a one-time event of deliverance. For Christians, this feature of Passover is also like Christ's once and for all defeat of death through his death and resurrection. In as much as we share in that event, we share in deliverance from the dominion of death and are set free in new life under his lordship. New Testament texts do describe cleansing from sin offered in Christ, but they draw on other OT sacrificial traditions (see, e.g., Heb. 10:1–22).

At the first opportunity to respond, **the people bowed down and worshiped.** They had heard that one day they would explain to their children that **the LORD . . . spared our homes.** They worshiped although they were not yet delivered. They worshiped because they believed that the Lord would follow through on these promises. The Lord's deliverance was not attributed to Moses' or Aaron's persuasive power, nor to the people's will to freedom. Even at the sea they murmured and complained (14:31). The text pushes the truth that it is the Lord who delivered them.

Additional Notes §13

12:8 / It is faster to cook meat by boiling it (a half hour vs. two to three hours)—the method for cooking most other OT sacrifices. The Deuteronomist amends this instruction for later observances of the Passover (Deut. 16:7; *bashal*, "boil"). Why roasted lamb? Because it can be done without pots that were necessarily packed for the journey. The NIV unfortunately glosses Deut. 16:7, translating the word "boil" (*bashal*) as "roast," apparently to harmonize it with "roast over fire" (*tseli ʾesh*) in v. 9. This harmonizing error is unfortunate (and unnecessary) since the Exodus instruction in vv. 1–13 is specifically for the first Passover, not for subsequent Passovers. The Greek OT also has "roast" (*optos*) in Exodus and "boil" (*epsō*) in Deuteronomy.

12:11 / The form *khippazon*, translated "haste," occurs only here, in Deut. 16:3, and in Isa. 52:12. Its root, *khapaz*, means something like "trembling in alarm" (see, e.g., Job 40:23; see also Jacob, *Exodus*, pp. 310–11).

12:14 / The Passover lamb was killed on the fourteenth of the month. The Feast of Unleavened Bread began on the day they left Egypt, **from the evening of the fourteenth day** (v. 18), technically the beginning of the fifteenth. It continued through the twenty-first (seventh day), which was the day of the concluding feast. There are further descriptions of the Feast of Unleavened Bread in Lev. 23:5–6; Num. 28:16–17; and Deut. 16:1–8.

12:20 / Matzah bread is made only with flour and water. It could be made from five species of grains: wheat, rye, barley, oats, and spelt (emmer). Ashkenazi Judaism forbade products during this feast that have traces of natural leaven: rice, corn, millet, and legumes (beans and nuts). In current Jewish practice, a family searches the home on the night before Passover with a feather and a spoon to collect pieces of leavened bread hidden to initiate the search (Sarna, "Exodus," p. 385).

12:21 / The people received Moses' words as from the Lord. For a brief summary of the variety of source critical theories on the compositional complexity of the liturgical and narrative elements in vv. 21–28, see Durham, *Exodus*, p. 161.

12:24 / Present-day Seder meals do not use a lamb because it can't be done properly. Sometimes a lamb shank is eaten, but often the meat is chicken. Only the Samaritans still roast an unskinned and uneviscerated whole lamb. The celebration is a *present* event, not just a memorial. It also looks to the future, sometimes leaving an empty place at the table for Elijah and the front door ajar. The Seder liturgy follows the pattern of describing the event of the original Passover, explaining its meaning, and celebrating with eating and drinking.

§14 The Devastating Blow and the Beginning of the Exit (Exod. 12:28–51)

The night of the exodus came. After the lengthy plagues, speeches, and extended instructions for the Passover and Feast of Unleavened Bread observances, the exit began. The second half of Exodus 12 continues to braid together the three themes of the Passover lamb, the death/life of the firstborn, and the necessity of bread without yeast. The narrative describing the beginning of the actual exit from Egypt forms the central panel (D) of the chiastic structure we saw in the previous chapter:

C First Passover instruction to the people (vv. 21–27)

    D *First historical Passover-unleavened bread event: The exodus* (vv. 28–42)

C′ Perpetual Passover ordinance to Moses (vv. 43–51)

The last part of Exodus 12 (containing C′) mirrors the former material (C) about the Passover.

12:28–42 / The people kept the first Passover vigil. After all the instruction leading up to it, the text marks the actual event by simply noting that **The Israelites did just what the LORD commanded Moses and Aaron.** They prepared the Passover lamb, sealed their houses, and ate the meal. What follows are seven succinct reports that read like a series of related news bulletins (vv. 29–30; 31–32; 33–34; 35–36; 37–38; 39; 40–41). The narrative is in a hurry. Pharaoh and the Egyptians were in a hurry. The people and their bread were moving out.

The first bulletin describes the Lord's action of striking the firstborn. **At midnight the LORD struck down all the firstborn in Egypt.** This action revealed the Lord of life and death for all to see. Judgment and grace were God's to distribute. From the highest throne to the lowliest place in Egypt, **loud wailing** was heard in every house and **all the Egyptians got up during the night.**

The second bulletin reports Pharaoh's response. He calls for Moses and Aaron in the middle of the night and gives them six quick imperatives: **"Up! Leave . . . Go . . . worship** ("serve") **the LORD . . . Take your flocks . . . and go."** He capitulates completely, saying "as you have requested" twice. He has given up on negotiating their "service" for himself. Pharaoh's last comment in the book of Exodus is not a command, but a request: **"And also bless me."** This time Pharaoh did not change his mind until they had begun their exit (14:4).

The third bulletin describes the people's hurry with their bread because the Egyptian people **urged** them **to hurry and leave the country.** With someone dead in each house, they were afraid more would die if the Israelites remained. In the midst of the havoc, the detail about the care of the bread may seem odd and out of place. Yet, it was the primary symbol of their deliverance (like the bread and chalice in the Lord's Supper). Even in this dark hour of haste, the Lord provided for the detail of daily bread in a unique way, **on their shoulders in kneading troughs wrapped in clothing.**

The fourth bulletin describes the grace of the Egyptian people toward the Israelites, who obeyed God in asking for portable wealth (*khen,* NIV "favorably disposed"). The emphasis here is on the Egyptian graciousness (also at 3:21). The word translated "plunder" means "delivered" (*natsal,* in the *pi^cel*; BDB, p. 664). The children of Israel delivered the Egyptians of their wealth, of their slaves, as well as of their guilt for the years of slavery (see additional comments at 11:2–3). The slaves were released with material goods to begin their new lives (Deut. 15:12–15). They would also have the materials necessary to build the tabernacle (38:24–31). The Lord had inverted the power structure.

The fifth bulletin describes the first journey of the exit from Egypt. There are two problems for modern readers in this report. First, the locations of **Rameses** and **Succoth** are not precisely known, and maps of the exodus vary. The general locale of a one-day journey out of Egypt limits the range. Succoth is usually assumed to be southeast of Rameses toward the Bitter Lakes.

More problematic is the declaration that **There were about six hundred thousand men on foot, besides women and children.** The clear reference to "strong men" did not include the elderly or youths. Estimates of the total group size reach two million people. The logistical impossibility of that many people has generated much discussion (see Durham, *Exodus,* pp. 171–72). The most common, though not conclusive, solution is to read the word for "thousand" (*ʾelep*) as "clan" or "troop" (see also Num. 1:16; Judg. 6:15). Yet Exodus 38:26 is quite clear that individual men were counted. Israel under Solomon's rule had this many people for the first time, which may suggest a retrospective attempt to include that population as a delivered people (Sarna, *Exodus*, p. 62). **Many other people** ("a great mixture") who were oppressed under Pharaoh also went with them.

The sixth bulletin describes their first meal on the road and why it was necessarily unleavened. They baked their bread before it leavened **because they had been driven out of Egypt.** They were driven out by the pharaoh's six imperative commands (vv. 31–32) and in part by the pressure of the Egyptian people (v. 33). Later, they would be driven by Pharaoh's chariots as they neared the sea (14:9).

The seventh and final bulletin offers a historical reflection on the **length of time the Israelite people lived in Egypt.** Again, scholars provide no harmonizing explanation for the exact number **430 years, to the very day.** The round number in Genesis 15:13 is 400 years (see Durham, *Exodus*, p. 172). Verses 17, 41, and 51 repeat the expression "to the very day."

A statement about the legacy of the Lord's breaking into history to bring the people out of Egypt concludes the central panel of Exodus 12 and 13. It changes everything **for the generations to come.** A deft repetition of words establishes the relationship between the Lord's vigil and Israel's vigilance in remembering. The word "vigil" means, literally, "a night of protecting," or "keeping," so the people protect or keep this night as a time to honor the Lord. The reference to future Passover vigils bridges this section to the following perpetual Passover statutes.

12:43–51 / These verses return to the concerns of perpetually keeping the Passover. They mirror "C" in the chiastic structure above, the "First Passover instruction" (vv. 21–27) as C′, the "Perpetual Passover ordinance." Here the Lord speaks to Moses and gives seven additional statutes designed to preserve the original purpose of the celebration: to form a community around the historical deliverance of God's people. These verses are sometimes treated as an appendix but, besides adding regulations to perpetual Passover keeping (vv. 24–27), they are also an integral part of a structure that centralizes God's action and the actual deliverance of the people. Additionally, they provided instruction for adjudicating future Passovers for the "many other people" who went with them (v. 38).

Of these seven laws (*torot,* "instructions"), five concern who should or should not share in the Passover meal. Every long-term resident, regardless of social position, could eat. If the resident were male, he had to be circumcised as a necessary sign of his membership among the people of God (like baptism for Christians; Gen. 17:10–27; see also Exod. 4:25). The five laws regarding participants are as follows: (1) **No foreigner is to eat of it.** (2) **A temporary resident and a hired worker may not eat of it.** These two categories refer to people who have not joined the community of faith, but who are temporarily associated with it. (3) **The whole community of Israel must celebrate it.** Those prohibited were not committed to the community through faith in the Lord. The excluded "foreigner" (*nekar*) especially refers in the OT to those who worship other gods. They might have been in the community for business purposes. This table was not open to idolaters. "Temporary resident" (*toshab*) could be translated "visitor," or someone who did not plan to be associated with the believing community for very long. The "hired worker" (*shakir*) was someone who was associated with the community only for the money he might earn. These three kinds of people were excluded from partaking of the Passover meal.

On the other hand, anyone who had joined the community of Israel through the life circumstance of debt slavery or conversion, as well as by circumcision, was considered an Israelite. (4) **Any slave . . . may eat of it after you have circumcised him.** (5) **An alien living among you who wants to celebrate the LORD's Passover must have all the males in his household circumcised; then he may take part like one born in the land.** The "alien living among you" differed from those who were excluded, in that a *ger* was a "landed immigrant." These families had joined the community permanently. Their circumcision was a sign, as it was for all Israelites, of the integrity of their decision before the Lord. In later texts the term *ger* refers to conversion to Judaism (Isa. 14:1; 56:3–8). Discrimination against the landed immigrant (NIV "alien") was strictly prohibited (v. 49).

Two further laws deal with other matters. (6) **It must be eaten inside one house.** This means that whatever home began eating in, one must stay in it. The house was to be sealed from beginning to end, like the first Passover. (7) **Do not break any of the bones.** This command reiterates in part the original instruction to cook the lamb whole (v. 9). It also includes not breaking the bones when eating it, to access the marrow (see also John 19:36; Ps. 34:20 [LXX])

The section ends with the report that all the Israelites obeyed these commands from the very first observance. Verse 51 echoes verse 41, reminding us that this was all done on that **very day the** LORD **brought the Israelites out of Egypt.**

Additional Notes §14

12:37 / Rameses was likely at tell ed-Dab ͨa, 80 mi. northeast of Cairo. For a summary of the possible locations of Rameses and Succoth see Hyatt, *Exodus*, pp. 59–60; see also my comment on 13:18–20 and in the Introduction.

12:44 / It may seem odd that Israelites, enslaved under the pharaoh, would themselves have slaves. Although chattel slavery existed in Israel, especially during and after the reign of King Solomon, the OT laws stand against it. The laws require the release of slaves every 7 years, assuming that any debt they owe or any cost the owner incurred would be paid by then. This was God's law regarding slavery although it apparently was not kept uniformly in Israel's long history. See the discussion of slavery laws at 21:1–17; see also Deut. 15:11–18.

§15 Unleavened Bread and Firstborn Redemption, Revisited (Exod. 13:1–22)

The first sixteen verses of Exodus 13 belong to the framework that begins in Exodus 12. They return to the themes of unleavened bread and the firstborn, completing the braided work of 12:1–13:16 (see an outline of this structure in §13). The observance of the Feast of Unleavened Bread (B') in verses 2–10, with Moses speaking the message to the people, mirrors God's words to Moses in (B), 12:14–20. The law of the firstborn redemption in verses 11–16 (A') mirrors the killing of the firstborn in Egypt and the protection of Israel's firstborn in 12:1–13 (A). The structure is thus A, B, B', A'. The remainder of Exodus 13 (vv. 17–22) begins the next stage in the story of the exodus. It gives us basic notes about their first travels in the wilderness before crossing the sea.

The rhetorically remarkable feature of Exodus 13 is the weaving of the Lord's past and future actions with the commands concerning the people's future remembering. The text includes specifically personal language to use in remembering. The Lord "brought you out" (vv. 3, 9), will bring you (vv. 5, 11), did this "for me" (v. 8), and "brought us out of Egypt" with "a mighty hand" (vv. 14, 16). God commanded the people to consecrate (v. 1), commemorate (v. 3), observe the service and eat unleavened bread (vv. 5–7), explain it to their children (vv. 8, 14), keep it year to year (v. 10), and give their firstborn animals and redeem their firstborn child (v. 13).

13:1–2 / The first two verses seem to belong with the other "firstborn instructions" given in verses 11–16. These verses may simply link the firstborn and the Feast of Unleavened Bread together as commemorations of the exodus salvation.

If we interpret the text in its present form, we may treat it as an interruption of the chiastic structure, broken only in these two verses. When biblical structures vary, it often indicates an emphasis on the intruding verses. In this case, it would stress that the

Passover is about the firstborn and God, declaring: "Your firstborn have been protected and are precious to God." All Israel is also called God's firstborn, as a created people among the nations of the earth. This message provides the contextual explanation for both the Feast of Unleavened Bread and the slaughter and redemption of the firstborn.

13:3–10 / Here, Moses' instructions for keeping the feast in perpetuity mirror the first Feast of Unleavened Bread instruction from the Lord (12:14–20). These verses simply repeat many of the features: **Commemorate this day** (12:14; 13:3); **the day you came out of Egypt** (12:17; 13:3); **Eat nothing containing yeast** (12:15; 13:3, 6); and **on the seventh day hold a festival to the LORD** (12:16; 13:6). Verse 7 repeats each of the three key terms from 12:15: **unleavened bread** (*matsah* = "matzah"); **nothing with yeast** (*khamets*); and **any yeast** (*se'or*).

The text focuses the main point ("eat matzah on those seven days") in two new ways—on the present and on their future location in the land. It is possible that the final editor was concerned with his situation and looked back at the exodus. The text itself timelessly looks to the present (**Today, in the month of Abib**), *the future* (**When the LORD brings you into the land**), and *the past* (**the land he swore to your forefathers**). The exodus is always interpreted in the context of the four-hundred-year-long promise to Abraham, Isaac, and Jacob (2:24; 3:6, 15–16; 4:5; 6:3, 8; 13:5, 11; 32:13; 33:1; see comment at 3:15).

Moses briefly centered the people's attention on the present with the words "Today . . . you are leaving." He gave them hope for the future and for the day by mentioning their promised destination. The land of the future was not a wilderness, but **flowing with milk and honey.** Neither was **the land of the Canaanites** unoccupied (3:8, 17; 13:5, 11; 23:23, 28; 33:2; 34:11). Moses gave them hope, but not unrealistic hope (see comment at 3:8). The "month of Abib" also looked forward, since it was the first calendar month of the Canaanites, among whom they would live. It meant "new grain" and began on the spring equinox.

To "eat matzah" was a tactile aid in the logistics of personalized remembering. It was a reminder of the hurried departure from Egypt that they would be rehearsing year after year. **On that day tell your son, "I do this because of what the LORD did for me when I came out of Egypt."** The remembrance was to be spoken in the first person, "I." Even future generations would say "for me." In telling their children, the parent made it clear that the Lord's redemption was for them in whatever historical time the family lived.

The words **a sign on your hand and a reminder on your forehead** that the law might **be on your lips** also invoked a bodily kind of remembrance. Orthodox Judaism takes this instruction literally, using phylacteries, or leather boxes with long straps containing Scripture texts, to bind the commandments to one's left arm and forehead (Deut. 6:8; 11:18). In a non-literal sense, the hand and forehead references meant that the observance of unleavened bread was to be very personal, close at hand, and on your mind so that you speak of it frequently. The section concludes with the refrain, **For the LORD brought you out of Egypt with his mighty hand** (13:3, 9, 16).

13:11–16 / Moses continues to speak to the people, establishing a perpetual ordinance for the redemption of the firstborn. The law of the firstborn redemption (vv. 11–16) mirrors the killing of the firstborn in Egypt and the protection of Israel's firstborn (12:1–13). This protection was established when the Lord passed over the houses to protect them from the destroyer (12:13b). Its relationship to the redemption of the firstborn in the Passover celebration is explained to a child in verses 14–15.

The details here establish the principles of the Lord's ownership as Creator of life and redeemer from death. The ordinance begins with **Consecrate to me,** meaning "set apart" or "sanctify" (*qadash*), because the **first offspring . . . belongs to me** (v. 2). The law is rooted in God's holiness, or "uncreatedness." God is the Creator. It continues in verse 12 with the words, **you are to give over to the LORD.** "Give over" (*'abar*) means to pass it on as it was received. In this context it could be paraphrased, "Give the firstborn back to the Lord" because they **belong to the LORD.**

The last details concern redeeming the firstborn rather than sacrificing them. The Lord did not desire their death, as from the outset God provided for their redemption. As with the first Passover, a lamb was the agent of redemption. **Redeem with a lamb** means "ransom" (*padah*) or "buy back" the firstborn from death. The text mentions donkeys specifically because they were the main means of transport for the Hebrews. They were exempt from death ("redeem with a lamb" **every firstborn donkey**) because they were so valuable. Later, in the book of Numbers, the tribe of the Levites was dedicated to the Lord in place of redeeming the firstborn with a lamb. Their animals became substitutes for sacrificing all the firstborn animals (Num. 3:11–13, 40–51).

13:17–22 / These verses introduce the next major section (13:17–15:21) that takes the Israelites to the wilderness by way of the sea. We return to the story of the exit from Egypt with three brief notes. First, we look ahead to the geographical route. Next, we look back in history to an oath made about Joseph. Then we are brought up to date on a new manifestation of the Lord's presence in cloud and fire.

The first note (vv. 17–18) concerns the route to the sea. The name **God** occurs for the first time since Exodus 10, reminding the reader that "the LORD" who had been close at hand in Egypt was still "God" as they leave it. The mentions of **Philistine country** and facing **war** were ominous in the ancient historical setting. Newly liberated slaves with their families were not prepared for this, though they would face it soon enough (17:8). The Lord's first concern was that they would not **change their minds and return to Egypt.** This would in fact be a temptation, as quick physical liberation does not necessarily result in the liberation of one's self-perception (14:10–14).

God's route was certainly not the shortest way. The primary trade and military road to Canaan was to the northeast, along the Mediterranean. An army on this route could walk to Gaza in only ten days. But **God led the people around by the desert road toward the Red Sea.** Like most English translations, the NIV continues to follow the Greek (LXX) "Red Sea" rather than the Hebrew "Sea of Reeds" (*yam sup*). This sea was a series of marshes and lakes between the Mediterranean and the Gulf of Suez where the Suez canal presently runs. The general consensus is that the people moved southeast, from Rameses to **Succoth** on the first day (12:37) and then from Succoth to **Etham on the edge of the desert** (v. 20). Archaeologists have not verified the exact locations of the camping places. (They may have traveled down the Wadi Tumilat to tell el-Maskhuta.) The translation "desert" is misleading, since *midbar* means seasonal pastureland where no one lives permanently. This definition makes better sense of the text because while a desert does not support livestock, they apparently found food for their flocks when they entered this *midbar.*

The translation **armed for battle** is peculiar since the Hebrew word means merely "in groups of fifty" (*khamushim*). This could indicate a "military" formation for orderly marching (as in "in their divisions," 6:26; 7:4; 12:17, 41, 51). The text says nothing about being "armed" with weapons, which Hebrew consistently expresses with another word (*khalats*, Num. 31:5; 32:21, 27, 29–32; Deut. 3:18). At most it could be translated "prepared for battle," a defensive strategy to divide the company in case of attack. It is most likely, however, simply a reference to the orderly exit of the people.

The note about **the bones of Joseph** (v. 19) looks back to an oath made by their ancestors (at the end of Genesis) hundreds of years before. The people remembered, and Moses finished this "old business" as a testimony to memory and memorial actions that build hope. Joseph's bones were physical history connecting them to the blessing he gave in Genesis 50:25. When they saw the physical reminder of Joseph, they heard the words again as a present voice of promise, **"God will surely come to your aid"** (Gen. 50:24–25).

The last note (vv. 19–22) uses the name **the LORD** (Yahweh) again, as God became visible and near the people to protect and guide them. Until now, only Moses had been given a visible manifestation of the presence of the Lord, in the bush at Sinai (3:2, 16; 4:5). Throughout their wilderness experience, the people would receive physical signs of the Lord's presence. The physical signs began with the practical help of columns of **cloud to guide them on their way** and **fire to give them light** ("to shine for them") **so that they could travel by day or night.** The remarkable statement is that **the LORD went ahead of them in a pillar.** The Lord did not leave them, day or night. God was a unique physical and visible presence (see also 24:15–17; 40:34–38; Ps. 18:9–13). This new reality would have further implications for their aid and for their judgment as the revelation of the Lord to the people continued in the wilderness and at Sinai.

Additional Notes §15

13:1 / The separation of the firstborn instructions in vv. 1–2 and 11–16 has been assumed by many scholars to be a source and redaction issue. Childs notes that this is widely accepted as a result of two different sources side by side (Childs, *Exodus*, p. 184).

13:8 / The word "son" has been interpreted in the Jewish tradition as "child." If no children are present, an adult receives the explanation. "What the LORD did for me" is the focus of the Jewish Passover Seder (see Tigay, "Exodus," p. 132).

13:15 / Present Jewish practice is to redeem the firstborn son by giving five monetary units (euro, dollar, shekel) to a descendent of a priestly family (*kohen*). This follows the "five shekels" injunction in Num. 18:16.

13:18 / The body of water, in Hebrew *yam sup* (sea of reeds), is found in most English versions translated as the Red Sea. (The Hebrew *sup*, "reed," refers to the papyrus that grew in the margins of fresh water.) In the region between Egypt and Sinai north of the present-day Gulf of Suez at the northern end of the Red Sea, the body of water furthest to the south and closest to the present Red Sea was the chain of Bitter Lakes. Further to the north were Lake Timsah, Lake Balah, and Lake Menzaleh. Understandably, the exact location of the sea crossing is a matter of debate, with proposed locations ranging more than 200 mi. apart. For the argument that the Sea of Reeds should best be translated as the Red Sea for liturgical and OT contextual reasons, see Fretheim, *Exodus*, p. 153.

13:19 / When he said, "God will surely come to your aid," Joseph used a term that means "God pays a visit" (*paqad*). The quality of this "visit" in Scripture depends on your relationship to the Lord. In Exodus the same word root is translated (NIV) as "I have watched over you" (3:16); "the Lord was concerned about them" (4:31); "punishing . . . for the sin" (20:5); "count them" (30:12); and "I will punish them for their sin" (32:34). See further discussion on 32:34.

§16 Crossing the Sea (Exod. 14:1–31)

The Lord set a strategic trap for Pharaoh in the exit from Egypt. God sent the people of Israel to a vulnerable location next to the sea and "hemmed in by the desert." This was part of the Lord's plan to draw the pharaoh out. Moses, the people, and Pharaoh all play their roles. The narrative is packed with action: the people obey the Lord's directions; the king pursues them with chariots; the people cry out in terror; Moses steadies them; the Lord directs them toward the water; the pillar of cloud/fire protects them; the Lord drives the sea apart; the people walk; Pharaoh pursues; the Lord fights; the charioteers panic; Moses raises his staff; the Lord sweeps the Egyptians away; and the people fear and trust the Lord.

Why did the Lord do this, when Israel was already out of Egypt and on the way? What was the purpose of drawing the Egyptian army into this trap? The Lord states a brief reason: "**I will gain glory** (or "be honored") . . . **through Pharaoh and all his army, and the Egyptians will know that I am the Lord.**" We find similar words in 12:17–18. This episode may seem like a superfluous show of strength after the plagues, but the persistence of the pharaoh is shown to be unrelenting. God's final demonstration of counterforce brought an end to all negotiations and clearly established the Lord's reputation for the world. In the ancient world, the name of Yahweh was not known. The witness of the text is that the Lord came down at this point in history to reveal who God is in a unique and unequivocal way. God's identity was greater than simply being the "God of the Hebrews, who wanted the people freed." God's purpose was not limited to manipulating a specific Pharaoh for one specific purpose. The scope of the Lord's action and self-revelation is, at once, historical and cosmic.

The drowning of the pharaoh's chariots and horsemen is unequaled in the history of OT revelation. It demonstrates that the Lord is God over all chaotic and oppressive forces that rule in the created world (see the discussion of these themes in Exod. 15).

The lordship of Yahweh means more than release for slaves; it means the coming end of the principalities that twist the world. The luring of Pharaoh into the heart of the sea revealed the Creator's move to redeem creation and restore it to the Creator. Escaping the pharaoh was not enough. His power had to be broken in such a way that the entire world would know who the Lord is and what God's sovereignty can mean.

14:1–9 / The Lord's baiting and Pharaoh's pursuit begins when God instructs Moses to turn back toward Egypt and encamp in a specific place by "the sea" (13:18; 15:4). The text is very precise about the location, giving a triangulation point, but the three places named have been lost in the sands of time: **near Pi Hahiroth, between Migdol and the sea . . . directly opposite Baal Zephon.** This place could have been by any of the four lakes that once stood to the east of Rameses (see additional note at 13:18). Verse 9 describes again the exact (presently unknown) location.

The plan was to entice the pharaoh to display his arrogance once more. He would think the people were confused and wandering about, **hemmed in by the desert.** This meant, literally, that he would believe "the wilderness had closed them in," as if the Lord was not also God of the wilderness.

Here in Exodus 14 the Lord hardened ("strengthened") Pharaoh's heart for the last time (vv. 4, 8, 17). The hardening occurs after Pharaoh began preparations for his pursuit, intensifying his resolve, but not "creating" his intent. The translation "I will gain glory for myself through Pharaoh and all his army" is, more accurately, "I will be honored because of Pharaoh and all his army." The Egyptians and the wider ancient world would hear of this display of Yahweh's power. The end of the chapter reports the immediate honoring that occurred:

> And when the Israelites saw the great power the LORD displayed against the Egyptians, the people feared the LORD and put their trust in him and in Moses his servant. (v. 31)

The people honored the Lord because they were saved from Pharaoh's attack. Pharaoh came after them with his entire war arsenal and the Lord defeated him. Israel came to fear and trust Yahweh through this traumatic experience of danger and rescue.

Pharaoh receives the report **that the people had fled,** which contrasts with the narrator's report in verse 8 that **the Israelites**

. . . were marching out boldly. "Boldly" is a good translation of the
Hebraism "with uplifted hand." In this context it does not mean
"defiantly" (Knight, *Theology as Narration*, p. 101; quoted in Durham, *Exodus*, p. 190) or "confident of their safety" (Durham, *Exodus*, p. 190). They marched out in orderly divisions of fifty (12:17,
41, 51; see also 13:18).

Powerful Pharaoh decided with his "servants" (*ᶜebed* NIV **officials**) that they had made a mistake in losing the Israelite's **services** (*ᶜabad* "serving us"). He pursued them with his entire army,
including **six hundred of the best chariots, along with all the
other chariots of Egypt.** Each of the chariots had **officers** (*shali-
shim*) or, more specifically, "commanders of three," perhaps meaning that the large chariots carried three men. Pharaoh took his
elite corps and everyone else: chariots, cavalry, and infantry. The
Hebrew word translated **troops** means simply "fighting force."
Exodus 14 describes this fighting force frequently (vv. 7, 9, 17, 18,
23, 28). They **pursued the Israelites and overtook them as they
camped by the sea.**

14:10–18 / The narrative comes to a crisis. An immov-
able object was pursued by an apparently irresistible force. The
ironies of this crisis point are rich. The Lord had not wanted them
to face war (13:17). Instead, they were now facing the unleashed
power of Egypt's army. Although the Israelites were trapped between the sea and the army, in fact, a trap had been set for the
Egyptians. Pharaoh was riding forth in all his might, but he had
never been so vulnerable. The chaos about to ensue would engulf
and transform everyone. It was the Lord's greatest self-revelation
to humanity up to that historical moment.

When the people **looked up** they saw the force of the chariots, riders, and infantry **marching after them.** The children of Israel **were terrified and cried out to the LORD.** Their next response
was against Moses. The complaints came rapid-fire in three sarcastic questions. **"Was it because there were no graves in Egypt
that you brought us to the desert to die? What have you done to
us by bringing us out of Egypt? Didn't we say to you in Egypt,
'Leave us alone; let us serve the Egyptians'?"** They had indeed
communicated such things in Egypt in their worst moments (5:20–
21; 6:9). The reference to "graves in Egypt" is ironic, considering
the proliferation of ancient pyramid tombs.

This would not be the last time that their situation was "too
much to bear." They would speak of preferring to serve and die in

Egypt twice again in Exodus (16:3; 17:3). Whom they would serve/ worship remained the issue in the midst of the crisis. Their experience of bondage had taught them to avoid these kinds of encounters with the Egyptians. Systematized bondage functions best by means of effective fear, not by mass murder of the labor force. The Hebrews were willing to return to that familiar fear, rather than endure the terror of God's bid for their freedom. Now, close to that freedom, they were not prepared to deal with the dangers of the plan the Lord had laid. The risks of serving the Lord and the dangers of transformation were a necessary part of the process of learning to trust and fear God (v. 31).

Moses' leadership was evident in his patience as he spoke an oracle of salvation for God. He did not defend himself against the accusations and sarcasm. He spoke rather to their fear and uncertainty. The plan had not yet been revealed to anyone. They had good reasons for fear, as their families huddled around them. Moses spoke confidently, with three imperatives: **Do not be afraid. Stand firm and . . . see the deliverance the LORD will bring you today.** Then he addressed the presenting issue of the Egyptian army. **The Egyptians you see today you will never see again.** The use of the verb "see" was Moses' school for them in changing perspectives: see the Lord's deliverance; you see the Egyptians today; and you will never see them again.

Then Moses finished his declaration of gospel: **The LORD will fight for you; you need only to be still.** The primary meaning of "be still" is "be silent." By implication this may have meant to simply watch "the LORD . . . fight for you" and do nothing, but it always meant to stop talking (e.g., Job 13:5). Moses was referring to their complaining to him when he said that they should be quiet and watch what the Lord would do (vv. 19–31).

The next verse has generated much discussion as the Lord asked *Moses,* **Why are you crying out to me?** The people "cried out to the Lord" in verse 10, but Moses answered them calmly. Moses had also just told the people to "be still." It has been suggested that this is simply an editorial seam between older sources (J/P). This possibility doesn't help us interpret the text we have. It is likely a general reference to the crying out in verse 10 in which Moses could have participated. We can also assume that, in the silence that followed verse 14, Moses would be fervent in private prayers. God asked him to stop praying and lead the people.

A second discussion regards the contrast between "be still" (v. 14) and "move on" (v. 15). Again interpreters invoke the editorial seam. The Lord may be correcting Moses' command to do nothing by telling them to "move on." This interprets "be still" incorrectly as "don't move" rather than "be silent" before the Lord. The plain narrative meaning is that silence before the Lord was necessary before they could hear the word to "move on."

The "plan" was finally revealed. Moses would raise his staff **over the sea to divide the water so that the Israelites can go through the sea on dry ground.** The army, chariots, and horsemen would follow. Clearly another miracle was in the offing. The imagery here, and even more powerfully in Exodus 15, is from the creation of the world in Genesis 1. It is a re-creation of part of the creation event, creating now a whole people who, for the first time in history, would trust and fear the Lord together (v. 31). Three phrases allude to the creation: as God's spirit hovered over the waters (Gen. 1:2) so Moses was told to raise his staff over the sea; as God separated the water (Gen. 1:7) Moses' action divided the water; and as God made dry ground (Gen. 1:9) so the people would go through the sea on dry ground.

Verses 17 and 18 repeat the Lord's claims of verse 4: **"I will harden"** and **"I will gain glory** (be honored) **through Pharaoh and all his army, through his chariots and his horsemen."** (See the discussion and additional note at v. 4.) The NIV omits the original emphatic claim that begins verse 17: "And I, Behold me! I will harden." This is the whole wonderful, troublesome point of the text. The Lord God, known only to the Hebrew slaves and barely trusted by them, would cause the greatest king of the ancient world to destroy his army through an ill-advised display of power. God said, "Look at me!" (or, "Behold me"). This is God's self-revelation, and after this the Lord would be known by the children of Israel, and the whole world, as greater than any earthly king.

Even non-Israelites **will know that I am the LORD.** Many in the future would honor Yahweh as the God who created, who creates new realities, and who redeems those who cry out to him. No one fought for the Lord; the Lord fought for them. Because God took this initiative of deliverance, defeating the powers of slavery and death for the Israelites, the people knew who in the world to honor as Lord and God. This is the preeminent self-revelation of God in the OT. Even as they died, Pharaoh's army brought honor to the Lord by revealing God's lordship over the forces of creation and military might. Even the rebellious gave honor to the Lord by their defeat and dying (Phil. 2:10–11; 1 Cor 15:24–26).

14:19–31 / The Lord fought for the children of Israel as promised (v. 14). God used the basic components of creation: the **pillar of cloud**, fire, wind, water, dry land, light, and the cover of night. The text mentions **the angel** (lit., "messenger") **of God who had been traveling in front of Israel's army** for the first time. "Messengers" were not pictured in the OT as winged creatures (an attribute of seraphim in Isa. 6:2) but in a variety of seen and unseen ways. In Exodus they were present *with* God in the burning bush (3:2), in the cloud (v. 19), and as an unseen protector, guard, and warrior (23:20, 23; 32:34; 33:2). In Genesis they appeared as men with God (Gen. 18:2, 22; 19:1). At the sea, the angel and the cloud worked interchangeably. The Lord was in the cloud/angel that **withdrew and went behind them.** The pillar of cloud was the messenger that protected them by standing between the "encampments" (*makhaneh*) **of Egypt and Israel** (not "armies," *khayil* as at v. 17).

The presence of the angel meant that it was not an ordinary cloud, but an effective protection so that **neither went near the other all night long.** Its special feature was its darkness on one side, so that night prevailed for the Egyptians while "lighting up the night" for the crossing of the sea on the Israelite side. One assumes that the Egyptian chariots attempted unsuccessfully to penetrate the cloud. It also kept any Israelite from crossing over to the Egyptians in panic at the sight of the army. Even in the context of a miracle, the Lord used ordinary elements of nature. This was not magic, but the creation responding to its Creator for a special purpose. Moses' staff did not part the water, but the Lord sent a wind to part it when Moses raised his hand/staff.

God created a new reality with the dry land in the midst of the divided water: **all that night the LORD drove the sea back with a strong east wind and turned it into dry land.** A special word turns up in "dry land" (*kharabah*). This is not the more common "dry ground" (*yabashah*) found in verses 16, 22, 29. This word means "wasteland" and sounds like the word for "sword" (*khereb*). This was the "sword" with which the Lord would defeat the chariots and horsemen of Egypt.

When the Israelites went into the midst of the sea on dry ground they had walls of protection **on their right and on their left.** The chariots could not attack them in a typical flanking maneuver. The Lord's pre-battle maneuvering had given this helpless people the advantage. The text does not mention that the cloud of protection followed them, but it may be assumed. On the dark side of the cloud **all Pharaoh's horses and chariots and horsemen followed them into the sea.** Then the Lord fulfilled the promise (v. 14) to fight for the Israelites in three actions. First, **During the last watch** (2 a.m. to 6 a.m.), the Lord threw the Egyptians **into confusion.** The Hebrew word here (*hamam*) means a chaotic, noisy panic. Second, God "turned the wheels of their chariots so that they had trouble steering."

The Egyptians decided to retreat. They finally recognized that the Israelites had the LORD . . . **fighting for them against Egypt.** The Lord often fought for the people from a storm cloud (v. 24). The clouds were God's chariot, riding on the wings of the wind (Pss. 18:9–14; 104:3). The Lord fought using the elements of nature against which no army could stand (1 Sam. 7:10; Judg. 5:4–5, 20–21). The Lord's third action had Moses stretch out his hand staff so that **at daybreak the sea went back to its place.** The repeated mention of the flow of water in verses 26–28 helps us to picture it: **the waters may flow back . . . the sea went back . . . the** LORD **swept** ("stirred") **them into the sea . . . water flowed back and covered the chariots and horsemen.** As the sun came up, the sea became the sword of the Lord in the wasteland.

Salvation and destruction came together. The sea of protection from evil was also the sea of destruction for evil forces. The Lord destroyed the Egyptian army. The confusion of the force of the chariots and horsemen was complete in their **fleeing toward** the water as it returned to its place. **Not one of them survived.** The water of the sea into which they drove their chariots killed them. This part was no miracle, since those that enter seas usually drown. The miracle was that the sea did not kill the Israelites. Like Jonah, they did not drown, but were re-created in the midst of the water (see also Rom. 6:4; Col. 2:12).

Yahweh did not choose to act alone to fight for Israel. The Lord could have directly sent the wind to blow the water apart, or to stop it, but did not. God instead allowed Moses' leadership to be maintained and strengthened in the midst of the salvation of the people. Moses was necessary at every stage of their deliverance. The people needed a human leader who was present to lead. Even after Moses' obvious role in the Lord's parting of the sea, the people would challenge his leadership (Num. 16). For now, however, the people **put their trust . . . in Moses his servant.**

The rhetorical effect of verses 29–31 is partly lost in translation. The phrase **the Israelites went through the sea on dry ground** appears to be a concluding repetition of verse 22 since it is identical in English. Yet "went" is literally "walked" in verse 29, indicating the participation of their feet in their salvation. Also, "on dry ground" comes emphatically before "through the sea" in verse 29: "the Israelites walked on dry ground," meaning "in perfect safety." They had walls of protection around them as well. Finally, the contrast between **the hands** ("power") **of the Egyptians** and **the great power the LORD displayed** is more obvious in Hebrew, which uses the same word in each phrase. Alternately one could translate the latter, "the great hand of the Lord," but either "power" or "hand" should be used for both words. The hand of the Lord cut off the hand of Egypt's violence.

The last verse of the chapter is the key verse. The whole point of the narrative witness is found in these words. **When the Israelites saw . . . the people feared the LORD and put their trust in him.** They were witness to their own salvation. While they were still slaves in Egypt the Lord called them to come out of Egypt through Moses. God gathered them in worship in the Passover and Feast of Unleavened Bread. Now, at the sea, God had enlightened them about who Yahweh is, Lord of creation and salvation. This was the work of the Lord's Spirit from the beginning: to call, gather, and enlighten the people.

The whole deliverance from Egypt was not through ordinary means, but it did involve ordinary people. This was not a revolution, nor was it salvation of the people's own making. The point of the narrative is that the Lord delivered them in extraordinary ways. Even the plagues did not convince the people that their deliverance was a good idea. At the sea they murmured and complained (vv. 11–12). The text tells us that it was only when they **saw the Egyptians lying dead on the shore** that they feared and put their trust in the Lord (see the comment on "fear of the Lord" at 9:20). The demonstration of the great power of the Lord against their enslavers was an antecedent to their belief. When they were free, they believed and they sang (15:1–21).

Additional Notes §16

14:17 / The NIV translates "And I, Behold me . . ." present in the Hebrew text simply as "I." God uses this exact expression only two other times, both in transformational events related to the flood (Gen. 6:17;

9:9). Jesus uses the parallel expression in Greek, *idou ego* ("behold, I"), when sending his disciples out for the first time (Matt. 10:16), promising to be with them forever (Matt. 28:20) and in promising to send the Holy Spirit (Luke 24:49).

14:19 / This is a "theophany" or "appearing of God." The text avoids thinking spatially in theophanies like this. One can never pin down the location of angels or the Lord. For some, however, thinking of the Lord and an angel together in the cloud may be a helpful oversimplification. See the discussion of theophanies in Exod. 32.

14:25 / **He made the wheels of their chariots come off.** The NIV interprets "turned from the path" (*sur*) to mean that the wheels came off (with KJV, NASV). Other translations follow the Greek with "clogged" (RSV, NRSV). This is a case of overtranslating. The word means to turn or "steer" off the path.

14:30 / On the fear of the Lord see comments at 9:20 and 20:20.

§17 Singing at the Sea (Exod. 15:1–21)

Worshiping the Lord was Israel's transition to a new existence. Exodus 15 links the experience of Egypt (chs. 1–14) and the trust-building journey of the first year in the wilderness (chs. 15–18). It ends the traumas of Egypt with a song to, and about, the Lord's victory over the chaos. Verses 22–27 describe the challenge of trusting Yahweh for basic provision and protection during their journey to the mountain of God (Horeb/Sinai).

This "Song at the Sea" has three stanzas (vv. 2–6; 7–11; 12–17), framed by an introductory and concluding verse (vv. 1, 18). Each stanza begins with two verses that witness to what the Lord has done (vv. 2–3, 7–8, 12–13), continues with two verses of narrative describing a scene and a comparison of sinking/being still like stone or lead (vv. 4–5, 9–10, 14–16a), and concludes with one verse of praise directly addressed to the Lord (vv. 6, 11, 16b–17).

The song is poetry. It does not purport to give literal descriptions of the events. Rather, broad sweeping images create a vivid picture of the Lord's actions. For example, the mention of God hurling a horse and its rider into the sea does not refer directly to any actual throwing by God, but casts the imagination to the rider, knocked down by the returning water. Verse 12, which says that the earth swallowed them, does not refer to anything other than the water closing in upon them.

As with other Hebrew poetry, this song does not rhyme (but see comment on v. 12) nor is it strict in meter. It uses varying parallelisms (bicolon, or tricolon, referred to here as triads) to build images. The second line (colon) may reinforce the first line as in, "He is my God, and I will praise him, / my father's God, and I will exalt him." A second line may also add more specificity to the first, as in, "the sea covered them. / They sank like lead in the mighty waters."

After the narrative note that "Moses and the Israelites sang this song to the LORD," the song of Miriam serves as the introductory refrain or musical bridge (see vv. 20–21). These lines could

have been sung as an introduction and between the three stanzas
of the hymn of praise.

"I will sing to the LORD, for he is highly exalted.
The horse and its rider he has hurled into the sea." (v. 1b)

15:1 / Moses and the Israelites **sang this song to the
LORD.** The natural response to their "trust" in the Lord (14:31) was
to sing to him. Its theme is praise. The song is technically neither a
celebration nor a description of the Egyptians' defeat. Rather, it is
a song "to the LORD." This distinction is vital for understanding
the nature and content of the text. Israel did not accomplish this
victory, the Lord did. Moses was not shy about describing the enemy's defeat, but he attributed everything to the Lord. The song
begins with the words "he has triumphed gloriously" (NIV **is
highly exalted**). It ends with the doxology, "The LORD will reign
for ever and ever." The stanzas of the song are built around bringing honor to the Lord.

15:2–6 / The first stanza of the song focuses on their experience of deliverance at the sea. Its last line summarizes it
theme: **Your right hand, O LORD, shattered the enemy.** The first
part of the stanza is a witness to the Lord's deliverance (vv. 2–3).
Its focus is on the Lord as **. . . my strength, my song, my salvation,
my God, my father's God . . .** and as **a warrior.** The singer bears
testimony to the saving power the Lord provided by intervening in
the historical circumstance at the sea. Yahweh (the Lord) **is his
name.** God fights to create and establish the people (Deut. 1:30;
3:22; 20:4; Josh. 10:14, 42; 23:3, 10). They have no army of their own.

God must be like a warrior to defeat an advancing army.
The descriptive narrative (vv. 4–5) further develops this image.
Parallel lines (v. 4) describe Pharaoh's chariots, army, and elite officers and their drowning. The Hebrew expression for **deep waters**
(*tehomot*) is similar to the word for the Babylonian chaos goddess
Tiamat. When the Lord is in the fight, chaos drowns chaos (see additional note on 15:18).

The narrative verses close (in all three stanzas) with the
enemy sinking **like a stone** (v. 5). The first stanza concludes with
praise directly addressed to the Lord (v. 6). Parallel lines praise
Your right hand, O LORD, a Hebraism referring to God's power on
display. God has thoroughly destroyed the enemy.

15:7–11 / The second stanza of the song describes the
attack by the enemy and moves to the theological exclamation,

Who among the gods is like you, O LORD? This stanza begins, as the first, with a witness to the Lord's deliverance (vv. 7–8). The image is the Lord's fire against his enemies: **it consumed them like stubble.** The firsthand witness returns to the walls of water in a poetic triad: **the waters piled up. The surging waters stood firm like a wall; the deep waters congealed in the heart of the sea.**

The descriptive narrative (vv. 9–10) tells how the **enemy boasted** in six ways (a triad of parallels). We hear the Egyptian's pride as they boasted of pursuing, overtaking, dividing, gorging, and drawing their swords and destroying. The boast, **I will draw** (*riq*) **my sword,** literally means, "I will clear the field of battle with my sword" by killing everyone. The narrative closes with the enemy sinking—not like a stone this time, but **like lead.** The stanza concludes addressing praise directly to the Lord in the form of a question (v. 11). It uses a triad of praise to express the unbelievable deliverance the worshiper has experienced: **Who is like you— majestic in holiness, awesome in glory, working wonders?**

15:12–17 / The third stanza shifts perspective away from the victory at the sea. It looks forward to the journey into Canaan and focuses on the themes of the Lord's new people in a new place. A longer conclusion of praise celebrates these themes, including the summarizing bicolon (v. 17): **You will bring them in and plant them on the mountain of your inheritance.**

The final stanza begins as the others did, with a witness of belief in the Lord's deliverance, past and future (vv. 12–13). The first line looks back; the second and third look forward. They add witness to their hope for the future to their praise for the past victory. Faith had been created in the midst of the people singing. There is another mention of the "unfailing love" (*khesed*) of the Lord, and this is not the last time (2:24, 6:4–8; 20:6; 34:6–7).

> **You stretched out your right hand and the earth swallowed them. In your unfailing love you will lead the people you have redeemed. In your strength you will guide them to your holy dwelling.** (vv. 12–13)

Verse 12 has been troublesome for interpreters. Why does it say the *earth* swallowed them when it was the sea? Some have suggested emending the text to say the depths of the earth swallowed them, meaning Sheol, the place of the dead (see the discussion in Durham, *Exodus*, p. 207). It may be a reference to the mud in the sea that swallowed them. The rabbinic commentators suggest that the phrase means the Lord properly buried the Egyptian bodies. It also could point forward to the deaths of the enemies who attack them in the wilderness (Goldin, *Song*, pp. 208–10).

Verse 12 is a poetic seam linking the past experience of victory with hope for future victories. Interpreters debate whether to include verse 12 as an addendum to the previous stanza, or to include it with the forward-looking last stanza. Hebrew construction often uses link verses or bridges between two related but diverse sections. The verse belongs with the third stanza. Verse 11 completes the previous stanza with praise. Adding verse 12 to that stanza makes it unnecessarily awkward. Further, the triad of lines "you stretched out," "you will lead" and "you will guide" rhyme in Hebrew (*natita, nakhita, nehalta*), binding verses 12 and 13 together poetically.

The narrative in the middle of the stanza (vv. 14–16a) describes the **terror and dread** of the peoples and leaders of Canaan (Philistia, Moab, Edom, Canaan). **The nations will hear and tremble.** This third narrative closes with the hope that the Lord's reputation, built at the sea, would cause the nations they are soon to meet to be **as still** ("silent") **as a stone.** Joshua 2:9–11 records this kind of effect (see also Num. 22:3).

This third stanza also concludes with praise directly addressed to the Lord (vv. 16b–17). It begins, however, with two interruptive prepositional phrases in 16b: **until your people pass by, O LORD, until the people you bought pass by.** These emotional outbursts form the poetic bridge that begins the praise of the Lord. As they complete verse 16, they communicate the awe and worship of this praise for God.

The richest Hebrew word in this culminating praise is translated in the phrase, "the people you bought" (*qanah*). The Hebrew means "acquired by some effort." It can mean "created" or "gave birth to," both requiring strenuous effort by the Creator or begetter (see also Exod. 4:22; Num. 11:2). It can also mean "acquired through cost" (such as the loss of life in Egypt) or through labor (as in the Lord's many interventions). All of the meanings are relevant in the Exodus story, which is the primary basis for our understanding of the word. In Exodus 20 the Lord uses a homonym (*qanna᾿*) when he says "I am a jealous God" (*᾿el-qanna᾿* see the discussion at 20:5). The Lord who had gone to so much trouble to redeem the people would not easily let them go.

There are three longing references to the place the Lord would take the people:

the mountain of your inheritance—
the place, O LORD, you made for your dwelling,
the sanctuary, O LORD, your hands established (v. 17)

These look forward to both Mt. Sinai (Horeb) and Mt. Zion (Jerusalem). At Sinai the people would meet the Lord and receive instructions for building the tabernacle, which means "dwelling." This dwelling of the Lord moved with them to the central ridge of the hill country of Judah and was the worship center for generations at Shiloh. Several hundred years later, David conquered Jerusalem and moved the tabernacle within its walls. This was where the Lord promised to dwell when Solomon built the temple in which the tabernacle was placed.

15:18 / **The LORD will reign for ever and ever.** In the witness of Scripture the Lord's victory over the pharaoh's chariots and horsemen at the sea was more than a historical victory for Israel. The celebration had a deeper cosmological context in the ancient Near East and a broader application in Scripture. This context and application can be seen in the powerful use of the words and images of this song in later OT texts. The deeper ancient Near Eastern context includes the background of the Babylonian creation myth that reflected the struggle to control creational disasters (storms, floods) and historical armies that could suddenly destroy life. The god of Babylon, Marduk, destroyed the goddess Tiamat (Chaos) by cutting her in half. In the Canaanite (Ugaritic) myth, the god Baal subdued the sea god Yamm (chaos of the sea). Still, monsters lurked in the dark depths, waiting to wreak havoc on anyone who ventured too close. Deep water and its monsters (Leviathan or Rahab) were symbols of chaos and objects of great fear in the ancient Near East.

15:19–21 / The narrative resumes by repeating the notice that the Lord defeated Pharaoh's chariots and horsemen as at the end of Exodus 14 (vv. 28–29). Then Miriam comes into view, with the women, singing with **a tambourine in her hand.** Miriam, the young girl who watched over the baby Moses (2:4, 7–8), is now called **the prophetess** (see also Num. 12:2). She is one of four who have this distinction in Scripture, joined by Deborah (Judg. 4:4), Huldah (2 Kgs. 22:14), and Noadiah (Neh. 6:4). Rabbinic tradition also names Hannah, Abigail, and Esther as prophetesses for a round seven (Sarna, "Exodus," p. 412).

Miriam's song is the refrain with which Moses' song began (v. 1). **Sing to the LORD, for he is highly exalted. The horse and its rider he has hurled into the sea.** The two songs work together to provide verse and refrain as well as call and response. The only difference between them is the main point. Miriam sang and called Israel to sing with the plural imperative (you all) "Sing!" while Moses sang, "I will sing." Miriam and all the women lead the singing and dancing in celebration of the Lord's victory and their salvation from the Egyptian army (see also Judg. 11:34; 1 Sam. 18:6).

Additional Notes §17

15:1 / James Muilenburg's rhetorical analysis is helpful for understanding the composition of this song (see Muilenburg, "Liturgy," pp. 238–50). Another proposal that many translations follow in blocking their English text is chiastic, with vv. 11–12 as the doxological center, but this is less convincing (see Brueggemann, "Exodus," p. 802). This song is the oldest known Hebrew composition, alongside the song of Deborah (Judg. 5).

15:18 / Scripture addresses the fears of natural and historical catastrophes in a unique way. It was unnecessary for Yahweh to subdue the sea because Yahweh made it. In Genesis, God hovered over the deep (Gen. 1:2) and divided it simply by speaking (Gen. 1:6). God gathered waters in seas (Gen. 1:9) and saw that it was good. In Exodus the Lord used the sea against the perpetrator of chaos for Israel, the pharaoh, dividing the sea again (14:16) and cutting down the pharaoh's army. The book of Exodus is fairly subtle about the connections, using the cognate for "deep water" (*tehomot*, vv. 5, 8) that is similar to the Babylonian Tiamat. Ezekiel, in a later context, is much more explicit.

> "I am against you, Pharaoh king of Egypt, you great monster lying among your streams. You say, 'The Nile is mine; I made it for myself.'" (Ezek. 29:3)

> "Son of man, take up a lament concerning Pharaoh king of Egypt and say to him: 'You are like a lion among the nations; you are like a monster in the seas thrashing about in your streams, churning the water with your feet and muddying the streams.'" (Ezek. 32:2)

Pharaoh and the sea are both chaos threats in Exodus (see Jer. 46:7–8). The Lord ironically used one to drown the other. The sea crossing sets Leviathan/Rahab (danger of a water catastrophe) within the perspective of God's control (see also Ps. 84:4; Isa. 30:7).

> There is the sea, vast and spacious, teeming with creatures be-
> yond number—living things both large and small. There the ships
> go to and fro and the leviathan, which you formed to frolic there.
> (Ps. 104:25–26)

> By his power he churned up the sea; by his wisdom he cut Rahab
> to pieces. By his breath the skies became fair; his hand pierced
> the gliding serpent. (Job 26:12–13)

> It was you who split open the seas by your power; you broke the
> heads of the monster in the waters. It was you who crushed the
> heads of Leviathan. (Ps. 74:13–14)

Other psalms more directly suggest the defeat of historic enemies
through the Lord's rule over the symbols of chaos. They often specifically mention the Exodus victory.

> You rule over the raging of the Sea; . . . You crushed Rahab like
> one of the slain; with your strong arm you scattered your enemies.
> (Ps. 89:9–10)

> The waters saw you, O God, the waters saw you and writhed; the
> very depths were convulsed.... Your path led through the sea,
> your way through the mighty waters,... You led your people like a
> flock by the hand of Moses and Aaron. (Ps. 77:16, 19–20; see also
> Ps. 114:1–7)

These songs of victory over the chaos of nature and history make the
point that the fear of the ancient Near East does not hold sway. The
Lord's victory over the pharaoh was also a victory over the symbols of
chaos in the ancient Near East. The prophet Isaiah draws once again on
these themes in preaching to the people in exile in Babylon.

> Was it not you who cut Rahab to pieces, who pierced that monster
> through? Was it not you who dried up the sea, the waters of the
> great deep, who made a road in the depths of the sea so that the
> redeemed might cross over? (Isa. 51:9–10; see also Isa. 50:2)

Fear of the chaos of natural and historical disaster is universal in human
experience. Chaos is both an external threat and an internal anxiety. In
calling Peter to walk on the stormy water (Matt. 14:22–34) the Lord demonstrated that he was the same Lord who mastered the causes of chaos at
creation, in the Exodus from Egypt, and in the return from Babylon. The
objective gospel is a consistent witness in Scripture: "The LORD will
reign for ever and ever." The question of trust or lack of trust in this Lord
ever remains.

§18 Journey from the Sea into the Wilderness (Exod. 15:22–27)

The next major section of Exodus is the journey from the sea to Sinai. It begins inauspiciously in verse 22 of Exodus 15 and continues through Exodus 16 and 17. During this journey the people encounter difficulties finding water and food. The Lord uses these opportunities to build new faith and trust. The NIV says God "tested" them, translating a word (*nasah*, v. 25) that means "trained" or "proved." The Lord proved that the people could learn to follow God's instruction for their own well-being. The training, which was not easy, could be described as "trial runs." In the narratives, however, the people did not pass or fail the "tests." They learned more about, and proved their trust in, the Lord. The texts give little negative comment about their grumbling apart from describing it as grumbling. Moses was impatient with them at the Wilderness of Sin, but the Lord responded with patience. This was not the case in the book of Numbers, when the people faced the same difficulties, complained, and suffered God's impatience with them over lessons they should have learned in Exodus.

The various "trial runs" in 15:22–17:7 focus on water and food. Enemy attacks on the Israelites, during which the Lord provides for their protection, precede and follow these "tests" (14:10–21; 17:8–16; see outline below). Within the brackets of that protection, the text describes these water and food trials. Each episode of trial follows this pattern: (1) the people grumble against Moses; (2) the Lord tells Moses he will find out whether they can follow instructions he gives them in their trial; (3) the Lord gives the instructions; (4) the Lord provides the water or food. This section of the text, then, follows the chiastic structure:

The Lord provides protection from the Egyptian army (14:10–21)

A water at Marah made sweet; twelve springs at Elim (15:22–27)

    B quail and manna provided in the Sin wilderness (16:1–36)

A′ water from the rock at Rephidim (17:1–7)

The Lord provides victory over the Amalekites (17:8–16)

The major theme is the provision of the Lord, with the bread and meat at the center. On either side of that provision is God's protection.

15:22–27 / The oases of Marah and Elim both provided water for the people. Marah was a challenge, but Elim was not. They traveled in the Wilderness of **Shur,** a location southeast from somewhere in eastern Egypt if the traditional location of Mt. Sinai in the southern part of the peninsula is accepted. At Marah the people **could not drink its water because it was bitter** (*marim*).

The **people grumbled against Moses** with a legitimate question, **"What are we to drink?"** Moses cried out and the Lord showed him a tree. God did the sweetening, but provided Moses with a visible means of maintaining his leadership. Moses participated in the transformation of the water at Marah. God reversed the fouling of the Nile waters in the first plague with this sweetening in the wilderness. The rabbinic midrash says that Moses asked God why God created brackish water. God replied, "Instead of asking philosophical questions why don't you do something to make the bitter waters sweet?" (Sarna, "Exodus," p. 413). This is precisely what Moses did.

The narrator reports, after the fact, that **he tested them** (v. 25b). The notice of testing accompanies a longer explanation (vv. 25b–26) of these trials in general. The Lord established a fixed principle of relationship between them, described as **a decree and a law for them.** These related words should be translated together as a guiding principle or standing prescription. They come in the form of courtroom case law that establishes precedent for future decisions. Its typical form is: if this happens, then this will happen.

The fascinating feature in this particular "law" is that God was the one bound by it. If the people acted in a certain way, then God swore to to keep them healthy. The freedom, even in relation to God, was given to the people. This is generally referred to by Christians as "grace," not "law." The law had four conditions that had to be met: **"listen carefully to the voice of the LORD your God and do what is right in his eyes, if you pay attention to** ("prove") **his commands and keep all his decrees."** This language leans forward toward the language of laws given at Sinai. It does not speak of specifics here, but of fostering an observant relationship with the Lord.

The Lord promised that if the people fostered this relationship, **"I will not bring on you any of the diseases I brought on the Egyptians."** This looks back at least to the plagues of boils and the death of the firstborn, but is stated more inclusively. Egypt was known as a land of diseases (Deut. 7:15). This is accompanied by the positive self-identification of God, **"I am the LORD, who heals you."**

The extent of the Lord's healing and protection from disease given in the Sinai law often goes unnoticed. Whether in physical healing, protection, freedom from slavery in a totalitarian regime, or public health, Yahweh was the source. At the end of the wilderness wanderings, just as they were about to enter the promised land, the Lord said again, "See now that I myself am He! There is no god besides me. I put to death and I bring to life, I have wounded and I will heal,..." (Deut. 32:39).

The Lord's self-revelation in the giving of the law was as "the Lord your healer." In the beginning of their life in service to Yahweh rather than the pharaoh, they were in need of healing and health. In the healing of the bitter waters at Marah, the Lord showed concern for safe drinking water. After that, God took them to the healing oasis at **Elim, where there were twelve springs and seventy palm trees, and they camped there near the water.** The text is silent about the repair done in these days. It simply implies that they stayed for several weeks (16:1).

Additional Notes §18

15:23 / Possibilities for the location of Marah include the Bitter Lakes or Hawarah, 46 mi. south of Suez. Elim may have been at Wadi Gharandel (62 mi. down the Suez Gulf) or Ayun Musa which has 12 springs (close to the top of the gulf). For possibilities of other proposed locations for Mt. Sinai see Durham, *Exodus*, pp. 212–13.

15:26 / The Lord's concern for health and healing in the 613 Sinai laws is extensive (Exod. 19–Num. 10:10). Community order in itself is a health issue. Keeping the Ten Commandments (e.g., you shall not kill, you shall not steal, you shall not bear false witness, you shall not covet) deeply reduces violent crime in any community. The Sinai laws are also full of legal procedures with extensive instruction on how to maintain a just court, establishing a system of rule by law rather than by force. The laws also addressed medical concerns, including quarantine for contagious diseases, washing requirements for those who handle corpses (not done in Europe until the nineteenth century; Num. 19:19). The laws governing sexuality provided for the possibility that sexually-transmitted diseases would be nonexistent. For further discussion of the role of the law in creating public health and a healthy community see Bruckner, "A Theological Description of Human Wholeness."

§19 Leadership, Learning, Manna, Meat, and the First Sabbath Rest (Exod. 16:1–36)

In Exodus 16, Israel begins learning to walk in the Lord's way (vv. 4b, 28b). The survival of the people depended on the transformation of their culture. The text presents a jumble of themes around this purpose, some for the first time in Exodus: the grumbling and lessons of the newly redeemed slaves; the status of Moses and Aaron's leadership; the Lord's visible presence with the people; and the Lord's provision of bread, quail, and rest. The chapter ends with instructions for the first Sabbath rest and a manna memorial for the generations after the manna ceases. The people were successful in learning to follow the Lord's instructions for their daily bread and weekly rest.

16:1–12 / The presenting issue was food, as the people were hungry and grumbling. The text takes us, however, to two deeper issues: Would the people learn to trust and follow the Lord's instructions for their daily life? And would they learn who was responsible for their assembly in this wilderness? The first twelve verses weave together the themes of the Lord's presence with and for the people, his visible "glory," and his instructions for receiving daily bread. Moses and Aaron received the complaints and reported the word of the Lord.

After several weeks at Elim's twelve springs, they set out towards Sinai and **came to the Desert of Sin**. The cycle of complaint, instruction from the Lord, and provision began when **the whole community grumbled against Moses and Aaron** about the shortage of meat and bread. Their complaint, in fear of hunger, was an exaggeration of their situation. It was the second of three times they would long for Egypt and speak of dying (see also 14:11 and 17:3). They remembered Egypt, where they had **pots of meat and ate all the food** they wanted. This was not exactly the truth about their experience, but they did ironically and unwittingly describe the abundance that the Lord would give them (see v. 8, "meat to eat . . . and all the bread you want").

The Lord used this grumbling as an opportunity to educate the people in walking in trust and following instructions. There is a similar kind of grumbling in Numbers, but it occurs after they have been to Sinai and following the Lord for a year. There the grumbling brought judgment against the people, because they had had time to learn the ways of the Lord. An overly negative judgment should not be superimposed on the exodus experience because of Numbers. In Exodus 15–17 the Lord was patient and tolerant of the missteps of the recently delivered slaves. Their failure to follow instructions did make Moses angry (v. 20), but the Lord only mentions their slow learning curve once and was successful in convincing them to change their pattern (vv. 28, 30).

The Lord shared the plan, the instructions for the people, and the thought behind it with Moses. God first addressed the presenting issue of hunger. The Lord would **rain down bread** (better than hail!).The people were to **gather enough** bread for **each day** for five days, and **On the sixth day** there would be **twice as much.** No one was told why they were to do it this way. They would learn to trust the Lord for what they did not know. In the middle of verse 4 the Lord brings the bigger, underlying theological problem to the surface. **In this way I will test them** ("prove their ability") **and see whether they will follow my instructions** (lit., "walk in my torah"). The Lord's plan was to form this assembly into a people who would bless the world through the way they lived. God was preparing them for the more comprehensive instruction (*torah*) at Sinai. Giving bread with instructions was a small beginning, but by the end of the chapter it proved effective. The people learned to follow the Lord in the matter of daily bread (v. 30). The Lord "proved their ability" to follow (*nasah*, NIV "test").

The second, deeper, issue was whether they would learn who was responsible for their assembly in this wilderness. Verses 6–12 bring this issue to the surface. Moses' and Aaron's words to the Israelites were, **"you will know that it was the LORD who brought you out of Egypt."** Almost every verse repeats the theme of the presence of the Lord: **you will see the glory of the LORD** (v. 7); **You will know that it was the LORD** (v. 8); **Come before the LORD** (v. 9); **there was the glory of the LORD** (v. 10); and **Then you will know that I am the LORD your God** (v. 12). Belief in the Lord's presence and provision is a primary theological problem throughout the book of Exodus. People set free from bondage are at risk of misunderstanding their freedom and turning to new forms of self-chosen bondage. At Sinai the primary issue would be their freedom to worship any god they choose, when they make the golden calf and say, "These are your gods, O Israel, who brought you up out of Egypt" (32:4).

In the Sin(ai) wilderness the error of the people was relying on Moses and blaming him for their situation (v. 3b). Moses knew better than to take credit or blame for what happened to them. Twice in two verses he questioned their presuppositions (vv. 7, 8). **"Who are we? You are not grumbling against us, but against the LORD."**

The status of Moses and Aaron's leadership was in question, but it was the Lord's leadership that was truly at stake. The people were willing to theoretically acknowledge that it was the Lord who protected them, who both took and gave life. They had seen this much in the plagues and in the crossing of the sea. Nonetheless, protection and provision of food and water were not the same thing. At the waters of Marah, their experience was that Moses sweetened the water (v. 25). Now they hold Moses responsible for feeding them. The Lord's lesson for them was that God not only delivered them but also cared for their daily needs.

God connected the people's experience of the deliverance at the sea with the provision of bread and meat by making the "glory of the LORD" visible for them both in the familiar cloud and in the new manna. The people were told that **in the morning** "you will see the glory of the LORD." The glory of Yahweh mentioned here has sometimes caused Bible readers and interpreters difficulty, and many rephrase the text in order to shape it to meet their preconceptions. In this text the manna was the new manifestation of the "glory of the Lord." In the *afternoon* the people saw the familiar cloud from the sea: "there was the glory of the LORD" **appearing in the cloud.**

The later command to place an omer of manna in the ark of the covenant corroborates the importance of the manna as a continual sign of God's presence and glory, even when the cloud was not visible. This was the first time the glory was said to be manifest in anything. The glory of Yahweh was manifest in the pillar of cloud many times after this first time, which makes it the most familiar visible referent (Mt. Sinai 24:16–17; tabernacle 29:42–43; 33:22; 40:34–35; temple 1 Kgs. 8:11). Here also the glory of the Lord was represented outside the pillar of cloud for the first time.

The tension in the narrative is great when Aaron confronts the **whole Israelite community** with the words **"Come before the LORD, for he has heard your grumbling."** For the reader who expects judgment at every juncture in the OT, these words sound ominous. Yet the Lord continued to establish the relationship. God used their grumbling to invite them to "draw near" (NIV "come before") to see and know for themselves that **I am the LORD your God.** They gathered and, as Aaron spoke, they were facing the desert. And **there was** ("Look!") **the glory of the LORD appearing in the cloud.** The Lord drew near to them with a visible sign of presence, as God had done at the sea. Then they heard the news of tomorrow: **"At twilight you will eat meat, and in the morning you will be filled with bread."**

16:13–20 / God provided both quail and bread. The text mentions the quail only briefly and focuses instead on the manna, an enduring sign of God's presence and their source of food for forty years. The manna appeared first as **a layer of dew around the camp.** It formed, like dew, without falling from the sky. Then **thin flakes like frost on the ground appeared,** either from or with the dew (see Num. 11:9). This was the manna, not named until verse 31, but vocalized first in the people's question *man hu'* translated **"What is it?"** The words, **"It is the bread the LORD has given you to eat"** reinforces the point about the Lord's presence from verses 6–12. The daily reminder of the Lord's glory in the form of manna was a continual sign of God's presence throughout the wilderness wanderings. The physical symbol of the Lord's presence in the bread of the Last Supper continued and added weight to this amazing theological initiative by God. This was a radically new kind of food, introduced as a staple.

Moses did not answer the question, "What is it?" for in asking the question the people had already named it. Instead he pressed forward with instructions that functioned as their discipleship school: **"Take an omer for each person you have in your tent"** (an omer is two quarts). They passed the first part: they **did as they were told.** The miracle was that they gathered randomly, some gathering more than others, but when they measured the amount gathered per tent, they had one omer per person.

Moses was not happy when some of them failed to follow the second part of the three-part directions (v. 4). **However, some of them paid no attention to Moses.** When they kept it until morning **it was full of maggots and began to smell.** In this way the Lord built in a natural consequence for inattention to instruction. It is too strong to call this disobedience, since the text does not. Disobedience will come later at Sinai (32:7–10). The so-called "test" and point of the text here is to see if they could follow instructions and reap the benefits in relation to the Lord (16:4; 15:25b–26). They only made this mistake the first time. Each day they gathered the manna again, and learned to trust the Lord daily for their bread. The success of the training must be kept in view, since it brought them to the mountain of the Lord.

16:21–30 / "Sabbath" or "rest" occur six times within eight verses (23–30; in vv. 23 [twice], 25, 26, 29, 30). The third part of the manna training commenced with the first Sabbath rest command, which Moses relayed to them in stages. God had commanded the people to gather manna six days but to refrain from gathering on the seventh day. They all followed the first half of the instructions and **On the sixth day, they gathered twice as much.** Then **the leaders of the community came and reported this to Moses,** since they had received this instruction without explanation of what would happen next (v. 22, note these were the "tribal leaders" rather than "elders"). These leaders then received the second stage of instruction from Moses: **"Tomorrow is to be a day of rest, a holy Sabbath to the LORD . . . Save whatever is left and keep it until morning."** That was all he told them until the next morning. They did what he said, completing the second stage.

The next day no **maggots** appeared. Moses told them to eat what they had saved and gave them the full command: **"Six days you are to gather it, but on the seventh day, the Sabbath, there will not be any."** They had almost completed the final stage of the training. Nevertheless, **some of the people went out on the seventh day to gather it.** They found nothing. The Lord's training related to the most basic of needs, daily bread. Again the Lord employed a form of "operant conditioning" to teach them to rest on the seventh day. When they kept the command to gather twice as much on the sixth day, they ate on the seventh. If they tried to gather food on the seventh day, they were disappointed.

"Revising" or "refusing to keep" the final stage of the Sabbath instructions was not the end of the story. The Lord kept them in dialogue and asked a relevant question, necessary for their success in bringing blessing to all the people of the earth: **"How long will you** ("you all") **refuse to keep my commands and my instructions?"** It was a question that made a positive difference for the people. God convinced them to change their ways. Thereafter, they **rested on the seventh day.** The Lord patiently explained that the Sabbath was a gift from God, who created the possibility of rest by giving them surplus bread. **Bear in mind that the LORD has given you the Sabbath; that is why on the sixth day he gives you bread for two days.** The Lord had succeeded in using their grumbling as a lever and opportunity to show God's own glory, to train them in trust, and to give them a source of daily bread as well as weekly rest.

We should not underestimate the weight and enduring influence of this gift and the command **no one is to go out** to gather bread (i.e., not to work). This first observation of the Sabbath not only provided a paradigm of working and resting, but it also established the previously unknown seven-day week. The impact of this paradigm is now known throughout the cultures of the earth. This was the beginning of the fulfillment of the promise to Abraham that his descendents would be a blessing to all.

Resting does require trust in the Lord to provide (see the discussion on 20:8). Resting demonstrates trust in God for daily needs and an acceptance of this gift. It acknowledges the work of God's holiness in one's life. Verse 23 says it was **a holy Sabbath to the LORD.** Keeping the Sabbath acknowledged that holiness is not earned or inherent, but a gift from the Lord. The people receive the Lord's holiness by doing nothing. This was the lesson the Lord tried to teach the people from the beginning. Exodus 31:13 makes it explicit: "You must observe my Sabbaths. This will be a sign between me and you for the generations to come, so you may know that I am the LORD, who makes you holy."

16:31–36 / Manna was so important in the formation of Israel's early relationship with the Lord that a memorial was commanded for **the generations to come, so they can see the bread.** The manna saved in a jar was a visible memorial to the manifestation of the glory of the Lord given on that first hungry morning. It was a reminder of the means by which the people learned to follow the Lord's instruction and the Sabbath gift that God revealed through it, even before Sinai.

The writer's description of manna endures long after the memory of its appearance and taste were lost. **It was white like coriander seed and tasted like wafers made with honey.** This should be read with a comma after the word "white." Coriander seed is gray or brown but the comparison describes its size and shape. Numbers 11:7–8 remembers the taste a bit differently (see also Ps. 78:24–25, where it is called "the bread of angels").

Verses 31–36 are an editorial postscript, referring to putting **the manna in front of the Testimony.** The "Testimony" is the ark of the covenant built later at Sinai (25:22, "ark of the Testimony"). The "Testimony" is also sometimes a more specific reference to the tablets of stone on which the commandments are written (31:18, "tablets of the Testimony"). Aaron puts the two-quart jar **(an omer)** of manna in front of the Testimony. This likely means in front of the tablets of stone, inside the ark of the covenant. The postscript also notes that they ate the manna for **forty years . . . until they reached the border of Canaan** (Josh. 5:12).

Additional Notes §19

16:1 / The Desert of "Sin" is related to the word "Sinai" and not to the English word "sin."

16:5 / The Hebrew says "it will be twice as much." The NIV interprets this to say "that is to be twice as much" meaning they should gather twice as much on the sixth day. This is based on v. 22, where it says plainly that they gathered twice the amount. Rabbinic tradition interprets it to say, "it will prove to be double," meaning the single amount gathered on the sixth day will miraculously double. In v. 22 they interpret "double" to mean that it doubled after it was gathered, which is the reason for the leaders' visit to Moses (see comment on v. 22).

16:7 / After the Lord's oath about the "glory of the LORD" filling the whole earth, Scripture describes other manifestations of the glory of the Lord in the creation (see, e.g., Pss. 19:1; 29; 97; 108:5; 145:8–17; Isa. 6:3b; 35:1–2; 1 Cor. 11:7; 15:39–45; 2 Cor. 3:18; Rom. 6:4; John 1:14).

16:12 / There are a number of verses in Exod. 16 that contain illogical sequences, awkward repetitions, and abrupt shifts. Many interpreters have followed the logic of source analysis by suggesting a rearrangement of verses, such as moving vv. 6–8 to follow vv. 11–12 to keep the quail verses together in more logical sequence. Quail, like this text, cannot be herded.

16:15 / Many have posited and discussed natural explanations for the manna and quail. The text claims that the Lord provided them at the right time and did not provide any manna on the seventh day. The question under consideration is "by what means did God provide this food?" Flocks of quail migrating between Europe and Africa still arrive exhausted on the Sinai Peninsula. Manna is thought by some to be a sweet excretion of some insects in arid climates (see Durham, *Exodus*, p. 224.).

16:23 / The command to observe a Sabbath ("rest") every seventh day appears here for the first time. "Sabbath" (*shabbat*) comes from the verb "rest" (*shabat*). It is not related to the word for "seven" (*shibʿah*). God *rested* on the seventh day after the creation (Gen. 2:2–3) but this is the first time the noun *shabbat* appears in Scripture. God explained the Sabbath commands more fully at Sinai and included rest for debt slaves, land, and the animals (20:8–11; 21:2; 23:11–12; 31:13–17; 34:21; 35:2–3).

16:30 / The first Sabbath command to rest comes with an ironic wordplay from 16:3: "all the food we wanted" (*sobaʿ*) sounds like the word for Sabbath (*shabbat*). What they wanted (bread), the Lord gave them. What they needed (rest), God commanded as a necessary gift.

§20 Quarreling, Water from a Rock, Amalekite Attack, and a Banner (Exod. 17:1–16)

The people continued their journey, **traveling from place to place as the LORD commanded.** It sounds like a good beginning. The Lord was their personal guide in the wilderness and they followed. Exodus 17, however, presents two new serious encounters, both rife with conflict. The people quarreled with Moses (vv. 1–7) and were attacked by the Amalekites (vv. 8–16). The internal and external threats provided new opportunities for growth. Their escalated quarrel with Moses revealed the internal dysfunction of their nascent relationship with the Lord and God's chosen leader. The external threat from Amalek confirmed the ongoing need for the Lord's protection and Moses' leadership. These crises also confirmed the leadership of the elders and Joshua and the presence of the Lord.

They camped at Rephidim, near the rock at Horeb (v. 6). They were in the shadow of Mt. Sinai. Numbers 10–36 will report the longer journey after Sinai, where they will return to Rephidim, renamed Meribah (Num. 20). Unlike the incident in Numbers, here Moses' leadership was exemplary. At Rephidim, water from the rock and the Amalekites' attack complete the structure of the Exodus journeys (see chiastic structure discussed in §18).

17:1–7 / The people tested the Lord, raising their grumbling to a new level of mistrust. As at Marah (ch. 15) and the Sin(ai) wilderness (ch. 16), the people grumbled and the Lord responded by instructing Moses and providing for the people. This time, however, the people **put the LORD to the test.** Essentially, they tried to train God to be at their beck and call. Rephidim is renamed here with two names, Meribah and Massah. Meribah means "place of quarrelling," coming from the root *rib* that refers to a courtroom-based civil lawsuit or the pre-court disagreement and conflict. **So they quarreled with Moses** (vv. 2, 7)—engaging in an unreasonable and confrontational dialogue. Massah means "place of testing" and comes from the root *nasah*. It refers to putting belief in the Lord's presence on trial. They "put the LORD to the test" (vv. 2, 7) by challenging the fact of God's presence with them: **"Is the LORD among us or not?"** The Hebrew is more explicit: "Is the Lord there? Perhaps the Lord is not there!"

The problem of water was real, but the means of addressing the crisis was problematic. The presenting issue was that **there was no water for the people to drink.** Once again, however, behind the lack of water stood the deeper issue of relationship to the Lord. Moses sensed this immediately when they made a demand: **"Give us water to drink."** By presenting an understandable need in an unreasonable way they exposed their false assumptions about the Lord and Moses. Their use of confrontational demand as a means to crisis resolution revealed their relational dysfunction. Moses dealt with this by bringing the Lord into the conversation: **"Why do you put the LORD to the test?"**

More than dysfunction or a bad attitude, their quarrel with Moses was based on at least two false assumptions. First, they did not wait on the Lord to provide for their need. They assumed, in spite of their recent experiences, that they must do something. Perhaps they thought that God did not know what they needed. Second, they assumed that if the Lord tested, or "trained" them, they also were free to test the Lord. This is what one did with other kinds of gods. If the god did not produce results, one changed gods. This was the original form of conceiving and creating a god that is one's personal "water boy." They challenged the Lord as if the Lord were a false god, suggesting that if they were still thirsty, then the Lord was not really there (v. 7).

The quarrel degenerated to accusations that bordered on death threats. The people posed an accusatory rhetorical question: **"Why did you bring us up out of Egypt to make us and our children and livestock die of thirst?"** This question implied that Moses intended to kill them from the beginning. Moses feared for his life in crying out to the Lord, **"They are almost ready to stone me."** God may have acknowledged the reality of this threat in telling Moses to **"Take with you some of the elders . . . and go."** The people's view of Moses would change radically at the next crisis, as they depended on him to survive the deadly attack from the Amalekites (vv. 8–16).

God responded to Moses and the people in a measured way. Contrary to some interpretations, the Lord's wrath is never in view here. Though God had cause to be angry after all of the acts of provision and deliverance, the text does not suggest any anger and we should not assume it is there. God follows a consistent pattern in these first wilderness encounters. Even in this escalated episode of mistrust, the Lord walked them through the crisis, demonstrating characteristic reliable and gracious provision. Later, when the people had had time to process and assimilate their experience, yet persisted in their challenges, God's righteous anger would strike against the perpetrators of rebellion. In this text, however, the Lord continues to lead with practical patience with this newly forming people.

The Lord gave Moses five steps for surviving this crisis. God told him to "take some of the elders of Israel" and walk **ahead of the people.** This could also be translated "walk in front of the people," which would make this a visible sign of Moses' leadership and support by some of the elders. The Lord also instructed him to **take in your hand the staff,** the symbol of Moses' original commission and the instrument with which he struck the Nile. The staff that Moses used to transform water to blood in judgment would here bring clear water from a rock.

The Lord moved Moses forward with the third imperative "go," followed by the promise to be with him, **"I will stand there before you by the rock at Horeb"** (Sinai). This promise was the fourth step for surviving the crisis, and the NIV does not completely translate it. The text says, "Look at me standing (*hinni ʿomed*) before you by the rock at Horeb." Although the Lord is visible to Moses, the text does not describe this presence, but it was essential to his success. The final step was to **"Strike the rock . . . in the sight of the elders of Israel."** The text does not even bother to describe the water coming out and satisfying the people. The outflow of water is the critical last step but the simple words **Moses did this in the sight of the elders** play down the outcome.

The point of the narrative is less the miracle of water, than it is the Lord's strategy for resolving the quarrel and its deeper issues of belief and witness. The elders, who the text has not mentioned since the selection of the Passover lamb, begin to play an increasingly important role (18:12; 19:7; 24:1, 9, 14). They support Moses by standing with him before the people. Consolidating his base of support, they become witnesses to the provision of water.

In the midst of providing, protecting, and creating a new people, the Lord's risk was that some would not believe. The people remained free to reject God's lordship. In this text, they are dismissive and inordinately forgetful of the Lord's past mighty acts of salvation. Their attitude commonly causes one of two strong reactions among readers. The first is to judge their ingratitude and lack of faith as ridiculous, causing the reader/hearer to feel superior. The second response may be closer to the intention of the biblical narrative: to recognize one's own enduring tendency to serve self-interest, not to recognize the Lord's presence, and not to trusting God for daily needs. This second response carries forward into the tradition to be sung by later generations in Psalm 95:7b–8: "Today, if you hear his voice, do not harden your hearts as you did at Meribah, as you did that day at Massah in the desert" (see also 1 Cor. 10:3–6).

The Lord's pattern of visible provision and presence in the midst of the people's struggle to understand and assimilate what they had experienced escalated as they drew near to Mt. Sinai. At the mountain the Lord's presence would be, as at the sea, powerfully manifest for all to see (19:16–25). The rejection of that presence would also escalate. There the question would change from, "Is Yahweh there, or not?" to "Do we want Yahweh there?" (20:18–19). The later crisis of rejection (32:1–4) would require an even greater intervention by God.

17:8–16 / The Amalekites came and attacked the Israelites at Rephidim. This simple statement expresses their continued vulnerability. Abruptly the text announces an unexpected attack and we hear about Joshua and Hur, called into action for the first time in Exodus, without any historical background. Moses gave directions and Joshua selected men. Moses, Aaron, and Hur prayed with uplifted hands on the hill as the men fought against the Amalekites and prevailed. The cooperative effort protected and saved the people through God's empowerment. The absence of God's dramatic visible presence (as at the sea) sets a new paradigm for Israel's protection. The Lord would fight behind the scenes through the people to protect them.

Joshua's name appropriately means "Yahweh saves." The text mentions Joshua as a new leader but does not herald him as the cause of victory, here or in later texts. In Exodus he accompanied Moses up Mt. Sinai (24:13; 32:17) and was with Moses when he met the Lord face to face in the tent of meeting (33:11). The Amalekites who attacked here were some of Esau's descendents (Gen. 36:16), a nomadic people centered northeast of Sinai in the Negev (Num. 13:29).

Moses said to Joshua, "Choose some of our men." The Lord gives no orders or directions to Moses here. Nonetheless, the Lord's intervention is visible when Moses takes up a position (*natsab*) saying, **"I will stand on top of the hill with the staff of God in my hands."** Moses and Aaron also took Hur with them (Caleb's son, leader of the tribe of Judah, who later shared administrative leadership with Aaron [24:14]).

As long as Moses held up his hands, the Israelites were winning ("stronger"). When Moses rested (NIV "lowered") his hands, the men of Amalek were stronger. Moses raised his hands to the Lord (vv. 15–16), who strengthened the limbs of the men of Israel. Moses' limbs also grew weak and he needed to sit down on a stone (v. 12) so that Aaron and Hur could use their hands to hold up his hands and the staff. Six hands **remained steady,** an expression that means "confirmed" (from which we receive the word "amen," *'aman*). In this acknowledgement of the Lord came strength. So, **Joshua overcame the Amalekite army with the sword.** "Overcame" (*khalash*) means "weakened" or "knocked to the ground." He did it with "the edge of the sword," which can be translated more graphically "mowed down" (RSV) or "totally defeated." It was a rout. The Amalekites were weakened by Joshua, who was strengthened by the Lord through Moses' hands of witness. Moses was strengthened by Aaron and Hur.

The Lord asked Moses, for the first time, to **Write this on a scroll,** so they would have a record of this great occasion of cooperative protection. God's redeemed people, attacked in their infancy, had been saved by a difficult and faithful action. God wanted future generations to remember the Amalekite attack and the promise that functioned like a curse. For the same reason, God said, **make sure that Joshua hears it.** Joshua was the heir to Moses' leadership position and would keep the oral memory of the Lord's protection through his men and Moses' prayer. Forty years later, Moses would remind the people of the merciless Amalekites (Deut. 25:17–18).

The tribe of Simeon wiped out the Amalekites in the days of King Hezekiah, more than five hundred years later (1 Chr. 4:43). It is ironic that no one would remember the Amalekites if this text did not preserve their memory.

Moses built an altar and called it The LORD is my Banner. This was the first altar Moses built for the sake of a thanksgiving offering. Abraham, Isaac, and Jacob also built such altars to share a meal with the Lord (Gen. 12:7; 13:18; 26:25; 35:1, 17). To give thanks for safety and deliverance, the blood and fat of the flock animal were given to the Lord (poured out and burned). The meat was shared among the people (Lev. 7:15).

At the sea the people sang, "The LORD . . . has become my salvation" (15:2). Now they offered thanks at an altar named "The LORD is my Banner" (*yhwh nissi*), which also functioned as a title for the Lord. The visual image of six hands holding Moses' staff looked like a banner, or battle standard, and served as a rallying symbol for fighting men. Moses, however, shifted the image, and with it the credit, to the Lord (see Ps. 60:4). Later, through Isaiah, the Lord promised to raise this banner to the Gentiles, to bring them into fellowship with God's chosen people (Isa. 49:22). Here, however, that banner simply defeated those who opposed them.

Additional Notes §20

17:2 / The Hebrew word for "quarrel" (*rib*) is also translated "lawsuit" (e.g., 23:2–3). It usually refers to a civil lawsuit. It also can mean a pre-court disagreement or a fight. See Gemser, "Controversy-Pattern," pp. 120–37.

17:7 / "You put the LORD to the test." The people are attempting to force God's hand in the way that Satan attempted to force Jesus' hand in Luke 4:1–13. See Fretheim, *Exodus*, pp. 189–90.

17:8 / The Israelites were attacked again in the wilderness on several occasions. The Amalekites and Canaanites successfully attacked some of the Israelites as a judgment from God when they tried to enter Canaan without the Lord's direction (Num. 14:45). Later they were attacked without provocation by the Canaanites (Num. 21:1), by the Amorite king Sihon who controlled Moab (Num. 21:23, 26), and by King Og of Bashan (Num. 21:33).

17:9 / In Numbers, Joshua is one of the 12 spies sent to Canaan and, with Caleb, gives a good report (Num. 13:16; 14:6, 30, 38). He became Moses' successor, receiving authority from the Lord to lead (Num. 27:18; Deut. 1:38).

17:14 / This is the first mention of writing as a way of remembering in Exodus. It is likely that it ended up in the *Books of the Wars of Yahweh*, a pre-biblical source that has been lost in time but is mentioned in Num. 21:14. Moses writes again at Mt. Sinai, as does God. See 24:4, 12; 32:16, 32; 34:1, 27–28.

17:16 / For hands were lifted up to the throne of the LORD.
Lit., "a hand was upon the throne of the Lord." Because of an odd spell-
ing of the Heb. word for "throne" (*kes* instead of *kisseh*), some translate
the word throne as "banner" (*nes*), which has a very similar shape in Hebrew. This changes the meaning to "a hand upon the *banner* of the Lord,"
referring to a call to arms for Israel. This emendation is unnecessary (see
Fretheim, *Exodus*, p. 193). Rabbinic tradition says the word for throne was
written defectively on purpose to show that as long as men like Amalek
are at work in the world, attacking the elderly and children who fall behind (Deut. 25:17–18), God's sovereignty will be incomplete (Sarna, *Exodus*, p. 422). In traditional interpretation Amalek comes to represent all
who want to kill God's chosen people.

§21 Father Jethro and God's Just Justice (Exod. 18:1–27)

Jethro, the non-Israelite, met Moses and the Israelites in peace. The first half of Exodus 18 describes the circumstances of Moses' reunion with his father-in-law Jethro, his wife Zipporah, and his sons. The conversation and action, however, focus on Jethro. Moses' witness to the Lord's deliverance is followed by a description of Jethro's belief and celebration meal with the elders of Israel. The second half of Exodus 18 describes Jethro's detailed advice to Moses concerning his legal administration. Brueggemann aptly notes that the combination of these two parts is more than incidental (Brueggemann, "Exodus," p. 829). The Lord's intention to bring blessing to the cultures of the world would require freedom *and* justice that provided for what the poorest people needed, not simply what they deserve. The Lord's liberation and justice are shot through with mercy.

This chapter provides a key for understanding the Israelite and non-Israelite relation to God. Structurally, Exodus 18 stands as a transition between the wilderness journey from Egypt to Sinai (chs. 15–17) and the first encounter with the new covenant at Sinai (chs. 19–23). Jethro's brief appearance and return to his "own country" mark the parting of a God-fearing Gentile from the midst of the Israelites. He offered them a structure for the administration of law that they readily accepted. They would continue to follow the Lord's leading and receive the laws of Sinai.

18:1–12 / The text once again calls Jethro **the priest of Midian** (2:16; 3:1; see comment on 2:18). What Jethro believed and came to believe is a matter of wide speculation, since the text tells us less than we would like to know. From it we can deduce that he was a priest for God (*'elohim*) but did not know *'elohim* as the *Lord* until Moses' witness about the exodus (see v. 11). In Genesis 25:2–4, Midian is identified as a descendant of Abraham and Keturah (his wife after Sarah's death), so Moses and Jethro had a common ancestor. Jethro was good to Moses from the outset of their relationship (2:20) and offered consistent support for Moses' calling.

In verses 2–4, Moses' family is reunited and we hear an update on **Zipporah.** Apparently, after the attack in which she saved Moses, he sent her back to Jethro because of the dangers of going to Egypt (4:24–26). The text implies that Jethro concurred with that decision. Now he brought **her and her two sons** back to her husband. **One son was named Gershom, for Moses said, "I have become an alien in a foreign land."** The reminder about Moses' son Gershom and the introduction of his son Eliezer also serve to briefly summarize Moses' personal experience. We met Gershom (meaning "an alien there") at his birth in 2:22 when Moses had been a resident alien in Egypt and had found a natural home in Midian. This serves as a paradigm for God's people as well. At Sinai, the Lord would continually remind Israel of their origins as resident aliens. This heritage would influence their laws concerning the treatment of *resident aliens* among them (e.g., 22:21; 23:9; see also 20:2).

Moses' and Zipporah's second son **was named Eliezer, for he said, "My father's God was my helper; he saved me from the sword of Pharaoh."** This is the only mention of this Eliezer (meaning "my God helped") in Scripture, but his introduction describes the second part of Moses' and Israel's experience. First they were aliens (Gershom), and then God helped them (Eliezer). Samuel later used the word "help" to name the altar Ebenezer ("stone of help") where the Lord saved them (1 Sam. 7:12). The psalmist also speaks of God as a "an ever-present help" (Ps. 46:1).

The personal detail of the meeting between Jethro and Moses is unusually warm and full of mutual respect. **Jethro had sent word,** but Moses did not wait for them to arrive. **Moses went out to meet** them. Because of the patriarchal setting, the text does not describe the meeting with Zipporah and the boys, but it mentions them three times each (vv. 2, 5, 6). The narrative describes Moses meeting with Jethro, respectfully bowing down and greeting him with a traditional kiss. Then they "each asked the other about their health" (*shalom,* NIV **greeted each other**) and entered Moses' tent to talk privately. This is a rare personal glimpse that adds credibility to Moses' narrative character. He had a peer, friend, and human counselor.

Moses told his father-in-law about everything the LORD had done and Jethro believed in the Lord. For the first time in

Scripture a non-Israelite is "converted" to faith in the Lord. It began with Moses' witness (v. 8). He described their protection through what the Lord **had done to Pharaoh and the Egyptians.** He also told about **all the hardships,** including the lack of water and food, the quarreling, and the Amalekite attack. The intervention and provision of **the LORD** in each case **had saved them.** Moses' witness was to the grace and historical intervention of Yahweh in their midst. The verb *natsal* is pressed into the narrative four times to carry the theme of saving and delivering (lit., "snatched from the jaws of trouble," vv. 8, 9, 10 [twice]; see also 3:8; 5:23; 6:6; 12:27).

Jethro believed in the Lord as God on the basis of Moses' testimony although he did not see any of the dramatic historical events himself. **Jethro was delighted.** More than simply believing the result he saw, he shared the joy (*khadah*) of what **the LORD had done for Israel in rescuing them.** Jethro acknowledged the source of their transformation and directed his praise to the Lord in classic parallel psalmic form.

> **"Praise be to the LORD,**
> **who rescued you from the hand of the Egyptians and of Pharaoh,**
> **and who rescued the people from the hand of the Egyptians."**

Jethro also confessed his conviction to Moses, saying **"Now I know that the LORD is greater than all other gods."** Previously a believer in God, maker of all things, he recognized the revelation of God's intervention in history on behalf of an oppressed people. He confessed the specificity of the name, Lord, as God's manifestation in the world. As a descendant of Abraham, he may have known the promises given him and seen the beginning of God's work through Israel. What the pharaoh and the Egyptians know (7:5; 14:4, 18) and the Israelites know firsthand (6:7; 10:2; 14:31), Jethro also claimed to know. The whole earth did not yet know but, with Jethro, the word had begun to spread (see comment at 9:14–16, 29).

The final part of Jethro's confession of faith was his **burnt offering and other sacrifices,** brought **to God** and eaten together with **all the elders of Israel.** Again the elders played a leading role, representing the community in relation to God (3:16, 18; 4:29; 12:21; 17:5, 6; 18:12; 19:7, 24:1, 9, 14). Jethro offered the two general types of sacrifices common in the OT: "burnt offering" (*ʿolah*) and "sacrifices" (*zebakh*). The former were wholly consumed by the fire in tribute to God. The latter were sacrificed with the blood and fat offered to God and the meat eaten by the people in a fellowship (*shalom*) or thanksgiving (*todah*) meal (24:5, 9–11; 32:6; Deut. 12:27; 27:7; Lev. 3:1). The giving of the burnt offering was more than a cultural exchange. It was an acknowledgement of one's devotion to God.

Jethro made the offerings and ate with the elders **in the presence of God.**

When Jethro offered sacrifices, however, they were to God (*ʾelohim*). The juxtaposition of the two names indicates that his path did not lie with this newly forming people of Yahweh. He did not follow the presence of the Lord to Sinai, or "serve" him with Israel. Instead he returned to Midian, believing in the Lord God. Jethro was a model of hope for Gentiles, very early in biblical tradition, that the promise God made to Abraham, Jethro's common ancestor with Moses, would be fulfilled. The placement of his narrative just before the giving of the law at Sinai and the Lord's specific covenant with Israel is not accidental. Israel would have a special relationship with the Lord because of its creation through the experience of the sea and its early formation at the mountain of God. By including the story of Jethro at this juncture, Israel's Scriptures acknowledged the possibility of righteous Gentiles who feared God and lived accordingly.

18:13–16 / Moses' first concern and all-consuming task had become administering God's law to the people. The Lord's justice, unknown in Egypt, was now critical. Historically, deliverance from oppression was often followed by new forms of bondage. Scripture tells the story of another possibility: rule by law rather than by force. This is one of the greatest gifts of Judaism to the civilized world. Jethro assisted Moses in establishing a just system of appellate courts with provision for choosing and vetting judges, and a process for appealing to higher courts.

The problem the narrative presents is that Moses' caseload was overwhelming. Moses' answer to Jethro's questions reveals the beginning stages of a transformed community. **Moses took his seat to serve as judge for the people, and they stood around him from morning till evening.** The same people who brought their quarrel (*rib*) against Moses in this very place (Rephidim, 17:1–7) now come to him to settle their disputes. When Jethro asked why Moses did this, his servant-hearted answer was, **"Because the people come to me."** The same people who said, "Is the Lord among us or not?" (17:7) now seek God's will through Moses. This was progress.

Verse 16 is replete with legal terminology: **"Whenever they have a dispute** (*dabar*, "legal matter" or "legal case"), **it is brought to me, and I decide** (*shapat*, "judge") **between the parties and inform them of God's decrees** (*khoq*, "statues," "ordinances") **and laws"** (*torah*, "instructions," "laws"). The terms "decrees" (*khoq*) and "laws" (*torah*) previously occurred in Exodus to refer to the observance of festivals (12:24, 49; 13:9) and the Sabbath (16:4, 28). Moses' reference, however, now includes the settlement of civil disputes, generally known as OT case (casuistic) law (see additional notes).

18:17–27 / Jethro's strong advice was to let justice roll down through just judges and "good" legal procedure. The presenting issue was the caseload, but Jethro helped Moses with more. He identified the various elements of the problem (v. 18) and gave Moses five points of advice (vv. 19–22) that would bring satisfaction and well-being (*shalom*) to the community (v. 23). He helped Israel establish justice in the community in part through a system of appellate courts.

Moses met Jethro's initial, astounded rhetorical questions (e.g., "What are you doing?!" v. 14) with a seemingly reasonable answer: "They come to me to seek God's will, I decide the dispute, and teach them God's laws." Jethro might have been impressed with the people seeking God's instruction, but he was certainly not impressed with Moses' lack of administrative savvy. His response was very direct: **"What you are doing is not good."** Moses was blind to his own limitations and the physical limitations of his simple procedure. He assumed that God's justice was all on his shoulders. He needed Jethro to explain that "good law" in a community must be accompanied by a good legal system of administration.

Jethro proposed five steps for consideration and approval. First, Moses should remain as the people's advocate (NIV "representative") **before God.** This he did later, with great effect, in Exodus 32–34. Secondly, he should **Teach** ("enlighten," "warn") **them the decrees and laws.** Moses had been teaching individuals, case by case (v. 16). Here Jethro describes a general teaching role, with Moses as the first law-school professor. His legacy in bringing the commandments to the people from Sinai quintessentially fulfilled this role. The first two foundation stones of justice were rule by law that was centered in God's instruction.

The last three steps of advice provided the best chance of a just court system. Jethro's third suggestion involved the selection ("discerning") of just judges. The people chosen through this discernment and vetting process were to meet certain criteria. They were to be **men who fear God** (respect and trust), **trustworthy men** (publicly acknowledged), **who hate dishonest gain** (would not take a bribe). The fourth step established something like district courts, even for the arbitration of disputes in a group of ten people. The **officials over thousands, hundreds, fifties and tens** established an appellate court system, in which the magistrate over ten people could send a difficult case to the magistrate over fifty, and so on. The final step was the supreme court, over which Moses himself would preside as a final appeal for the **difficult cases** (v. 22, "complex cases;" v. 26, "hard" or "severe cases").

Jethro concluded his advice by saying that **God so commands.** The text implies that God approved Jethro's advice to Moses. This was not special revelation, but nonetheless revelation given through Jethro's wisdom and experience (see also Acts 15:28). **Moses listened to his father-in-law and did everything he said.** Moses implemented Jethro's advice, as the text reports almost perfectly verbatim (vv. 25–26; Deut. 1:9–18). This text demonstrates God's radical commitment to, and insistence on, just judges, good procedure, and the process of appeal to a higher court. Justice is quickly perverted among people who do not have legal recourse.

It is ironic that a non-Israelite advises Moses concerning the administration of God's law. Not all revelation is so administratively oriented and transforming of culture at the same time. The establishment of a functioning justice system is critical in a community that has been ruled, in contrast, by the will of violent men. Jethro's prediction was partly fulfilled and partly an anticipatory hope to which the community that fears God still clings: "**all these people will go home satisfied**" (*shalom*, "in peace," "contented").

Additional Notes §21

18:1 / Several theories have attempted to explain the nature of Jethro's priesthood: Jethro was the originator of belief in Yahweh (Kenite theory); alternatively, Jethro and Moses both learned Yahwism from the

Kenites. See Durham's summaries of four speculative theories (Durham, *Exodus*, p. 241).

18:5 / In the narrative context, **near the mountain of God** refers to Rephidim. In 17:6 they were close to the "rock at Horeb." In 19:2 they leave Rephidim to go right up to the base of Mt. Sinai.

18:12 / Some commentators suggest that Jethro did not believe in Yahweh, since he offered sacrifices to God instead of Yahweh. The text does not support this assertion (see vv. 9–11), but is differentiating between Moses' path to Sinai and Jethro's path to Midian. *ʾElohim* and Yahweh are not two different gods, but explicitly the same, one, holy, and eternal Lord God. This is a central assertion of the book of Exodus. Exodus 18:12 and 24:9–11 are literary and theological reflections of each other on either side of the first giving of the law on Mt. Sinai. In both texts the elders of Israel come before *ʾelohim* with burnt offerings and sacrifices. In both they eat a meal in God's presence. The meal is a part of the formal acceptance of the Sinai covenant in Exod. 24 (see comment at 24:11). The former, however, is pre-Sinai, initiated by Jethro and a confirmation of his non-Israelite faith (see Bruckner, "Law before Sinai," p. 92).

18:16 / The grounding of God's law in the pre-Sinai biblical narrative has largely been overlooked (see Bruckner, *Implied Law* and "Law before Sinai").

18:23 / The creation-based wisdom that Jethro brings to Moses is implied as God's command in the context, **and God so commands,** even if this is translated to mean "if God so commands." See the excellent discussion of Jethro's brand of revelation in Fretheim, *Exodus*, pp. 198–200.

§22 Meeting God at Sinai (Exod. 19:1–25)

Exodus 19 is the theological and literary pivot of Exodus. Nowhere do we find a fuller revelation of God in relation to the people. In the preceding chapters Israel had been "let go" from serving the pharaoh so that they might serve/worship the Lord. Here they serve/worship at the place of Moses' original calling and receive their own call to be God's "kingdom of priests" to the world (chs. 25–31; 35–40).

The larger literary structure of Exodus 19–24 comprises a chiasm (see below) and gives a context for the meeting between the people and God at Sinai. There is a close relationship between the laws and the story of the people's redemption. This relationship is critical for a more general interpretation of the function of law. In addition, the proximity of the giving of the laws to the visible presence of the Lord declares their divine origin.

   A Narrative: conversation with the Lord, visibly present on Sinai (19:1–25)

      B Laws: Ten Commandments (20:1–17)

         C Narrative: Moses mediates between the Lord and the people (20:18–21)

      B′ Laws (20:22–23:33), including book of the covenant (21:1–23:19)

   A′ Narrative: conversation with the Lord, visibly present on Sinai (24:1–18)

Brueggemann observes that the juxtaposition of the Lord's visible presence (theophany, A, A′) and the giving of law (B, B′) places the law outside of Israel's historical horizon. "[It is] beyond the reach of Moses or of any king . . . Israelite life is mandated from the awesome region of heaven . . . [and is] neither a historical accident nor an ordinary political entity, but a community willed and destined by God" (Brueggemann, "Exodus," p. 831).

The laws of the Lord are set in the midst of the narrative of God's gracious provision and deliverance. The laws preserved and equipped the people for their mission in the world. The Lord had called them, snatched them from Pharaoh's lordship, established them through the Passover, and provided for their needs in the wilderness. God had patiently guided them through their own grumbling, protected them in danger, and had brought them to Sinai. Now the people would see the Lord revealed personally to them at the mountain of God (see comments on the narrative context of the laws at 19:4–5 and 20:1).

Exodus 19 contains the most dramatic event in Exodus since the crossing of sea, with the manifestation of the visible presence of Yahweh on Mt. Sinai. As mighty as the Lord's acts of deliverance had been, the experience at Sinai presented an even more powerful revelation of the Lord's presence. God had been present with them to this point as their redeemer, provider, and protector. At Sinai the Lord had an additional proposal for them regarding their mission and their worship/service in the world. A pyrotechnic theophany ("visible presence of God") accompanied the Lord's message.

19:1–2 / Israel camped there in the desert in front of the mountain. The people had finally come to serve/worship the Lord. Moses returned to this place, as the Lord had described to him at the burning bush: "this will be the sign to you that it is I who have sent you: When you have brought the people out of Egypt, you will worship God on this mountain" (3:12). All of the narrative to this point in the book of Exodus has been preparation for this key chapter, and not least the refrain, "Let my people go, so that that they may worship me" (5:1; 7:16; 8:1, 20; 9:1, 13; 10:3). The people had now arrived, through the Lord's grace, at the mountain. They would begin to serve/worship the Lord through the laws that God gave and through the building of the tabernacle.

19:3–6 / God . . . the LORD called to him from the mountain. The Lord's first words to Moses upon his return to Sinai contain the formality of poetic parallelism: **say to the house of Jacob / tell the people of Israel.** The short but powerful speech that follows this introduction contains the primary themes and the structure of Mosaic faith (Muilenburg, "Form and Structure"). Brueggemann called it "the most programmatic for Israelite faith that we have in the entire tradition of Moses" (Brueggemann, "Exodus," p. 834). Rabbinic tradition notes the inclusivity of the parallel

address, with "house of Jacob" specifically referring to the households of women and children.

The Lord's intentions with regards to this redeemed people
are immediately clear. God asks them to declare their intentions.
Verse 4 describes the three stages of their journey and the Lord's
provision in it. The second part of God's speech (vv. 5–6) presents
an invitation to a special vocation in the world. God attaches a
conditional promise to this offer to serve the Lord as intermediary
between God and the other nations of the earth. God called Israel
to be his holy nation and a kingdom of priests to the world.

This call begins with a description of God's grace in three
stages: bringing Israel out of bondage, providing for them in the
wilderness, and guiding them to an encounter with God that
would continue to transform their lives. The Lord reminds them
that they had indeed been witnesses to these gifts. They had seen
**"what I did to Egypt, and how I carried you on eagles' wings and
brought you to myself."** The Lord spoke very personally, saying:
"I did," "I carried you," and "I brought you to myself." The point is
that it was the Lord who brought them out of bondage, who carried them through their fears in the wilderness, and who brought
them beyond those external and internal forms of oppression to
worship God. They did not seek God before God sought them.
They did not begin by keeping laws or making sacrifices. They
simply cried out for help. Their relationship with God began with
God's own unexpected mercy and provision. Moses expands the
reference to the Lord carrying Israel on "eagles' wings" in his song
at the end of the wilderness sojourn in Deuteronomy 32:10b–11.

The second part of the Lord's first message for the people at
Sinai was an invitation for a reciprocal relationship. It begins with
the conditional statement, **"Now if you obey me fully and keep
my covenant."** The most obvious reference is to the covenant that
was about to be given: the book of the covenant (21:1–23:19). The
people's agreement to this condition in verse 8 could be read as a
declaration of their intent to receive that covenant. On the other
hand, the Abrahamic covenant was also clearly on the table in
Exodus, both before and after the meeting at Sinai. The reference
to the Lord's covenant need not be read exclusively. God's work in
the world extended through the exodus and at Sinai, but this did not
supersede the earlier covenants. Sinai's grounding in the promises made to the cultures of the world through Abraham would
become dramatically evident in 32:13–16. During the golden calf
crisis, the appeal to the Abrahamic covenant was enough for the

Lord to preserve Israel and the Sinai covenant. Moses had also previously imparted case law from the Lord (18:15–16), the Passover and Feast of Unleavened Bread and firstborn statutes (12:1–11, 21–27, 43–50; 13:1–16), and the Sabbath commands (16:16–30).

The result of their acceptance of the covenant was not, as is sometimes assumed, simply their salvation. Rather, it indicated something larger that encompassed the Lord's mission for the whole earth and all the peoples.

> **"out of all nations you will be my treasured possession.**
> **Although the whole earth is mine,**
> **you will be for me a kingdom of priests and a holy nation."**

The meaning of "treasured possession" is found in the parallel line that further defines it, "you will be for me a kingdom of priests and a holy nation." This is something new. For the first time in Scripture since the mention that God would bless all the nations of the earth (Gen. 12:3; 22:18), the Lord adds a dimension to the relationship between God and other peoples. Israel would be a treasured possession among all nations as a holy nation in as much as it was a kingdom of priests. The phrase "kingdom of priests" provides an interpretive key to the Lord's offer. Priests mediate God's law and grace. If they were all priests, then their calling was to mediate, through all that they were and communicated (e.g., written Scripture), the word and life of God to the world. The context for Israel's mediating work would be the kingdom of Israel, the political reality in which some in each generation lived faithfully, preserving God's social vision for the world and God's written word.

A second interpretive key is found in the phrase "Although the whole earth is mine" (v. 5). In the Exodus context, that the "whole earth" belonged to the Lord meant the reversal of the domination of chaos and the proclamation of the Lord's reputation, that the Lord might be known "in all the earth" (9:16)

Another, better, translation is: "because the whole earth is mine, I choose you to be a kingdom of priests in order to bring it blessing." This reading uses the immediate and the broader Genesis–Exodus context. Israel is thus not seen over against less honored nations, but as a nation chosen in order to bring the blessing (Fretheim, "Whole Earth," p. 237).

The transformation or restoration of the nonhuman creation often accompanies the transformation of God's people in Scripture. Because the whole earth belongs to the Lord, the wilderness

that the people initially experienced as an inhospitable place was
made hospitable. God transformed undrinkable water at Marah.
Bread rained down from heaven and quail abounded in the Sin
wilderness. A waterless place burst forth with abundant water at
Horeb. Isaiah described a similar transformation in the promise of
the people's return from Babylon (Isa. 35:6–7; 41:17–18; 43:19–21;
48:21). Paul described the transformation of the nonhuman creation as bound up with human transformation in the new creation
(Rom. 8:21–23). The whole creation was thus at stake and involved in the Israelites' decision at Sinai.

   "These are the words you are to speak to the Israelites."
The Lord wanted Moses to repeat these words immediately to the
Israelites. God wanted them to declare their intentions regarding
this offer for them to enter into a partnership for the world's sake.
This served as Israel's call narrative, mirroring Moses' own call
(3:10–12).

   19:7–9 / Moses made a mediating trip down the mountain, heard the peoples' affirmative response, and brought it back
to the Lord. He spoke first to the elders. The text implies that they
took it to the people who unanimously responded, **"We will do
everything the LORD has said."** In the immediate context, the
Lord had not asked them to do anything specific. Their response
was a formulaic agreement (see also 24:7) that functions here as a
declaration of intent to enter into a further formal covenant with
Yahweh (as in a wedding service). The actual details of that covenant would require more than half of the Pentateuch to describe
(Exod. 20:1–Num. 10:10).

   Back on the mountain, Moses reported the response and
heard the Lord's portending words about the coming of God's
own visible presence to the mountain: **"the people will hear me
speaking with you and will always put their trust in you."** The
coming **dense cloud** was similar to the cloud column that led
them, but more massive still and accompanied by a much more
powerful display (vv. 16–19). After Sinai, the cloud of the presence
would again descend on the tent of meeting and on the tabernacle
(33:9–10; 40:34–38). On Sinai, the Lord said that the people would
see the presence and hear the voice of the Lord speaking to Moses
(vv. 9, 11, 16–19).

   19:10–15 / Preparation for the theophany of Yahweh
began. The Lord gave instructions for the people to prepare themselves for the powerful event of the Lord's descent to Mt. Sinai in

their sight and hearing. God gave Moses three days to **consecrate them.** The text describes three elements of their consecration. They washed their clothes (vv. 10, 14). They abstained from sexual contact (v. 15; see also Lev. 15:16–18; Deut. 23:10–11). They established a boundary at the foot of the mountain that they did not cross (vv. 12, 21–24). This sort of consecration is external in nature. The boundary also functioned to consecrate the mountain ("set apart for a special purpose").

The Lord insisted that the people **"not go up the mountain or touch the foot of it."** Touching the mountain brought the threat of death by stoning or arrows. This extreme measure served to reveal the great distance between the purity of the Lord and the impurity of the people. In order to go even to the foot of the mountain they had to abstain from sexual relations and wash all their clothes. In preparation for worship at the tabernacle, the people would need to follow similar protocols. The established boundary served as an external limitation to preserve human life and make the face-to-face encounter possible. The act of touching the mountain would be so powerful a rebellion that no one was permitted to touch anyone who did touch the mountain, even to kill them. Stones and arrows were to be used so that this kind of theological death would not be transferred physically to anyone else.

The people were asked to wait in the camp until the Lord sounded the horn. The "ram's horn" (*yobel*, v. 13) and "trumpet" (*shopar*, vv. 16, 19) are synonymous (see Lev. 25:9–10). The horn was their signal to approach the boundary at the foot of the mountain (vv. 16–17). **"Only when the ram's horn sounds a long blast may they go up to the mountain."** Later the shofar was used in worship to imitate the sound of the Lord (2 Sam. 6:15; Ps. 47:5). At Sinai, God was the one who gave this signal.

19:16–19 / **On the morning of the third day** the Lord came down to meet the people. Earthquake and dense smoke accompanied the sound and light to fully engage, even overpower, all five senses. The people **trembled.** It began with double sight and double sound in the **lightning, with a thick cloud over the mountain, [thunder] and a very loud trumpet blast.** The Hebrew words for "thunder and lightning" are plural, indicating a continuous manifestation. When the trumpet sounded the signal, **Moses led the people out of the camp to meet** *ʾelohim.*

The people approached the boundary set at **the foot of the mountain.** They "took their stand" here since this was the line they could not pass. The smell and taste of smoke increased as the mountain lit up, in addition to the lightning, **because the LORD descended on it in fire. The smoke billowed up from it like smoke from a furnace.** The experience must have been overwhelming when the earthquake began. The trembling (*kharad*) of the mountain matched the trembling (*kharad*) of all the people (see Rom. 8:22–23; Pss. 18:7; 68:8). Then the trumpet began moving closer (*halak*, lit., "was walking," omitted by the NIV) and **grew louder and louder.** God was walking down the mountain toward them.

Then Moses spoke and the voice of God answered him. Moses was standing with the people at the boundary at the foot of the mountain. He spoke to God in their hearing and the people witnessed the Lord's response. The text does not reveal whether this first voice was articulated speech or like thunder (Pss. 18:13; 29:3–5). It simply says that the Lord intended to speak with Moses in their hearing so that they "will always put their trust in you" (v. 9).

God appeared in visible form many times in the OT (see comment on 33:11). The encounter at Mt. Sinai, however, was the only time God appeared and spoke to all the people. Previously the people had seen the sign of God's presence in the cloud that led and protected them. Now, amazingly, the Lord was determined to appear "in the sight of all the people" (v. 11) and be heard speaking with Moses (v. 9). The people saw and heard with their own eyes from 19:16–20:18. After hearing the Ten Commandments, the people asked the Lord to stop speaking directly to them (see 20:18–19).

19:20–25 / The warnings about forcing one's way to the Lord were reinforced. These verses interrupt God's speaking in the hearing of the people. (Direct speech with the people resumes in 20:1.) The interruption has a necessary theological character. It begins by repeating the description of the Lord's descent from verse 18: **The LORD descended . . . and called Moses to the top of the mountain.** God did not again descend. God was already there. When God called, Moses climbed the mountain and was immediately sent back down with an urgent message (v. 20; v. 24 is emphatic in Hebrew). The Lord pressed two issues: one for the people and one for the priests. God was concerned that the people might disregard the warning and **force their way through to see the LORD and . . . perish** (lit., "fall dead," either by stones and arrows or by the Lord, see v. 24). Even to Moses, God seemed overly concerned. Moses objected that they had already been warned and that he had obediently **"Put limits around the mountain"** (v. 23).

This "overly-cautious" interruption of the appearance of God reinforces the warning about trying to force one's way to the Lord. It may be intentionally awkward for emphasis. The extra warning highlights the human inclination to control one's way to holiness (Gen. 3:5–6). Moses underestimates how natural it is to be dismissive about what God actually says. The narrative demonstrates repeatedly how easily people reconfigure their relationship to God on their own terms. The propensity to trust one's own judgment and bend instructions, even those given by God, is embedded as a self-referring and self-serving human default. The Lord knew that setting limits and giving warnings was never enough. Some of the people would not recognize the powerful reality and danger of not actually listening to God's word. Out of carelessness or fervor, cavalier curiosity or religious intensity, they would attempt to break through and get some holiness for themselves.

The second issue the Lord pressed with Moses concerned the priests. They received special warnings, perhaps because their interest in holiness was even greater than that of the rest of the people. The mention of priests may be anachronistic, as Aaron's sons were not commissioned until 28:1, but this disjuncture gives emphasis. The Lord reminded them that they were not exempt from the washing and abstaining instructions: **"Even the priests, who approach the LORD, must consecrate themselves."** They, too, were to prepare to meet the Lord, lest they view themselves as inherently consecrated. The Lord was also concerned that the priests would **force their way through** (v. 24). In approaching the boundary in worship, Aaron's sons would have led the people forward to the foot of the mountain (rabbinic tradition identifies the "priests" here as all firstborn sons). The ones who wanted to be "closest to the Lord" were a special problem in God's eyes. Whether for status or genuine piety, they were willing to put themselves and their families at risk in order to pursue their own personal holiness. (vv. 22, 24; see also Matt. 11:12)

The chapter concludes with the Lord's insistence that Moses go down immediately to warn the people and priests again to observe the limitations that had been set. Perhaps in concession to the holiness-hungry priests, God asked Moses to **bring Aaron up** when he returned. **So Moses went down to the people and told them.** Moses has gone up/down Mt. Sinai six times by the end of Exodus: 19:3/7; 19:8/14; 19:20/25; 20:21/24:3; 24:9 (further up in 24:13)/32:15;

34:4/34:29. This was his third climb down. The next words are the Ten Commandments, given as Moses stands with the people at the foot of the mountain boundary.

Additional Notes §22

19:1 / The people are at Sinai from ch. 19 through the end of Exodus, through Leviticus, to Num. 10:10. In this narrative context of camping at Sinai for almost a year, the Lord delivered 613 commands, by rabbinic count.

19:2 / "Desert" occurs three times in the first two verses, but the Hebrew *midbar* means "wilderness" or "seasonal pastureland where no one lives permanently." The people lived here for a year and had a good supply of water, finding food for their flocks. It is not possible to confirm the location of Mt. Sinai/Horeb. The traditional site, since the 4th c. A.D., is Mt. Musa (7,488 ft.), one of the highest peaks in a mountain range in the south central region of the Sinai Peninsula. Others argue for Mt. Serbal, 20 mi. to the NW, which stands dramatically alone near Wadi Feiran. Still others look north on the Sinai Peninsula to Mt. Sin Bishar because it is within three days' walk from Egypt. Rabbinic tradition notes that it is blessedly unknown, like Moses' grave, so that these sites do not become places of veneration in Judaism. (A Christian monastery, however, was built at Mt. Musa.)

19:4–6 / Some scholars consider this meeting with the Lord to be the birth of Israel (e.g., Brueggemann, "Exodus," p. 835; Durham, *Exodus*, p. 262). If we are to use the metaphor of the birth of Israel as a people and take the Lord's version of the story into account (v. 4), they were born when they cried out in Egypt and the Lord delivered them through the sea; they were nurtured as an infant in the wilderness (see Deut. 32:10; Ezek. 16:4–6); and brought by God to be presented, ready to respond to the Lord, at the end of their "childhood," at Sinai. In this analogy, the giving of the law is the beginning of their responsible adulthood, not their birth.

19:5 / The expression "treasured possession" occurs most often in Moses' sermon in Deuteronomy. See Deut. 7:6; 14:2; 26:18–19; Ps. 135:4; Mal. 3:17. I am indebted to Fretheim for his close theological reading of this text in Fretheim, "Whole Earth," pp. 229–39. Israel was not free from the obligations of the law given later in Exodus, but the law was not the basis of their relationship through history. A generation could reject the offer to be the Lord's "treasured possession" in relation to the world, but the promises of God to them did not fail. The NIV phrase "Although the whole earth is mine" translates the conjunction *ki* in a fairly uncommon way, as a concessive, rather than in its most common causal meaning, "because" (see Williams, *Syntax*, §§444, 448).

19:6 / The expression "kingdom of priests" does not occur elsewhere in the OT, but the concept develops in the synonymous and misunderstood term "holy nation." Israel is "holy" in that God "sets apart" the people (31:13) for the mission of witness to God among the nations (Isa. 61:4–7; 62:10–12). Zech. 8:23 carries a literal and remarkably personalized version of this idea. The NT also understands the Jewish people to be mediators of God's truth, fully revealed in Christ. OT texts demonstrate this priestly role. See Rom. 15:8–12; Acts 13:47; 15:14–18; Gal. 3:8–9. The expression "kingdom of priests" refers to Christians in 1 Pet. 2:5–9 and serves, with Exod. 19:6, as a foundation for Luther's formulation of the "priesthood of all believers." For a summary of the biblical concept of holiness, see Bruckner, "Ethics," pp. 226–27.

19:13 / Some translate "they may go up on the mountain," preserving this as a supposed contradiction that the people could climb Sinai. The NIV ("up to the mountain") removes the contradiction. Since mountain approaches also "go up" mountains, "they may go up the mountain" (to the boundary) is the preferred meaning. The boundary would not have been a distinction between flat ground and elevated ground. That is not how mountains are. The people went partway up the mountain, up to the boundary. They could not, however, go up on the mountain heights.

19:22 / Some scholars interpret this reference to priests (not consecrated until Exod. 28:1) in relation to "approaching the Lord" at the altar, later in Exodus. The burden, however, is to interpret it here, in the context in which the redactor placed it.

§23 Ten Commandments: First through Fifth (Exod. 20:1–12)

Most people have some awareness of the Ten Commandments as a set of rules or laws but are less familiar with the significance of their relational context. Interpreters have also frequently examined the commands (law) in isolation from the narrative of Exodus 1–19. In the biblical context the commands *are not* abstractions of ethical principles. They are woven into a specific account in which the Lord had delivered, forgiven, redeemed, and formed the people. In the preceding chapter, the Lord had invited them into a special relationship as a "kingdom of priests" in relation to the world (19:5–6), and the people had accepted this invitation.

The formation of Israel as the people of God began with their dramatic deliverance from bondage and continues in Exodus 20–23 with the giving of the first Sinaitic laws. The laws provided boundaries and instruction that protected and sustained the freedom introduced by the exodus. These laws were not the basis of the people's relationship with the Lord, as we have seen, but rather the Lord's salvation was the basis of the laws.

Verse 2 directly confronts the temptation to interpret a disconnected legalism: "I am the LORD your God, who brought you out of Egypt, out of the land of slavery" (see also Deut. 6:20–25). Salvation is the gracious a priori of God's law. This initiative (Exod. 1–19) is the necessary foundation for understanding Exodus 20. The laws secured a new community order and a means of remembering, through future generations, that they were a delivered people. They remained "delivered" because they were also a "commanded" people.

The rabbis noted that the commandments were God's second act of creation. The first creation separated chaos and order. The second act created a people by revealing the separation of right and wrong (Plaut, *The Torah*, p. 521). The positive commands prescribe specific behavior. The negative form ("You shall not") of eight of the ten commands conversely sets positive outer boundaries that secure the safety and health of individuals and the community (Fretheim, *Exodus,* p. 204).

Some commentators have argued that the sociality of the commandments was a "Bill of Rights" that sustained the newly delivered community. The commandments provided a way for the liberated slaves to maintain order and guaranteed the benefits of their freedom. The command against idols prevented the false bondage of Egypt's prolific statuary. Sabbath rest provided respite for all workers. Honoring parents protected the integrity of extended families, intentionally broken in slave economies. No stealing and no false witness mitigated against economic exploitation. The purpose of the commands was to restrict the forces and tendencies that would diminish healthy freedoms in human society.

Wright notes that the values of modern society have reversed and inverted the commands. Coveting is our priority, we expect sexual license, ignore extended family, and view God as irrelevant. The commands provide for God, family, faithful sexuality, and property protection in that order (see Wright, *Deuteronomy,* p. 66).

20:1 / Exodus 20 begins as the Lord speaks amidst the storm and blowing trumpet (19:16–19; 20:18). **And God spoke all these words.** The Ten Commandments hold a special place among the six hundred and thirteen laws in the OT. They are the only commands the Lord spoke directly to the people from the mountain (19:7–19, 25; 20:1; Deut. 5:22). They are the first commands God gave at Sinai and are separated from those that follow by narrative discourse (vv. 18–22). God wrote them on tablets of stone (31:18; 34:1, 28; Deut. 5:22). They are given the title "The Ten Words" (NIV "Ten Commandments," 34:28; Deut. 4:13; see also Deut. 5:22; 9:10) and they are later placed in the ark of the covenant with a second title, "the Testimony" (40:20; Deut. 10:4–5).

20:2–3 / The first commandment is, **"I am the LORD your God, who brought you out of Egypt, out of the land of slavery. You shall have no other gods before me"** (see also Deut. 5:7). This direct speech personally addresses the reader in the second person, "you." Israel recited and remembered the exodus event as the basis of their monotheism. While others worshiped minor gods or competed for the attention of God's people, the Lord had no equal (Deut. 4:35, 37). The assumption was that the Lord would deliver each new generation from slavery to other gods and those who would control them. In the same way, this command also declared all human power to be relative. Neither was the individual to be his or her own god, a slave to the "self" and its fulfillment. This command insisted instead that the true and sustained freedom of the created people of God was, and would be, established and maintained when you have no other gods "before me" (lit., "before my face"). Not even the projection of our best humanness can replace God (Brueggemann, "Exodus," p. 843).

We can see the *external* measure of keeping this command in what a person or community confesses about the Lord in relation to other gods and philosophies. The psalmist elucidated this measure during Israel's monarchy by specifying the gods of the ancient Near East: "You shall have no foreign god among you; you shall not bow down to an alien god. I am the LORD your God, who brought you up out of Egypt. Open wide your mouth and I will fill it" (Ps. 81:9–10). The prophet Jeremiah, who recognized that an external confession of faith in the Lord might be a deceptive cover for one's true loyalties, pressed the *internal measure* (see Jer. 7:4, 8–11).

The Lord measured the internal keeping of the first commandment by broadening it and specifying that it include many of the other commands (see also 22:20; 23:24; 34:14, 17; Deut. 13:1–18).

20:4–6 / The second commandment continues the first, but more specifically (see additional notes). **"You shall not make for yourself an idol in the form of anything in heaven above or on the earth beneath or in the waters below. You shall not bow down to them or worship them."** The veneration of images made to represent powerful experiences of the creation was, and is, found throughout the cultures of the world. God commanded Israel not to make gods of any earthly power or experience, nor to make an image of their experience of God in the exodus (see Wright, *Deuteronomy*, p. 70). They were to experience the world as created by God, never to create gods themselves. This command protected them from the binding or enticing promises of the power of idols they had experienced in Egypt and which surrounded them on every side.

The prophets echoed this prohibition, railing against Israel's struggle with idolatry through the generations. The gods of the Canaanites and Moabites and, later, the gods of the Assyrians and Babylonians became temptations as the people sought to control their own lives. The gods of money and prosperity (the Baals), sexuality (the Asheroth), and the safety that comes with military power (Molech, Asshur, Marduk) took different forms in different nations, but they always vied for the people's allegiance. Isaiah's classic oracle from the Lord that mocked gods created by human beings reminded the people that the Lord was both their Creator and redeemer (Isa. 44:8–22).

The other laws made this command against other gods more specific: Do not mention their names (Exod. 23:13). Execute their prophets (Deut. 13). Divination practices are prohibited (Lev. 19:26; 20:6, 27, 31; Deut. 18:10). Sacrificing children to gods is forbidden (Lev. 20:1–5; Deut. 12:31; 18:10). Destroy the places of worship of idols (Deut. 12:2–5). See also Exod. 34:17; Lev. 19:4; 26:1; Deut. 4:9–12, 16, 23, 25; 27:15 and Miller, "Decalogue," p. 235.

In developed civilizations, the manipulation of created things to produce life-changing technologies, prosperous economies, and the freedom to pursue individual self-realization continues to entice and enslave the people of God. Luther broadened and internalized this command by summarizing its meaning: "We are to fear, love, and trust God above anything else" (*Smaller Catechism*).

The command against idols has a motive clause that includes a personal warning and a promise: **"for I, the LORD your God, am a jealous God, punishing the children for the sin of the fathers to the third and fourth generation of those who hate me, but showing love to a thousand generations of those who love me and keep my commandments"** (also Deut. 5:8–10). The translation "punishing . . . for the sin" is, literally, "visiting the guilt" of the fathers to the third generation. Without God's special intervention, the moral repercussions of idolatry sticks to families for several generations by the Creator's decree. By contrast, loving God results in God's showing love for time immemorial, thus making the wiser choice obvious.

God's "showing love" (*khesed*) is a different word in Hebrew and richer in meaning than the human love ("who love me," *'ahab*) in this verse. The best translation of *khesed* is "unrelenting love." It is often appropriately translated "steadfast love." Its context includes God's everlasting loyalty to the promises and commitments God made to the people, even when one generation or another fails to respond to that love. While unfaithfulness results in negative consequences for a time, God's promises abide exponentially through the generations. God would never abandon creation or those who would remember their redemption (see comment on 34:6–7, below).

God's "jealousy" has sometimes troubled readers, as human jealousy is not necessarily a positive attribute. God's jealousy in Scripture, however, is part of the positive bond between God and the delivered people. We can only understand the Lord's jealousy in the context of the exodus itself. God came down, delivered, guided, and created them as a people. In response they brought their gold to Aaron, who made a calf and they said, "These are your gods, O Israel, who brought you up out of Egypt" (32:3–6). God's deliverance and their betrayal is the primary context for understanding the Creator and redeemer's jealousy.

Praise for the deliverance of their lives properly belonged to God. God's jealousy is not like human jealousy, but rather has an ultimate truthful grounding in God as the Creator and redeemer. It requires that human beings, who are created and redeemed, tell the truth about their situation and not pose as creators of their own redeemer. The homonym *qanna*ʾ means "possession" in its noun form (see comment on 15:16). God is rightly jealous, because the people "belong to" God, who has "paid for" or "purchased" the people, even though they pretend otherwise. The exiles in Babylon also founded their hope on God's jealous love (Zech. 1:14–16; see also Isa. 42:8–17).

20:7 / The third commandment is, **"You shall not misuse the name of the LORD your God, for the LORD will not hold anyone guiltless who misuses his name"** (see also Deut. 5:11). "Misuse" is, literally, "lift up in vain." The "name of the Lord" is "Yahweh," given to Moses and the people as their deliverer and the Creator of their new life. This is a direct reference to remembering who had delivered them. God's reputation was tied to God's name in the exodus. Its "use" or "lifting up" in a positive way declared God's works of grace and deliverance. To speak of the Lord after Sinai was also to declare that God's laws were formative for the new community of faith. To speak of God without reference to the creating law and redeeming gospel could be a vain use of God's name, that is, God's reputation.

People also used the Lord's name as a means of swearing to tell the truth in court. Corrupting the legal process by lying would be a specific violation of this command as well (Lev. 19:12; Deut. 6:13; 10:20; see also Lev. 6:3–5). The prophets further developed this command by internalizing the prohibition. They exposed the vanity of using the name of the Lord in worship when an individual's or community's life was based on the exploitation of others

(Amos 5:21–24; Isa. 1:11–17). This radicalized application meant that someone could publicly be a devout person, in prayer and regular worship, but be "lifting up" *the name* "in vain."

The Jewish tradition made the application of this command more specific by "fencing" *the name*. They spoke the tetragrammaton YHWH in the public reading of the Hebrew Scriptures as *hashem*, "the name," or *ʾadonay*, "my lord" so that the four consonants were never articulated either as "Yahweh" or in any other fashion. (On the continued protection of this specific name in Christian tradition, see commentary at 3:13–15.) Luther applied the prohibition of misuse to the common corruption of personal speech: "We are to fear and love God so that we do not use his name superstitiously, or use it to curse, swear, lie, or deceive, but call on him in prayer, praise and thanksgiving" (Luther, *Small Catechism*, p. 3).

20:8–11 / The fourth commandment, is **"Remember the Sabbath day by keeping it holy. Six days you shall labor and do all your work, but the seventh day is a Sabbath to the LORD your God. On it you shall not do any work, neither you, nor your son or daughter, nor your manservant or maidservant, nor your animals, nor the alien within your gates."** "Sabbath" (*shabbat*) comes from the verb "rest" (*shabat*). It sounds like, but is not related to, the Hebrew word for "seven" (*shibʿah*), the day of the resting. God now expands the Sabbath command given first with the manna (16:21–30). This command is unique in the ancient Near East. It required that the people trust that they could survive without working every day. God, the owner of all of time, provided the seven-day week. God's gift of the Sabbath gave the former slaves the gift of rest, but it was to be rest in the God who gave it.

The Sabbath day *belongs* to the Lord. This positive command came with an unusual motive clause that pointed back to the creation. **"For in six days the LORD made the heavens and the earth, the sea, and all that is in them, but he rested on the seventh day. Therefore the LORD blessed the Sabbath day and made it holy"** (see also Deut. 5:12–15). The motive is obtuse, based in the Lord's hallowing of the day. It is pure gift, implying that to rest is to share in the life of God, who also rested.

The Sabbath command is also unique in requiring rest for servants, animals, and resident aliens. This expansion of the wilderness command was only the beginning of the broadening of the law by specifying other applications. For more on the release of debt slaves every seventh year, letting land lie fallow, and weekly rest for the animals, see 21:2; 23:10–12. The Sabbath has been called the "greatest worker protection act in history" (Wright, *Deuteronomy*, p. 76). It established a community where the most powerless living thing, the nonhuman earth, could rest in the life of God. Nothing was outside the purview of this command. Debts were to be cancelled every seven years (Deut. 15:1–18). Lost land was to be returned every forty-ninth Jubilee year (Lev. 25:8–55). Among the Ten Commandments, Sabbath is the most broadly specified (see 31:12–17; 34:21; 35:1–3; Lev. 19:3; 23:3; 25:1–7; 26:2; Num. 15:32–36; Deut. 15:1–18).

Jesus offered a radical interpretation of the Sabbath rest command when he declared that it was "made for man" (Mark 2:23–3:5; Matt. 12:1–13; Luke 6:1–10; see also John 9). The Lord healed on the Sabbath, giving rest and respite from disease, rather than following a strict observance of the gift as a law. The preacher in Hebrews 4:1–11 further broadened the hope of rest in God.

20:12 / The fifth commandment is, **"Honor your father and your mother, so that you may live long in the land the LORD your God is giving you"** (see also Deut. 5:16). The integrity of the newly formed community required that the adults honor parents who were no longer an economic asset in the family. While later applications (by adults) have focused this command on preadult children, the original context was a covenant with the *adult children* in the community (Deut. 27:20). Young children learned (or not) to honor their parents through the honor (lit., "weight") they saw adults give to their elders. This commandment mentions both mother and father (mother first in Lev. 19:3), in contrast to the Akkadian Code of Hammurabi (1750 B.C.) that only expressed concern for the father. The attached promise of long life in the land demonstrates the central value God placed on extended families for the health of the community.

Specific laws offer details describing what it meant to radically dishonor one's mother and father. Children should not attack or curse their parents (21:15, 17; Lev. 20:9; Deut. 21:18–21; 27:16). The commandment, however, is positive, instructing that honor (or "weight," *kabed*) is due parents simply because they are one's mother and father. This is not a question of subordination, but of giving serious weight to parents' concerns and needs. Leviticus 19:3 adds that children should give "respect" (*yare*ʾ). There is no mention of "earning" the respect. The elder was also liable before God for keeping the six hundred and thirteen laws. The new sociality was based on the command of God, not on social contracts. This commandment does not address the abuse of parental authority. We see this, rather, in the commands against killing (physical abuse), adultery (sexual abuse), and false witness (verbal abuse).

The advice of Proverbs 4:1–27 demonstrates the positive role of the father with a preadult child, guiding the child to a life of wisdom (see also Prov. 10:1; 13:1; 15:5; 19:18). The NT specifically links good parenting and the command to honor parents when it quotes the fifth commandment (Eph. 6:1–4; Col. 3:20–21).

Additional Notes §23

20:1 / For a clear discussion of the special place of the Ten Commandments in Scripture see Miller, "Decalogue," pp. 229–42. For a fuller discussion of the Ten Commandments as a bill of rights that establishes and sustains a liberated people see Harrelson, *Ten Commandments;* Wright, *Deuteronomy,* pp. 64–66; Fretheim, *Exodus,* p. 222.

20:2 / For the broadening and specifying applications of the Ten Commandments I am indebted to a helpful article by Miller, "Decalogue," pp. 229–42.

20:4 / The numbering of the Ten Commandments varies according to religious tradition. The Reformed and Eastern Orthodox churches separate "no other gods" and "no idols" as numbers 1 and 2. The Lutheran, Roman, and Anglican churches combine them as number 1 and separate "no coveting" into number 9 (house) and number 10 (wife and servants). The Jewish tradition reads the prologue itself ("I am the Lord your God") as number 1 and combines "no other gods" and "no idols" as number 2. Scripture itself does not number the commandments. This commentary follows the Reformed tradition.

20:5 / The word "jealous" (*qanna³*) is also sometimes translated "zealous." It is repeated in God's extended name, or title, in Exod. 34:14, where God's self-description includes the words *yhwh qanna³* and *³el qanna³* ("jealous Lord" and "jealous God"). See also Deut. 4:24; 5:9; 6:15; Josh. 24:19; Nah. 1:2. On "a jealous God," see also Goldman, *Ten Commandments,* pp. 146–47. On idolatry see Barton, "The Work of Human Hands."

20:8 / For further discussion of the sabbatical principle in Scripture see Miller, "Human Sabbath." On the theological import of the Sabbath see Heschel, "A Palace in Time."

§24 Ten Commandments: Sixth through Tenth (Exod. 20:13–26)

20:13 / The sixth commandment is, **"You shall not murder"** (see also Deut. 5:17). The verb translated "murder" (*ratsakh*) is sometimes rendered "kill" (e.g., RSV, although the generic Heb. word for "kill" is *harag*). Scholars have made various arguments for both translations of *ratsakh*, but English does not have one word that clearly suffices. ("To murder" is too specific and "to kill" is too general.) The word refers to killing without proper authority. That is to say, it refers to the act of killing defined by its relation to a context of illegal action, that is, killing outside of God's law. In the OT *ratsakh* refers to a range of unacceptable killing, including high-handed killing (premeditated murder), homicide of various kinds, and manslaughter through various levels of negligence (intentional and unintentional). Numerous laws that God gave the people at Sinai specify these differences (21:12–14; Num. 35:30–34; Deut. 19:1–13).

The law provided for exceptions to this general prohibition against killing, for example, to executing a high-handed murderer (Deut. 19:11–13). The misadministration of justice was a grave concern, and therefore God specified that cities of refuge be set up immediately to shelter those who killed another without malice or forethought (21:13; Deut. 4:41–42; Josh. 20:3). The law prohibited killing without forethought, but those administering justice were to take into account the motivation for the crime, and so it was important to provide a place where judges could render a just judgment and an appropriate sentence. God also made an exception to the law against killing in the war against the Canaanites (Deut. 20:1–18). Only God, however, could provide the exceptions.

The new community's experience of and response to unlawful death was grounded in two realities. The first was the biblical-juridical principle of an "eye for an eye" and "life for a life" (see the discussion on 21:22–25). God's community had to respond juridically to unlawful death. An individual homicide could easily debilitate a community, especially when the perpetrator was not called to account by an honest system of justice. The community was to hold violent persons responsible for the results of their actions, regardless of their social position (Num. 35:31; Lev. 19:15). Scripture views the malicious "spilling of blood" as an anti-creational act (a sin against the Creator) that affects even the earth (Gen. 4:10–12; Num. 35:33–34; Deut. 21:1–9). God's law governed the "eye for an eye" principle, and the courts adjudicated it.

The second response of the biblical community to unlawful death was the early call to practice a better justice: "I am the LORD. Do not hate your brother in your heart . . . Do not seek revenge or bear a grudge against one of your people, but love your neighbor as yourself. I am the LORD" (Lev. 19:16b–18). The underlying principle is theological: "life belongs to God" (Lev. 17:11; Gen. 9:6). God admonished individuals and the community not to seek revenge for bloodshed themselves, since this too destroyed the community. The Sinai law itself addressed this by pairing the commands "do not hate" and "do not seek revenge."

Restorative practices of justice (*iustitia salutifera*) existed precisely to avoid cycles of personal vengeance. The healing of a community that suffered homicide was possible only when hate and revenge were quelled in the knowledge that life and justice belong to God. Jesus echoed Leviticus 17 and 19 when he commanded the same (Matt. 5:21–26, 38–47).

20:14 / The seventh commandment is, **"You shall not commit adultery"** (see also Deut. 5:18; 22:22; Lev. 18:20; 20:10). The law against adultery meant that sexuality was not a private matter, but constitutional for the good of the newly created community of God. The promise to bless the nations of the world through Israel could be fulfilled only if the people sustained the integrity of their marriages, families, and thus the community of faith, over the millennia. Laws regulating sexuality are common in the ancient Near East, but the death penalty for adultery in Israel was especially severe (e.g., Deut. 22:22). Adultery was a high-handed sin against God (Gen. 39:9).

In a limited sense, "no adultery" meant sexual fidelity within marriage. In the most limited sense it meant that no one except her husband was to have sexual relations with a married woman. Whatever the primary social structure in Israel at a given time, (polygamy or monogamy), the bond of marriage was limiting.

The Sinai law corroborates the Lord's concern for a strong community and healthy sexuality with numerous specific prohibitions regarding other forms of sexual behavior (Lev. 18:1–30; 20:10–23; Deut. 22:23–29). A woman was expected to be a virgin when she married (Deut. 22:13–21). This, together with the law against adultery, also removed the option of promiscuity for a young man. The prophets attacked adultery as evil and detestable, because it brought external devastation to the individual and the community (Jer. 23:10; Ezek. 18:10–13; Hos. 4:2; Mal. 3:5).

Jesus removed the penalty of stoning for adultery, but he did not soften the demand of the law, clearly labeling it as sin (John 8:1–11). At many points he intensified and internalized the command, suggesting that hell was the end result (Matt. 5:27–28, 30b). Jesus' interpretation of the Sinai law was more radical than the law itself.

Jesus also criticized the legal loopholes found in the Sinai law for divorce and equated divorce with the faithlessness of adultery (Matt. 5:31–32, continuing the trajectory of Mal. 2:16). Jesus allowed for the possibility of divorce only in the case of the unfaithfulness of a spouse (Matt. 19:3–9). The father's warnings to the son in Proverbs 5:1–23; 6:23–35; and 7:7–27 spell out the devastating effects of adultery.

The prohibition against adultery generally defends the integrity and emotional stability of the family for the sake of the children, wife, and husband. It preserves the trust that is foundational to healthy familial relationships. The integrity of the family protects the most vulnerable in society, the children, whose emotional security is always at risk.

20:15 / The eighth commandment is, **"You shall not steal"** (see also Deut. 5:19). The law prohibits theft in order to protect the goods and livelihood of the people and to sustain freedom and trust. Stealing is incompatible with living under God's protection (Ps. 50:16–18) and is a kind of blasphemy (Prov. 30:9). It marks a city as corrupt (Isa. 1:10–23) and brings a curse on the thief and the one who protects him (Zech. 5:3–4; Prov. 29:24).

The law against stealing is common in many cultures. The remarkable feature of Sinai law was that it primarily countered the destructive effects of stealing in a community not by violent suppression of the thief, but by restitution. In other ancient cultures the loss of a hand could result, and penalties for theft were most severe for those in lower economic classes. In biblical law, if restitution was not possible, the severest penalty was debt slavery (until the debt was paid, or for seven years).

The book of the covenant, beginning in Exodus 22, began to establish case law to deal with restitution in specific cases or situations (see the discussion at 22:1–12).

This inner-biblical expansion of the law against stealing created a trajectory that shifted the burden to every level of society. The poor must not steal, but the privileged should make sure it was not necessary for them to steal by "stealing" hope. It was also possible to correlate this move with the exercise of generosity (Job 31:16–40; Ps. 112:1–9). Jesus corroborated this expansion and intensified it by putting the weight of the final judgment on whether or not one cared for the poor materially (Matt. 25:32–46).

20:16 / The ninth commandment is, **"You shall not give false testimony against your neighbor"** (see also Deut. 5:20). Sinai law renders the commandment against false witness more specific with detailed instruction concerning conduct in public court. It broadens the law to include gossip and slander against one's neighbor in general. You must not lie about your neighbor, in or out of court. Leviticus 19:11–12 combines the public courtroom and private deceit contexts: "Do not lie. Do not deceive one another. Do not swear falsely by my name and so profane the name of your God. I am the LORD" (see also Lev. 19:15–16). The command reflects the original context of courtroom law and translates literally as, "You will not answer against your neighbor with a false testimony." In Egypt God's people had been victims of exactly this crime. Pharaoh's false testimony against them was that they wanted to worship God because they were too "lazy" to work. He accused them of lying and offered his own version of the situation. His powerful "false witness" led to the law of increased labor (see comment on 5:7–12, 15–19). God's new community was to be a place where the truth was told (see Gen. 18:18–19).

The Sinai law also addressed the perpetual problem of false witnesses in court. It provided for the vetting of suspect witnesses before both priests and judges with an extreme penalty for perjury (Deut. 19:16–21). The prophets of the eighth and seventh centuries B.C. attacked those who gave false witness as a means of profit. The intimidation of truthful witnesses, giving false witness against the poor for gain, bribe taking, and manipulation of property law were all serious problems (Amos 5:10–15; Isa. 5:23–24; 10:1–2; see Hos. 4:1–3; Jer. 5:1, 26–28; 7:5–10).

The law also addressed the broader problems of deceit, gossip, slander, and lying about members of the community (Lev. 19:11, 16). The following succinct command generally sums up God's law on these matters: "Do not spread false reports" (Exod. 23:1). The psalmist also lamented the perpetual problem of spreading false reports (Ps. 5:8–10; see Ps. 27:12–14). In Psalm 50 the Lord takes lying personally (Ps. 50:19–22; see also Ps. 15:2–3).

The book of Proverbs is replete with admonitions against the wrongful and destructive use of the tongue. The NT carries this trajectory forward, reinforcing the necessity of telling the truth in every case (Jas. 3:1–18; 4:11–12; 1 Pet. 3:10).

20:17 / The tenth commandment is, **"You shall not covet your neighbor's house. You shall not covet your neighbor's wife, or his manservant or maidservant, his ox or donkey, or anything that belongs to your neighbor"** (see also Deut. 5:21). Most commentary on this commandment notes its unique internal and radical nature. Covet means "desire" or "to take pleasure." Some see this focus on internal desires as an extension of the law against stealing, false witness, or adultery, or as a combination of them. Others see it as a general law supporting the first nine commandments. It stands against the internal source of all sin: longing for things that cannot be rightfully yours. The word used about Eve, who saw that the fruit was "pleasing" and took and ate, is the same as the word translated "covet" in Deuteronomic law (ʾavah, Gen. 3:6; Deut. 5:21; the synonym, used in Exodus, is khamad). In its extreme form, coveting becomes a consuming appetite that is never satisfied.

Already this command is radical, internal, and very broad. Inner-biblical development, interpreted by the rabbinic and NT traditions, pushed its meaning into the public and observable realm. No one could be sure to keep this command if "coveting" were not also an observable offense. Leviticus specifies examples of observable coveting. The sequence of Leviticus 19:11–13 recites and expands on the eighth (v. 11a), ninth (v. 11b–12), and tenth (v. 13) commandments. The text reports and expands the tenth commandment as follows: "Do not defraud your neighbor or rob him. Do not hold back the wages of a hired man overnight."

The rabbinic tradition reinforced this second meaning of "covet" in the Mishnah. "You shall not covet" came to mean "You shall not defraud." The rabbis interpreted coveting in relation to the commandments against taking interest on a loan from the poor (Exod. 22:25–26; Lev. 25:36–37). Neither was an employer to withhold the wages of a day laborer, who was by definition poor and in need of the day's wage (Lev. 19:13–14). The development of this tradition of interpretation can be traced through the apocryphal writings between the end of the OT and the NT. Jesus supported the rabbinic tradition of "you shall not defraud" as well as the radical internalized meaning of not feeling desire for one's neighbor's goods. In his conversation with the rich young ruler he accepted the ruler's recitation of the law, that included "you shall not defraud" (*apostereō*), rather than (*epithumeō*) "covet" (Mark 10:17–22).

It is helpful to remember both the outward and the radically internalized applications of the commands found in Scripture. The laws of God ought to be kept, and we can keep them in their outward form. This is necessary for the sake of ordered life in the community and the well-being of individuals. In the biblical tradition, this is especially necessary for the sake of the weaker members of society, and for the protection of children. Simultaneously, we must acknowledge that we cannot keep God's commands wholly. When we plumb our hearts and motivations, we discover we are fugitives from the law. We are driven by this discovery from God's holy law to Jesus and the cross in order to obtain forgiveness and freedom.

20:18–21 / *Do not be afraid, but fear God.* The text immediately reminds the reader here that the people were standing at the foot of the mountain listening to God deliver the Ten Commandments. The power of the encounter that began in Exodus 19 continued with the sound of the **trumpet** of the Lord, **the thunder and lightning and . . . the mountain in smoke, they trembled with fear.** These verses mention twice that they stayed at a distance (vv. 18b, 21), as a result of their fear as well as in response to God's concern that they would rush onto the mountain (19:12–13, 23–25). The story of this powerful and personal encounter with the Lord who had so recently delivered them surrounds the commandments. Apart from the context of this story, the people cannot understand or keep the commandments.

The words, **"Do not be afraid. God has come to test you, so that the fear of God will be with you to keep you from sinning,"** express a vital theological distinction. No other passage in Scripture places *being afraid of God* and *fearing God* in such obvious juxtaposition. They come from the same Hebrew verb. The "fear of the Lord"

or "fear of God" is an essential characteristic of a person in right relation with God. "Fear of the Lord" is sometimes translated "reverence" or "respect." It is certainly not the same as "being afraid." The
midwives were the first to "fear the Lord" (1:17, 21). Pharaoh's officials who protected their servants when warned about the hail-
storm feared the word of the Lord (9:20). "Capable men" were
those who were trustworthy and "feared the Lord" (18:21).

This "fear of the Lord" includes an element of ultimate awe
as well as trust in the One who inspires the awe. At the crossing
of the sea, trust in the Lord and "fear of the Lord" are parallel in
the summary statement: "when the Israelites saw the great power
the LORD displayed against the Egyptians, the people feared the
LORD and put their trust in him" (14:31). Being afraid at the mountain was a natural response. Only trust in the Lord could begin to
transform being "afraid" into "fear of the Lord." The stated goal,
that they would be kept from "sinning," reveals that being afraid
is not enough of a motivation. Sin is endemic enough that one
must also *trust* the Lord who gives commandments as part of the
"fear of the Lord."

The people make an important decision in this brief narrative report. The close encounter with the Lord was more than they
could endure. They asked Moses to serve as an intermediary to receive the remainder of the laws. **"Speak to us yourself and we
will listen. But do not have God speak to us or we will die."** God
and Moses honored their decision. From this point forward, **Moses
approached the thick darkness where God was** and the people
kept their distance (see 34:29–35). This request established Moses
as the prophet of God for the people (Deut. 5:23–28). God continued to use prophets and judges as intermediaries to speak to the
people throughout the next thousand years (Deut. 18:15–22).

20:22–26 / Exodus 20 continues with Moses' conversation with God. It serves as a transition to the lengthy legal corpus
called "the Book of the Covenant" in 24:7. These verses function as
a preamble to the law code, reminding the people that the Lord
was not a created god, but had **spoken to you from heaven.**

The description of the Creator's altar answered the implied
question, "If the Lord is not a created god, how will our liturgical
worship be similar to and different from the worship of created
gods?" The beginning of the answer to this is found in the altar requirements. **"Make an altar of earth for me."** After they left the
wilderness the people built altars from whatever material was

available, earth or stone (e.g., Judg. 6:24; 1 Sam. 14:35). If they made an altar of stone, they were not to use cut or **dressed stones** (Deut. 27:5–6; Josh. 8:30–31; see also 1 Kgs. 6:7). They used no images of God or created things, in keeping with the second commandment. The stones were to be natural (as they were created), not "defiled" by a craftsman's (idol-maker's) tool. This distinguished them from altars to other gods, demonstrating their allegiance to the Creator of all things and not to some worshiped aspect of the creation.

The person offering the sacrifice was to be modest. **"do not go up to my altar on steps, lest your nakedness be exposed."** This instruction stands in contrast to ancient Near Eastern practice as well. Ritual exposure and nakedness were common, with a priest climbing stairs to an altar with a short tunic, or naked, garnering the worshipers' attention. God's altar was not the place for a priestly show. Steps up to the altar were forbidden. When God established the priesthood, undergarments were part of the requirements (28:42).

Additional Notes §24

20:13–17 / What is the authority of the law today? The exodus from Egypt provides the theological foreground for the question "How should we live?" The first concern of the Pentateuch is what God has done in creating, promising, and delivering a people. The second question involves who we shall be in response to God's actions. The question "What should we do?" necessarily follows. A more accurate formulation of the question would be, "What does the text say we should do, now that we are free to act?" In light of God's gracious acts to deliver and restore the people, what is found in the laws of the Pentateuch to guide a responsible life? A perspective of faith requires that the interpreter walk the line between "antinomism" (against the law) and a new "nomism." Since Christ has fulfilled the law, do we, therefore, "nullify the law by this faith? Not at all! Rather, we uphold the law" (Rom. 3:31). The law in general, therefore, retains authority, but the nature of this authority remains a subject of debate. See survey in Bruckner, "Ethics," pp. 224–40.

20:13 / For a clear exposition of the command "You shall not murder" as the basis for just-war theory, see Simpson, "Thou Shalt Not Kill."

20:14 / The death penalty for adultery was for both the man and the woman. On the relationship between the severe penalty and the stakes for God in familial integrity see Wright, *Deuteronomy,* pp. 80–81. For a discussion of the shifting definitions of adultery in the OT see Bosman, "Adultery." Concubines were given "rights" within the family system and could not be sold as slaves. Biblical law did not outlaw polygamy, which continued in limited practice in Judaism. Monogamy became a legal requirement in Judaism around 1000 A.D. Monogamy (marriage between one man and only one woman) became the norm after the 6th c. B.C. On the actual and metaphorical layers of Proverbs' warnings against adultery for the young man, see Koptak, *Proverbs,* pp. 162–66.

20:15 / When Sinai law further specified laws against stealing it moved toward describing culturally systemic theft. John Calvin developed this application of the command, using many of the laws in Deuteronomy (Wright, *Deuteronomy,* p. 83). This broad description of theft included laws against moving property landmarks, exploiting workers or resident aliens, false weights and measures, bribery, preventing gleaning by the poor, loan-sharking, vandalism, and withholding the sabbatical forgiveness of debt. At one time the prohibition of theft was thought to have originated as a law against kidnapping (stealing a person) in order to sell him or her into slavery (Alt, "The Origins of Israelite Law," pp. 101–71 and rabbinic interpretation; see Exod. 21:16; Deut. 24:7). Scholars of biblical law do not presently think it was defined this narrowly, although kidnapping was probably part of the general rubric. In this regard, see the interpretation of this commandment by M. L. King regarding stealing a man's freedom in Anderson, "The Eighth Commandment."

20:16 / Later specific laws address many concerns that corrupt justice: do not help the wicked by being a malicious witness; don't be swayed by popular opinion; don't favor people just because they are poor (23:1–3); don't deny justice to the poor in a lawsuit; don't accept a bribe for testimony; don't oppress resident aliens, for you were aliens in Egypt (23:6–9); don't pervert justice; and don't show partiality to the poor or favoritism to the great, but judge your neighbor fairly (Lev. 19:15). Never show partiality: if a family member or close friend entices you to evil, you must bring them to court (Deut. 13:6–11).

20:17 / For a survey of the law against covetousness in the OT, Apocrypha, rabbinic sources, and its use in Jesus' conversation with the rich young ruler, see Bruckner, "On the One Hand."

§25 Covenant Laws I: Debt Slaves and Capital Offenses (Exod. 21:1–17)

Israel's law codes have a unique context. Other ancient Near Eastern cultures had laws that were similar in form and content, but none were integrated into an account of deliverance. Israel's law is unique in that it is embedded in the story of the Lord's salvation and desire to ensure the well-being of the people. In Exodus, narrative sections both precede and follow the Ten Commandments and the book of the covenant. Later, the biblical text interweaves the story of God's people with distinctive priestly law in Leviticus–Numbers and Deuteronomic law. The narrative setting provides an important interpretive context for the more difficult laws.

The preamble (20:22–26) and postscript (23:20–33) of the book of the covenant contain warnings against idolatry, pointing forward to the golden calf incident in Exodus 32. After that event, the text reiterates a briefer form of the book (32:12–26) as a renewal of the covenant that the people broke.

The contents of the book seem jumbled, with unrelated laws in various forms. The sequence has raised questions and created tension for casual readers and scholars alike. The book includes laws regarding slavery, human violence, injury by dangerous oxen, restitution for theft and property damage, limiting the use of power over the most vulnerable, worship, integrity in the face of corruption or hate, Sabbath laws to protect the poor, and rules for religious feast days. The text lists these sequentially and without explanation. The legal forms include a mixture of case laws ("if . . . then," or casuistry), prohibitions, positive commands, decrees, and the *lex talionis* (law of retribution, law of retaliation, often expressed as "an eye for an eye"). We will refer to this law of retaliation by the relatively uncommon English word "talion," or by its more common terminology, the Latin *lex talionis*.

The preamble of the book (20:22–26) comes before the official superscription (21:1) and the conclusion (23:20–33) is after the subscription (23:13). The commentary that follows organizes the laws by section: I. 21:1–17; II. 21:18–36; III. 22:1–31; IV. 23:1–33. Olson has called this collection of laws in Exodus "jagged edged laws" (see additional notes).

Many of these laws make the reader aware of the great historical distance between the ancient culture and our own. They reflect the setting of most of Israel's history, that is, early agricultural life in Canaan. The lower status of women and implicit acceptance of slavery (in whatever form) are disturbing and require the reader to understand the cultural limitations of that specific time. Concerns about the assumptions certain laws make have caused some to dismiss the authority of biblical law or the OT in general. The historical context may require a reader to carefully evaluate the way the authority of these laws functions in a modern context. Self-serving interpretations have used some of these laws as a crude club. It is essential to remember that no single law can be understood as God's word in isolation from the whole corpus of 613 laws or from its three-thousand-year history of interpretation.

Biblical law is dramatically distinct from other ancient Middle Eastern legal documents in its combination of religious, ethical, and social laws, as well as their unique placement in the narrative. A comparison between the laws and the forms of the laws and other ancient Middle Eastern legal documents reveals both similarities and differences in the laws themselves. The nature and timing of the influence of other ancient Middle Eastern law codes is a matter of wide debate. Some have seen an inner tension in the book between sustaining the inherited cultural practice of slavery and the Israelite tradition of liberation (release from slavery) that God begins in the exodus. This may be too facile, but it demonstrates the tension within the book and takes the narrative context into account in interpreting the laws. In general, Israel's law made fewer class distinctions in its punishments for crime, paid more attention to subjective factors such as protection for perpetrators, and generally specified punishments that were less harsh (for a few exceptions see Blenkinsopp, quoted in Olson, "Jagged Cliffs," p. 256). Israelite law was unique in protecting the rights of resident aliens and the poor, "for you were aliens in Egypt" (22:21; 23:9–13).

21:1–11 / The civil and criminal laws of the book of the covenant begin with the words **"These are the laws you are to set before them"** (21:1–23:19; see 24:7). The first laws provided for the protection and occasional release of debt slaves. Debt-slavery was not synonymous with chattel slavery (life-time forced labor). Debt-slavery was the lot of the destitute in the ancient world. A person who could not pay a debt could "sell" themselves or a family member as compensation for that debt. Kidnapping and selling strangers (i.e., the acquisition methods of chattel slavery) were forbidden (v. 16).

These and other biblical laws deal with protecting slaves (e.g., Deut. 15:11–18) rather than abolishing slavery, which most modern readers would prefer. Further, the release of debt-slaves applied only to Hebrews. Others could become part of an owner's household for a lifetime (Lev. 25:39–55). The implied approval of slavery points to the limitations of any culture in manifesting the righteousness of God. God regulated, rather than prohibited, the practice in order for these laws to work in the context of the ancient world. (See Jesus' comments on the issue of cultural concessions in the law of Moses in Matt. 19:8; Mark 10:5.)

Taking slavery as a cultural norm, these laws began a gradual trajectory of limited freedom and protection for slaves. The major case of the first group of laws (vv. 2–6) established the seventh-year release of Hebrew debt slaves. Any slave could be in danger of becoming permanently bonded, but God's basic law was against such servitude since the Lord had "purchased" their freedom from Egypt (Lev. 25:53–55). Freedom from slavery is a primary context of the book of Exodus.

Verses 2–5 arrange the first five laws in a typical fashion. They begin with the major case law that established the general governing principle of the seventh-year manumission (release) of male Hebrew slaves. The laws immediately following provide for four contingent cases, each beginning with the word "if": **"If he comes alone"; "if he has a wife"** (in which case she went free with her husband); **"If his master gives him a wife and she bears"** children (in which case the wife and children stayed with the owner as his [original] property), or **"if the servant declares, 'I love my master and my wife and children and do not want to go free.'"** If a bond slave preferred the bondage of his employment (in order to stay with his family) he had to make that decision after the sixth year. Incentive to leave and the "stability" of a life-long arrangement were legislated. The piercing of the ear with an awl at the doorpost of the house was a symbolic act that opened the ear of the servant always to hear the master's request.

The first and major case of verses 7–11 preserved the social position of a woman who had been sold by her father as a maid-servant (*ʾamah,* often "concubine," as here). **"If a man sells his daughter as a servant, she is not to go free as menservants do."** She was not "freed" in the seventh year because the basis of her protection was her legal status as a wife. The four contingent cases indicate that she had been "sold" with the status of a wife/concubine and must remain married. **"If she does not please,"** her family might redeem her; the master could not secondarily sell her to strangers. **"If he selects her for his son,"** she has the rights of a daughter. **"If he marries another woman, he must not deprive the first one of her food, clothing and marital rights."** Finally, **"If he does not provide,"** she owed him nothing and was free to go.

21:12–17 / What constitutes a capital offense sheds light on the foundations and values of a society. In biblical law the death penalty is reserved for offenses against life, not against property (as in other ancient codes). These verses give four capital offenses in a participial case law form (22:18–20 give three more). The introductory "Anyone who strikes" is a common alternate form, stylistically different from, but functionally equivalent to, "If anyone strikes."

Two case contingencies follow the first capital offense, **"Anyone who strikes a man and kills him shall surely be put to death"**—one for manslaughter (unintentional homicide) and one for premeditated murder. The sentence for the latter was death but the former defendant was allowed to flee to a city of refuge where he would be given due process of law, protection from vengeance, and possible incarceration (see Num. 35:10–15, 22–28; Deut. 4:41–43; 19:8–10; Josh. 20:6). Alternatively, he could take refuge at the Lord's altar (see 1 Kgs. 1:50; 2:28). Hittite laws, by contrast, provided that a murderer of means could buy back his life from execution, a practice that Numbers 35:31–32 specifically legislates against.

The second and fourth cases concern grown children attacking either their mother or father. **"Anyone who attacks his father or his mother must be put to death."** The Code of Hammurabi §195 provided no protection for a mother and called for cutting off the hand of the one who struck their father. The penalty of death for **"Anyone who curses his father or mother"** was radical. This law demonstrates the strength of the foundational value of the family for Israel. The word traditionally translated "curse" has been shown to mean more than a verbal imprecation (Brichto, quoted in J. Sprinkle, *The Book,* p. 77). It means to denigrate, repudiate, and abuse. The case of the rebellious son of Deuteronomy 21:18–21, who was given a warning (did not heed discipline), might have been an expansion of this case law. A warning, or "second chance," would have mitigated the chances of execution, if the death sentence was in fact administered.

The third capital case was also indirectly related to parents, since it was often children who were stolen from them to be sold. **"Anyone who kidnaps another and either sells him or still has him when he is caught must be put to death."** This law strongly legislated against any slave trade, a practice common in the ancient Middle East, thus preventing its development in Israel (2 Kgs. 5:2; Judg. 5:30).

Additional Notes §25

21:1 / See Olson, "Jagged Cliffs," also Hanson, "The Theological Significance," and Paul, *Studies.* For 10 points on the relationship between law and the biblical narrative context see Fretheim, *Exodus,* pp. 201–7. For a newer source critical argument that the book is not the oldest of the biblical law codes see Van Seters, *A Law Book.* For excellent discussion of the laws and an extensive bibliography on the book, see Sprinkle, *The Book.* For an erudite analysis of the laws within the book see Houtman, *Exodus,* III, pp. 78–269. For a focus on composition history, see Crüsemann, *The Torah.* The seven extant law codes of the ancient Middle East include two Sumerian documents: that of king Ur-Nammu of the third dynasty of Ur (ca. 2100 B.C.), and that of King Lipit-Ishtar of Isin (ca. 1900 B.C.); two from Akkad: that of Dadusha king of the city of Eshnunna (ca. 1800 B.C.) and that of king Hammurabi king of the city of Babylon (ca. 1750 B.C.); and three national law codes not associated with individual kings: those of the Hittite Empire (eastern Turkey, ca. 1300 B.C.); those of the Assyrian Empire (primarily northern Mesopotamia, ca. 1100 B.C.); and those of the Neo-Babylonian Empire (all of Mesopotamia, ca. 600 B.C.). The law codes from the kingdoms of Eshnunna and Babylon have the most similarities with biblical law. For example, the Law Code of Dadusha of Eshnunna §§54–55 and the later Code of Hammurabi §§25–52 each have laws about an ox that gores that are similar to Exod. 21:28–32.

21:4 / At times the law included both men and women in the release, as Deut. 15:12–18 indicates. See the equal protection of male and female in Exod. 20:10, 17; 21:20, 26–27, 32.

21:10 / The sale of daughters into marriage for financial reasons was also a Mesopotamian practice (Van Seters, *A Law Book*, p. 95). The Code of Hammurabi provides more compensation for divorced women, but none for those sold as slaves/concubines.

21:17 / Was the death penalty carried out in these cases? The sentence in Heb., *mot yumat* (infinitive absolute with the *hopʿal* imperfective) can be translated, "may be put to death." The NIV translates the same words "shall surely be put to death" and "must be put to death." While "may" is not likely, it is grammatically possible, functioning as a strong rhetorical deterrent. Some rabbinic opinion takes *mot yumat* to be God's prerogative ("he will surely die") and the isolated *yumat* an execution by human judges (e.g., 35:2; on the other hand, see Num. 35:21; Deut. 17:6; 19:15). Verse 17 does not specify the executer, method, and timing. Gerstenberger has argued that this was only a legal form and did not establish the practice of capital punishment. See Gerstenberger, "(He/ They) Shall Be Put to Death," pp. 43–61.

§26 Covenant Laws II: Personal Injury, Bulls, and Oxen (Exod. 21:18–36)

The second section of laws concerns intentional or accidental injuries and the offenses are organized from more to less severe (Sprinkle, *The Book,* p. 105). While verses 12–27 address offenses by humans against humans, the following sections concern various offenses of animals (oxen) against humans (vv. 28–32), followed by offenses of property against property (vv. 33–36), and humans against property (22:1–16). We need to interpret each law in light of those surrounding it.

21:18–27 / This section highlights five cases concerning human violence and injury, with three providing protection for slaves. Each of the cases has historically been applied to both men and women, even though the verses do not specifically mention women, since the laws that do mention both men and women treat them equally (vv. 20, 26–29). A strict legal penalty punished even the most powerful for human violence against the most vulnerable (pregnant women, slaves).

In the first case, **"If men quarrel and one hits the other with a stone or with his fist"** and one of them is **"confined to bed"** there were two possible results. If **"the other gets up and walks around outside with his staff,"** the perpetrator was "not responsible" (free from guilt) except that he must compensate the man **"for the loss of his time"** and for any expense involved with his healing. Verses 23–27 imply and address the second possibility, that the victim remained bedridden. In that case the perpetrator would have been guilty (responsible to a greater degree) and subject to the *lex talionis* (see §25 and v. 26). Rabbinic law provided that the one who injured the other was liable for five kinds of restitution: for the injury, for pain, for medical expense, for lost income, and for mental anguish and humiliation (see Sarna, "Exodus," p. 460).

In the second case, the law protected a man or woman slave from mortal harm. This applied to any slave, whether Hebrew or foreign, a temporary debt slave or lifelong servant (v. 21). The text presents two possible outcomes. If the man or woman died, the law required that the owner be **punished.** "Punished" is, literally, "avenged," which meant death for death. The owner could not ransom his life with wealth (Num. 35:30–31). The death penalty for the murder of a slave was unique to Hebrew law (v. 12). The second outcome, if the slave got up **after a day or two,** was that the owner was not punished (i.e., executed as a murderer). If an owner seriously injured a slave, that owner was under the *lex talionis,* as in verses 23–27.

The third case introduces the *lex talionis* and is thus particularly significant. The case concerns an injured pregnant woman, whose child "came out" as a result of the injury. This law provided a strong deterrent to harming a woman and her unborn child, whether intentionally or unintentionally. It begins, **"If men who are fighting hit a pregnant woman and she gives birth prematurely."** The NIV preserves the general meaning "gives birth prematurely" (lit., "her child comes out"). Two results and sentences were possible for the court in the case of premature birth (live birth or miscarriage). If there was **no serious injury** (to child or mother) the offender paid a fine. The *lex talionis* principle allowed for monetary substitutes for bodily injury and debilitation (see comment below at v. 26).

The second possibility was that of **serious injury,** death or permanent debilitation. "Serious injury" meant accidental injury, and included intentional harm, for while the blow was intentional, the permanent injury to the mother or the child was accidental. In the case of mischievous injury, the *lex talionis* was invoked, setting a precedent of protection for the weakest members of society. "Life for life" was usually enforced only for intentional injury (vv. 12, 14). If death (of the mother or the child) was the result, it was treated as murder: **"you are to take life for life."** This was the same penalty as for capital offenses (attacking parents or murder, vv. 12–17). The detail of **eye, tooth, hand, foot, burn, wound,** and **bruise** turned attention to the possible debilitating effects on surviving premature babies. Whether intentional or not, the death or injury of a woman or her child was the biblical test case for the protection of life and limb. It introduced the *lex talionis.*

The concept of retributive law is sometimes identified by the biblical "an eye for an eye." Other times the same idea is called "talion," an English word derived from the Latin *talio, talionis,* "retaliation." The *lex talionis* ("law of retaliation," or "law of retribution") or "talion formula" was an attempt to make the punishment fit the crime. Leviticus 24:17–22 and Deuteronomy 19:21 reinforce the idea. It serves as a legal attack on violence in general, but it stands especially against violence towards slaves. The introductory case is the injured pregnant woman, but the two cases that follow are an interpretive key to the talion law concerning slaves. They form the most important protective law for owned persons in Scripture. Mesopotamian law also contained *lex talionis,* but it was not applied evenly to nobles, freemen, and slaves (Code of Hammurabi §§194–201; §§209–214).

Shalom Paul argued that this law was not, as previously thought, a primitive law (Paul, *Book of the Covenant,* pp. 70–79). Rather, it served as a correction to violent abuse by slave owners who could afford to pay fines and still sustain their cruel behavior. In rabbinic practice the owners paid monetary equivalents in the place of the retributive maiming, but were not allowed to do so in the case of murder. The metaphoric reading of "an eye for an eye" is found in the very next verse (v. 26). No application of physical talion is found in Scripture.

The fourth and fifth legal cases provide an interpretive key to the talion formula by giving two examples of violence against slaves (vv. 26–27). They demonstrate that this talion principle was not taken literally, but was established as a guarantee that injury would be compensated. In the case of a slave, it was "freedom for destroying a slave's eye" and "freedom for destroying a slave's tooth." *Freedom* would be the obvious preference of a slave, rather than taking the master's eye or tooth. This sets a trajectory of better and more restorative justice. Giving freedom to a slave who had lost his eye by a violent master was more effective compensation for the slave as well as the master, who would keep his eye, but forfeit the worker he had abused. These two cases establish a precedent for applying the law of talion *restoratively* rather then *strictly.* This level of protection for all slaves (vv. 20, 26–27) had no parallel in ancient Middle Eastern law codes.

21:28–36 / Dangerous bulls and the protection of bulls are the subjects of the last four major cases in the chapter. Bulls were essential to Israel's economic life in the land of Canaan for a millennium. They provided power for plowing and hauling and represented a significant investment. These nine verses mention "a bull" nine times. While the law protected their economic value, it also placed animals in proper perspective to human life. Two of the cases addressed human death caused by a bull and two provided deterrents against injury to bulls, providing compensation for their loss to the owner.

The first major case states that "**If a bull gores a man or a woman to death, the bull must be stoned to death, and its meat must not be eaten.**" This basic provision represents an economic loss for the owner, who was otherwise **not . . . held responsible** for the blood of the woman or man. It was an accidental death. A contingent case follows this major statute. "**If, however, the bull has had the habit of goring**" and the owner knew of this past behavior and had done nothing, he was guilty of negligent homicide. The penalty was the death of the bull *and* the death of the owner. The rabbis in this case interpreted the owner's death as the prerogative of heaven, not a human court. (This is the case wherever an infinitive does not strengthen the Hebrew verb.) In the event the owner was deemed to have known of the bull's past behavior, a member of the victim's family could demand payment in the place of the owner's death. The owner of the animal must pay **whatever is demanded.** This was not a ransom for murder, which biblical law forbade. The man was liable, but not a murderer.

The death of the bull by stoning was unique to Israelite law. The burial of the bull under a pile of stones (after the stoning) made profit from the meat impossible, treated the death of a person by an animal as abhorrent, and marked the location of the crime for all to see. Verse 31 amends the major case and the contingent case to include children who were killed by bulls. This reflects a higher value on the life of *all* children than in the Code of Hammurabi, which called for the execution a servant's child as vicarious punishment for the death of a freeman's child.

The second major case addresses a similar situation, "**If the bull gores a male or female slave.**" Because of its brevity, it is easy to misread this law. It assumes both of the situations of the first case (accidental death and negligent death). The bull would be killed in either case. By contrast, Mesopotamian law did not require that a bull be killed for the death of a child or a slave. In contrast to verse 30b, he must pay **whatever is demanded,** here "**the owner must pay thirty shekels of silver to the master of the slave.**" The slave's master did not receive the same consideration as the family in the first case; but note that the law does not mention the family of the slave.

The third and fourth cases provided for the protection of donkeys and bulls (Heb. *shor* throughout vv. 28–36; the NIV oddly uses "ox" only here). The third case served to warn property owners against negligence: **"If a man uncovers a pit or digs one and fails to cover it and an ox or a donkey falls into it."** The compensation included the meat of his animal as well as the funds to buy a new one. The fourth involved two bulls: **"If a man's bull injures the bull of another and it dies."** The parties were to settle this accidental death by an equal division of the meat and an equal division of the value of the live animal. The contingent case which follows creates a balance to the first contingency of the first case on bulls: **"if it was known that the bull had the habit of goring"** and the owner was negligent, he kept nothing. The owner of the dead bull kept all the meat and took possession of the live bull. The chapter ends with an application and reminder of *lex talionis:* **"the owner must pay, animal for animal."**

Additional Notes §26

21:22 / Interpreters have deeply contested this single verse on injury to a mother/unborn child because of the Hebrew words *ʾason* (probably lit. "calamity causing sorrow of another," NIV "serious injury") and *veyatsʾu yeladeyha* (lit., "and her children come out," NIV "and she gives birth prematurely",) which are ambiguous. The plural "children" may be a plural abstraction of a child not fully formed, but it may also mean miscarriage (as in some Mesopotamian law). It is ironic, considering the ambiguity, that the rabbis use this text as grounds for the legality of abortion. They argue that serious injury only refers to the mother, and they assume the death of the child. Since a fine was considered an adequate compensation for the death of a child (v. 22), they argue that a premature child's death could not have been considered murder, which always required death as a penalty (Num. 35:31). But the question remains, how could the death of an unborn child not be considered a serious injury requiring a greater penalty, at the very least, to the child's mother? (see Sarna, "Exodus," p. 461). The LXX clarifies the more reliable original meaning of injury to the child: "If two men strive and smite a woman with child, and her child be born imperfectly formed, he shall be forced to pay a penalty" (v. 22a). Houtman, *Exodus,* III, pp. 160–71, discusses the extensive secondary literature (see also Sprinkle, "Interpretation," pp. 233–53).

21:24 / Jesus amended the application of "an eye for an eye" for individuals responding to violence against them. He admonished his disciples, "Do not resist an evil person" (Matt. 5:39).

21:26 / The NIV oddly confuses the legal material by using "manservant" and "maidservant" where it previously used "male slave" and "female slave" (vv. 20–21). The Heb. words (ʿ*ebed* and ʾ*amah*) are consistently the same throughout.

21:28 / The "goring ox" case laws have parallels in the Akkadian laws of Eshnunna (53–55) and the Code of Hammurabi §§250–52. This has led to extensive secondary literature comparing them. See Finkelstein, *The Ox*; Sprinkle, *The Book*, pp. 104–28.

21:33 / Commentators have puzzled and suggested many reasons for the placement of this third legal case, which seems out of place because it begins, "If a man" rather than "if a bull." However, these last two cases deal with bulls that are killed and provide a just compensation for the owner.

§27 Covenant Laws III: Property Rights, Capital Offenses, Using Power, Relationship to God (Exod. 22:1–31)

Exodus 22 continues with the casuistic laws of the book of the covenant. These case laws protected property in cases of theft or negligent damage and established civility between neighbors by setting limits of liability for another's property. They continue through verse 17, after which the legal form changes to commandments (apodictic law). The commandments address three more capital offenses, limitation of the use of power with the vulnerable, and one's relationship to God. The Lord established law and the rule of law through the courts and judges, building a just society under God's rule (vv. 8–9, 11).

22:1–17 / Eleven major cases of theft and damage here establish legal precedents for dealing with the loss of property, safeguarding personal property rights. Limits on punishment contrast with some Akkadian (Mesopotamian) laws by providing protection for the perpetrator. The first four cases deal with liability and restitution for theft (vv. 1–4). The next two deal with restitution in the case of negligence (vv. 5–6). Cases seven through ten and their various contingencies regulate liability in second-party possession of an owner's goods (stored, loaned, lost, or stolen; vv. 7–15). Two remarkable verses (vv. 10–11) focus on restoring and maintaining relationships between neighbors who have experienced conflict over the loss of property. The eleventh case concerns virgins who were seduced (vv. 16–17).

The first of four cases on theft (v. 1) links Exodus 21 and 22 by using the words "steal" and "ox." While the prior laws concerned injuries from, and damage to, an ox, the laws in Exodus 22 concern theft (see comment on 21:33). **"If a man steals an ox or a sheep and slaughters it or sells it,"** the penalty was fivefold for oxen and fourfold for sheep. Missing oxen meant lost labor so their theft was a greater liability. For most thefts the penalty was simply double, but the value of the animals and therefore the greater loss/potential for profit increased the penalty.

The second major case (v. 2) limits the liability of the homeowner who used violence in protecting his home at night. **"If a thief is caught breaking in and is struck so that he dies, the defender is not guilty of bloodshed."** The contingent case holds the homeowner liable for the bloodshed if he killed the intruder in the daylight. This allowed for the factor of darkness and the increased fear of what cannot be seen at night and the increased possibility of harm to the victim. Traditional interpretation allowed that homicidal intent (on the part of the thief) might be assumed at night, when residents were certain to be at home and were therefore more vulnerable.

The text briefly states the third major case (v. 3). If someone steals, they **must certainly make restitution.** Its contingency, **if he has nothing,** forced him into debt slavery, which also served as an option to stealing for the indigent poor. The Code of Hammurabi §8 called for the execution of a thief who could not pay and also inflicted heavier fines (30 times and 10 times the value) depending on the social status of the victim. Hebrew law never imposed death for violation against property. The fourth case (v. 4), concerning theft, returns to the subject of stolen animals and established the double restitution standard (vv. 4, 7, 9): **"If the stolen animal is found alive in his possession . . . he must pay back double."** In this case, the animal would be restored to its owner in addition to the fine.

The fifth and sixth cases (vv. 5–6) deal with restitution in the case of negligence. **"If a man grazes his livestock . . . and lets them stray . . . in another man's field,"** he must restore an equal amount of whatever was lost, **from the best of his own field or vineyard.** Negligence with **fire,** which the people used in a controlled way to clear fields, might have led to the destruction of a neighbor's harvest or **standing grain.** They used **thornbushes** as fences between fields. Again, the negligent party was liable for the loss, but only in an equal amount since the outbreak of fire was not intended.

The more complicated cases of property law involved three parties (borrower, owner, and thief). If one's property was stored by or loaned to a second party and was stolen, who was liable? Cases seven through ten and their various contingencies regulated liability in such situations (vv. 7–15). The seventh case (v. 7) repeats the general rule of the thief's double liability: **"the thief, if**

he is caught, must pay back double." It set up the contingency, **if the thief is not found** (v. 8). In that situation, **the owner of the house** (borrower) was not liable for the silver or goods unless it could be proven that he had stolen them himself. The laws were realistic about human nature, considering first whether the borrower had actually stolen the item. He was liable to appear before the judges for scrutiny. They would clear his reputation or convict him and impose the double penalty. The eighth case imposed the double penalty for anyone convicted of the possession of "lost" or stolen property. The judges (jury) decided rightful ownership, guilt, and declared the typical double restitution.

The ninth case (vv. 9–13) focuses mainly on the relationship between neighbors. As in the seventh case, the problem here is a loss of goods that had been given to a second party for safekeeping (sometimes called the "bailor"). But this case deals specifically with animals that died, were injured, or disappeared for unknown reasons (theft, death by wild animals, wandering off). This law limits the liability of the second party, if he was not at fault, and addresses the attitude of the first party who had lost his animal. If the second party, the safekeeper or "bailee," was innocent of theft or abuse of the animal(s), he took an **oath before the LORD** (i.e., using the name of the Lord). The first party **is to accept this, and no restitution is required**. The law required that the injured party keep no grudge.

The law offered a contingency if the animal was known to be stolen by an unknown third party. Then the second party was liable for the value of the animal since he was responsible for its safekeeping (v. 12). The rabbis assumed that the first party had paid the second party for his services. If, however, he could produce the remains of death **by a wild animal** he was not liable, since this kind of protection was beyond what was required.

The tenth case (vv. 14–15) addresses liability in the case of an animal borrowed for use in plowing or hauling. If **it is injured or dies while the owner is not present, he must make restitution.** This stands in contrast to accepting liability for the animal given for safekeeping (vv. 10–11). Since the second party borrowed this animal for the purpose of labor, he is liable for overworking the animal or for placing it at risk during labor. This law also provided for the protection of the animal.

The contingency was that **if the owner is with the animal, the borrower will not have to pay.** Presumably, the owner would take care that the animal would not be injured or die through risk or overwork. Death would have been natural or accidental and the owner would bear the cost of the loss. A second contingency on the major law was that **the money paid . . . If the animal was hired** covered the "restitution" required if the "owner was not present." The owner assumed the risk of renting his animals.

The final case (vv. 16–17) concerns a man who **seduces a virgin** (*betulah*). This law was attached to those concerning the protection of property since seduction was a kind of theft (stealing a girl's reputation) and negligence on the part of the man. The law protected unmarried women who were seduced, holding the men liable. The law guards the reputation of a virgin **who is not pledged to be married** in as much as the man **must pay the bride-price, and she shall be his wife.** The assumption here is that if she was pledged to be married, the man would be guilty of adultery and under threat of death (as in Deut. 22:23–27). The stated contingency was **"If her father absolutely refuses to give her to him, he must still pay the bride-price for virgins."** In this case, the law required no marriage to take place.

22:18–27 / This section combines case law (casuistry) and commands (apodictic law) to form a transition from the casuistry of the first part of the book of the covenant (21:1–22:17) to the commandments of the latter part (22:28–23:1–19). The text gives three more capital offenses (vv. 18–20; see 21:12–17). Each of them prohibits the twisting of the Creator's prerogatives and intentions for the created order. **"Do not allow a sorceress to live"** prohibited perverting the powers of the created world through magical manipulation. The condemnation in the Hebrew is not as strong as the NIV implies. Literally, "she shall not live." It is the mildest warning in the three laws found here. It does not necessarily refer to execution but, as in Deuteronomy, can mean "do not let him/her live among you" (see also Deut. 18:9–14). Leviticus 20:27 prescribes stoning for diviners and enchanters who remain "among you." Sorcery attempted to exercise power that belonged to the Lord alone (7:11). The word "sorcery" seems generally to include divination, casting spells to alter outcomes, and manipulating created forms. Deuteronomy 18:10 condemns male sorcerers.

The second capital offense law here, **"Anyone who has sexual relations with an animal must be put to death,"** prohibits the perversion of God's intended use of sexuality. It strengthens the threat of death using the divine retribution formula, "will certainly die" (*mot yumat*; see additional note on 21:17). The NIV's "must be put to death" again is stronger than the Hebrew and blurs the progression of severity in these three offenses. Leviticus 20:15–16 (see also Deut. 27:21) specifically requires execution.

The third offense carries the most strongly stated penalty: **"Whoever sacrifices to any god other than the LORD must be destroyed."** Here the penalty was unequivocal execution (*kharam* is "the ban" or "elimination"). This is another form of the second of the Ten Commandments, prohibiting the false attribution of praise and honor that belong to God alone.

Four laws in verses 21–27 address the wrong use of power over vulnerable and marginalized people. Two prohibitions regarding resident aliens, widows, and orphans (vv. 21–24) are followed by two case laws concerning poor debtors (vv. 25–27). Nowhere else in the book of the covenant does God speak about any law so personally and passionately. Justice was not an idea that worked itself out in the ups and downs of this life. In relation to God justice was not a passive concern but immediate and active.

> **"Do not mistreat an alien or oppress him, for you were aliens in Egypt. Do not take advantage of a widow or an orphan. If you do and they cry out to me, I will certainly hear their cry. My anger will be aroused, and I will kill you with the sword; your wives will become widows and your children fatherless."** (vv. 21–24)

God informed and shaped Israel's relationship with other vulnerable people by insisting that they not turn the tables of power and function as the oppressor. Through the act of remembering that they were "aliens in Egypt," God's deliverance from oppression became a paradigm for Israel (3:7, 9). The words "If . . . they cry out . . . I will certainly hear . . . and I will kill you" reveal that God was bound to the law. From the very beginning Israel needed to remember that it had no monopoly on God's compassion. God followed through on this threat to "kill you with the sword" when using Assyria and Babylon to attack Israel in the eighth and sixth centuries B.C.

Two case laws also specifically protected poor debtors (vv. 25–27; see also Lev. 25:35–38; Deut. 23:19–20; 24:10–13). **"If you lend money to one of my people among you who is needy, do not be like a moneylender; charge him no interest."** Again the address is personal and direct. The phrase "do not be like a moneylender" is not necessary, but it puts the finger on the agent who might act fairly but not compassionately. Other ancient Near Eastern laws do not legislate compassion. Interest rates could be ruinously high (up to fifty percent). The second law uses a question that appeals to common humanity and then offers God's own compassion as a model for behavior. **"If you take your neighbor's cloak as a pledge, return it to him by sunset, because his cloak is the only covering he has for his body. What else will he sleep in? When he cries out to me, I will hear, for I am compassionate"** (vv. 26–27; see Deut. 24:12–13; Amos 2:8).

22:28–31 / The concluding four laws of the chapter directly address one's relationship to God. They begin the latter portion of the book of the covenant, which is almost entirely in commandment form (22:28–23:19). The first law has two parts: **"Do not blaspheme God or curse the ruler of your people."** Both "blaspheme" and "curse" refer to more than speech (see comment at 21:17; Brichto, in Sprinkle, *The Book*, pp. 167–68). They indicate speech and actions, that is, gestures that demonstrated contempt for God or a ruler. By comparison, the expression "blasphemes the name" (Lev. 24:16) comes from another word root (*naqav*) that means "utter a condemnation." The "curse" against the ruler can also refer to using one's power to bind the ruler's ability. Since all of these activities undermine the rule of God in the world, the law prohibits them.

The last three laws deal with acknowledging God as the source of income and life itself. Deuteronomy 18:4 and 26:2 also describe offerings from **granaries** and **vats**. The phrase **firstborn** of **sons** and animals echoes the commands God gave *before* Sinai (13:1–16). The final command begins with the injunction **"You are to be my holy people."** Exodus 31:13b, "I am the LORD, who makes you holy," is the best way to understand holiness (see also additional note on 19:6). One of the external signs of that distinction that the Lord gave was avoiding **the meat of an animal torn by wild beasts.** "Torn" (*terepah*) is the general term for "not kosher" (not properly bled in slaughter), meaning that the blood had not been acknowledged as God's in the animal's death. Leviticus 17:15 states that anyone who eats an animal killed by another animal must wash his clothes, bathe, and wait until sunset before he could be considered "clean."

Additional Notes §27

22:18–27 / The prophet seemed to have these verses in mind in Mal. 3:5.

22:18 / Each of the first three laws in this section concern cultic relation to the Lord. Sprinkle identified an alternating pattern of cultic/ social justice groups as follows: 22:18–20 cultic; 22:21–27 social justice; 22:28–31 cultic; 23:1–9 social justice; 23:10–19 cultic (Sprinkle, *The Book,* pp. 163–165). The alternating pattern demonstrates that the sociality of the people is not separate from their relation to the Lord.

22:24 / Scripture never accepts a passive view of justice for the vulnerable who are oppressed. Instead it describes justice as God's personal passion for those who are denied basic resources and dignity of life. God says "I" or "me" 8 times in 5 verses. When people cry out to God for help, God leans towards them. God also expects the people who follow God to perform just acts (e.g., Isa. 1:17; Jer. 7:5; 22:3). God demonstrates a special concern for "widows and orphans," which is a way of expressing "the most vulnerable." Scripture speaks of God's concern for the "the poor" more than 400 times. Perhaps the most well-known summary of this reality is the following: "Justice was not equal justice but a bias in favor of the poor. Justice always leaned toward mercy for the widows and the orphans" (Niebuhr, *Pious,* p. 92). See also Heschel, *Prophets,* I, pp. 200–201.

§28 Covenant Laws IV: Corruption, Poverty, Three Festivals, God's Promises (Exod. 23:1–33)

The book of the covenant concludes with laws that establish judicial integrity (vv. 1–9); Sabbath laws that protect the poor and beasts of burden (vv. 10–13); and the institution of three yearly festivals (vv. 14–19). Then the text returns to the narrative of God's promises to Moses (vv. 20–33). The alternating pattern of social justice legislation with laws about the people's relation to God continues.

23:1–9 / This first set of laws seeks to establish the integrity of witnesses and judges in the face of corruption or hate. These juridical procedural laws require extreme impartiality. Five imperative commands open the sequence (vv. 1–3; see also Lev. 19:15–18). Two illustrative cases (vv. 4–5) follow, and five more imperative commands (vv. 6–9; see Sprinkle, *The Book*, pp. 178–79) conclude the section. The general command, **"Do not spread false reports,"** echoes the ninth commandment about bearing false witness (20:13). A more specific, court-based, version follows: **"Do not help** (lit., "join hands with") **a wicked man by being a malicious witness"** (Lev. 19:11, 16; Deut. 19:15–21). The next two commands concern the power of public opinion and the necessity of impartiality for a witness or a judge: **"Do not follow the crowd in doing wrong . . . do not pervert justice by siding with the crowd."** "Crowd" may also mean "the mighty" (*rabbim*). In either case, it is clear that one ought not to be swayed by whatever powers are in play. The rabbis interpreted this to mean that the tyranny of literal applications of biblical law was not to sway competent and impartial judges. Nor were they to claim to special revelations from God, but rather use an impartial weighing of circumstances with the law (Tigay, "Exodus," p. 158).

The fifth law in this first sequence is surprising: **"do not show favoritism to a poor man in his lawsuit."** The context of 22:21–27 and the Lord's partiality to the vulnerable have led some interpreters to consider this a mistake. Several have emended it to read "to a great man," but the rhetorical impact of this verse drives home the point of this whole block of laws: never show partiality, ever. Verse 6 then provides a balance: **"Do not deny justice to your poor people in their lawsuits"** (see Sprinkle, *The Book*, p. 180). The call was never to show favoritism, but always to practice justice. The Lord's preference for the poor demonstrated in 22:21–27 was for the vulnerable poor who were being oppressed. To say that the Lord is partial to the poor in general puts too much weight on the idea. If a poor person sues someone, the judge should examine the case simply on its merits.

The two case laws between the first and last five commands illustrate the principle of impartiality. They also are surprising in two ways. They are not courtroom laws and they require helping one's enemy. They drive home the Lord's concern for justice. In these cases, the help was for animals that were in trouble. Animals could not go to court, but they were vulnerable. One's human relationships are not supposed to interfere with the objectivity of taking action to do the right thing: **"If you see the donkey of someone who hates you fallen down under its load, do not leave it there; be sure you help him with it."** Beyond the concern for the safety of animals, this legislates that God's people are to take substantial positive action to lessen the potential animosity of an enemy. Even in the face of hate, impartial judgment and action may bring about better justice (see also Matt. 5:43–45; Prov. 25:21–22; Luke 6:27–38).

The last five juridical procedure laws return to the problem of corrupt legal systems that uniformly put the vulnerable at a disadvantage. Verses 6–9 especially mention the poor, the honest, and the immigrant. Each of these contains motive clauses: a personal threat from the Lord, a warning about becoming blind to justice, and an appeal to the experience of vulnerability. This combination represents a broad sweep of possible motivations. The one (e.g., a witness or a judge) who is responsible for the death of an innocent person sins against God: **"for I will not acquit the guilty."** Bribes **blind** and **twist** words (Deut. 16:19; 27:25; Isa. 5:23; Prov. 17:23). This set of laws concludes with the reminder of the humbling experience of being an immigrant or resident alien: **"Do not oppress an alien; you yourselves know how it feels to be aliens, because you were aliens in Egypt."** These laws apply the Lord's general concern in 22:20–26 to courtroom procedure.

23:10–13 / The two Sabbath laws in this part of Exodus differ from the other three Sabbath texts in their motivation (16:23; 20:10; 31:15–17). The others state the purpose of the Sabbath in relation to God's holiness and resting in creation. Here the focus is on providing for the poor and for beasts of burden. The seventh-year rest for fallow fields, **"let the land lie unplowed and unused,"** applies also to the **vineyard** and **olive grove.** In this way **"the poor . . . may get food from it, and the wild animals may eat what they leave."** A parallel text in Leviticus 25:1–7, 20–22 emphasizes the Lord's provision. The seventh-day rest also points to those who bear the heaviest labor. Rest **"so that your ox and your donkey may rest and the slave born in your household, and the alien as well, may be refreshed."** The Lord's concern for sustaining and restoring the most vulnerable, the poor and the non-human creation, is again at the forefront.

Verse 13 is more than a general summary to **"do everything I have said to you."** The admonition, **"Do not invoke the names of other gods,"** speaks against the Canaanite religion the people would encounter. The prohibition directly refers to the worship of the ba‘*alim* (of the field, groves, vineyards, springs, and weather) and ʾ*asherot* (fertility goddesses) and their non-sabbatical agricultural and labor practices. The "other gods" of the Canaanites also stood in contrast to the God-centered laws of the three festivals that follow. Rain and temperature governed the agricultural year in Canaan, and thus all who lived there had the same harvest times. The focus of the celebrations, however, was quite different. Naming other gods in gratitude was the temptation of prosperity. The Creator's personal command was to celebrate the festivals "to me" (v. 14).

23:14–19 / These verses introduce three festivals commonly known in the OT in legal form (also noted in 34:18–23; Lev. 23:1–44; Deut. 16:1–17). They were harvest pilgrimage festivals, specifying that every man was to appear "before the Sovereign LORD." The burden for women traveling with children may have been too great (see Deut. 16:11, 14). The first festival, **the Feast of Unleavened Bread,** was celebrated (with Passover) **in the month of Abib** ("green grain" or "barley"), the month of the spring barley harvest. The text is clear, however, that the motivation for the first celebration was not the harvest, but rather because **in that month you came out of Egypt.** (On the Feast of Unleavened Bread see the comments on chs. 12–13.)

Seven weeks later they harvested wheat and other grains and celebrated **the Feast of Harvest.** It was also known as "the day of firstfruits" (Num. 28:26), "the Feast of Weeks" (*shabuʿot* Deut. 16:10), and Pentecost (50 days after Passover). It became the celebration of the giving of the Sinai law ("Festival of the Giving of the Torah" and, later, Rosh Hashana). The third festival was **the Feast of Ingathering,** the final harvest of orchards, vines, and gardens in late autumn. It became known as Sukkot, variously translated as "Booths" or "Tabernacles." It was a remembrance of living in tents and the Lord's provision in the wilderness (Lev. 23:42–43; see also Num. 29:12–39; Zech. 14:16–21). **"Three times a year all the men are to appear before the Sovereign LORD."** For the first several hundred years in the land, before the building of Solomon's temple, they were to appear at the tabernacle (see ch. 40).

The formal laws of the book of the covenant conclude with four laws concerning food and food offerings. These four also appear together in 34:25–26. The people practiced them throughout the year, but they particularly correspond to the festivals just mentioned. The prohibition of yeast with a sacrifice related to the Feast of Unleavened Bread. The command that no fat from a festival offering was to be left over until morning was also generally true of the Passover lamb (see the comments on ch. 12). They were to bring **"the best of the firstfruits of your soil"** all year, but this was especially important during the Feast of Harvest (Lev. 23:16–20; Deut. 26:1–11).

The final law may refer to the preparations for the final harvest feast, during which the tenderizing effects of milk may have been sought as a special contribution to the festival. The Sinai laws repeat the injunction **"Do not cook a young goat in its mother's milk"** twice more (34:26; Deut. 14:21). It shares a common concern with other laws the Creator gives for sensitive treatment of the nonhuman creation. Other laws protect the mother-offspring relations of lambs, calves, and kids (22:29; Lev. 22:27–28; see Exod. 23:4–5, 11–12; Deut. 22:6–7). Some commentators see a reaction in this law against either Canaanite, Dionysian, or magical practices (e.g., Durham, *Exodus*, p. 334).

23:20–33 / These verses are a formal narrative conclusion to the book of the covenant. They provide a balance to the introduction by reiterating the theme of the Lord's first-person concern for true worship of the Creator and redeemer of Israel (20:22–26). Scholars have noted a shift to a Deuteronomic style.

The text immediately drives the narrative forward toward the land of the Canaanites. While Abraham's name does not appear here, the enduring promise of the land renewed at the burning bush is in the forefront (3:6–8; 23:23, 31). God promises to provide a guardian angel and to help in the conquest of the land of Canaan. God also warns against the Canaanite's false gods.

The chiastic structure of these promises and warnings has blessing at the center. A' and B' expand on the promises and warnings given in A and B.

> A *Promise* of the Lord's angel's help in securing the land (vv. 20–23)
>
>> B *Warning* against false gods (v. 24)
>>
>>> C *Blessings* of the Lord your God (vv. 25–26)
>
> A' *Promise* of the Lord's help in securing the land (vv. 27–31)
>
>> B' *Warning* against false gods (vv. 32–33)

The promise of a guardian **angel** to guide them is a reminder of the protection God provided at the crossing of the sea in the pillar of cloud and fire (14:19). The **Name** (capitalized as shorthand for Yahweh) is in the angel means that the angel was powerful, effective, but as a messenger, not capable of forgiving **rebellion.** The people would rebel against the angel's guidance in 32:23, and the Lord had to intervene to forgive (34:6–7). The angel was not the Lord, but would deliver the guidance and protection of the Lord. The alternate use of the angel and "I" (the Lord) as subjects in verses 22–23 is typical of the interaction of the Lord and angels with people in Scripture. In the end, Moses' conversations were always directly with the Lord and never with the angel. The effectiveness of the presence of the messenger was that he would **oppose those who oppose** the children of Israel. Verses 27–31 describe the details.

The Lord had **prepared** a **place**, which was the land of Canaan. The Lord does not hesitate to say **I will wipe them out** ("blot out as nations"). The purpose of the deliverance from Egypt was that the people could serve the Lord in the land of the **Amorites, Hittites, Perizzites, Canaanites, Hivites and Jebusites.** God's intent throughout Exodus is consistent—to drive out the people of the land for their abominations and to give the land to Israel. In this way God would redeem the people and redeem the land (Lev.

18:24–27). The fulfillment of this promise meant the dispossession of another people group.

The first warning against **their gods** comes in five pithy instructions: **"Do not bow down . . . or worship . . . or follow their practices. You must demolish them and break their sacred stones to pieces"** (v. 24). The adoption of the false gods of the peoples of the land was an enduring problem. The worst offenses of their practices were child sacrifices to Molech (Deut. 12:31; 18:9–12) and detestable sexual practices (described in Lev. 18:3–30). The words "break their sacred stones" refer to the Canaanite veneration of sexuality and fertility. The Canaanites erected single stone pillars as dwellings for local gods (see also 34:13; Deut. 12:3–4). The physical act of breaking the pillars of false gods demonstrated their impotence (see also Judg. 6:25–32). The section we labeled B' above (vv. 32–33) expands this warning against "their gods."

The central section (C) describes the *blessings* of worshiping **the LORD your God** (vv. 25–26). It is the positive counterpoint to the rejection of the gods of Canaan. Worship of the Creator promised to bring a fourfold blessing: nourishment, health, fertility, and long life. The Lord of creation promised great gifts. For **"his blessing will be on your food and water. I will take away sickness from among you, and none will miscarry or be barren in your land. I will give you a full life span."** The Lord made a similar promise of health at Marah, after the Israelites crossed the sea. Deuteronomy 7:12–26 and 28:1–14 expand these blessings. The promises were bound to the worship of the true God, a central concern of Exodus.

Section A' again promises that the Lord will act to take the land from the Canaanites (vv. 27–31). Here the text does not mention the angel and the Lord directly explains the plan for fighting for them. Seven times the Lord says, "I will." **"I will send my terror ahead of you . . . throw into confusion . . . make all your enemies turn their backs and run . . . send the hornet ahead of you . . . drive them out before you** ("little by little") **. . . establish your borders . . . hand over to you the people who live in the land."** The Lord's commitment to fight meant that there would not be any significant military opposition to settling in the land. The confusion of the Lord (along with hailstones) defeated the five kings of the Amorites when they attacked at Gibeon (Josh. 10:10–11; see also Exod. 14:24; 1 Sam. 7:10; 14:15; Isa. 24:17–20; Jer. 48:44). The Lord's promises end with the expectation that the people would have to participate in driving them out.

The book of the covenant concludes as it began, with a reiteration of the warning against false gods (20:23; 23:32–33). **"Do not make a covenant with them or with their gods"** was a warning against breaking the covenant that was about to be confirmed (24:7–8) between the people and the Lord. Here we see a fuller revelation of the Lord's will for the people fleshing out the covenant with Abraham, Isaac, and Jacob (2:24; 6:4–5) which formed the foundation for the exodus. Any covenant the people would make with the Canaanites or with their gods **will certainly be a snare** to Israel and **cause** them **to sin against** the Lord. The first enticement would come sooner rather than later, in Exodus 32:4, 8. After that crisis, God will repeat and elaborate upon these words (34:11–16).

Additional Notes §28

23:10–11 / The seventh-year releases in vv. 10–11, Lev. 25:2–7, and Deut. 15:1–11 are excellent examples of three perspectives on a similar law. In Exodus, the motivation for the release is a singular concern for the poor and for animals in an agrarian economy. The well-being of God's creation is the primary concern. In Leviticus the Sabbath year is for the land and to the Lord. Time and space (land) are sacred because the Lord says, "the land is mine" (Lev. 25:23). The land will produce what they need when they allow it to rest. The concern reflects an ecological principle of the Lord's care for the nonhuman creation. Deuteronomy 15:1–11 does not mention the land but instead specifies a seventh-year release of general debts (release of debt slaves follows in vv. 12–18). This reflects a more urban setting and concern for the poor man, "your brother . . . in your town." The motive is general prosperity and remembrance of God's grace in redemption.

23:28 / The great Spanish rabbi of the Middle Ages, Moses Maimonides (ca. 1338–1204) extended this law to separate the preparation and serving of all kinds of meat from dairy products (e.g., using two sets of utensils and dishes).

23:23 / Only God has the proper authority to give land and displace people. The Native American perspective on the dispossession of a people by another people seeking liberation from the religious oppression of Europe is an important corrective in interpreting this feature in Exodus. Warrior has rightly noted that using the exodus simply as a paradigm of liberation is problematic, since the liberated people have to displace another people in order to be established as a people (Warrior, "Native American Perspective"). The God of Exodus cannot be separated from the God of Joshua. Only the Lord can justly take the prerogative to displace a people. God also takes the land from Israel (Lev. 24:26).

23:24 / Archaeologists have found many sacred stone monuments. The people sometimes used single-stone pillars to worship the Lord. See Gen. 28:16–22; Isa. 19:19. God forbade the people to use them for this purpose because of their association with false gods in Deut. 16:22.

23:28 / "Hornet" follows the LXX. The Heb. *tsir'ah* means "panic" (see also Josh. 24:12). Hornets in the vanguard would certainly be effective in bringing panic. The list of people groups is abridged from v. 23. This is common practice in Exodus and carries no special significance. The few represent the whole. Compare 3:8, 17; 13:5, 11; 23:23, 28; 33:2; 34:11.

23:31 / The idealized "borders" here are from the **desert** (the Negev wilderness) to **the River** (the Euphrates) and **the Sea of the Philistines** (the Mediterranean) to the **Red Sea** (Sea of Reeds). The "Red Sea" is taken to mean the Gulf of Aqaba because as a SE limit it stands opposite the Mediterranean as a NW limit. Even the largest kingdom of Solomon did not include all this territory (from Egypt to Mesopotamia).

§29 The Covenant Is Received and Sealed (Exod. 24:1–18)

Exodus 24 is reminiscent of the beginning of the Sinai journey, where the Lord also was present visibly and conversed with Moses. (See the structural outline of Exodus 19–24 in the introduction to Exodus 19.) The narratives of Exodus 19 and 24 serve as bookends for the law of Exodus 20–23, setting the covenant-giving in the midst of the story of God's grace and guidance. With the covenant, as in the exodus itself, the people initially followed God's instruction and accepted his provision by faith (19:8; 24:3, 7).

Moses' conversation with the Lord on the mountain continued briefly before Moses went back down (vv. 1–2). The people immediately agreed to the Lord's proposed covenant and three acts of confirmation followed. First, the people participated in a ceremony of acceptance (vv. 3–8). Then, seventy-four men partially ascended the mountain and ate a meal in the Lord's presence (vv. 9–11). Moses then ascended to the top to receive the stone tablets, while the people watched the fiery cloud of the Lord's glory surround him. Moses remained on the mountain for a longer period this time, in order to receive detailed instructions.

24:1–8 / God outlined the threefold confirmation of the book of the covenant before Moses' descent (vv. 1–2). The people would confirm it first, then the elders and, finally, God with Moses alone. **"Come up to the Lord, you and Aaron, Nadab and Abihu, and seventy of the elders of Israel . . . but Moses alone is to approach the Lord . . . And the people may not come up with him."** God asked Moses to climb up while the elders, Aaron, and two of his sons worshiped at a distance. God alone controlled the terms of access. Yet all in this group were close enough to see "the God of Israel" (v. 10). At the end of the chapter all the people saw "the glory of the Lord" (v. 17).

In order for Moses to bring the elders up, he first had to go down to the people. This was his fourth trip down the mountain and his fifth climb up (up/down in 19:3/7; 19:8/14; 19:20/25; 20:21/ 24:3; 24:9, further up in 24:13/32:15; 34:4/34:29). His fifth climb involved three stages: with the elders; with Aaron and sons part way; with Joshua a bit further (v. 13a); and alone to the top (v. 13b). He stayed on the mountain for forty days (v. 18; 32:15). The text mentions for the first time here that there were seventy elders, having referred to them earlier as "capable men," chosen at Jethro's counsel to serve as judges and administrators of the people (18:21–26; see also Num. 11:16–17, 24–25; Deut. 1:9–18).

The first confirmation of the book of the covenant began **When Moses went** down the mountain and **told the people all the LORD's words and laws.** The "words" (20:1) referred to the Ten Commandments (lit., "ten words," 34:28) and the "laws" referred to the ordinances of the book of the covenant (21:1). The people responded exactly as they had at the first theophany of thunder, trumpet, and lightning: **"Everything the LORD has said we will do"** (19:8; 24:3, 7).

The people then confirmed their verbal agreement to accept the covenant in six responsive actions. It began when Moses **wrote down everything.** Their agreement with the Lord would be based on written law. Secondly, Moses **built an altar . . . and set up twelve stone pillars** as a place for them to gather before the Lord. The altar represented God's presence and the "twelve stone pillars" represented the twelve tribes and were also gathering points for each of the tribes. God had forbidden such pillars as objects of worship in 23:24. But these represented the tribes of the people, not gods.

The third responsive act was the preparation of whole **burnt offerings** and the roasting of **young bulls as fellowship offerings** (on offerings, see comment on 20:24). Moses sent **young Israelite men,** since no priesthood was yet in place (28:1). The people ate the fellowship (*shalom*) offerings as a sign of communion with the Lord and their acceptance of the covenant. As always, all the fat and **the blood** belonged to the Lord. Moses saved **half of the blood and put it in bowls** for the ritual sprinkling in verse 8.

The fourth act of the people was to listen to Moses' reading of the book (20:22–23:33 in its final form). Previously the people had heard his oral report and affirmed it (v. 3). In a similar way, the people publicly and unanimously approved the formal document, now named the **Book of the Covenant,** as the fifth response. The people added the words **"we will obey"** (*shamaʿ*, or "we will listen").

The most dramatic action was the sixth: **Moses then took the blood, sprinkled it on the people and said, "This is the blood of [the book of] the covenant."** The people agreed to live in a newly ordered society, governed by the words of the creating and redeeming Lord. The people's confirmation of the book of the covenant was an important purpose of the exodus. The book would be read aloud yearly in Canaan as a covenant renewal ceremony (see Josh. 24:25–27; 2 Kgs. 23:2; Neh. 8:5–9).

The sealing of the agreement with the powerful symbol of lifeblood in this context represents the life God gives in the laws of the book of the covenant (Lev. 17:11, 14; Deut. 12:23). The law was life. "Young men" and "young bulls" emphasize this symbol. The lifeblood of the animal that God created communicated this gift of new life in the just ordering of relationships in the book (see comment on 23:10).

Under other circumstances the people were never to touch sacrificed blood, which belonged to God alone. The sharing of the blood with God bound them to the Lord's gift. In Leviticus, by contrast, blood cleansed people from sin. In the NT, Jesus said, "This [cup] is my blood of the covenant," combining the image of the meal of the elders (v. 11), the sprinkled blood upon the people, and the Levitical cleansing from sin (Matt. 26:28; Mark 14:24; 1 Cor. 11:25).

24:9–18 / The second confirmation of the covenant involved the elders eating a meal of celebration and communion with the Lord (vv. 9–11; see additional note on 18:12). Eating and drinking together was a common way to confirm a covenant (Gen. 26:28–30; Deut. 27:1–8). Following instructions (v. 2), Moses, Aaron and his two sons, **and the seventy elders of Israel went up and saw the God of Israel.** They partially ascended and worshiped "at a distance" (v. 1), eating and drinking with God in view (v. 11). God took a physical form that could be seen, as the text repeats, using two words to say, "they saw" God (v. 10 *ra'ah*, v. 11 *khazah*). The second word denotes an intense perception of what is actually there and is true.

The claim that they saw God is surprising, but so also is their awareness that this was a potentially dangerous situation. **God did not raise his hand against these leaders.** It was commonly known that one could not see God and live (33:20; see also Judg. 6:22–23). Yet God remained free to make exceptions, taking a visible physical form as with the seventy, later with Moses (33:11), and in the incarnation. Although **they saw God, and they ate and drank,** the text focuses on God's feet and **something like a pavement made of sapphire, clear as the sky itself** (lit., "sapphire like the bones [essence] of heaven in clarity"). "Clear as the deep blue sky" also communicates the Hebrew combination of the blue of sapphire (lapis lazuli) and the clarity of the sight.

The third confirmation of the book of the covenant was Moses' call to receive **the tablets of stone.** The final content of the tablets he would receive is not clear in this text, which refers to nonspecific **law and commands.** He did not descend from the mountain for eight chapters (32:15). When he descended, the tablets, described as two tablets, were called the Testimony, and inscribed with the Ten Commandments' "ten words" (32:15; 34:28–29). Moses' forty days on the mountain provide a major segue for the addition of detailed instructions for the tabernacle.

Leaving the elders, **Moses set out with Joshua** for some unspecified distance. Then Moses continued **up on the mountain of God** to the top for the fifth, but not the last, time. We do not hear about Joshua again until they both come down in 32:17. In their absence, Moses arranged for the smooth administration of justice by appointing **Aaron and Hur** as the highest court of appeal. Even in the midst of a theophany, an intact justice system was an important concern. Apparently the elders were close enough to the Israelite camp that **anyone involved in a dispute** could **go to them.**

Moses ascended to the top while the people saw the fiery **cloud** of the Lord's glory around him. The people witnessed Moses' forty day meeting with the Lord by means of the visible **glory of the LORD.** To the people and the elders it **looked like a consuming fire on top of the mountain.** After their experience with the trumpet, thunder, and lightning in Exodus 19, there could be no doubt that Moses was with the Lord (see also 40:34–38).

This has been called an ideal end to the Sinai narrative (see additional note). God had delivered the people from bondage and brought them through the trials of the desert; they had agreed to serve the Lord and received the book of the covenant and, in Exodus 24, they had unanimously confirmed their allegiance to the Lord. The confirmation meal was a celebration of a new gift and beginning for the emerging people of God. The laws of the covenant provided the possibility of life within the created order and with the blessing of the Creator. Yet the exodus from Egypt was not at an end, nor was their experience complete. They would doubt and rebel again, to their peril. They would also celebrate again. The Lord's forgiveness and further self-revelation after the crisis of the calf would draw them into the exuberant building of the tabernacle (36:3, 6–7).

Moses did not leave the mountain for **forty days and forty nights.** Waiting this length of time became an issue for the people. Six weeks was a long time to wait, and they would fear that Moses had died (32:1). Meanwhile, God dedicated the time on the mountain to giving Moses detailed instructions for a place of worship for the people. God did not intend to stay on the mountain, but to travel with them. The instructions for the tabernacle, which begin without further introduction (25:1), are the focus of most of the remaining chapters of the book of Exodus.

Additional Notes §29

24:4 / Writing the book of the covenant is Moses' second of three works (17:4; 24:4; 34:27–28). The Lord also writes, in stone (v. 12; 32:15–16). Moses may have written on leather or papyrus scrolls or on clay tablets. The Heb. expression "cut a covenant" (NIV "made a covenant") in v. 8 may refer to cutting words into clay or stone or to cutting an animal skin, or even the animal itself as a confirmation offering.

24:8 / The use of blood in the consecration of priests (Lev. 8:30) has led commentators to view the sprinkling of blood at Sinai as the consecration of the whole people as a holy people (19:6; E. W. Nicholson, "The Covenant Ritual in Exodus XXIV 3–8," VT 32 [1982], 74–86). Priests also used sprinkled water (mixed with a little ash from a burnt offering) in rites to purify unclean people (Num. 19:17–22). The author of Hebrews compared the "sprinkled blood" of Jesus' death to blood sprinkled on the altar (Heb. 9:7, 12; 10:19; 13:11–12) and to the cleansing of the people (Heb. 9:13–15; 19–22a; 10:22).

24:10 / The discomfort that the words "saw God" caused is evident in early translations of this text. The LXX has "saw the place" and the Targumim have "saw the glory."

24:16b / Even Moses, who had led the people out of Egypt, suffered their complaints, and received the Lord's instructions on the mountain many times, was required to wait. Not until the seventh day did the Lord call to Moses from within the cloud.

24:18 / Durham calls Exod. 24 an ideal end rather than the real end, which comes in Exod. 32–34 (Durham, *Exodus*, p. 247). I would suggest that chs. 32–34 are also short of the real ending, which comes after the Lord's forgiveness in Exod. 34. It even comes after hearts were moved (35:21) and "people continued to bring freewill offerings morning after morning" (36:3b). The real end to the Sinai narrative in Exodus comes in Exod. 40 when the people have built and consecrated the tabernacle, they know and keep the book of the covenant, and the glory of the Lord fills the tabernacle, day after day in the sight of all Israel.

§30 Introduction to the Tabernacle (Exod. 25–40)

The thirteen chapters that describe the tabernacle have posed a challenge for interpreters since the time of Philo (d. 50 A.D.). In *The Life of Moses* Philo gave a symbolic reading that has influenced interpretation to the present day. For him, the tent of meeting represented the spiritual world and the courtyard signified the material world. The colors (blue, purple, crimson and white) represented the basic elements; the seven lights of the lampstand were the seven planets; and the twelve precious stones were the twelve signs of the Zodiac. Josephus and the early Christian interpreters Clement and Jerome, who wrote after the destruction of the temple in Jerusalem, interpreted it in a similar way. Origen added a symbolic moral dimension that held sway through the Middle Ages: the gold, silver, and bronze respectively represented faith, the preached word, and patience. The Protestant tradition continued the symbolic interpretation for the Christian church. The holy of holies was a sign of the invisible and triumphant church of Christ and the courtyard was the visible and militant congregation. The most complete attempt to deal with all the details of the tabernacle as symbols was by Baehr in 1837 (Childs, *Exodus*, pp. 547–48). A more recent theological reading of Christ and the tabernacle is Poythress, *The Shadow of Christ*.

The nineteenth century brought literary criticism to bear upon the text. Scholars in this tradition identified the tabernacle description as the work of the so-called P (priestly writer) and discredited it as a "pious fiction" of priests writing in the postexilic period. It was thought that the verisimilitude of the detail was an attempt to justify their craft in Israel. Not until the twentieth century did interpreters seek to recover the positive role of the priestly writer. The current consensus among historical scholars is that the tent of meeting and the ark-tabernacle traditions have ancient roots. Much more could be said with respect to the scholarly debates on this subject. For further information on the priestly role, see Eichrodt, von Rad, et al. who argued for the positive priestly role. Childs summarizes the scholarship in *Exodus,* pp. 530–37, 550. Scholars still debate the process of writing and editing the tent and tabernacle traditions. See Durham, *Exodus,* p. 353, for a clear discussion; see also Haran, "The Nature of the *'ohel mo'edh.*" The final form of the tabernacle description would have been a comfort and source of hope to the people in the Babylonian exile. See Fretheim's seven points on the value of the repetitive detail (Fretheim, *Exodus,* pp. 264–65).

Interpreters are just beginning to recover a theological interpretation of the tabernacle of Exodus that provides a middle road between metaphorical imagination and historical dismissals.

There is a scriptural context for the tabernacle. "Then have them make a sanctuary for me, and I will dwell among them. Make this tabernacle and all its furnishings exactly like the pattern I will show you" (25:8–9). The tabernacle was a new paradigm for God's relationship to the people. God took the initiative to live among them in a very specific way. The Lord would not remain on the distant horizon in a cloud, or unapproachable on a mountain, but would be present in the midst of the camp. God was not geographically fixed at Sinai, but was and would be mobile, traveling with them in the wilderness toward the land of promise.

Creation and the tabernacle. Many elements of the tabernacle texts also occur in Genesis 1–2. This intentional reflection of the creation weights the significance of the tabernacle as a new creation of the Lord. Rabbinic interpreters have long recognized the echoes of creation in a variety of texts. The Creator was doing something new in directing the building of the tabernacle. The Spirit of God, present at creation (Gen. 1:2) filled Bezalel and the craftsmen who created the tabernacle with creative gifts (Exod. 31:1–11). Israel made the tabernacle, even as God made the world, as a dwelling place for God (Exod. 25:8–9; Ps. 104:1–4). God instructed them to erect the tabernacle on New Year's Day to underscore this new beginning (Exod. 40:2, 17).

The extended description of the tabernacle also mirrors the seven days of creation in Genesis 1. Seven times the Lord spoke to Moses about what the people should make (25:8; 30:11, 17, 22, 34; 31:1, 12). The Hebrew word for "make" (*'asah*) frequently refers to the Lord's making the world (Gen. 1:7, 16, 25, 26, 31; 2:3–4, 18; 3:21). In the seventh speech about the tabernacle the Lord speaks about the Sabbath rest (Exod. 31:12–18).

When the people had completed the tabernacle, Moses spoke words that were similar to God's assessment of creation ("and

God saw that it was good"). Moses inspected and "saw" that they had made the tabernacle, "just as the LORD had commanded" (39:43; 40:16, 19, 21, 23, 25, 27, 29, 32). Jon Levenson concludes that "the depiction of the sanctuary as a world, that is, an ordered, supportive, and obedient environment" corresponds to the description of creation in Genesis 1 (Levenson, *Creation*, p. 86). Fretheim adds, "The tabernacle is a microcosm of creation, the world order as God intended it writ small in Israel, a beginning in God's mission to bring creation to the point where it is perfectly reflective of the divine will" (Fretheim, "Whole Earth," p. 238; see also Fretheim, *Exodus*, pp. 268–72).

The clearest representations of the creation come from the detailed descriptions of the tabernacle itself. Exodus 25 begins with raw materials: metals (gold, silver, bronze), linen (flax), goat's wool, leather hides, dyes (red from grubs, blue from snails, purple mixed), acacia wood, olive oil, semiprecious gems, spices for fragrant oil, and incense imported from around the ancient Near East. Other materials are present as images: almonds, trees, flowers, and pomegranates. The construction of the tabernacle required the gifts created by artists and artisans: spinning, weaving, sewing, dyeing, metallurgy, woodworking, lapidary, making perfume, and tanning. Even the specific dimensions of objects may be tied to the creation: those given for the ark of the covenant and its cover (at the center of the tabernacle) are 5:3, which is very close to the so-called "golden ratio" (phi = 1.618) found in the spiral of sea shells, pine cones, the head of a daisy, the proportions of the human face, and many other natural objects.

The daily work within the tabernacle involved the basics of human life: light, oil, bread, water, meat, fire, and the protection of the cherubim, represented on the ark and woven into garments. The tabernacle engaged all five senses: the sound of bells on Aaron's hem; the smell of the fragrant oil that anointed everything; the sight of brightly-colored blue, purple, and scarlet curtains; the taste of meat from the altar, the only source from the domestic herds; and the texture of the curtains that formed the tabernacle walls. The tabernacle was, like the creation, simple yet opulent in its furnishing.

The tabernacle and incarnation. The tabernacle provided, for the first time since Eden, a place for the visible presence of God in the midst of the people. The Gospel of John provides a window that helps Christians interpret the significance of the tabernacle in relation to the incarnation. John 1:14–18 uses the words and images of the tabernacle in order to describe what God was doing in Jesus: "The Word became flesh and made his dwelling among us. We have seen his glory" (John 1:14–15a). The specificity of the person of Jesus walking in the flesh among the people matches the detailed descriptions of the tent of meeting as a location of God's presence (Exod. 25:22; 29:42–43; 30:6, 36). The phrase "made his dwelling (lit., "tented") among us" echoes the repeated words of the Lord, "Make this tabernacle" and "I will dwell among them" (25:8-9; 29:45–46). In Greek, "dwelling" is literally "live in a tent." John's words "We have seen his glory" also reflect Israel's experience, first on the mountain (24:16–17), but more substantially in the tabernacle (29:42–46; 40:34–38). The glory of the Lord "settled" (lit., "dwelt," or *shakan*) on the tent of meeting (40:35). The Lord "dwelt" (*shakan*) with Israel in the tabernacle (*mishkan*, lit., "dwelling place") for over 300 years before the building of the temple in Jerusalem. Many other echoes of the tabernacle texts are present in John 1 (see Hooker, "Johannine Prologue"). Exodus 34:6 is especially well represented in the words "full of grace and truth" (John 1:14) particularly resonate with Exodus 34:6. See also Exodus 33:18–23 as a background to John 1:18.

Revelation continues with the theme of the Lord's "tenting" with the people. God spread his tent of the new heavens over the people (Rev. 7:15; 21:3). The book of Hebrews draws on the pattern of heaven (Exod. 25:9, 40) focused on the new creation and the image of the eternal tabernacle in heaven where Christ has become the high priest (Heb. 8:2–5; 9:11).

The tabernacle and the golden calf. The worship of God, who has created and redeemed Israel, is a primary concern of this section. We can see this clearly in the narrative flow and structure of Exodus 25–40.

A   Exod. 25–31 tabernacle *instructions*

B   Exod. 32–34 golden calf, the people's (in)decision

A' Exod. 35–40 tabernacle *building*

God gave the instructions for the tabernacle to Moses on the mountain, while the people waited below. Their anxiety and impatience led to flagrant rebellion. In the aftermath of all God's activity on their behalf, the people said of the calf: "These are your gods, O Israel, who brought you up out of Egypt" (32:4). At the people's initiative, Aaron commanded that the gold be brought.

They built this calf without planning or lengthy labor to give the people immediate access to a visible, impersonal god.

Only after Moses' lengthy intervention and God's decision to forgive and remain with the people does the narrative return to the joyful and thankful building of the tabernacle. At this juncture, voluntary obedience by the people was the only worthy response. The materials were a freewill and heartfelt offering (as God instructed in 25:2). They fashioned the various elements of the tabernacle through a lengthy creative process. The design reflected the holiness of the invisible, personal, and active God (Fretheim, *Exodus*, p. 267). The calf was a humanly controlled object of worship, but the tabernacle was a place to meet the living God.

God is in the details. The lists of materials for curtains, supports, rings, bases, beams, and supports in these thirteen chapters (one third of the book) have seemed tedious to some interpreters. In addition to the extensive detail, Exodus 25–31 and 35–39 essentially repeat much of the same material. This intimate attention to detail, however, is exactly the point. If readers view this minutia only as a "problem," they will miss the value of its rhetorical impact. When God broke into history to deliver a specific people, the details were the story. Exodus gives great detail concerning Moses' call, the oppression, the plagues, the escape from Egypt, and the laws of the book of the covenant. It devotes even more detail to weaving, metallurgy, and leatherwork and many other details of the tabernacle. These chapters reveal much about God in relation to the world.

It is difficult to imagine how God would live in the midst of a people who had said to Moses, "Speak to us yourself and we will listen. But do not have God speak to us or we will die" (20:19). God's concern for the detail in the tabernacle is partly a response to this problem. God's intention was to be present without overwhelming the people. God sought the intimacy of daily relationship (as in the details of the law) and presence, yet also required differentiation from the people. God is *immanent* as well as *transcendent*. We can see this reflected in the physical detail that God designed (25:9; 40; 27:8).

As in all of Exodus, as God instructed the people concerning the details of the home they were to build (25:2; 31:3) so God gave quite specific instructions, leaving gaps where the creative work of Moses or the craftsmen could move forward. God would not dwell among them as a trumpet blast and lightning storm, but neither would God dwell as a common member of the community. Only the creation of the world and the incarnation match the weight of this radical historical and theological move. It is the mid-point in God's self-revelation and thus appropriately occurs in the book of Exodus. God was and is a redeemer who dwells among those God loves.

The detailed description of the tabernacle demonstrates more than the general axiom "God is in the details" (however true that may be). Rather, the details are there precisely because God wanted a tabernacle that was beautiful in a specific way, marked with gold almonds (not silver) and curtains made with three colors (blue, purple, and crimson). God came down to dwell in a place designed according to what God personally desired. The text claims to teach about God's preferences, not simply to record how to construct, reconstruct, or imagine Israel's portable worship space.

If we interpret Exodus 25–31 and 35–40 solely by means of sociological-religious categories, we will not understand the full impact of the text. Readers have rarely taken the text at face value for what it says about itself. More often than not, the text has suffered from interpreters' preoccupation with its historical context (variously exilic, Davidic, or Second Temple) as Israel's idealized worship space. Scholars differ widely on the sociohistorical setting, in part because the text is not interested in giving any clues about it. The plan is from God (25:9). The pressure for commentators to make a sociohistorical decision, especially in this case, has often prevented theological reflection that takes the physical details of the tabernacle as a serious theological revelation. (For an exception see Jacob, *Exodus*, pp. 758–934.)

§31 I Will Dwell Among Them: Materials, Ark, Table, and Lampstand (Exod. 25:1–40)

The lengthy instructions for the tabernacle highlight the overarching purpose of the deliverance from Egypt. It was a movable, physical place for the people to worship and serve the Lord. God designed the place for God's presence in their midst for daily service and worship. At center stage was the ark, containing the Ten Commandments, and the ark cover, for the "covering" of sins.

The terminology we will use here attempts to be consistent with the primary uses of the words in the biblical text. Therefore we use the word *tabernacle* (*mishkan*, lit., "dwelling place") to refer to the whole structure including the encompassing courtyard curtains, the altar of burnt offering, the bronze washing basin, and the "tent of meeting" (*ʾohel moʿed*). The tent of meeting includes the holy place (with the bread table, lampstand, and incense altar) and the holy of holies containing the ark of the covenant. Exodus 26 uses a few of these words in a special sense: "tent" (*ʾohel*, 26:7) refers to the outer goat hair covering of the tent of meeting; and "tabernacle" here refers only to the inner linen layer (26:1).

Moses had used an earlier version of the "tent of meeting" to meet with Yahweh before they constructed the tabernacle court. "Now Moses used to take a tent and pitch it outside the camp some distance away, calling it the 'tent of meeting.' Anyone inquiring of the LORD would go to the tent of meeting outside the camp" (Exod. 33:7). The tabernacle brought the place of meeting into the midst of the camp. The Lord designated the entrance to the tent of meeting and the space above the cover of the ark specifically as the places of meeting (25:22; 29:42–43; 30:6; Num. 12:5; Deut. 31:14–15).

25:1–9 / The Lord instructed Moses to take a freewill offering to supply specific materials for this dwelling place in the midst of the camp. These verses provide a key for understanding Exodus 25–31 and 35–40. The enterprise was to begin with an offering from the heart. **"You are to receive the offering for me from**

each man whose heart prompts him to give." Since the Lord would be very specific about the design and artistry of the tabernacle, this list of raw materials was also very specific. The patterns, in uniquely specific detail, were God's (vv. 9, 40).

The metals were **gold, silver and bronze.** "Bronze" is sometimes translated copper, but interpreters deduce the harder alloy (primarily copper with tin) from the context. The gold was of two grades. They used "pure gold" (*zahab tahor*) for the ark, cover, lampstand, table, and incense altar. They used ordinary gold for the cherubim, the molding and poles of the ark, the table and incense altar, and the gilding of the planks and pillars of the frame for the tent of meeting.

God specified four different materials for making the four-layered walls and ceiling of the tent of meeting. Two were cloth: **fine linen** and spun and woven **goat hair** (see 35:26). Two of the materials were leather: **ram skins dyed red and hides of sea cows.** "Dyed red" may simply mean "tanned," which has a reddening effect. Interpreters have found a variety of possibilities for "sea cows," but it was very likely fine dugong leather which would have been available from the Red Sea.

Three different dyes created three colors of linen thread: **blue, purple and scarlet.** The blue was probably from a Mediterranean mollusk (*murex trunculus* snail) and the scarlet from grubs (Heb. "red worm," probably from *coccidae*).

The NIV use of the word **yarn** with the colors is misleading, as it does not appear in the Hebrew text. Translators have puzzled over verse 4 because it seems to be missing a noun. The separation of the words for "colors" and "fine linen" with the conjunction *vav* (that is often, but by no means always, translated "and") has been the source of this confusion. Thus the NIV supplies "yarn *and* fine linen" (RSV "stuff and fine twined linen;" NASB "*material*, fine linen;" NKJ "*thread*, fine linen"). The conjunction, however, is most likely the *explicative*, meaning "specifically" (Williams, *Syntax*, §434). A working translation of this list-like form would be something like "blue, purple, and scarlet; specifically linen." The words are reversed, but have the same meaning in 26:1—fine-spun linen; specifically blue, purple, and scarlet. If it is necessary to supply a noun, thread (in italics) would perhaps be best, since they would have used flax thread in weaving linen. Since the text doesn't mention any colors for the fine linen outer walls of the tabernacle courtyard (27:18), we assume that they were not dyed but left white. This may also account for the fact that the supply list mentions the colors separately from the fabric.

The "fine linen" was made from flax. Egypt was famous for its weaving of extremely fine linen (200 threads per inch). Some of the Israelites would have likely gained this skill while working in Egypt (26:1, 31; see also Gen. 41:42; Ezek. 27:7). "Fine linen" (*shesh*) is an Egyptian loanword that also means "six" in Hebrew. The Egyptian word for six had a similar sound (two letters "s," also known as byssus). The word may have meant that the spun flax threads were six-ply (six strands per thread). They then wove these threads of *shesh*. Thinner strands and threads made finer linen fabric.

The **acacia wood** was from a tree widely used in Egypt and found in the Sinai wilderness, represented by hundreds of species, some straight enough to make lumber. They used this hardwood, which was relatively light in weight, for the framework of the tabernacle and tent, for the structure of the ark, and also for the other furnishings (table, incense altar, and burnt offering altar).

The **olive oil for the light** was for the golden lampstand and its service, which Aaron's sons were to keep burning all night (27:20–21). The **spices for the anointing oil** were myrrh, cinnamon, fragrant cane, and cassia (30:23–25). They were to anoint everything (30:26–30). God's dwelling was a fragrant place in the midst of other wilderness smells. God also specified that they use these spices in a precise recipe for **the fragrant incense** (30:34–36) for the incense altar in front of the curtain to the most holy place (30:6–8).

Craftsmen were to engrave the two **onyx stones** with the names of the tribes of Israel and mount them on Aaron's **ephod**. Onyx is a kind of fine quartz (see 28:9). The ephod was the high priest's vest-like garment made of gold and linen, over which he wore the **breastpiece**. Exodus 28:6–21 describes these articles of clothing and the twelve various **gems** mounted on the breastpiece.

Verses 8–9 are a necessary guide to understanding the purpose and function of the tabernacle (see Introduction to the Tabernacle in §30). **"Then have them make a sanctuary for me, and I will dwell among them. Make this tabernacle and all its furnishings exactly like the pattern I will show you."** The people were to participate in the creation of the tabernacle and all its furnishings. This word for "make" (vv. 8, 9) occurs in Genesis to refer to God's creating. The people participated in this creation, then, by using the materials God had designated.

The words "a sanctuary for me" mean "a place set apart" or "holy place" for the Lord to dwell among them. This was not primarily a congregational space. While it was also a space for meeting God, it was first of all a space for God in the midst of the camp. In the midst of their living, eating, and sleeping place would be God's dwelling place. It was holy because of God's presence. God was the people's source of holiness (31:13; Lev. 20:8; 21:8; 22:32).

The Lord asked them to make "this tabernacle and all its furnishings exactly like the pattern I will show you." The people built the tabernacle based on God's model (or blueprint). "Pattern" means "building plan" or "construction plan," and so God was the architect. God showed Moses the plan while on the mountain, in addition to describing it (25:40; 26:30; 27:8). Because God was to live there, God had a stake in the specific simplicity of furnishing and quality of materials and workmanship.

The Hebrew word for "tabernacle" (*mishkan*) means "dwelling place," built from the verb root used in verse 8, "I will *dwell* among them" (*shakan*). The Hebrew root for "dwelling place" is not the verb *yashab* ("sit," "remain for a while") but the verb *shakan* ("settle down," "abide"). The Lord did not come for a visit, but rather to live among them. On the other hand, God did not live *in* the tabernacle but dwelt among the people (v. 8), visibly descending to and ascending from the sanctuary. The text reveals the enduring presence as well as the mobility of God. Later Jewish tradition used the same root for the word *shekinah* to refer to the dwelling presence of the Lord.

25:10–22 / God begins the instructions by describing a chest called **the ark of the Testimony** (v. 22, or "covenant"). In Exodus the ark was important because it contained the "Testimony" of the Ten Commandments on tablets of stone (v. 16). Secondly, **the cover on top of the ark,** under the protection of the cherubim, was the place where God would meet Moses and, through him, Israel (v. 22). Leviticus 16 more fully describes the atoning function of this meeting place. From this place, God would make known and demonstrate to Israel the forgiveness of sin, year after year. This means of grace would continue to make it possible for the people to live with the Lord in their midst.

The ark was a **chest of acacia wood.** "Chest" (*'aron*) is a generic word for any box. It refers to a "coffin" in Genesis 50:26 and a "treasure chest" in 2 Kings 12:10. (The word for Noah's "ark" is different—*tebah*.) The ark measured **two and a half cubits long, a**

cubit and a half wide, and a cubit and a half high. A "cubit" ("fore-arm") was the distance from the elbow to the end of the middle finger. The ancient world used various measures, but the generally accepted length of a cubit was between seventeen and a half and eighteen inches. The ark was approximately forty-five inches by twenty-seven inches by twenty-seven inches. The ratio between its length and width is five to three—close to what, as we have seen, has recently been termed the "golden ratio."

They were to cover the ark **with pure gold, both inside and out.** The **gold molding around it** would have been decorative, but it probably also functioned as a rim to secure the lid, that had the same dimensions as the box. The design was left to the artisans who made it. God also left the design of the **four gold rings,** the dimensions of the **poles** that fit into them, and the **four feet** (or "corners") to the artisans. The poles were also made of **acacia wood** and overlaid with ordinary gold. They were perpetually **to remain in the rings of this ark.** In this way the Lord's meeting place would remain as mobile as the people (Num. 9:22).

The Testimony (i.e., the tablets of stone with the commandments) would be a reminder of the covenant God made with the people at Sinai. Its words reminded them that the Lord had delivered them from Egypt and made them into a people belonging to God. The **atonement cover of pure gold** (*kapporet*) was literally "a cover" for the ark. The translations add the word "atonement" because of its function in Yom Kippur (lit., "day of covering" or day of atonement) described in Leviticus 16:11 as a "covering of sin." The same root word (*kapar*) is translated "atone" in 32:10 and 32:30, which the NIV does consistently in the OT (see the use of the "sprinkled blood" in the discussion of 24:6–8). Martin Luther was the first to translate "cover," based on its function, as "mercy seat." The NT developed the understanding of Christ's "covering" sins (Gk. *ilastē-rion,* Rom. 3:25–26) with the metaphor "clothed in Christ" (Gk. *enduō,* Gal. 3:27; Rom. 13:14 and *epikaluptō,* Rom. 4:7–8).

The artisans were to make the two cherubim of ordinary **hammered gold . . . of one piece with the cover,** wings touching, facing **each other.** Their wings formed a canopy, **overshadowing the cover.** The text does not describe the features of the cherubim in further detail, but it is certain they were not the chubby winged boys of European art. Ezekiel pictures them with four faces each (man, lion, ox, eagle; Ezek. 10:14) and also with two faces (man and lion; Ezek. 41:18–19). Tradition describes them as having the face of a man and the body of a bull or lion (like a sphinx). Their functions are to guard holy things and attend the Lord. In Genesis 3:24, cherubim guarded the entrance to the garden of Eden, in order to protect the tree of life. The cherubim are the Lord's chariot in Psalm 18:10, and also in Ezekiel 10.

Exodus pictures the cherubim as part of the throne where the Lord comes to meet with Moses (see 1 Sam. 4:4). Like the seraphim in Isaiah 6:2, they did not look up at the Lord, but cast their eyes downward **toward the cover** with their wings shielding their eyes from the Lord's presence. God was unseen and the ark contained no image of the Lord. But God told Moses, **"There, above the cover between the two cherubim that are over the ark of the Testimony, I will meet with you."** As a result, tradition has called the ark cover a "footstool" throne, with the throne suspended invisibly between the wings of the cherubim. In other texts, the Lord's throne is *above* the cherubim. It is both locally between and high above the cherubim wings, in the heavens (Pss. 80:1; 99:1; 103:19; 123:1; see also Pss. 89:14; 93:2). The Lord was present, but always mobile. Psalm 11:4 and Isaiah 6:1 suggest that the throne's footstool was on earth, specifically in the temple, symbolized by the ark. The "feet of the Lord" touched the earth first with the ark and later, also accompanied by angels, with the incarnation.

Verse 21 gives us the key to understanding the function of the ark of the covenant. **"Place the cover on top of the ark and put in the ark the Testimony."** The "cover" was the place of the Lord's forgiveness from sin and of meeting the Lord. The "Testimony" was the Ten Commandments. Thus the ark was the place of God's grace and God's law. The ark was in the holiest place (holy of holies) inside the tabernacle. By contrast, the altar of sacrifice was not the holiest place or even in the holy place, but in the courtyard.

Within the holy place were the symbols of God's provision (the light of the lampstand, the bread of the Lord's presence, and the incense altar). But the most holy place held the commandments, the seat of forgiveness under the wings, and a place where Moses could meet with the Lord (25:22; 29:42–43; 30:6, 36). Exodus established that living under God's law, forgiveness, and meeting with the living Lord were the foremost purposes of the tabernacle. Describing the ark first also indicates this superlative position.

25:23–30 / The Lord instructed Moses to make a table, a lampstand, and an incense altar. The ark and its covering were the only items in the holiest place of the tent of meeting. The table, lampstand, and incense altar were the only furnishings in the holy forecourt of the tent, providing light, food, and good fragrance. The table had plates, dishes, pitchers, and bowls that likely held the bread, incense, oil for the lamps, and probably wine for the daily libation (29:40).

The Lord told Moses to **Make a table** to hold the **bread of the Presence** and the **pitchers and bowls for the pouring out of offerings** (vv. 29–30; 37:16). This table has several names in the OT, including "Table of the Presence" (Num. 4:7; see also Lev. 24:6; 2 Chr. 13:11; 29:18; 1 Kgs. 7:48). It was, like the ark, to be made **of acacia wood** (see comment on the wood at v. 5). It was a small table with four legs. The dimensions were ordinary, **two cubits long, a cubit wide, and a cubit and a half high** (approximately 36 in. by 18 in. by 27 in.; see comment at v. 10). Like the ark and its covering it was overlaid **with pure gold** and had a decorative **gold molding around it.** Its unique feature was a decorated **rim a handbreadth wide** (approx. 3 in.). This rim rose above the edge of the table to keep anything from sliding off. The table also was to have **four gold rings** attached high on the **four legs** to hold the two gilded poles for carrying the table.

The function of the table was to hold "the bread of the Presence" in **plates and dishes of pure gold.** The spirit-filled artisans under Bezalel's direction were to design these dishes (31:1–6; 35:30–35). Some dishes held incense for the altar. The Lord describes the twelve loaves of bread in Leviticus 24:5–9.

The priests would eat this unleavened bread in the Lord's presence and replace it every Sabbath. It also had a function in the ordination of priests, where they "waved" it before the Lord (called "shewbread") and added it to the burnt offering (see 29:23–25). This was the bread that David's men ate when they were running from Saul (1 Sam. 21:3–6). The table also held **pure gold** pitchers and bowls for **the pouring out of offerings.** The presence of bread and drink on the table in the tent echoes the meals the elders ate on Mt. Sinai in the Lord's presence (18:12; 24:11). In other ancient Middle Eastern cultures people offered bread and drink to their gods daily. In the tent of meeting the priests consumed the bread (and probably drink, since the bread was a week old) as a sign of relationship with God.

25:31–40 / In the holy place, on the south side of the tent of meeting, stood the **lampstand,** opposite the Table of the Presence. The lampstand (*menorah*) was made of approximately thirty-five kilos (75 pounds, a talent) of pure gold **of one piece.** The text does not give dimensions, leaving the design to the artisans. The talmudic tradition says that it was just over four feet tall (Plaut, *The Torah,* p. 613). It was similar in shape to a sage plant that still grows in the Middle East (*salvia moriah*) but was decorated as an almond tree. It had a central **shaft** from which **Six branches** extended, three on each side, opposite each other. The seventh lamp was in the center on top of the shaft.

Decorative instructions included **Three cups shaped like almond flowers with buds and blossoms** along each of the **six branches.** The central shaft was also to be decorated with **cups shaped like almond flowers,** placed just below each of the sets of opposite branches, with a fourth on the top, just below the lamp. The cupped flowers served to catch any oil that ran down the candlestick. The oil lamps themselves were made separately and placed on the stand.

The function of the lampstand was to **light the space,** providing light in the holy place for the service of the bread of presence and the incense altar. Leviticus 24:2–4 describes its use further. Aaron (and his consecrated sons) kept the lamps burning all night, every night. By contrast, the holiest place with the ark and its covering were pitch black.

The Hebrew word for lampstand is *menorah,* but it differs from the menorah presently used at Hanukkah which has eight lights to commemorate the eight days during which the oil did not run out of the seven lamps in the temple lampstand in the days of the Maccabees (talmudic tradition; see 1 Macc. 4:50). The Talmud prohibited making any other seven-lamp menorah, resulting in six- or eight-branched menorahs (Heb. *menorot*) in synagogues (Tigay, "Exodus," p. 167).

The chapter ends with the reminder that the Lord was critically interested in the design of the lampstand, the table, the ark, and its cover. **"See that you make them according to the pattern shown you on the mountain."** Exodus 26 turns to instructions for creating the space in which the people are to place these furnishings.

Additional Notes §31

25:1 / Some commentators refer to the tent of meeting as the "tabernacle" and the larger structure as the "tent" but this is not consistent with primary biblical usage.

25:3 / For a complete accounting of the materials and their uses see Jacob, *Exodus*, pp. 869–72.

25:5 / A dugong is closely related to the now extinct (Bering Sea) sea cow and in the same order as the western hemisphere manatee (*sirenia*). It eats the grasses near the shore. Other suggestions for translation have included dolphin, porpoise, seal, badger, and dyed goat leather. Dugong still live along the coast of the Indian Ocean.

25:10 / For a thorough discussion of the ark in relation to the ancient Near East see Haran, *Temples*, pp. 254–59.

25:21 / Throughout Exodus *the ark* is known as "the ark of the testimony," referring to the Ten Commandments that were in it. In Numbers it is known by both "ark of the Testimony" (Num. 4:5; 7:89; see also Josh. 4:16) and "ark of the covenant" (Num. 10:33; 14:44; see also Deut. 10:8; 31:9, 25–26; Josh. 3:3, etc.). Aaron's almond-bearing staff (Num. 17:1–11) and a jar of manna (Exod. 16:33–34) were later added to the ark as testimonies to the covenant.

25:22 / On the Day of Atonement (Yom Kippur), see Lev. 16. Once a year God removed the guilt of all the people through the sprinkling of blood on the atonement cover and by sending a live goat bearing the sins of the people into the wilderness.

25:37 / In Solomon's temple, three of the lamps on ten lampstands were never allowed to go out (27:20; see 1 Kgs. 7:49). Later synagogues that continued this practice called it the "perpetual light." The Roman church also adopted the practice. The Second Temple returned to the tabernacle pattern of one lampstand (1 Macc. 1:21; 4:49). The Roman Caesar Titus took this to Rome and represented it on his arch of triumph (Plaut, *The Torah*, p. 613).

25:40 / This chapter includes all the furnishings of the holiest and the holy place except the altar for incense, the description of which is found in 30:1–6 (as if an afterthought).

§32 Instructions for Making the Tent of Meeting (Exod. 26:1–37)

26:1–14 / Exodus 26 deals with the inner four-layered tent of meeting, including the holy place and most holy place. The small "t" **tabernacle** in verse 1 refers to the *tent of meeting,* not the larger structure that includes the courtyard (27:9–19). Four distinct Hebrew words describe various fabric creations woven for the tabernacle. (The NIV translates all of them "curtain.") The woven cloth for the tent of meeting is *yeri'ah* meaning "tent fabric," from a verb that means "quiver" (vv. 1, 7). The "veil" in front of the ark, dividing the holiest place from the holy place within the tent of meeting is *paroket,* meaning "veil," from a verb that means "shut off" (25:31). The "entrance screens" to the tabernacle and to the tent of meeting are *masak,* meaning "screen," from a verb that means "hide" or "shade" (v. 36; 27:16). The "hanging curtain" that encompassed the courtyard is *qela'.* This is the only word that really means "hanging curtain" (lit., "slung," 27:9). We will use the more precise terminology (indicated in quotes above) in order to avoid confusion.

God instructed that artisans were to weave the ten panels of "tent fabric" of **finely twisted linen,** specifically, **blue, purple and scarlet** thread (NIV has "yarn"). This phrase, with slight variations, appears twenty-four times in Exodus 25–40. Translators and rabbinic scholars have interpreted the somewhat ambiguous Hebrew in a variety of imaginative ways, trying to make sense of the fiber arts involved. (See the additional note below and comment on 25:4 for specifics on the translation of this phrase.) Most likely the twisting describes the process of spinning flax into the thread to then use in weaving. "Blue, purple and scarlet" describe three different colors of what was probably linen thread used in the weaving. The weavers could have used one color for the warp and two colors alternating in the weft (perpendicular threads) in a pattern. The result would be a regal tricolored cloth into which they wove, or worked in by some other method, the cherubim design. The dimensions of each of the ten panels of "tent fabric" were to be **four cubits wide** (approx. 6 ft.) by **twenty-eight cubits long** (approx. 41 ft.).

The fabric featured **cherubim worked into them by a skilled craftsman.** "Worked into them" is, literally, "a work of ingenuity." It means "designed skillfully" or "designed intelligently." Weaving a cherubim design into the cloth would have been a work of great artistry and mathematical skill. The Hebrew word translated "craftsman" means a "weaver of colors" or "variegator" in 35:35 and 38:23, although the word is most often translated "an embroiderer." The two textile processes are quite different. The instructions for the tabernacle mention these "skilled" artisans who did the work many times (vv. 1, 31; 28:3, 6, 8, 15; 29:5; 31:3, 6; 35:10, 25–26, 31, 35; 36:1–4, 8, 35; 39:3, 5, 8).

Joining the pieces together required two steps. First, they would join together two sets of five lengths each (each length was 28 by 4 cubits = 42 by 6 ft.). This would create two large sections, each measuring twenty-eight by twenty cubits (42 by 30 ft.). The Hebrew calls these two large sections "sisters" (v. 6, NIV "together").

The second step was to connect the two large sister sections. They made fifty **loops of blue material** along one twenty-eight cubit **edge** of each large section, sewing in a loop about every ten inches or so. They then joined the two sisters together with **fifty gold clasps** to make the tent of meeting. The result would be a single tarpaulin measuring forty cubits by twenty-eight cubits (approx. 20 by 14 ft.) that could be laid over the tent frame creating a floor space of thirty cubits by ten cubits, covering the (flat) roof and three walls with one end left open. The clasps created a cross seam one-third of the way from the back of the tent. From this hung the veil that blocked the holy place from the most holy place.

Over the linen tent fabric was a second layer of "tent fabric" for the tent of meeting, to be made of spun and woven goat hair. Exodus 35 reports, "all the women who were willing and had the skill spun the goat hair" (v. 26). Spun and woven goat hair was a common covering for bedouin tents and was not dyed. They were to weave **eleven** lengths of this "tent fabric" (NIV "curtains"). Each length, **thirty cubits long and four cubits wide,** was two cubits longer than the innermost layer. The longer thirty-cubit sides reached the ground. (The first linen layer was 28 cubits over a 30 cubit frame, so the fabric on each side ended one cubit above the ground.) As before, they joined the panels to form two tarp sections: **five of the curtains together into one set and the other six into another set.** The sixth panel provided four extra cubits. The extra material of the longer and wider tarpaulin provided a weather shield by folding the end double above the entrance (v. 9b). What remained was to hang down at the rear on the ground (v. 12). The two woven goat hair sections were joined together in the same way as the inner linen tent, with **fifty loops.** The **clasps** were **bronze** instead of gold and were hidden from view, since this curtain was sandwiched between the others.

The descriptions of the third and fourth coverings for the tent are very brief. We know only that both were leather: **"Make for the tent a covering of ram skins dyed red, and over that a covering of hides of sea cows."** The ram skins would be reddened simply from the tanning process. "Sea cows" probably means the sea mammal dugong (related to the manatee) rather than dolphin or dyed goat leather (see note on 25:5).

26:15–30 / The **upright frames** for the tent of meeting (NIV "tabernacle") were made of **acacia wood** (see 25:5). The confusing expression **two projections set parallel to each other** simply means the vertical frames were not solid wood but made of **two boards** (or "studs") joined together. The two boards were set parallel, **a cubit and a half** apart (27 in.), and connected (or "runged," *shalab*), probably by wood, at the top, middle, and bottom, like a ladder with big steps. The bottom of each board was cut as a tenon to fit into mortised (deeply grooved) metal bases. All the upright frames were **to be ten cubits long** (approx. 15 ft.).

God further instructed that the wooden frames be erected side by side and touching, the whole length of the wall (so the stud frames were about 24 in. on center). The **north** and **south** sides of the tabernacle had the longer walls, thirty cubits long (45 ft.), made of **twenty frames** each (by 1.5 cubits wide). The **west end of the tabernacle** was ten cubits wide (15 ft.), and was made of eight frames: six regular frames plus two special corner frames that would have been half a cubit (9 in.) wide each.

Scholars are divided about the construction of the corner and translate it quite differently. The NIV is helpful here: **"At these two corners they must be double from the bottom all the way to the top, and fitted into a single ring."** The corner frames were solid wood made of two boards joined tightly at the top by a gold ring. This hints that the studs themselves were a quarter cubit in width (4.5 in.). Their silver bases held them together at the bottom. Each upright board had its own silver base, **two bases for each frame, one under each projection.** The three sides had a total of ninety-six silver bases. The foundation of the tent was, thus, pure silver.

The wooden **crossbars** (with gold overlay) were to be long horizontal braces to tie the vertical frames together. The text does not say where they were to attach the crossbars or how the **gold rings** that held them in place were attached. Each of the three walls had **five** crossbars, with the **center crossbar** (the third of the five) extending **from end to end at the middle of the frames.** The other crossbars apparently could be in shorter pieces, but the middle one was a single piece of lumber extending thirty cubits along the long walls. God instructed that all the frames and crossbars be overlaid with ordinary gold. At the end of this description of framing, the Lord again reminded Moses to follow **the plan shown you on the mountain.** It was neither the first nor the last reminder that God had an important stake in dwelling in the midst of the people (25:9, 40; 26:30; 27:8).

26:31–37 / The Lord described two woven dividers for the tent of meeting: the "veil" (*paroket*) in front of the ark in the holiest place and the "entrance screen" (*masak*) that functioned as the door to the holy place (NIV uses "curtain" for both). God also explained the positions of the ark, the table of the bread of presence, and the lampstand.

The veil was to be **of blue, purple and scarlet . . . finely twisted linen, with cherubim worked into it by a skilled craftsman** (NIV adds "yarn," see translation discussion on 25:4). God gave similar instructions for the fabric of the whole tent of meeting (v. 1). The word for "veil," however, is different because of its unique function. The woven cherubim were an indication of the entrance to the holiest place, a preview of the cherubim on the ark cover. It was to be hung from **gold hooks** that were attached to **the clasps** of the roof fabric. The clasps were the same clasps that held the two large sections of the first layer of the tent of meeting together (v. 6). The seam ran exactly along the path of the veil. The **four posts of acacia wood overlaid with gold** in **silver bases** were to be placed alongside the curtain, probably evenly in front of the curtain in the holy place.

This word *paroket*, "veil," occurs *only* when referring to the special "curtain" around which everything else was positioned in the tent of meeting. The Lord instructed Moses first to **place the ark of the Testimony behind the curtain** ("veil"). Its primary purpose was to create a place of honor for the Ten Commandments ("the Testimony"). The curtain also created **the Most Holy Place** for the **atonement cover,** a place for meeting the Lord and receiving forgiveness. The "veil" secured both God's law and the Lord's gift of grace for the emerging people of God. A copy of this "veil" in the Second Temple was torn at the time of Jesus' death, signaling the availability of the gracious atoning forgiveness to all peoples of the world through him.

Outside the "veil" Moses was to place the furnishings for the daily work of the Aaronic priests: **the table** on **the north side** and **the lampstand opposite it on the south side.** The entrance to the tent of meeting and to the tabernacle faced east, so the table was on the right side as the priests entered and the lamps on the left. Again here there is no mention of the incense altar. The text and their locations in the tent reflect the prominence of the ark, the table of the bread of presence, and the light of the lamp.

The Lord also commissioned an "entrance screen" (*masak,* NIV "curtain") for the doorway into the tent of meeting. Its fabric and colors were to be similar to those of the veil and the tent itself, but without the cherubim, signifying that this was a holy place, but not the *most* holy place. The text adds that it is the work of a weaver of colors (known as a "variegator"). The NIV has **work of an embroiderer,** as do other translations, but embroidery and weaving color are not the same art. The text mentions the description of this workmanship six times (v. 36; 27:16; 28:39; 36:37; 38:18; 39:29). Oholiab was the master weaver, skilled in weaving colored patterns into fabric (38:23). The details for making **gold hooks for** the entrance screen and for positioning the **five posts of acacia wood overlaid with gold** were left to the artisans. They placed the five posts in cast bronze bases (rather than silver). The metals specified are decreasingly valuable from the center to the outside of the structure. The fabrics also become less intricate.

The skill and labor necessary to make the tent of meeting would ensure it was an intensively creative event. The investment of time and goods by the people to build a dwelling place for the Lord would have been very significant. The spinning, dyeing, weaving, carpentry and metal work would require immense ability and industry. God had high expectations of the creative potential of his newly delivered people.

In making the tabernacle God called the people to join the Creator in creating a beautiful place. The Lord's intention from the beginning of creation had not changed. God made the animals and then engaged Adam in naming them. Within God's creative activity, Adam had complete freedom to be creative. "He brought them to the man to see what he would name them; and whatever the man called each living creature, that was its name" (Gen. 2:19b). In detailing the tabernacle design, God revealed that the original intention for the human creation had not changed. God desired to enter into a joint creative enterprise that would influence the future of the world.

Additional Notes §32

26:1 / The "tabernacle" described here is the tent of meeting. Exodus also uses "the tabernacle" in two ways. Sometimes "tabernacle" refers to everything encompassed by the tabernacle courtyard curtains and sometimes, as in v. 1, it refers only to the tent of meeting. For definitions of my (consistent) usage see Introduction to the Tabernacle. The tent of meeting described in 33:7 (where Moses regularly met with God before the building of the tabernacle) and the tabernacle's tent of meeting, described here in Exod. 26, were physically different tents. Their basic function as a meeting place with God was the same. Exodus calls them both "tent of meeting" (*ʾohel moʿed*). The word "yarn" is an NIV addition to the Heb. text that seems to be missing a noun. See notes on the translation and meaning at 25:4, that relate to the list form I have used in this passage. Some interpreters believe that the whole material was woven of one kind of thread created by twisting one white linen and three colored (one of each color) wool strands together. Exodus never mentions wool (*tsemer*, see also Lev. 13:47–52). Numerology has motivated the interpretation of four-stranded threads (see Plaut, *The Torah*, p. 607; Jacob, *Exodus*, pp. 871–72). The law in Deut. 22:11 prohibited the combination of linen and wool.

§33 Instructions: Altar, Courtyard, Lamp Oil (Exod. 27:1–21)

27:1–8 / The description moves immediately from the tent's entrance screen to the bronzed altar that would stand in the courtyard. It would stand in the middle, halfway between the entrance screen of the tent of meeting and the entrance screen of the larger tabernacle. Worshipers brought whole burnt offerings and sacrifices in which animals were cleanly slaughtered for their meat to this altar. The blood (representing life) and fat (representing abundant provision) of every animal belonged to the Lord (see Gen. 4; Lev. 17:10–16). The people would be acknowledging this reality daily at this altar.

The people were to frame the altar with **boards** so that the center was **hollow** from top to bottom and light enough to carry. The wood was from **acacia** trees (see comment on 25:5). The frame was large enough to accommodate a cow or a bull: **five cubits long and five cubits wide** (7.5 ft.) and **three cubits high** (4.5 ft.). There is no information about the shape and length of the **horn at each of the four corners.** The carved wooden horns provided a place to demonstrate proper public acknowledgment to the Lord for the life of the animal (29:12). The **bronze network grating** was more than a simple grill grate. It probably had two or three tiers and held the **firepans,** and the meat above that. In this way the heat would be elevated above the heat-vulnerable, bronzed, wooden altar.

They were to overlay the altar **with bronze.** Everything related to the altar was also bronze: **its utensils, pots to remove the ashes, shovels, sprinkling bowls, meat forks** and firepans. Nearly all of the metal for the creation of the courtyard, including the tent pegs, was to be bronze (27:19; except the curtain, which was hung from silver hooks). The hierarchy of metals (gold, silver, bronze) demonstrated the relative holiness and importance of the furnishings.

The altar had two main functions. First (according to Levitical law, also given at Sinai), it provided the only place to "cleanly" slaughter animals for meat, since all blood belonged to the Lord. Only there could the people properly and humanely kill animals for food. The word "altar" (mizbeakh) comes from the word "slaughter" (zabakh). Some commentators underestimate the importance of this first function. The bronzed courtyard altar was the only source of meat for the people, providing properly bled beef, lamb, and goat meat. That is why this description mentions the "meat forks." All meat came from the hand of God and the people acknowledged this in thanksgiving "offerings" before they could consume the meat (see also 1 Sam. 14:32–35). The people cooked and ate the majority of offerings in thanksgiving to the Lord. The altar was also the place where they gave whole burnt offerings in preparation for meeting the Lord, which was the primary function of the tent of meeting.

The bronze altar was portable, like the furnishings inside the tent of meeting. The Lord's instructions continually pointed to the Lord's mobility through the wilderness. God was not tied to geography or a single cultural identity, but instead created a new culture of relationship, in part, through this mobility. The altar was to have bronze rings **at each of the four corners . . . under the ledge . . . halfway up the altar.** These were for the bronzed poles made to carry it.

God reminded Moses again to pay attention to the details he had seen **on the mountain** (25:9, 40; 26:30; 27:8). As God spoke these words Moses was still on the mountain. This may imply that the Lord showed Moses a visible plan or model in the six days of silence before the verbal instructions began (24:16b). It may also be translated, "that I have now shown you on the mountain."

27:9–21 / The next set of instructions described a **courtyard** to encompass the tent of meeting, the bronze altar, bronze basin, and a space for presenting animals for slaughter or whole offering to the Lord. The south, north, west, and east sides of the courtyard were each to have hanging **curtains** (qelaꜥ) **of finely twisted linen.** The linen was not dyed, so it was presumably an off-white flaxen color. The people were to hang them from the posts (probably made of acacia wood and perhaps overlaid with bronze) **with silver hooks.** The Hebrew is list-like: literally, "posts . . . and bases: bronze." They added silver **bands** around **the posts** for attaching the curtain hooks. Silver capital tops protected them against rot (38:28). They were set in **bronze bases.** The posts were not connected to each other except by the curtains.

The curtains were **five cubits high** (7.5 ft.), providing a visual barrier from the encampment all around them, but only half as high as the tent of meeting. The Lord specified the dimension of each side of the courtyard curtains individually. The total area was **a hundred cubits long and fifty cubits wide** (approx. 11,250 sq. ft.). The **south** and **north** sides were longer, with **twenty posts** each, spaced every five cubits (7.5 ft.). **The west end** had **ten posts,** spaced every five cubits.

The entrance to the courtyard faced east, **toward the sunrise.** Its screen (*masak,* NIV "curtain") was centered, flanked with **curtains fifteen cubits long** on either side (22.5 ft.). The posts were spaced every five cubits, three on each side. The entrance screen was made of **finely twisted linen,** but it was to be dyed **blue, purple and scarlet,** as was the entrance curtain to the tent of meeting. Again, the Hebrew text says that this is to be the work of a weaver of colors (see comment on 26:36). This entrance curtain was **twenty cubits long** by five cubits high (approx. 30 by 7.5 ft.). It was hung on **four posts** in **four bases.**

The last two verses of Exodus 27 return attention to the children of Israel, the **Tent of Meeting,** and the **Testimony** (Ten Commandments). The people were to bring the purest olive **oil** for the lamps in the holy place. **Aaron and his sons** were to keep them **burning before the LORD from evening till morning** (also Lev. 24:2–4). The light would be a sign of the presence of God among them, even through the night. This was to be **a lasting ordinance** among the children of Israel. Other "lasting ordinances" for the Israelites included the Feast of Unleavened Bread, the Passover, and the Sabbath (12:17, 24; 31:16). The return of attention to the Lord in the tent serves as a preliminary conclusion to the description of the tabernacle.

The instruction for the lamps may seem out of place here, as they concern priestly service in the tent of meeting (Durham, *Exodus,* p. 380). Rather than being part of the description of the golden lampstand (25:31–40), the text includes it here as a transition to the next two chapters about priestly service. The priests would move between service in the courtyard and the tent of meeting. Exodus 28–30 describe Aaronic vestments, priestly ordination, and priestly service.

Additional Notes §33

27:2 / Archaeologists have found several horned altars: see Biran, "Horned Altar," pp. 106–7, and Aharoni, "Horned Altar," pp. 2–6. Worshipers may have used the altar horns in some instances for binding a living animal as Sarna and Enns suggest, but this is not clearly the case in Exodus and Levitical law. They were to present and probably slaughter the animal before they divided its parts and arranged them on the altar (29:10–11; see also Lev. 1:1, 8, 11). The Lord only specified that bird offerings be brought directly to the altar (Lev. 1:15). Enns and Sarna are referring to Ps. 118:27 (see Enns, *Exodus,* p. 523; Sarna, *Exodus,* p. 172).

27:3 / The meat forks and firepans were for burning (whole offerings) and cooking the meat (sacrifices). It is the "altar of burnt offering" for the daily offering of two lambs (29:38–43; 30:28). The people did not feed God as in pagan sacrifices, rather God fed the people. They did not take any of the meat into the tent of meeting.

27:20 / Some scholars have noted the lack of olive trees in Sinai and concluded that this is part of a later retrospective idealization (or pious fiction) of the wilderness tabernacle. It is possible that traders were a source of olives and other supplies.

27:21 / This chapter describing the courtyard ends without mention of the bronze basin that stood between the bronze altar and the tent of meeting. Perhaps, like the omitted incense altar in Exod. 26, the basin was a priestly detail without a central theological function (30:18; see also 30:1).

§34 Instructions: Priestly Garments (Exod. 28:1–43)

28:1–5 / The Lord gave Moses specific instructions about creating **sacred garments for your brother Aaron.** Aaron and his sons would wear four layers: linen undergarments, a tunic (lightweight robe), a robe, and an ephod. The vest-like ephod had a small double cloth breastplate and a waist sash. A turban and its engraved medallion brought the number of garments to eight. The priests officiated with bare feet (3:5; 30:19; Josh. 5:15). The longest descriptions concern the ephod and the breast piece, the most complex and visible articles (vv. 6–30). Verses four and five serve as a table of contents for Exodus 28: **These are the garments they are to make: a breastpiece** (vv. 15–30), **an ephod** [vest] (vv. 6–14), **a robe** (vv. 31–35), **a woven tunic, a turban, and a sash** (vv. 36–40). Verse 5 contains a list of materials: **Have them use gold** (for the chains, breastplate, and turban medallion) and **blue, purple and scarlet;** specifically, **fine linen.** The material for the priest's garment was like that of the tent of meeting in which he ministered. It is also possible that they used gold thread (see comment at 28:6–14).

The chapter describes the purpose of the vestments in various ways: the garments are **so they may serve me as priests** (vv. 1, 3, 4); the two engraved onyx stones on the ephod vest and the twelve precious stones on the breastplate were "to bear the names" of the tribes of Israel before the Lord (vv. 12, 29); the Urim and Thummim on the breastplate were so the high priest would "always bear the means of making decisions . . . before the LORD" (v. 30); the bells on the hem of the robe were so that he "will be heard" and "not die" (v. 35); and linen undergarments were a modest covering, "so that they will not incur guilt and die" (v. 43). The engraved golden plate on the turban declared "HOLY TO THE LORD" (see vv. 36–43) and thereby expanded the primary theological explanation of the vestments.

God instructed Moses to bring Aaron and **his sons Nadab and Abihu, Eleazar and Ithamar** from among the Israelites for the practical purpose of measuring them for the priestly garments (vv. 1, 4). **"Tell all the skilled men to whom I have given wisdom in such matters . . . to make garments."** Exodus 28 focuses on Aaron's complex vestments. The sons are also fitted for fine white linen tunics, colored sashes, headbands, and undergarments (vv. 40, 42–43).

28:6–14 / Aaron would wear the **ephod** (*'epod*) as a vest-like outer garment. It was probably knee-length, as it had a **waistband** but had to be short enough to see the significant hem of the robe underneath it. It was probably open under the arms since the text says that the shoulder pieces held the front and back together. The garment was to be **made with gold, and with blue, purple and scarlet** material, which is as ambiguous in English as it is in Hebrew. The people used gold for the rings and chains, and many think the thread for weaving also contained gold (see 25:4). The text mentions the **skilled craftsman** again, particularly with regard to making the waistband (vv. 3, 6, 8, 15).

They were to **engrave two onyx stones** with **the names of the sons of Israel** for the **shoulder pieces** of the ephod. One tradition says that these shoulder pieces were clasped together by the onyx stones like a brooch, but the text does not describe this. The craftsman was to **mount the stones in gold filigree settings** and attach them to the shoulders of the ephod by **two braided chains of pure gold, like a rope.** They probably attached the other end of the chains to the gold rings sewn into the shoulders of the ephod vest (see v. 22).

The Lord described the engraving and its purpose in detail: engrave **the way a gem cutter engraves a seal;** engrave the names, **six names on one stone and . . . six on the other, in the order of their birth;** their purpose is that Aaron **bear the names on his shoulders as a memorial before the LORD.** Aaron represented the whole community before the Lord. For further detail, see the discussion in the following section.

28:15–30 / Aaron's **breastpiece for making decisions** was attached to his ephod-vest. It represented a twofold burden that Aaron was called upon to bear **over his heart** (vv. 29–30). Aaron was to enter **the Holy Place** daily to attend to the lamps (27:20–21). So **whenever he enters the presence of the LORD** he is to wear the breastpiece with its twelve precious engraved stones and the Urim and Thummim. The first burden that Aaron bore on the breastpiece consisted of the engraved names of the tribes of Israel. The precious stones on the breastpiece, like the two onyx stones on the shoulders of the ephod, were **a continuing memorial before the LORD.** Their purpose differed slightly. Aaron was to wear the breastpiece specifically for entering the tent of meeting. The precious stones were related to the **breastpiece of decision,** a reminder that critical future decisions were dependent on the Lord's revelation. The onyx stones, worn continually, would serve as a reminder of the Lord's initiative in choosing the people.

The second burden that Aaron bore "over his heart" (in the breastpiece) consisted of **the Urim and the Thummim . . . the means of making decisions.** Scholars have understood these to be stones (perhaps black and white) kept in the pouch formed by the doubled breastpiece and drawn out as lots to answer specific questions. This was a way for the Lord to communicate "yes," "no," or "wait" (see 1 Sam. 23:6–12). While the Sinai law forbids other kinds of divination, God made this provision for Israel's guidance in the wilderness tradition. In this way the leaders of Israel could inquire of the Lord in critical matters that involved the whole community.

Craftsmen were to fashion the breastpiece from the same material as the ephod, with **gold,** and **finely twisted linen** in **blue, purple and scarlet.** It was to be **a span long and a span wide** (9 in.) **and folded double,** forming a pocket for the two decisions stones. The twelve precious stones were set in **gold filigree** (like the onyx), each engraved with one name of one tribe, and mounted in four rows of three on the breastpiece.

The **square** breastpiece also had four gold rings, one at each corner. The top corner rings of the breastpiece were connected to two gold rings at the shoulders of the ephod vest by **braided chains of pure gold.** The onyx stone chains were likely attached to the same rings. The bottom corner rings of the breastpiece would be attached by a short **blue cord** to two more gold rings sewn into the sides of the mid-waistband seam of the ephod. This was so the breastpiece would **not swing out from the ephod.**

28:31–35 / God instructed that the hem of Aaron's blue robe be decorated with **gold bells** and **pomegranates of blue, purple and scarlet** material. The material was probably linen, but tradition assumes it was wool (see comment on 25:4). Aaron wore the robe under the knee-length ephod vestment, so the hem of the robe would be the main visible surface. God specified only the basic pattern: **entirely of blue cloth, with an opening for the head** and **a woven edge like a collar** (or "like leather"). The words **so that it will not tear** expressed concern for durability. The description does not mention sleeves.

The melodic repetition of the Hebrew in verse 34 (*paʿamon zahab verimmon paʿamon zahab verimmon*), literally, "a golden bell and a pomegranate, a golden bell and a pomegranate," communicates the beauty of the alternating pomegranate and golden bell pattern. Pomegranates were widely known as a symbol of abundance (Num. 13:23; 20:5) and were widely used in Solomon's temple (1 Kgs. 7:18–20; 2 Kgs. 25:17; Jer. 52:22–23). On the other hand, the bells were a warning against approaching the raw power of the holy place unannounced. The bells would ring as Aaron walked, to announce his entrance and exit from **the Holy Place before the LORD,** when he entered daily to attend to the oil lamps (27:20–21). The bell ringing, washing before entering, and wearing of undergarments were all necessary, **so that he will not die.** The people and priests demonstrated respect for God in these practical ways. The rabbis associated the bells with the practice of always knocking, or announcing one's presence, before entering anyone's home or room.

28:36–43 / Aaron's linen turban, and especially its engraved medallion (NIV "plate") with the **pure gold . . . seal: HOLY TO THE LORD** declared the theological importance of the vestments. They belonged to the Lord. As the bells announced Aaron's physical presence, the seal declared the presence of the grace of the Lord that made the people's gifts **acceptable to the LORD.** The engraved medallion is, literally "a blossom," which may refer to its shape or its brightness.

The Lord's prevenient forgiveness continually covered any mistake or faults in the offerings, **whatever their gifts may be.** The people did not need to fear to approach the Lord. That Aaron would **bear the guilt** meant that the words "HOLY TO THE LORD" were themselves a sign of forgiveness and sanctification. These words on Aaron's turban were a daily reminder of continual access to God. The words, along with the explanation in this text (vv. 38–39), indicate that the visible declaration of the Lord's forgiveness was enough. The name of the Lord, borne by one man, made the gifts acceptable and holy.

The parallel in Christ is unmistakable for Christians. Aaron himself, as a high priest bearing God's name, became the conduit to grace. The author of Hebrews makes the connection to Aaron in order to explain the necessity of Jesus' humanity. In the flesh, God's son experienced human weakness and was thus qualified to be a high priest, bearing guilt before God on behalf of others. This act of bearing guilt before God makes the removal of guilt possible through forgiveness. Someone must be the agent of transferring the guilt from the people to the God who forgives it. Jesus' humanity made it possible for him, like Aaron (and high priests after him), to become that necessary human agent (priest). Because Jesus was also God, however, he could accomplish this transfer from the people to the throne of grace once and for all, perpetually as the high priest in heaven (Heb. 2:17; 4:15).

Exodus 28 concludes with instructions for linen tunics, sashes, and undergarments for **Aaron and his sons** (vv. 39–43). Craftsmen were to **Weave** the **tunics** of undyed **fine linen.** Aaron's was worn under his ephod and robe. The sashes were to be colorful, the work of a weaver of colors (see comment on 26:36). The Lord asked also for **headbands for Aaron's sons.** The investiture of Aaron with the garments was requisite before Moses could **anoint, ordain,** and **consecrate** them as priests before the Lord. The Lord gave instructions for their ordination (ch. 29) and Leviticus 8–9 describes the service.

Wearing the garments was **to be a lasting ordinance for Aaron and his descendants.** Exodus names three other "lasting ordinances" (*khuqqot ʿolam*) for Aaron and his descendants: the priesthood itself (29:9); washing hands and feet before ministering (30:19–21); and wearing **linen undergarments** (vv. 41–43). Attention to physical cleanliness and modesty for the ministers was not outside the scope of God's concern. Physical cleanliness (purity) was a central feature of Levitical law. The undergarments were a response to the overt sexuality of ancient Near Eastern religious practice (see comment on 20:26). The overarching concern was for the **dignity and honor** of ministers before the Lord, which the Lord's own instructions provided (vv. 40–41). Their dignity and honor were not for their own sake, but, as the Lord said, so that **"they may serve me."**

Additional Notes §34

28:1 / Scripture mentions Aaron's and Elisheba's four sons, Nadab, Abihu, Eleazar, and Ithamar, together several times (28:1; 6:23). The younger two, Eleazar and Ithamar, served as priests with Aaron until he died (Num. 3:4). The older brothers, Nadab and Abihu, were with Aaron and the 70 elders on Mt. Sinai (24:1, 9) but did not survive their own ordinations. Lev. 8–10 records the ordination service, where the Lord provided the fire for the burnt offering. In the wake of the miracle, Nadab and Abihu took it upon themselves to parade with incense among the people: "they offered unauthorized fire before the LORD, contrary to his command. So fire came out from the presence of the LORD and consumed them, and they died before the LORD" (Lev. 10:1–2). God saw their improvisation as self-aggrandizement. Their actions illustrated the common temptation of ministers and priests to abuse their authority among the people.

28:9 / Onyx is a semiprecious stone of chalcedony quartz that can be engraved. It is sometimes dyed black. Artisans also use the white variety for cameo backgrounds.

28:11 / Filigree is delicate and intricate ornamental work, here created with gold.

28:17–20 / Translators disagree on the kinds of stones used, but the NIV has **a ruby, a topaz and a beryl; a turquoise, a sapphire and an emerald; a jacinth, an agate and an amethyst; a chrysolite, an onyx and a jasper** (see Osborne and Hatton, *Handbook,* pp. 660–61, for full lists of options).

28:30 / Scripture does not mention the Urim ("light," or "truth") and Thummim ("integrity," or "illumination") after David's reign (ca. 1000 B.C.) until briefly in the time of Ezra (4th c. B.C.; Ezra 2:63; Neh. 7:65). There is no biblical description of them. Josephus believed that God illuminated the 12 precious stones on the breastpiece when Israel was to be victorious in battle. One talmudic tradition held that the *shekinah* (glory of the Lord) illuminated the letters on the names on the stones to spell out answers to questions (see Lindblom, "Lot-Casting").

28:35 / The text gives no credence to the religious practice of warding off evil spirits by wearing bells (Frazer, "Folklore in the Old Testament," pp. 263–78). The point of the text is that all respect is due the Lord, who is much more powerful, good, and dangerous to the arrogant than any spirits. The Christian practice of ringing bells to announce services originated in this description of the bells on Aaron's robe.

28:36 / Deuteronomy describes the holiness of the children of Israel, chosen from among all the peoples of the world to be holy to the Lord (Deut. 7:6; 14:2; 26:19). They were not "holy" because of their own righteousness, obedience, or superiority (Deut. 9:4–6). This is religion's definition of holiness, not the Bible's description. Israel was "holy" because the Lord called, delivered, guided, instructed, and declared them "set apart" as the people of God. God says, unequivocally, "I am the Lord, who makes you holy" (Lev. 20:8; 21:8; 22:9, 16, 32).

The word *tsits* describes the pure gold, engraved medallion attached to the turban. When they pray, observant Jews wear a kind of *tsits* in the form of a phylactery as a frontlet, a small leather box with the commandments in it, attached to the forehead.

§35 Instructions: Aaron's Consecration, the Altar Consecration, and Daily Sacrifices (Exod. 29:1–46)

"After you put these clothes on your brother Aaron and his sons, anoint and *ordain them*. Consecrate them so they may serve me as priests" (28:41). Exodus 29 contains specific instructions for the priestly consecration and ordination ceremony, including three sacrifices and the consecration of the bronze altar. It also includes instructions for the ongoing daily sacrifice of two lambs. Verses 1–9 describe methods for the preparation of the animals, the vestments for the consecration, and the ordination ritual. Verses 10–14 describe the first offering, a young bull for the removal of sin. The second offering was a ram as a "gift offering" to God (vv. 15–18). The third animal was the ordination ram brought as a "fellowship offering" (vv. 19–37). Verses 38–42 describe the perpetual daily sacrifices (lambs), that were "worship offerings." Verses 42–46 give the theology behind the consecration and the key to the context of the ordination sacrifices. All of this was to prepare for the reality of the Lord dwelling among the people.

The people carry out most of the other instructions the Lord gives in Exodus 25–31 and in Exodus 35–40. Leviticus 8–9, however, records Aaron's consecration and ordination.

With regard to the offering of blood sacrifices, the OT practice is foreign to many readers and is often maligned. In addition to atonement for sins, the Lord provided a broad range of gifts through blood sacrifice. These gifts included: protection from death (see 12:21–27); confirmation of the possibility of a new life (see 24:8); cleansing from physical disease or uncleanness; covering over unintentional sin; forgiveness of sins against others or God; meals of fellowship and thanksgiving in the Lord's presence; and a means to express worship and adoration. The elaborate sacrificial system was a means of conversing and living with a holy God. It may still serve a pedagogical function for understanding aspects of human relationships with the Lord. In Aaron's consecration, God called for three blood sacrifices with three different purposes: forgiveness, praise, and a fellowship meal with God.

Why did God ask for the sacrifice of animals from the flock as an offering for sin? The Lord established sacrifice on a view of reality that included four facts of human experience. First, the world was created as a place of goodness and well-being (Gen. 1–2). Whole relationships were the Lord's intention from the beginning. Second, intentional and unintentional decisions and actions easily shattered relationships and well-being (*shalom*, Gen. 3). People experienced this brokenness as anxiety and alienation from others, from God, within oneself, and from the nonhuman creation. Scripture and the sacrificial system call this brokenness "sin." The third fact is that the restoration of well-being for an alienated or anxious person is not easy. Unresolved sin leads to an intensification of anxiety, fear, hurt, and anger. This usual state of affairs makes reconciliation even more difficult. People tend to resist the restoration of whole relationships because it costs something. Forgiving another, forgiving oneself, or seeking the forgiveness of another is costly. In sacrifice for sin, the lifeblood and the economic cost of the best animal from one's flock visibly and physically represented that cost. Fourth, then, the sacrifice of an animal from the flock was a fitting representation of the relational situation. In the slaughter, the people saw the alienation (the sin); absorbed the personal cost (sacrifice); and experienced the reality of the struggle for life against death (blood).

The people therefore offered the best animal from their flock in the presence of the Lord, who was the source of well-being from the beginning. Only God could supply the forgiveness and reconciliation that they sought through these physical entities that God provided as representations. Only God could remove the anxiety and restore the well-being of those who offered their animals as prayers to the Lord. In Christ, God became the perfect sacrifice in as much as God became the sin, alienated on our behalf; Jesus became the sacrifice, which cost him his life; and he shed his blood, demonstrating that the struggle for eternal life and death was at stake. Because Christ was also the Lord, his sacrifice brought an end to the need for sacrifice once and for all (Heb. 7:27; 9:12, 26; 10:10; Rom. 6:10; 1 Pet. 3:18).

29:1–18 / The Lord begins by describing the basic preparations for the consecration and ordination of Aaron and his sons.

Moses was to present three animals and three kinds of bread at the Lord's dwelling place (tabernacle). **Aaron and his sons** were not to come on their own, but Moses was to bring them **to the entrance . . . and wash them with water.** The washing reflects the general Levitical relationship between cleanliness and holiness (see 30:17–21). Moses was then to **dress Aaron** in the garments of his service: **the tunic, robe, ephod** and **breastpiece** described in Exodus 28. Like the tent of meeting itself, Aaron was to wear four layers. The text here does not mention the undergarments, perhaps because they were put on in private. Moses was also to **Bring his sons and dress them in tunics . . . headbands** and **sashes.** Exodus 30:22–33 further describes the anointing with oil. Verses 29–30 reiterate the inheritance of Aaron's family as priests and the possession of the garments as a **lasting ordinance.**

The first offering was a young **bull** presented for the removal of sin. Generally a "sin offering" (*khatta²t,* v. 14) was made when the people confessed sin and received forgiveness. The offering provided cleansing from defilement, or "covering" of specific unintentional sin. The priests cooked and ate the meat of regular sin offerings (Lev. 4:27–35; 6:24–29). The burning of the blood and fat of the animal signified that the fire had consumed the sins. Sin offerings for the whole congregation or the sins of a priest were not eaten or even turned to smoke inside the tabernacle. The priests offered the fat and blood on the altar, but they took the meat outside the camp and burned it where the altar ashes were usually dumped, as a sign of the disposal of the more serious sins (Lev. 4:3–21). This "removed" the sin. The offering at Aaron's consecration (vv. 10–14) was just such a sin offering.

The **hands** of Aaron and his sons on the **head** of the young **bull** were a sign of participation. The physical contact in this **sin offering** signified the transfer of sin to the animal, as to the scapegoat on the Day of Atonement (Lev. 16). The flames would consume the sins with the young bull. They were to make sin offerings (v. 14) for confessed sin, for cleansing from defilement, and for covering specific unintentional sin. Moses was to **pour out** the blood at **the altar** and the fire consumed the fatty parts of the animal, signifying the purification from sin. The kidneys and liver may have been included as "fatty parts" because of the ancient practice of using them for divination. Blood **on the horns of the altar** was a visible sign of giving the sins to the Lord for cleansing. The meat and other remaining parts were taken **outside the camp,** thereby removing any trace of Aaron's or his son's sins.

The second animal in Aaron's consecration was **one of the rams,** presented in worship and adoration. They burned all of this **burnt offering** (a gift offering, *ʿolah* v. 18). Often the phrase **a pleasing aroma** (e.g., vv. 18, 25, 41) accompanied the description of these offerings. No one ate any part of it. A burnt offering was a voluntary sign of the worshipers' love, adoration, devotion, commitment, and surrender to the Lord (vv. 15–18). Laying **hands** on the **head** of the ram was, as in the first offering, a sign of participation. By laying hands on a whole burnt offering, Aaron and his sons would communicate their willingness to participate in their ordination, approaching God in the rising of a great volume of smoke to the sky. The **entire ram** was to be turned to smoke (NIV "burn") **on the altar.** The declaration in this consecration context was similar to the declaration of intent at a wedding. The repetition in **offering to the LORD,** "a pleasing aroma," **an offering made to the LORD** reflects the voluntary surrender of the whole burnt offering and the Lord's pleasure in receiving it.

29:19–37 / The **ordination ram** (v. 27) was the third animal God told Moses to bring to the altar. They ate this ram in a fellowship meal in God's presence. It was a "wave offering" (*tenupah*), more commonly known in Leviticus as a "fellowship offering" (*zebakh shelamim,* Lev. 7:28–36). As always, they gave the blood and fat to God on the altar, but in the ordination Aaron and his sons ate the lean meat in the Lord's presence. A fellowship offering was generally a voluntary act of worship, thanksgiving, and fellowship with God. For the third time, **Aaron and his sons shall lay their hands on its head.** In the case of the fellowship offering, the hands on the head signified the transfer of their specific dedication to serve the Lord as priests. They would also eat part of the ram in the Lord's presence as a demonstration of their fellowship and solidarity with God's call on their lives.

The least familiar part of the ordination service is the application of the **blood** of the ram. Moses was to touch Aaron and his sons with the blood **on the lobes of their right ears . . . on the thumbs of their right hands, and on the big toes of their right feet.** He also was to **sprinkle** it not just on **the altar** but also, with the **anointing oil,** on them in **their garments.** The rabbinic commentary suggests that the blood on the ear teaches that the priest must listen to the people; on the thumb teaches that he must act for their good; and on the toe teaches that he must live among them (Sarna, "Exodus," p. 513). The appendages may simply represent their whole bodies. They were consecrated ("set aside") from head to foot. Once the blood had been applied, **Then he and his sons and their garments will be consecrated.**

The transition from the consecration portion of the ceremony to the actual ordination comes in verse 22. The editors of the NIV have placed the notice of the shift in parenthesis: **(This is the ram for the ordination.)** Verses 22–27 and 31–34 describe the procedure for the meat of the ordination ram. They were to take all **the fat** and the **right thigh** and **wave them before the LORD.** They turned to smoke with the first ram (the burnt offering) with three kinds **of bread.** From the remaining meat that they were to eat, they were to separate **the breast of the ram, wave it before the LORD,** and give it to Moses for his **share** to eat. The "breast" of a ram is just behind the front legs and includes the brisket. Verse 28 serves as a concluding admonition to follow the Lord's instructions.

Verses 28–30 interrupt the flow from the ordination distribution of meat to eating the fellowship meal. The Lord established three perpetual statues regarding future fellowship offerings, the sacred garments, and future ordinations. First, in future regular fellowship offerings, the breast that was Moses' share and the right thigh that was burned to the Lord should be given to **Aaron** or his descendents as their regular portion to eat (see also Lev. 7:28–36). Second, instructions for the inheritance of the costly priestly garments established the perpetuity of the Aaronic priestly family. Third, God instructed that the sons of Aaron to succeed him in the future should wear the priestly clothing continually for **seven days** when they were to be ordained. This may have been some deterrent to seeking the position since the garments were extremely heavy.

The ordination meal was to be only for Aaron and his sons. The remaining meat of the ram was to be cooked ("boiled") and eaten by those who were ordained in the courtyard (**a sacred place**). What they could not eat in one day was to be burned, because it was **sacred.** The **ordination** sacrifices lasted for **seven days.** The text is not clear as to whether they performed the ordination rite seven times; whether they performed the rite just once, somehow over a period of seven days; or whether they performed the rite in one day followed by six more days of bull sacrifices (sin offerings). In any case, they offered a full-grown bull every day for each of the seven. During the seven days of ordination they also consecrated the bronze **altar.** The text is unclear, but it is likely that the seven bulls, sacrificed over the seven days of ordination, also served to make **atonement** for the **holy** altar. The holiness (lit., "set apart") of the altar meant that it could not be used for anything except what God designated.

29:38–46 / With the details of ordained priests and a consecrated altar in place, the Lord immediately added a description of the *perpetual daily sacrifices* and their purpose (vv. 38–43). The **two lambs** were worship offerings—offerings not for sin—but nevertheless offerings wholly turned into smoke to demonstrate devotion. In this way the people daily acknowledged the presence of the Lord (vv. 42–43). They offered one lamb at dawn and one **at twilight,** both with bread (about seven cups of flour) and **wine** (about one liter). This was the foundation of the whole sacrificial system (*tamid,* or "regular" offering). The Lord explained that the lambs did not **consecrate** or hallow the place—God's own **glory** did that. The lambs functioned as a preparation for meeting **at the entrance to the Tent of Meeting before the LORD. There I will meet you and speak to you; there also I will meet with the Israelites.** The people did not summon the Lord. God's grace both initiated the relationship and provided for its maintenance. The people could only prepare for it (40:34; Lev. 9:4–6, 23–24).

God gave the theological context of Aaron's ordination in verses 44–46. The Lord, not Moses, would be the prime mover in the consecration of the altar, priests, and tent of meeting. The actions would have a sacramental character. God had given the instructions and would be present in the actions. In order to reinforce this, the Lord says **"I will"** seven times (vv. 43–45).

Two **"I am"** statements follow the "I will" statements, so the reader does not think that animal sacrifice has replaced the initiative of God to dwell with the people. The whole point of the public demonstration of sacrifice was so that **They will know that:**

> I am the LORD their God,
> who brought them out of Egypt so that I might dwell among them.
> I am the LORD their God. (v. 46)

God's expressed purpose, that "they will know," hearkens back to the exit from Egypt itself and its purpose: that people would *know* the Lord. The sacrifices and consecration were for the sake of daily remembering that the Lord had delivered them from Egypt. Regardless of the abuses that led to the end of the sacrificial system in Jesus' day, the Lord gave the system for the good and sustaining provision of God's newly emerging people in the wilderness.

Additional Notes §35

29:10 / They presented the animal to the Lord and slaughtered it in the Lord's presence at **the front of the Tent of Meeting**, 25 cubits (37.5 ft.) west of the altar.

29:14 / The NT compares Jesus, who was crucified "outside the camp," to this kind of offering. "The high priest carries the blood of animals into the Most Holy Place as a sin offering, but the bodies are burned outside the camp. And so Jesus also suffered outside the city gate to make the people holy through his own blood" (Heb. 13:11–12).

29:16–17 / The sprinkling of blood in this case was simply a public sign that all lifeblood belongs to the Lord. The washing of parts that were to be burned was again a sign of the relationship between cleanliness and the Lord's holiness.

29:27 / The "wave offering" (*tenupah*) was an elevation or lifting of the breast as a presentation of the meat to God. They then ate the breast as a means of fellowship with the Lord who had not just provided the meat, but symbolically brought it to the meal as a special contribution to the table fellowship. The older language of "heave offering" (*terumah*, KJV, NASB) is equal to the word "presented" in the NIV. This refers to the thigh, that they also waved. J. Milgrom has shown that the root *rum* in this context does not mean "heave" or "lift" but "give" or "contribute" (Milgrom, *Leviticus 1–16*, pp. 461–81).

29:46 / Verses 45–46 provide the context and purpose connecting the sacrificial system to the overarching narrative. The persistence of faithful Judaism beyond the destruction of two temples (587 B.C. and 70 A.D.) makes clear the temporary nature of the sacrificial system, even for Israel.

§36 Instructions: Incense Altar, Money, Water, Anointing Oil, and Incense (Exod. 30:1–38)

Exodus 30 includes instructions essential to priestly service in the tabernacle: making the gold incense altar for the tent of meeting (vv. 1–10); collecting the tabernacle census tax (vv. 11–16); making the bronze basin for the courtyard (vv. 17–21); the anointing oil ingredients (vv. 18–33); and the incense recipe (vv. 34–38).

30:1–10 / The small gold incense altar (one cubit square, two cubits high) was for the continuous burning of incense in the holy place. The description of its construction exactly follows the rubric for the table of the bread of presence (25:23–28) that was located in the same room. The text presents the details of its materials, size, horns, overlay, molding, rings, and poles in order. The position of the incense altar was a clear marker of the entrance to **the ark of the Testimony**, the Ten Commandments, and **the atonement cover**. It was also one of the sensory aspects of meeting with the Lord (v. 7). The text does *not* describe incense as a means of prayer, but it has been traditionally understood as a practical sweet-smelling counterpoint to the aroma of the burnt offerings.

The Lord also describes its use and limitations to Moses here. Aaron was to add incense twice daily, at dawn and at twilight, so incense would **burn regularly before the LORD for the generations to come.** Nothing else could be burned or poured on the altar. It would be consecrated once a year on the Day of Atonement (Yom Kippur, Lev. 16:16). The word "atonement" (*kippur,* "covering" of sin) appears three times in verse 10. Aaron was to daub blood from the **atoning sin offering** on the horns of the altar to make it holy to the Lord.

30:11–16 / The Lord instituted a tabernacle census tax for two purposes. First, it was to be yet another reminder that God, as Creator, was the source of their individual lives. Their lives, purchased out of slavery, belonged to God. They were to recognize this reality each time a census was taken. At the time of a census, the community would be tempted to take pride in the power of its fighting force (as in Num. 1:2–3; 2 Sam. 24:1–2; 1 Chr. 21:1–5; see also 2 Chr. 2:17–18). At this time God required each man to **pay the LORD a ransom for his life.** The Hebrew word for "ransom" is from the same root as "covering" or "atonement" (*kippur*). The men **twenty years old or more** would stand in a line and would **cross** the courtyard, placing **a half shekel** (about 5 grams/.2 oz. silver) in the collection box. Each would be counted as he paid **the atonement money** that "covered" his life. It was not a measure of personal worth, but a token acknowledgement of the Lord's action in giving him life.

The second purpose of the tabernacle "atonement money" was to cover expenses of **the service** (or "work on") **of the Tent of Meeting,** which explains its place in this tabernacle text. The **rich** and **poor** alike were to give an equal amount in this "offering to the LORD." In the requirements for other offerings, God gave special consideration to those who could not afford the standard costs of the sacrificial system (e.g., Lev. 5:7–13). In this case, however, everyone was to take equal pride in their contribution to maintaining the Lord's dwelling in their midst (and not in their military power).

30:17–21 / The **bronze basin** or "laver" was to be for the priests to wash in the courtyard. God gave little detail to Moses beyond that it was to be a "bronze basin" in a **bronze stand.** The bronze basin was to stand between the entrance to the tent of meeting and the bronze altar in the courtyard, a space of about thirty-six feet. Aaron and his sons were **to wash their hands and feet with water from it. Whenever they enter the Tent of Meeting** to light the lamps or to replenish the incense or the bread on the table. They were to wash also **when they approach the altar** to make an offering **by fire.** Washing was a sign of respect for the holiness of God and their appointed task. Twice the Lord added the weight of the warning, **so that they will not die.** Two of Aaron's sons died at their ordination for modifying the Lord's intentional ordering of the world within the tabernacle (see Lev. 10:1–2).

30:22–38 / Producing the anointing oil required large amounts of **fine spices: . . . liquid myrrh, . . . cinnamon, . . . fragrant cane, . . .** and **cassia.** The Lord's recipe called for a total of fifteen hundred *shekels* (approx. 38 pounds) of spices and one **hin of olive oil** (perhaps six quarts). "Myrrh" is a resin from the sap of a shrub of southern Arabia (*commiphora*). "Fragrant cane" is produced from an aromatic reed (*calamus*). "Cassia" is a type of cinnamon.

The priests were to use this fragrant oil to **consecrate** everything in the tabernacle: **the Tent of Meeting, the ark of the Testimony, the table and all its articles, the lampstand and its accessories, the altar of incense, the altar of burnt offering and all its utensils, and the basin with its stand** (see Lev. 8:10–11). The fragrant oil also anointed and consecrated Aaron and his sons when Moses poured it on their heads (29:7; 40:15) and sprinkled it on their garments (29:21).

The Lord declared the fragrant anointing oil **sacred** (*qodesh*, "holy," see additional note on 28:36). It was set apart and no one was to use it for common things. The Lord told Moses specifically to tell the Israelites to consider it sacred, not to pour it on **men's bodies**, and not to make it at home as a **perfume**. The accompanying threat is not death, but that offenders will no longer be considered part of the Israelite community ("cut off"). **It is sacred, and you are to consider it sacred.**

The Hebrew word *qodesh* and its verbal form occur eleven times in verses 22–33 and is translated many ways in English, including the following in various contexts: consecrated, holy, sacred, sanctuary, sanctified. The basic meaning of *qodesh* is "set apart" for a special purpose. In any case, it was the Lord who conferred the change in status from common to holy. The Lord declared the fragrant anointing oil holy. It was the visible and fragrant means by which God conferred holiness on other objects and people. It had a sacramental character, that is, God acted through it.

The second recipe from the Lord was for **a fragrant blend of incense** made by a **perfumer**. The **spices** (*besamim*, better "fragrances") were primarily solid resins. Resins are produced from the sap of trees or plants. They probably refined **gum resin** from the sap of a balsam tree; **onycha** is uncertain but thought to come from a mollusk gland; **galbanum** is a resin from a plant of Persia and Crete; **and pure frankincense** is a resin of a plant from Arabia (*boswellia*). These costly imported fragrant resins were to be mixed **in equal amounts, salted** (or "refined" or "tempered"), and ground **to powder.**

This refined blend was expressly for the incense altar **"in front of the Testimony in the Tent of Meeting, where I will meet with you."** The details, even of the incense, were always connected to the Lord's Testimony (Ten Commandments), meeting, and presence. Like the anointing oil, the Lord declared the incense sacred and called on Israel to treat it as holy.

Additional Notes §36

30:1 / In some religions incense is thought to ward off evil spirits. Some have thought the clouds of incense functioned to "cover" or hide the presence of God in mystery (see Mendenhall). The text says simply that incense is to "burn regularly before the LORD" (v. 8). The enjoyment of its fragrance is the main point in v. 38, and hence the warning against making it for personal use in v. 38.

30:11–16 / The Heb. words for "atonement" (*kippur*, "covering" of sin) and "offering" (*terumah*) each appear three times in these verses.

30:12 / Some interpreters sense in this verse an ancient superstition against counting people in the plague warning. Counting coins that people give, instead of counting the people themselves, was sometimes understood as a means of avoiding exposure to supernatural danger. Censii were generally not welcome in the ancient Near East, as they were often part of the process of enforcing a military draft, forced labor, or taxation.

30:13 / The half-shekel offering has led to the practice of using one half the common currency (e.g., 50 cents) as a basic offering amount in current Jewish practice. They "must pay" (v. 12) is a palindrome in Heb. (*wntnw*) that the rabbis took to mean that charity was a two-way street.

30:23 / A shekel varied in weight. The OT shekel may have been 11.4 g./.4 oz. The "sanctuary shekel" in v. 13 may have been closer to 10 g. The NT shekel was 14.5 g./.5 oz. They used the weight to produce the monetary shekel of silver weighing .5 oz. Estimates of the quantity of a *hin* vary from 4 to 6 quarts.

§37 Instructions: Bezalel and Sabbath (Exod. 31:1–18)

The tabernacle instructions conclude with the appointing of the master craftsman Bezalel (vv. 1–11) and a Sabbath reminder that the Lord is the source of their holiness (vv. 12–17). The creation of holy space and holy time come together. When the instructions are complete, the Lord gives Moses "the two tablets of the Testimony, the tablets of stone inscribed by the finger of God" (v. 18). This chapter unites the themes of the Lord's gifts to Israel: God's creating; the indwelling Spirit; creative human ability; conferred holiness; rest; life protected and ordered by God's law; and holy time and space (Gen. 2:1–2; Lev. 19:30).

31:1–11 / The Lord chose **Bezalel** and **Oholiab to make artistic designs . . . and to engage in all kinds of craftsmanship.** This text is important for understanding the relationship that the Creator seeks with creative and skilled people. The Lord created a beautiful and good world. God called people, gifted them, and filled them with the Spirit to participate in bringing beauty into the world as God continues to do in every generation. **Also I have given skill to all the craftsmen.** They came from every tribe, qualified by their created and developed ability. The construction of the tabernacle required all kinds of skilled people: spinners, weavers, tailors, dyers, metallurgists, silversmiths, woodworkers, lapidaries, perfumers, and tanners.

The Lord identified Bezalel, the master craftsman, in a special way. **I have filled him with the Spirit of God** (*ruakh 'elohim*, as in Gen. 1:2), **with skill** (or "wisdom"), **ability** (or "intelligence") **and knowledge in all kinds of crafts** (or "workmanship"). He was able to fully employ his created gifts when he was filled with God's Spirit. Exodus 35:30–36:2 records the beginning of his work in the Spirit and we find a record of his success in 38:22–23.

Exodus 30:7–11 contains a complete summary of the elements of the tabernacle and its furnishings. God told Bezalel,

Oholiab, and the skilled people **"to make everything just as I commanded you."** Exodus 25–30 gives fairly specific details of all the tents, furnishings, and vestments. Nonetheless, many significant details are missing (e.g., the height and thickness of the lampstand; the configuration of the posts for the veil). The wisdom and skill of the artisans would be part of the creative process (see also Durham, *Exodus*, p. 410).

31:12–18 / The Lord told Moses to remind the people of the gift of **Sabbath** rest, that God established in the creation, and of God's holiness, conferred upon them. They were to remember that the Lord created the world in six days and rested on the seventh. The people were about to begin the creation of the tabernacle as God's work in the world. The Lord made the earth as a dwelling place for them. Now they were going to make a dwelling for the Lord. They, too, must rest from making the tabernacle each week, remembering the Creator as the source of all things. Weekly "holy time" remembering the Lord takes precedence even over building the holy space. The Sabbath command would be Moses' first word to the people of all that the Lord had shown him. No one was even to build a cooking fire on the Sabbath (35:2–3; see also 34:21; Num. 15:32–36; Jer. 17:21).

The tabernacle instructions ended with a Sabbath reminder. The Lord said that the Sabbath rest was to be kept **"so you may know that I am the LORD, who makes you holy."** Only in experiencing rest before the Lord would they come to know that their holiness was truly a gift from God. Christians and Christian theologies widely misunderstand holiness in Scripture as religion rather than relationship to the Holy One. Holiness is not something to achieve, but to receive. One can prepare to meet and receive the Lord but one cannot presume to possess "holiness." Leviticus is quite clear that "holiness," being set apart by the Lord's redeeming work, is a gift from God. The words "I am the LORD, who makes you holy" occur often in Leviticus (Lev. 20:8; 21:8, 15, 23; 22:9, 16, 32).

Sabbath rest was so important for the relationship between **the LORD** and **the Israelites** that two threats of **death** for those who did not rest on the Sabbath (vv. 14–15) accompanied the commandment. The Sabbath was **holy to the LORD** (16:23; 20:11; 31:15), therefore it should be holy to God's people (20:8; 31:14; 35:2). Even after the destruction of the temple, Sabbath-keeping remained the distinguishing mark and anchoring identity for God's people. The Lord said it was **a lasting covenant** between **"me and the Israelites forever"**—that is, grounded in the creation itself (v. 17).

Here the Lord finishes giving Moses the instructions for the tabernacle that began in 25:1. Exodus 31 concludes with a return to the gift of the law that will be a gateway to life for the newly formed people. **The LORD . . . gave him . . . the tablets of stone inscribed by the finger of God** (v. 18).

The **two tablets of the Testimony,** the tablets of stone, were the Ten Commandments (34:28). Often the word "Testimony" is an abbreviation for the Ten Commandments. When the text refers to the "ark of the Testimony" it means the ark that contains the Ten Commandments. The word "testimony" occurs quite often (16:34; 25:16, 21–22; 26:33–34; 27:21; 30:6, 26, 36; 31:7, 18; 32:15; 34:29; 38:21; 39:35; 40:3, 5, 20–21). Exodus 24:12, where God first invited Moses up the mountain to receive them, mentions the two tablets. In 34:1–4 Moses receives the second set of "two tablets." The following texts also refer to the tablets: 24:12; 31:18; 32:15–16, 19; 34:1, 4, 28–29. Exodus 32:16 associates the "finger of God" with the "writing of God." It marks God's personal investment in the law.

The narrative style of the first part of Exodus resumes in this last verse and continues in the crisis at Sinai (32:1–34:35). If not for the golden calf, the text could have moved directly and smoothly to 35:1. Instead, Scripture reveals how vulnerable the emerging people of God are to their own agendas. It is fitting that the tabernacle description ends with its center, the Ten Commandments, handed from the Lord to Moses. These commandments, the presence of the Lord, and the future of God's newly formed people will be at risk in the next three chapters.

Additional Notes §37

31:1 / "I have chosen Bezalel." The Heb. *be-tsal-ʾel* means "in-protection of God." The root *tsal* is "shade," meaning "protection." "Moreover, I have appointed Oholiab" (v. 6), whose name means "my father's tent." It is possible that this means that "God is my shelter" (lit., "my father is my tent").

31:3 / The exact term "Spirit of God" (*ruakh ²elohim*) is found relatively few times in the OT: of the creation in Gen. 1:2; of Joseph in Gen. 41:38; of prophecy in Num. 24:2; 1 Sam. 10:10; 11:6; 19:20, 23; 2 Chr. 15:1; 24:20; Ezek. 11:24; of Job in Job 33:4; and of Bezalel here in v. 3 and 35:31. Its Greek form (*pneuma theou*) occurs in the description of Jesus' baptism in Matt. 3:16.

31:12 / This section begins with the words, **Then the LORD said to Moses.** Commentators have long noted that these words occur here for the seventh time in the tabernacle instructions (25:1; 30:11, 17, 22, 34; 31:1, 12). This is appropriate for a reminder about the seventh day. The word "Sabbath" (*shabbat*) means to "stop" or "cease" labor. The expression "be refreshed" (*napash*) or "breathe" accompanies the word in 23:12 and v. 17. The Sabbath created breathing room from daily labor. The word in 20:11 is *nuakh,* meaning "rest," as in "free" from work.

31:13 / Sabbath rest is a major theme of the book of Exodus. It stands at the beginning of the Sinai instructions (Exod. 20) and here at its first ending (Exod. 31). It is the first instruction Moses gives after the golden calf crisis in 35:2. God gave the first Sabbath with the manna in 16:23–30. God further explicated the Sabbath commands at Sinai and included rest for debt slaves, land, and the animals. See comments at 20:8–11; 21:2; 23:11–12; 35:2–3. For a discussion of holiness as a foundation for ethics see Bruckner, "Ethics."

31:14 / On the extreme threat of death as a legal form, see comment in the additional note on 21:17. This threat occurs in Exodus at 19:12; 21:12, 14–17, 29; 22:19; 31:14–15; and 35:2.

§38 Crisis at Sinai: The Golden Calf (Exod. 32–34)

Exodus 32–34 forms an important watershed for understanding God's relationship to the world. The Creator had sought to redeem, form, and live among the people. To this end God delivered them out of Egypt, brought them to Mt. Sinai by going with them in the fiery cloud, and provided for them in the wilderness. At Sinai God set about forming them into the sort of community originally intended: in trust and fidelity with the Lord, with each other, and with the nonhuman creation.

During their time at Sinai, the people had again witnessed a dramatic revelation of God as Lord of creation. The detailed laws of the book of the covenant demonstrated God's concern for every aspect of human life. The people accepted this covenant in 24:3, 8. Then Moses had climbed the mountain again and was gone for forty days and nights (24:18), during which time God described the tabernacle, where God would continue to dwell among them, at great length.

In Moses' absence, the people did not know that God intended to dwell with them in the tabernacle. Without Moses, and left to their own offhanded devices, they had asked a priest (Aaron) to throw together a god (32:24). By repeating the lie, "these are your gods, who brought you up out of the land of Egypt," they chose to live in a convenient darkness of their own making rather than in the light of God's presence. While they were doing this, God was unveiling a perfect plan to invite the whole community to join in creating a beautiful dwelling place, a cooperative enterprise with the Creator. In this context, Aaron's "meanwhile-building" of the golden calf is a paltry and ironic act.

At first God honored their choice to reject the Lord. Then, in conversation with Moses, God "relented" (32:14). This "change of mind" is in itself a theological revolution and reveals the radical nature of the God of the Bible. This particular decision to relent led to an eternal change in the way God relates to the world. A series of difficult conversations between God and Moses reveal God's anguish and struggle (32:7–34:7, as we will see below).

The Lord's decision to be a forgiving God had a lasting effect on how God would relate to the wider world through Israel. It meant that God would not, hereafter, always punish the wicked in the world promptly. It meant that even God's people could choose sin without immediate (and just) repercussions. It also meant that forgiveness and reconciliation were possible, even in the worst cases, for those who turned to the Lord. It meant that God would unrelentingly pursue recalcitrant people.

God's four major decisions provide a framework for the extended narrative of Exodus 32–34. The long process of dialogue and action reveal God's anguish over the faithlessness of the people. God's final decisions resolve to take more responsibility for the relationship with them. Even in their rebellion, God would not forsake the people (see also Hos. 11:1–9).

The Lord's first decision after the golden calf incident was whether or not to "consume" the people and be finished with them. Moses interceded for the first time and the Lord "relented" concerning the threatened "disaster" (32:9–14). This decision was limited only to not destroying the people. Repentance, forgiveness, reconciliation, and renewal of the covenant were not yet in view. The people were still celebrating their calf-god. The question was simply what the Lord would do about it. God ruled out annihilation.

The Lord's second decision after the golden calf incident concerned whether or not God's presence would go among them (32:30–33:6). God said, "I will not go with you" (33:5). Instead, God decided to send a protecting angel in front of them. Having determined not to be finished with Israel, God would at least provide for their protection. Moses' second intercession (32:30–34) was a request for forgiveness on Moses' terms. The Lord did not grant it but was still deciding what to do with people who rejected the source of their life and deliverance (33:5). The turning point in the Lord's decision to go among them follows the description of Moses' face-to-face relationship with the Lord "as a . . . friend" (33:11). Moses' personal friendship with God was the basis on which the Lord reversed his second decision. The Lord's presence would go (33:14, 17). The unresolved tension at this point in the narrative is how the Lord would go among them without forgiving them.

The Lord's third decision after the golden calf incident was whether or not to forgive the people. The biblical text in no way takes this for granted. The Lord agreed to show Moses God's glory as he hid in the cleft of the rock. That "glory" was more than a visual show. It was the revelation of the identity of God to this emerging, failed, and faithless people. In this dramatic event the Lord declared God to be the one who forgives "wickedness, rebellion and sin" (34:7). Yet God "does not leave the guilty unpunished." This juxtaposition of forgiveness and punishment will require further explanation (see comment on 34:7). In any case, the crucial point is that the Lord decided to go among the people, forgiving them.

The Lord's fourth decision after the golden calf incident concerned how to start over with them to accomplish God's intended mission in the world. God would make a covenant, making promises based on God's own faithfulness to God's own word: "I will do wonders . . . how awesome is the work that I, the LORD, will do for you" (34:10). The previous Sinai covenant in the book of the covenant and the tabernacle instructions remained, but God now placed these laws on a new foundation. God's forgiveness, faithfulness, and promises would secure the future of the people. God's word cannot fail, even though hindered by human rebellion and sin.

Exodus 32–34 generally moves from the crisis of rebellion to judgment, to uncertainty at the center, and finally to reconciliation with God.

A   32:1–6 Crisis of the golden calf

   B   32:7–14 Moses intercedes and God relents concerning the disaster

      C   32:15–29 Confrontations through Moses' leadership

         D   32:30–35 The plague: Will God forgive them?

         D'   33:1–6 God will not go with them. How will the Lord be present?

      C'   33:7–11 Face to face: Tent of meeting

   B'   33:12–17 Moses intercedes again and God decides to dwell with Israel

A'   33:18–23 God's glory: God will be gracious

Exodus 34 provides for Israel's restitution and future with the Lord. The self-revelation of God occurs in a new way in time and history. The structure of Exodus 34 is as follows:

vv. 1–4	New stone tablets
vv. 5–9	The name of the Lord
vv. 10–28	A new covenant
vv. 29–35	Moses' radiant face

These vital three chapters separate God's tabernacle instructions (chs. 25–31) from the people's tabernacle building (chs. 35–40). The people's creation of the tabernacle demonstrated their true repentance after the golden calf crisis (36:3–7; 39:42–43). God showed forgiveness by dwelling in the midst of Israel's camp at the conclusion of Exodus (40:34–38). The fact that the crisis and the Lord's further revelation separate the instructions from the building of the Lord's dwelling place highlights these three chapters as a prominent theological revelation of the nature of reality.

As Moses was receiving the instructions on the mountain, the people had no idea of God's detailed plan for living in their midst. They could not conceive of the preparations God was making for them and for their future.

Additional Notes §38

32–34 / Critical scholarship has explained the disjunctures in the extended narrative of Exod. 32–34 as a redaction of separate independent sources (JE). This commentary follows the inclination to interpret the sense of the whole text (Childs, *Exodus*, pp. 557–81). Moberly demonstrates the logic of the final redactor in forming a narrative that moves from sin (ch. 32) to dialogue (ch. 33), to new covenant (Exod. 34; Moberly, *Mountain*). Brueggemann summarizes the progression: "Israel receives an articulation of God's fierce, unwarranted graciousness in the face of a profound act of disobedience. This is precisely the theological conclusion that would be most important to the exilic makers of canon" (Brueggemann, "Exodus," p. 927).

32:1–6 / The creation of the golden calf god who had supposedly "delivered the people from Egypt" temporarily "set the people free" to serve themselves. Their self-made religion created not only a new god (v. 1), but also a new version of their story of freedom and a new kind of celebration (vv. 4, 6b). It was a perverse reflection of what the living Lord had *done for* them and *promised to* them.

Their falsely created faith began with the slippery lie that some other god had led them out of Egypt (v. 4). Exchanging the truth for this lie impoverished the freedom they did have. It resulted in a broken covenant (v. 19), the removal of the true God's presence (33:3) and, for some, death (vv. 28, 35). Their celebration ended in the loss of their freedom to serve the true God altogether (see 33:3–5). They displaced God's initiative on their behalf with their own. They replaced a place to meet their Creator and redeemer with a small object of worship. A visible, controlled, and inanimate calf-bull became a substitute for the tabernacle and the Lord's invisible and living presence in their midst. They not only made the god; in making it they became their own gods. They twisted God's intended freedom for them to serve the Lord into a new form of self-slavery.

They asked for **"gods who will go before us."** The expression "who will go before us" means a god who "will lead and protect us." Up to this point in the narrative, the Lord had been that leader and protector through the cloud and an angel. The people's request was an attempt to usurp that leadership, forgetting the past. The people quickly dismissed their memory of the facts of their exit from Egypt, survival in the wilderness, and covenant-making at the mountain. Instead of recalling the Lord's mighty acts on their behalf they disparagingly referred to Moses, literally, as **"this fellow Moses [the man] who brought us up out of Egypt."** (The NIV unfortunately omits "the man.") They were implying that Moses was the one who delivered them and then they dismissed him because he had been on the mountain so long. They also conveniently forgot that they had previously accepted (24:3) the prohibition against making any other gods (20:4–5; 22:20), especially of gold (20:23).

The narrative reports that **Aaron answered them** without reflection or argument. He responded to their demand with his own demand that drove the idol-making forward. Demanding imperative voices (vv. 1–2) dominated the conversation. In contrast, God requested that the requirements for the tabernacle materials be given in a freewill and heartfelt offering (25:2; 35:4–9, 20–29). The translation of Aaron's words **"Take off the gold"** is a weak rendering of the verb *paraq*, which means "grab," "tear," or "plunder." It is a synonym of the so-called "plundering" of the Egyptian gold that the Lord arranged through Egyptian generosity (*natsal*, 3:22; 12:36). The gold was to be a resource for building the tabernacle. Now they "plundered" *themselves* to make another god. They used their gold to *make* their god, rather than *honoring* the living God with their gold in the making of the tabernacle.

The people's response was enthusiastic. **"These are your gods, O Israel, who brought you up out of Egypt."** They expressed the central and most egregious lie of the crisis. It falsified their whole existence as a people and had the potential to destroy all of them. God considered destruction as an option, based on the law that made this a capital offense (22:20). Aaron continued to attempt to be relevant to the cultural situation. Led by his best intentions, he **built an altar in front of the calf and announced,** for the following day, a **festival to the Lord.** The use of seemingly appropriate religious words created a half-truth. The biblical text does not exonerate Aaron of responsibility (see comments on vv. 21–25).

A "festival to the Lord" could have been a good thing. God had asked for a remembrance of the Exodus as a festival to the Lord in the Feast of Unleavened Bread (*khag leyhwh*, 12:14–17; 13:6–8). Their sin was not their celebrating, singing, or dancing. Rather, it was worshiping a god of their own making and celebrating it on their own terms. They had reduced the revelation of the living God to an image they could control. Having done so, they did not even mind that Aaron called the calf "the Lord." Their newfound religion looked a lot like Yahwism and sounded similar to the festivals the Lord had asked for in the building of the tabernacle. The insidiousness of their rebellion was in its half-truths. The form of what they did looked similar to what the Lord commanded: they **sacrificed burnt offerings and presented fellowship offerings;** they remembered their deliverance; **they sat down to eat and drink;** and they celebrated. But they based the object of their worship and its content on a self-serving lie.

Since they had already replaced the living Lord with a golden calf that they called by the same name, they also felt free to improvise in their celebration. When they had finished eating, they **got up to indulge in revelry.** They created a new aspect of their festival that did not resemble any of the festivals in the book of the covenant (23:14–17). Their revelry included (potentially good) dancing and singing (vv. 18–19). The last time the people danced was after the crossing of the sea, in celebration of the Lord's deliverance. They danced and sang again here, but the tone was different. The Lord called the celebration "corrupt" (v. 7). They celebrated what they had made as the "authors" of their own deliverance and salvation. In this move, they celebrated themselves as if they were their own saviors. Their revelry was the natural result of a self-serving celebration.

32:7–14 / God's first decision was whether or not to destroy the people. The Lord sent Moses down the mountain to intercede. God severed any association with them, telling Moses that **"your people, whom you brought up out of Egypt, have become corrupt."** This shift in pronouns suggests that the Lord's passion against self-serving betrayal was as strong as God's passion for those who were faithful (see 2 Sam. 22:26–28). The NIV translation here is too passive ("have become corrupt"). It is better read, "have corrupted themselves" (reflexive *pi'el* of *shakhat*, "ruined," "destroyed"). God implied that Moses might be able to do something. God's accusation was that the people **"have been quick to turn away"** from the prohibitions against worshiping other gods and making idols (20:4–6, 23; 22:20). The Lord noted especially that they had said, **"These are your gods, O Israel, who brought you up out of Egypt."** God then said, **"I have seen these people."** Idolatry and all kinds of intentional sin are the result of living as if God cannot see (Ezek. 8:12; 9:9; Pss. 14:1–2; 53:1–2).

God continued with the request, **"Now leave me alone so that my anger may burn against them and that I may destroy them."** God's anger did not burn simply because they rejected the Lord. It burned because they had known God as their savior from slavery, provider in the wilderness, and giver of their new life together in the covenant. They spurned God's friendship and grace.

The Lord's anger burns most fiercely when the redeemed live as if they had not been redeemed.

God's words to Moses, "Now leave me alone," revealed that God would not act in judgment unless Moses refused to intercede. The Lord thus gave Moses an opening to leave God alone or to stand in the gap. God asked Moses' permission and opened a window of hope for the rebellious people. What Moses did next made all the difference for some, but not for all (vv. 25–27). In Israel's refusal to be loved they had rejected God's love. Moses argued for their lives using two warrants: God's reputation as a redeemer and the Creator's promise to Abraham, Isaac, and Israel.

But Moses sought the favor of the LORD his God (lit., "sought to make the Lord's face pleasant"). Moses did not make excuses for the Israelites. He himself would see that the worst offenders were executed (see comment on v. 26). Yet he appealed for an outcome other than judgment alone. God had already decided to bring judgment but had not yet determined its extent. Moses took the opening that God gave by interceding for the people.

Moses began by asking the Lord questions about the salvation from Egypt and God's reputation with the Egyptians. God had made so much progress. The Lord had delivered the people **"with great power and a mighty hand."** The Egyptians had come to know (and potentially all the earth would come to know) that the Lord was the Creator and redeemer. Moses was shockingly direct: **"Why should the Egyptians say, 'It was with evil intent that he brought them out, to kill them in the mountains and to wipe them off the face of the earth?"** The sin of the people had put the reputation of the Lord's salvation at risk. Moses and the Lord are quite open about the crisis of the salvation of the world.

Then Moses made several appeals to God's openness to relationship. He did not challenge the justice of God's anger, but asked the Lord to **Turn** away from it, **relent,** and **"not bring disaster on your people."** Moses knew that behind the circumstantial wrath of this apostate situation was the Lord's redeeming love for creation. Moses appealed to the Lord's promises, made out of this steadfast and unrelenting love. Faithfulness to promises is one of God's attributes. Moses reminded God of this when he spoke of **"Abraham, Isaac and Israel, to whom you swore by your own self."** God swore by what was ever true: "your own self." Moses quoted God's own promises back to God (v. 13; Gen. 15:5; 22:17; 26:4; Deut. 9:26–29). While God might have fulfilled the promises through Moses (v. 10b), the Lord chose not to start over.

God responded to Moses' questions and appeals because what God had already accomplished in delivering the people was significant (see also Phil. 1:6). God's reputation among the unbelieving nations mattered because God had bigger plans than Israel (Col. 1:15–20). The Lord's response demonstrated unending faithfulness to fulfilling God's own promises.

The narrator reports the first decision of the crisis: **"Then the LORD relented and did not bring on his people the disaster he had threatened."** The older translations use the expression "God repented of the evil" (KJV, RSV). The NIV has, more accurately, "relented . . . the disaster." When God is the subject of the verb *nakham* it is best translated "had compassion" or "relented." The basic meaning of the verb is "have compassion" or "feel sorrow." When people feel sorrow, or are "sorry," the context of sin often warrants the translation "repent." *Nakham* means "repentance" in the sense of feeling sorrow. When God feels sorrow, however, the word cannot mean "repent" since God does not sin. Rather, it indicates God's sorrow for the consequences people must face as a natural result of their sin and the Lord's justice in the world order. God expresses this "sorrow" in compassion and in "relenting."

32:15–29 / Moses' confrontation with Aaron and two confrontations with the people once again mark his skill as a leader. As Moses went down the mountain with Joshua, he carried **the two tablets of the Testimony.** The text places the Ten Commandments at the center of the narrative (also at 31:18). Two verses (vv. 15–16) mention the tablets and the writing on them three times each. They represented the agreement the people had made with the Lord in the book of the covenant (24:3). The work of the living God in history and in the lives of these specific people is at stake. Whether hope remained for God's project in time and space depended on what happened next.

Joshua, who was with Moses (24:13), **heard the noise of the people shouting** and thought it was the **sound of war** (or "fighting") **in the camp.** The mention of Joshua helps to validate his future leadership role. His focus on war is typical. Moses responded in poetic verse:

> not victory's singing sound
> not defeat's singing sound
>   singing sound I hear (v. 18; author's translation)

Twelve Hebrew words in verse 18 tell the truth about the "celebration" of the calf. It was not a victory for the people. They had thrown down and shattered the gift of new life they had previously accepted (24:3–8). Neither was it a defeat. They had not lost a battle with an enemy. No one had forced them to abandon the Lord. Moses' point was that the singing was meaningless. It was an empty party ("random singing," so Durham, *Exodus*, p. 424).

Moses . . . saw the calf and the dancing. Again this contrasts with the celebration of the people at the sea. After their deliverance, there had been singing and dancing to celebrate their deliverance through the Lord's victory over the pursuing Egyptians (15:20). The singing and dancing were not the issue. The emptiness of the singing and dancing, and its false object, the self-made calf, were the problem. They had tossed away meaningful life and hope for the future. Like the Lord, when Moses saw them, his **anger burned** (vv. 9–10; 19), because so much was being lost.

Moses responded with appropriate symbolic actions in his first confrontation with the people. He **threw the tablets . . . breaking them to pieces.** The original covenant with the Lord was shattered in the same place it had been made, **at the foot of the mountain** (v. 19; 24:4). The tablets contained the Ten Commandments, but they also represented the whole book of the covenant (24:3–7). The people had already agreed to the terms of the book, in order that they could be the people of God. God might dwell in their midst, but they had now annulled the relationship. The exodus project, the blessing of the nations through the Israelites, was in jeopardy and God would have to start over (v. 10). The Lord did just that (34:10).

Then Moses **took the calf . . . burned it in the fire . . . ground it to powder,** and **scattered it on the water.** Gold, of course, melts when fired and is too soft to be ground into powder. The Hebrew words used here for burned, ground, and scattered convey total destruction. These verbs constitute a formulaic sequence also found in the annihilation of a Ugaritic god. The action was practical as well as symbolic. Whatever the melted and fragmented result was, Moses put it in water and **made the Israelites drink it.** This resembles a trial by ordeal in which people were observed as they drank in order to discern the guilty from the innocent (Num. 5:16–22).

After his first confrontation with the people, Moses also confronted Aaron for leading them **into such great sin** (vv. 21–24; "great sin," *khata'ah gedolah*, see comment on v. 30). Aaron began with Moses, as Moses had begun with the Lord, by asking him not to be **angry** (vv. 10, 22). Aaron even called Moses "Sir" (NIV **my** lord; *ʾadoni*, not *yhwh*, "Lord"). The similarity ended there. While Moses had immediately turned to God's redeeming power, Aaron proceeded to make excuses and put all the blame upon the people "for their tendency to **evil**" (vv. 11–12, 22). He recounted for Moses what had happened between himself and the people (vv. 1–3; 23–24a). His description of how he made the idol was, however, a lie: **"I threw it into the fire, and out came this calf!"** (v. 24b). In fact he had made the "idol cast in the shape of a calf, fashioning it with a tool" (v. 4). He had also built the altar in front of the calf and announced the festival (v. 5). To Moses, he claimed that the calf had somehow magically self-generated. Moses later recounted that the Lord was angry enough to destroy Aaron too, but did not (Deut. 9:20).

The text does not exonerate Aaron of guilt. He made the calf and acted as its priest (vv. 2–6, 21–25, 35). He tried to be relevant to the people's expressed need in Moses' absence, but in doing so he lost the core of faith itself. The Lord's restitution of Aaron and his ordination as the high priest may seem a bit scandalous. As a result, some interpreters have sought to explain Aaron's actions in the kindest way, suggesting that he was forced to act as the people wanted. Others have suggested that the death of his two sons at their ordination somehow atoned for Aaron's sin. None of this is in the biblical text. The scandal is the scandal of God's grace. God's decision to live among people the Lord knew to be rebellious extended to Aaron. It revealed the reality that the most devout are prone to the greatest sins. No one is exempt from turning away from the Lord, and no one is beyond God's forgiveness, though unalterable consequences may endure (see the comments on 34:6–7).

Moses' second confrontation with the people was necessary because they still **were running wild.** He began by standing at the gate, the traditional place of court proceedings. A just administration of courtroom procedure lies between the lines of this text. This is also what one would expect after having read the concern for justice in the book of the covenant. Zeal for God's law stood behind what followed, but the text does not condone wanton zealotry.

Moses stood **at the entrance** ("at the gate"). The due process of law had already begun as Moses stood at the place of judgment. The people had heard the law against idolatry and agreed to it (20:4–6; 22:20). Moses had confronted them with the tablets of the covenant (v. 19), destroyed their idol, and made them drink its failure, probably as a public trial (v. 20). Still, they persisted in "running wild" and **out of control**. Again Moses warned them, this time standing at the gate of judgment. He called out, **"Whoever is for the LORD, come to me."** This was the second opportunity for repentance. Once they had made and confirmed their choices, Moses commissioned the Levites with a third and final confrontation. Those who persisted were slain.

The Levites' killing may also be understood as an action to stop the wild behavior. Not necessarily vengeful, it was a battle to wrest control of the community from the lawless who would not stand down. The anguish of Moses' words reveals an absence of vengeance, **"each killing his brother and friend and neighbor."** The specific mention of each Levite killing his brother and friend and neighbor tells the truth about the pathos of the situation. Those who would not stop wantonly "running wild" were executed by people they knew. They were "out of control" as individuals and as a crowd.

The creation of a people who would bless other nations seems hopelessly lost at this point in the narrative. The main concern was to bring the wild celebration of a false god to an end. The Levites had the crucial role of ending the riotous situation. As a result Moses commended them: **"You have been set apart to the LORD today"** (better, "Set yourselves apart today," see additional note on v. 29), and **"he has blessed you"** is literally, "He gives you a blessing" because of what you did. They were not blessed by the awful action of executing men, but God blessed them for suffering their role in restoring law and order to the community.

32:30–35 / Would God forgive the people? God's second and third decisions concerned whether God's presence would go among the people (ch. 33) and whether God would forgive them (ch. 34). Exodus 32 ends with a preview of these issues. In both cases, the preliminary answer was "No." God's angel would lead them and the Lord would not forgive the guilty.

Moses spoke to the Lord about what **a great sin** (*khataʾah gedolah*) the people had committed, repeating what he said to the people: **"You have committed a great sin"** (lit., "You, you have sinned a great sin"). This great sin is reminiscent of the sin in the garden of Eden. There, the Lord's instructions had been clear about the limits of human freedom. Adam and Eve could eat of all the trees, including the tree of life, but God asked them to accept their limitations regarding the tree of knowledge of good and evil.

At Sinai, the Lord asked that they make no false gods but trust the Lord alone. In both cases the narrative reports the sin in a painfully casual way. In Genesis 3, "the woman saw that the fruit of the tree was good for food and pleasing to the eye, and also desirable for gaining wisdom, she took some and ate it. She also gave some to her husband, who was with her, and he ate it" (Gen. 3:6). At Sinai, the tone of the people's remarks is similarly cavalier: "Come, make us gods who will go before us. As for this fellow Moses who brought us up out of Egypt, we don't know what has happened to him" (v. 1). The excuses they give are also casual in tone (Gen. 3:12–13; Exod. 32:22–24). The offhanded manner in which they dismiss God's concern intensifies the reader's experience of the insidious, rationalizing nature of the sin. Alienation from God and blaming others is "sin" in the original sense—the sin has corrupted all relationships and yet the sinner defends the behavior as normal.

Moses told the people that he would try to **make atonement** for their sin with the Lord. This atonement (or "covering") had nothing to do with blood or sacrifice. Moses' best possibility for restoration was by means of God's friendship and through conversation. He made an either-or request: **"please forgive** (*nasa*ʾ, "lift the consequences") **their sin—but if not, then blot me out** (*makhah*, "erase" or "wipe out") **of the book you have written."** God did not accept either of Moses' alternatives. Rather, God would be selective: **"Whoever has sinned against me I will blot out of my book."** The Levites killed only a small percentage of the guilty (see additional note on v. 28). Many had ceased their revelry at Moses' first confrontation (vv. 19–20).

The Lord knew who had sinned. The final word of the Lord was, **"when the time comes for me to punish** (*paqad*), **I will punish** (*paqad*) **them for their sin."** Hebrew does not have a word for "punish." The same word, *paqad*, is used for God's "visitation" that brings blessing or punishment. The difference depends on the relationship one has with the Lord. Literally, the text says, "when I visit, I will visit their sin upon them." The difference between "visiting" their sin and "punishing" for their sin may seem subtle, but it is important for understanding the consequences of sin in relation to God. This distinction is crucial for understanding God's identity described in 34:6–7 (see comment below). The Lord's visitation on those who sinned was in the form of **a plague** that **struck the people.**

At the end of Exodus 32, the people had shattered their covenant with the Lord. The ugly work of the Levites in killing **three thousand** recalcitrant Israelites and the plague that followed put God's reputation at risk. Yet God took responsibility for killing and making alive, in history and in the flesh of a specific people. In Christ, the Lord would take on the scandal of God's own death. God's grace abounds, but judgment attends those who do not seek refuge in the Lord (34:6–7; Rev. 19:11–16).

Additional Notes §39

32:1 / "Make us gods" may also be translated "make us a god" (*'elohim*). Hebrew uses the simple plural form in a royal way throughout this text. The text even refers to the single calf-bull idol in the plural (v. 4b, NIV "these are your gods"). This can also be properly translated "this is your god."

32:4 / The "idol cast in the shape of a calf" (*'egel*) was a bull-calf, a symbol of power and fertility. Usually in the Canaanite representation of the god El, sometimes called "Bull-El," the god stood on top of the calf-bull. Ancient worshipers represented the god Hadad in a similar way. See also 1 Kgs. 12:26–33 for the bulls Jeroboam erected at Bethel and Dan. Jeroboam misused the words of v. 4 as a positive precedent. The inclusion of the detail that Aaron made the idol, "fashioning it with a tool," heightens the foolishness of creating a "god" by one's own hand. See Isa. 44:9–20.

32:6 / The celebration of worship in front of the calf is similar to the sin in the garden of Eden. Adam and Eve also sought to establish themselves as authors of their own futures by eating from the tree (see comment on v. 30 above). The Heb. word "revelry" (*tsakhaq*, in the *pi'el*) usually means "mocking" or "teasing." The sexual connotations sometimes attributed here stem from a comparison with a positive use of the word referring to sexual relations between Isaac and Rebecca in Gen. 26:8. It is more likely that the mocking was rooted in the knowledge that the calf-bull was in their control and they were free to do anything they liked. The unrestrained sexuality is a more likely reference in v. 25, "running wild" (*para'*) that also means "uncovered."

32:9 / God called them **a stiff-necked people** three times in this crisis (v. 9; 33:3, 5). God makes sure that Moses tells them so (33:5). When God forgave them, it was not because they were no longer stiff-necked. God forgave them in spite of their stiff necks (34:9–10). On the importance of the term "stiff-necked" in this context see Moberly, *Mountain*, pp. 89–93. See also Deut. 10:16; 31:27; Jer. 7:26; 17:23; 19:15.

32:10 / See Childs' discussion of "Let me alone" in *Exodus,* p. 567; also Fretheim, *Exodus,* pp. 283–84.

32:14 / For a good discussion of the translation issue of *nakham* as "repent" (people) and "relent" (God), see Craig, *Poetics,* p. 34. Note also that the older translations "of the evil" also misunderstood the reliance of the word *ra'ah* upon its context. "Disaster" is correct. It may be experienced as an "evil" by those who are caught in sin because of its catastrophic results. The word does not in itself refer to intrinsic evil.

32:22 / When Aaron later wore the medallion on his turban that says "HOLY TO THE LORD," it did not mean that Aaron was holy in himself (28:36; 39:30). It meant that God had conferred upon Aaron the Lord's own holiness. The only indications in Scripture of Aaron's participation in God's judgment (or even in his forgiveness) were that he remained silent when the Lord destroyed his two arrogant sons and that he refused the meat that was due to him by law (Lev. 10:3, 16–20).

32:25 / The expressions "running wild" and "out of control" are from the same root, *para',* meaning "broken loose." The text leaves the details of the wildness to the reader's imagination. Commentators have concluded that it entailed drunkenness, violence, and sexual abuses of all kinds. They had become **a laughingstock** (*shimtsah*), literally, "a shamed whisper" or "derision."

32:27 / Moses said, "This is what the LORD, the God of Israel says." The narrative does not record God's instructions to Moses. The Lord had already given the legal grounds for these executions in the book of the covenant: "Whoever sacrifices to any god other than the LORD must be destroyed" (22:20). The Lord referred to this law in speaking with Moses (v. 8).

32:28 / The "three thousand" people the Levites killed were 0.5% (1 in 200) of the 600,000 men who left Egypt (12:37) The percentage is even lower in relation to all who left Egypt.

32:29 / The LXX has the reflexive, "You have ordained yourselves," implying that the killing by the sword "filled their hands," which implies that they took the responsibility of being priests into their own hands. The Heb., however, has the imperative *mil'u yedkem* ("fill your hands," meaning "ordain yourselves"). It means that they should hereafter consider themselves as set apart for special service to the Lord. God described the ordination of the Levitical priests of Aaron's family to Moses in Exod. 29. The Deuteronomist considers all Levites to be priests (Deut. 18:1–8).

32:30 / Verses 21, 30–31; and 2 Kgs. 17:21 mention "great sin" (also "sin" or "sinned" in vv. 32, 33, 34). Choosing not to trust the Lord at both Eden and Sinai had consequences that shaped the persistence of evil in the world and the Lord's strategy to bring all creation under God's rule. In both cases God decided, in response to foolish human choices, not to terminate the project to bless the creation. Rather God took on more responsibility, including more vulnerability to human accusation and disbelief. God decided to forgive, to be long-suffering, and to continue to provide, even for those who rejected God. After the "great sin" it is increasingly clear that only God's initiative and unrelenting love for creation will be able to save any of it.

32:32 / Exodus does not elsewhere mention "the book you have written." It may be similar to "the book of life" (Ps. 69:28; Phil. 4:3; Rev. 3:5; 20:12–15; 21:27) or the "scroll of remembrance" (Mal. 3:16–18).

§40 Crisis: Will Yahweh Go with Them? (Exod. 33:1–23)

Following Moses' discovery of the golden calf, Moses and the Lord engaged in conversation as God decided what to do (v. 5). The primary question was whether the Lord would continue to go with them personally (vv. 3, 5, 12, 14–16; see also 34:9). Exodus 32 had ended with the Lord's immediate negative reaction to their betrayal (32:33–34). God initially decides not to go with them, but two realities, described in the first half of Exodus 33, turn the conversation: the people's demonstration of repentance; and Moses' close relationship with the Lord. In the second half of Exodus 33, Moses intercedes further and the Lord decides to go with them and promises to reveal God's glory and goodness. The following outline reveals the developments in these relationships and conversations:

vv. 1–6	The Lord refuses to go with the stiff-necked people and the people mourn
vv. 7–11	Face to face in the former tent of meeting
vv. 12–17	Moses intercedes again; Yahweh *will* go with you
vv. 18–23	God promises to reveal divine glory and goodness

33:1–6 / The Lord repeats the instructions from Exodus 32 in more detail (see 32:34a): **"Leave this place . . . go up to the land . . . I will send an angel before you."** The Lord reminded them of the oath to Abraham and the land of the Canaanites **flowing** with milk and honey, taking Moses back to the words of the original promise God made at Sinai (3:6–8, 16–17). At this point, God had partially answered Moses' petition to restore the people (32:13) so the second half of verse 3 comes as a shock: **"But I will not go with you, because you are a stiff-necked people"** (see additional note on "stiff-necked" at 32:9). The Lord had told them to **"take off your ornaments"** ("adornment" or "finery"). They **stripped off**

(*natsal*) **their ornaments,** as they had "stripped" the Egyptians (3:22). Jewelry remained the symbol of the golden calf that they had made from their earrings. This stripping of ornaments and their mourning in verse 4 (*'abal,* grief as at a funeral) were both signs of their repentance. They accepted the reality of their condition as "stiff-necked" and relinquished the "plunder" of their deliverance from Egypt.

33:7–11 / These verses establish the depth of God's friendship with Moses. They are key to understanding the transformation of the Lord's relationship with the people described in verses 12–23 and 34:1–10. The repeated expressions "I know you by name," "I am pleased with you," and "you have found favor with me" (vv. 12–13, 16–17; see comment there) characterize Moses' friendship with the Lord. Friendship was the foundation on which the restoration of sinful Israel was built.

Now Moses used to take a tent and pitch it outside the camp some distance away, calling it the "tent of meeting." The friendship of God with Moses in the tent of meeting became the new paradigm for the Lord's friendship toward all Israel. When the people completed the tabernacle, the new "tent of meeting" became a place for the presence of God to remain among them. Moses' original tent, and the relationship it represented, rescued them in this crisis through the conversation it afforded. The tabernacle tent, made after this crisis, would sustain the people throughout their history, even when they sinned, by its existence at the center of community worship.

Before the crisis of the golden calf, the text describes an idealized relationship with the Lord. At that that time, **Anyone inquiring of the LORD would go to the tent of meeting outside the camp** (v. 7) as part of their normal relationship with their redeemer. When **Moses went out to the tent, all the people rose and stood at the entrances to their tents** in respect for the Lord (v. 8). At that time, **the pillar of cloud would come down . . . while the LORD spoke with Moses** (v. 9). When the people saw it, they **stood and worshiped** in front of their tents (v. 10). The Lord would speak to Moses **as a man speaks with his friend** (v. 11). After the crisis of the calf, only one relationship had not changed. The Lord still spoke with Moses as a friend. God used the reality of that friendship as a foundation for traveling with them (vv. 12–15) and for establishing that the people had a forgiving God in their midst (34:5–7).

Concern about seeing God face to face is critical in Exodus 33. **The LORD would speak to Moses face to face,** "as a man speaks with his friend" (v. 11a). Some interpreters dismiss this as an idiom or as an older (incorrect) tradition, but a few verses later God gives a clear warning that creates a paradox: "you cannot see my face, for no one may see me and live" (v. 20; see Gen. 32:31; Exod. 19:21; Judg. 6:22–23; 13:22; Isa. 6:5). In this well-known encounter, Moses was able to see the Lord's back as God passed by him. Yet the deep friendship of God in face-to-face encounter is corroborated in Numbers 12:7–8: "my servant Moses . . . is faithful in all my house. With him I speak face to face (lit., "mouth to mouth"), clearly and not in riddles; he sees the form of the LORD."

The first time Moses *saw* the Lord, at the burning bush, he was afraid to look (see comment on 3:6). This is the major tradition in Scripture. One cannot see God and live, but God can be seen. Abraham and Sarah saw God speaking through "three men" (Gen. 18:2) who became "two messengers" (Gen. 19:1) and spoke as the Lord (Gen. 18:10, 13). Fretheim calls this and other theophanies an "oscillation" because the Lord is present and speaking, represented as a human-looking messenger (*mal°ak,* sometimes translated "angel"). Hagar has a similar experience and says, "Have I really seen God and remained alive after seeing him?" (Gen. 16:13; RSV). The seventy elders also saw the God of Israel (see comment on 24:10), yet "God did not raise his hand against these leaders" (24:11). We witness the same concern over seeing someone and speaking to the Lord in Judges 6:22–23 and 13:22. God remained free to make exceptions to the rule, and allowed these people to live (24:10–11; see Num. 12:8; Deut. 34:10; Ezek. 1:26–28).

Fretheim comes to three conclusions about the OT claims that people saw God: (a) God can be seen. The issue is not visibility, but whether or not you live through it. (b) God is capable of allowing God's self to be seen, and does it. People live to tell about it because God grants an exception to the rule. (c) People may not see God's "fullness." Nonetheless, people do sometimes see, hear, and speak to God in human form. Fretheim concludes that, for Israel, there is no such thing as a non-incarnate God (Fretheim, *Suffering,* pp. 91–93; 105). The continuity of the OT with the fuller revelation of the Lord's commitment to corporeality in the incarnation and bodily resurrection of Jesus is obvious (see comments on the "dwelling glory" of God in "Tabernacle and Incarnation" in the introduction to Exodus 25).

33:12–17 / Moses intercedes again for the presence to go with them. He expresses a natural concern for how he would lead so many people without the Lord. Moses' reminder that **"this nation is your people"** was an expression of his frustration (v. 13). The Lord reversed the decision not to go with them (v. 3b) based on this personal friendship with Moses (v. 17). **"My Presence will go with you, and I will give you rest"** (v. 14). Moses reacted as though he could not believe what he had just heard. His emotion is palpable as he vents his anxiety and relief together in verses 15 and 16. Then the Lord assured him and confirmed this decision to personally go with them (v. 17).

Two Hebrew phases repeated throughout verses 7–11 define Moses' friendship with the Lord. They are translated: **"You have found"** grace (NIV "favor," vv. 12, 13, 16, 17) and **"I know you by name"** (vv. 12, 17). The basic meaning of the word *khen* ("grace," or "favor") is a heartfelt response toward someone who has a need but no claim upon the giver (see additional notes). "I know you by name" is God's summary of the reality the narrator reported earlier, that Yahweh would speak to Moses face to face as a man speaks with his friend (v. 11). As we have seen, the restoration of Israel was built on friendship with the Lord.

Moses had been in a relationship with the Lord long enough to discover God's friendship and grace. God's faithfulness made it possible to bring blessing to the people and to the world through them (v. 16b). God would hereafter extend this grace and friendship shared with Moses to the whole nation. The Lord revealed the full extent of this friendship when Moses saw God's glory and goodness (vv. 18–19; 34:5–7). How the Lord would go among them without forgiving them remained unresolved until then (34:7).

33:18–23 / **Then Moses said, "Now show me your glory."** Moses asked to see God's glory, as he had previously (see comments on 16:7; 24:16). He sought assurance of God's promise to be present with them, asking for what he had previously seen: a theophany of God's presence. The Lord gave Moses what he wanted (glory) and what he needed (knowledge of God's goodness; 34:6–7). The text mutes the importance of the glory (34:5a), as God knew what Moses and the people needed was to know God's **goodness** and **name** (i.e., God's character, v. 19). The Lord's response to Moses did not even mention glory. God said, **"I will cause all my goodness to pass in front of you, and I will proclaim my name,**

the LORD, in your presence." What Moses saw would simply serve to support what he had heard (34:5–7).

The Lord gave a preview of 34:6–7 in verse 19b. **"I will have mercy** (*khanan*, "be gracious") **on whom I will have mercy, and I will have compassion** (*rakham*) **on whom I will have compassion."** This expansion of the name Yahweh is still in a brief form. It comes as a promise that anticipates the further revelation of the identity of the Lord to Moses in 34:5–7. (See comment there on the meanings of the words "mercy" and "compassion.") The Lord's gifts of mercy and compassion, given to Israel in the exodus and at Sinai in the law, remained God's own prerogative. They were, like friendship, the jurisdiction of a personal God. Through Israel the Lord had revealed mercy and compassion to the world. It was not to be taken for granted. The Lord declared here that God's goodness was not abstract, but personal and relational.

The final verses of Exodus 33 (vv. 20–23) give the logistics of the anticipated revelation of the fullness of God's identity (v. 19, "all my goodness"). The Lord reminded him, **"you cannot see my face . . . and live."** But God will be seen. The Lord would make it possible by providing every necessity: **"a place near me . . . you may stand on a rock . . . I will put you in a cleft . . . and cover you** (*sakak*, "shield") **. . . I will remove my hand . . . you will see my back."** In the event itself, what Moses *saw* had less impact (34:5) than what Moses heard and experienced. The Lord stood there with him and spoke. The friendship between Moses and the Lord led to establishing new and enduring foundation stones for God's friendship with the people: the commandments (34:1–4) and all the goodness of God's name (34:5–7).

Additional Notes §40

33:3 / The essential conversations concerning the Lord's decisions are in vv. 3, 12–19 and 34:5–10. They form the structure and themes that the other sections of the text support.

33:4–5 / They "stripped off their ornaments at Mount Horeb" (Sinai). The tradition took the removal of ornaments to mean a perpetual ban on ornamental "jewelry." For the rabbis, the initial removal was a sign of repentance. The perpetual ban demonstrated their awareness of their tendency toward evil.

33:7–11 / The theme of the friendship of God in Exodus contrasts with that of God as a stranger. When the Lord says, "leave me alone so . . . that I may destroy them" (32:10), God's distance and estrangement from the people is evident. God sought friendship with those who were willing, but was a dangerous stranger to those who lived as though the Lord did not exist. Jesus continued this stranger/friend theme in his teaching on caring for the destitute. To those who do not show mercy he will say, "I was a stranger and you did not invite me in." Not knowing the friendship of God leads, in the judgment, to despair and permanent estrangement (Matt. 25:43–46).

33:7 / The different style and content of vv. 7–11 has led to an extensive unresolved discussion among source critics. For a summary of that discussion see Durham, *Exodus*, p. 440. This part of the text has a critical role in the flow of the narrative and in the theological revelation of Exodus 34 (Childs, *Exodus*, pp. 589–93; Fretheim, *Exodus*, p. 295). It ought not be considered as intrusive, misplaced, or parenthetical, regardless of its origin. Its contrasting style and content is exactly the "intrusion" needed to resolve the conflict between God and the people. The paragraphs that follow (vv. 12–23) demonstrate the kind of intimacy these verses describe.

33:10–11 / The best discussion of the theophany texts is by Fretheim, "God in Human Form," in *Suffering*, pp. 79–106. He demonstrates that from Genesis onward we can see God in human form. For a theological interpretation of the face-to-face theme in 2 Cor. 4:6 see Ford, *Self and Salvation*, pp. 193–202.

33:13 / The NIV conflates/elides the literal "If, please, I have found grace *(khen)* in your sight" to read "If you are pleased with me." The Heb. word *khen* actually means "grace." In vv. 12–17, the NIV has either "pleased with" (vv. 12, 13, 16, 17) or "find favor" (vv. 12, 13), which is too weak for grace in relation to God. It is better translated "grace" (so KJV, LXX, *charis*). In other places, the NIV does translate words from the same root verb as "mercy" (v. 19) and "gracious" (34:6).

33:15 / Moses was not pressing the point further. The singular "with you" in v. 14 is commonly used for the singular "people." Moses was not worried that God would only go with him and not with the people, contra Enns, *Exodus*, p. 581.

33:18 / Commentators vary widely in their interpretation of Moses' request to see God's glory. This was not an expression of Moses' ecstasy, daring, impertinence, or spiritual longing. Moses was looking for reassurance by asking for what he previously had seen. The NIV does not help by omitting the word "please" (*na³*, particle of entreaty; v. 18 is, lit., "cause me to see, please, your glory").

33:19b / "I will have mercy on whom I will have mercy" uses the same form of repetition of the Lord's original self-revelation to Moses in 3:14, "I AM WHO I AM." It is an expansion of the name Yahweh (see Childs, *Exodus*, p. 596).

33:22 / The description, "When my glory passes by, I will put you in a cleft in the rock and cover you with my hand," powerfully expresses the combination of the friendship of the Lord and the glory of God's presence. The OT traditions of the visible glory of God and the friendship of the Lord come together again in the NT to explain who Jesus was after his resurrection from the dead. See John 1:14, 16 and 2 Cor. 4:6; see also Num. 12:8; Ps. 17:15. The OT assumes that God has a human form that can be seen (Tigay, "Exodus," p. 188).

§41 Crisis Resolved: The Name of the Lord (Exod. 34:1–9)

Exodus 34 is the theological center of the book of Exodus. The stone tablets with the Ten Commandments, which Moses broke in anger in Exodus 32:19, are remade (vv. 1–4, 27–29). The Lord proclaims the divine name with a full description of who God is in the world. God responds to the golden calf crisis by promising to be a forgiving God in their midst. The Lord then describes how this forgiveness would function (vv. 5–9). The text reiterates representative laws from the book of the covenant and the Ten Commandments (vv. 10–28). Finally, we see the glory of God revealed in Moses' radiant face (vv. 29–35). The summaries and resolutions of tension in this chapter serve as a microcosm of Exodus. The richly layered narrative combines themes of the confrontation of sin as sin, God's provision of detailed instructions, the juxtaposition of God's transcendence and immanent friendship, and the persistence of God's intention to be present in the world in a specific way. All that remains is the building of the tabernacle (Exod. 35–40).

34:1–4 / The Lord asked Moses to **"Chisel out two stone tablets like the first ones"** so that God could once again **"write on them the words that were on the first tablets."** It was imperative that God's commands were readily available to guide the people. This brief "interruption," before the appearance God had promised in 33:22, serves an intentional purpose in the narrative. It emphasizes that the commandments would remain at the center of Israel's life, symbolically placed in the ark of the covenant in the holy of holies. They were not peripheral to the "sign" of the Lord's appearance. God's presence was a confirmation to Moses of the commands and promises that God was about to renew. It was not an abstract theophany or epiphany. The verses about the commandments serve to bind the chapter together (vv. 1–4, 27–29, 32, 34).

Once again the text emphasizes the Lord's transcendent otherness ("holiness"), for **"not even the flocks and herds may graze in front of the mountain."** The particulars that the text gives also highlight Moses' labor and participation. Moses **chiseled the stone,** climbed **Mount Sinai** (for the sixth time), and went **early in the morning** as he **carried the two stone tablets in his hands.** God integrated human endeavor and friendship into the re-creation of the people (see also Gen. 2:19).

34:5–7 / The proclamation of the identity ("the name") of the Lord echoes the call of Moses and the revelation of the Lord's name in Exodus 3. After many struggles, the Lord reveals a fuller description of the divine characteristics and attributes. It is difficult to overemphasize the importance of verses 5–7. Yahweh's identity itself became the basis for Israel's continued existence as a sinful and forgiven people. These verses are the heart of the chapter that is the theological core of Exodus. They functioned as a confession of faith in God and God's redeeming work throughout the OT. Throughout their history, Israel frequently repeated this credo, or portions of it, in a wide variety of formats and contexts.

Then the LORD came down in the cloud and stood there with him and proclaimed his name, the LORD. God had promised to show Moses the "glory" of the Lord (33:18, 22). Now that the time had come, the "glory" is barely noticeable in the brief mention of **the cloud.** The Lord's greater glory was found not in this visible manifestation, but rather in the relationships proclaimed in his name.

Many texts use verses 6–7 as a touchstone in an amazing variety of ways and formats. The descriptive praise of Psalm 145 exults in the generational blessings of creation because of the faithfulness specifically revealed in verse 6 (see Ps. 145:8–13). David relied on the Lord's reputation, twice quoting verse 6 in his cry for deliverance (Ps. 86:5, 15). He knew that though the arrogant were attacking him for his failings, the Lord would still receive him. "But you, O LORD, are a compassionate and gracious God, slow to anger, abounding in love and faithfulness." The psalmist also used verse 6 as the basis for praising God for removing transgressions from us "as far as the east is from the west" (Ps. 103:8, 12).

King Hezekiah used the same credo to appeal to the northern tribes to return to the Lord after the Assyrians had devastated their land (2 Chr. 30:8–9). Joel quoted verse 6 as a call to forgiveness. He reminded the people that it was not too late to repent, because of God's reputation: "Rend your heart and not your garments. Return to the LORD your God, for he is gracious and compassionate, slow to anger and abounding in love, and he relents from sending calamity" (Joel 2:13). After the people had returned from exile in Babylon and rebuilt the wall of Jerusalem, they gathered to rededicate themselves in confession to live faithfully before God. The Levites used verses 6–7 as the basis of their prayer of repentance, petition, and renewal of their covenant with God (Neh. 9:17, 31). Jonah quoted God to God in his complaint about the Lord being slow to anger, forgiving the wicked, especially the violent Ninevites (Jonah 4:2).

And he passed in front of Moses, proclaiming,

> **"The LORD, the LORD, the compassionate and gracious God, slow to anger, abounding in** unrelenting **love and faithfulness, maintaining** unrelenting **love to thousands** of generations; **forgiving** (lifting the burden of) guilt-**wickedness** (sin that leaves a lasting negative impact, *ʿawon*), **rebellion and sin. Yet he** *certainly will not clear (the effects), visiting the (ongoing effects of) guilt-wickedness of the fathers* on **the children and** *grand***children . . . to the third and fourth generation."** (vv. 6–7; author's translation; variation from the NIV in italics; see the comments below)

God is **compassionate.** The Hebrew word for "compassionate" (*rakhum*) is from the same root word as "womb" (*rekhem*). The word means "to be soft like a womb." It is illustrated by the soft compassion of a mother for her child in the womb. The relationship of compassion is based on the Creator-created relationship: the Lord remembers that we are made of flesh and fade easily (Ps. 78:38–39). The Creator bases this compassion on an original love for the creation (Gen. 1:31). The NT uses the corresponding Greek word, *splanchnizomai,* to describe how Jesus was moved to "compassion" when healing the crowds (Mark 1:41).

God is **gracious** (*khannun*). God's grace means that the Lord often acts generously, giving gifts freely, without asking for anything in return (see comment on 33:12). God illustrated the meaning of the word in the law against taking collateral for a loan to a poor person: "If you take your neighbor's cloak as a pledge, return it to him by sunset, because his cloak is the only covering he has for his body. What else will he sleep in? When he cries out to me, I will hear, for I am *gracious* (NIV **compassionate**)" (22:26–27).

The NT cites God's grace as the source of Jesus' incarnation (Luke 2:40; John 1:14–17; Rom. 3:24; 4:16; 5:15–17).

The LORD is **slow to anger.** The Hebrew idiom "burn with anger" is, literally, "nostrils burn" (*kharah 'ap,* 4:14; 11:8). "Slow to anger" is, literally, "lengthened nostrils" (*'erek 'apayim*), indicating that God's anger cools before dealing with the people's sin. God's anger is always in response to human sin, riled when people destroy God's beloved creation, especially when it involves self-destructive, sinful actions. The key text in Exodus for understanding the delay in punishing sin comes just after the golden calf rebellion in which the people threatened to destroy their relation to God through idolatry (32:10–14, 33–35). God's anger would be tempered, as in that case, until a later day (Rom. 2:5–8).

The LORD is **abounding in love** (*rab khesed*). *Khesed* is more than generic "love," for which Hebrew has another word (*'aheb*). "Steadfast love" is a better translation, but *khesed* is even stronger than that. "Unrelenting love" or "pursing love" is closest to its meaning when God is the one loving. Technically the word means "tenacious fidelity in a relationship, readiness and resolve to continue to be loyal to those to whom one is bound" (Brueggemann, "Adjectives," p. 217). The richness of this rich has led to translations that include "steadfast love," "mercy," and "grace." Psalm 136 uses *khesed* as its powerful refrain, "His love (*khesed*) endures forever" (see also Ps. 103:8). This is the only adjective that occurs twice in this text (v. 6, "abounding in love," and v. 7, "maintaining love"). The Lord's reliable and unrelenting love stands at the center of God's self-disclosure at Sinai.

The LORD is **abounding . . . in faithfulness** (*rab 'emet*). The Hebrew word for "faithfulness" here (*'emet*) has the basic meaning "truth" or "true." It means "completely reliable and trustworthy." Psalm 119 uses the word *'emet* to speak of the eternal foundation of the Lord's law as a source of life (Ps. 119:142, 151, 160). The two words *khesed* and *'emet* function as a pair quite often in the OT, vouching for the reliability of God's love (Gen. 32:10; Pss. 25:10; 26:3; 115:1; Isa. 16:5).

The LORD is **maintaining love to thousands** (*notser khesed la'alapim*). This is better translated "to a thousand generations" (see additional note on v. 7). God "maintains" (*natsar*) or "guards" and "protects" this love forever. The "love" is *khesed,* making "unrelenting love" the only word repeated in this description of the Lord. This phrase forms the central line of the Lord's self-disclosure (see also 20:6). It also serves as the transition from the list of adjectives describing who the Lord is to the text explaining how God will deal with sin. God's dealing with sin begins with love *(khesed)*. God abounds *(rab)* in love and protects *(natsar)* that love to a thousand generations (= "forever").

Verse 7 deals with God's forgiveness and the enduring consequences of the people's behavior after the golden calf incident. God had to decide how to treat the people when they sinned. Verse 7 is difficult to translate, but its meaning is vital to understanding the Lord's relationship to the ongoing sin of the people. The verse describes three aspects of this relationship (variations from the NIV are in italics):

> 1. Forgiveness of three kinds of sin: "forgiving/*lifting the burden* of guilt/ wickedness *with ongoing negative impact* (*ʿawon*), rebellion and sin."
>
> 2. Guilt: in this narrative, all are guilty (except Moses and Joshua), but not all seek repentance/restoration.
>
> 3. Enduring consequences: *punishing/visiting the wickedness* (*ʿawon* "guilt" or "consequences/impact of the wickedness") *of the fathers* on the children and *grandchildren* . . . to the third and fourth generation.

One traditional interpretation of this juxtaposition of forgiveness and so-called "punishment" has been that God forgave those who repented and punished (the children of) those who did not. Although some argue for a distinction between those who love and seek God and those who hate God (based on the phrase in 20:5 "of those who hate me"), this meaning is not congruent with the narrative or grammar of this verse. At this point the Lord is speaking to Moses about how to deal with the guilty who are seeking restoration. The grammar does not make a distinction between sinners (wicked/unrepentant/punished) and the righteous (forgiven/repentant), since the same "wicked" and "wickedness" (*ʿawon,* or "guilty") are forgiven in verse 7a (**forgiving wickedness**). Who needs forgiveness if not the guilty/wicked? This text does not directly address the problem of unrepentant sinners, many of whom were slain in 32:27–28, 35. Rather, it addresses the realities of life (consequences) for repentant and forgiven (guilty/ wicked) sinners.

Those who seek to be faithful to God still sin and incur guilt. The point in this text is that they also incur the enduring consequences of sin, though God may forgive them for it. Forgiven people live with the consequences of the sins of others or their own forgiven sins every day. Some kinds of sin have consequences that last a lifetime and beyond, into the lives of children and grandchildren. God's forgiveness may restore right relationship with God, but the consequences for human relationships are stickier. Numbers 14:18–23, where Moses quotes God to God, corroborates this interpretation. Moses tests God's "new" reputation by quoting Exodus 34:6–7 in asking for forgiveness for the people's sin (*ʿawon*, "wickedness"). Based on this *khesed* (unrelenting love) God forgave the people, but that generation nonetheless suffered the consequences of their rebellion by remaining in the wilderness.

Another view of this apparent paradox is the concept of partial forgiveness. Interpreters holding this view say that God's forgiveness means giving a lighter punishment to those who are forgiven (Tigay, "Exodus," p. 189). Again, this interpretation rests on what the text means by "forgive" and "punish."

Forgiving wickedness, rebellion and sin. "Forgiving" (from *nasaʾ*) means "lifting a burden and carrying it away." Exodus uses the same word to refer to the removal of locusts (10:19). It is the same verb used of Isaiah's Suffering Servant: "Surely he took up (*nasaʾ*) our infirmities" and "he bore (*nasaʾ*) the sin of many" (Isa. 53:4, 12).

The Lord forgives guilt-wickedness (*ʿawon*). The Hebrew word has two aspects: the guilt of the sin itself and its enduring physical consequences. This word describes the kinds of sins that have permanent results, even though the sinner may be forgiven.

The Lord forgives "rebellion" (or "betrayal," or "transgression," *pashaʿ*). This word refers to violations of an agreement between two parties. This is the Lord's complaint against Israel through the prophets (Isa. 1:2, 28; Hos. 8:1).

The Lord also forgives "sin" (in a generic sense, *khattaʾah*). This covers a host of actions against God and others. The general meaning of the Hebrew word *khattaʾah* is walking off the Lord's path. The point of the Lord's using the three major words for *sin* is that God will forgive every kind of sin. Being forgiven by God does not mean that a person did not commit sin. It means that God's grace, love, and faithfulness restore the person to relationship.

Yet he does not leave the guilty unpunished. This difficult phrase is better translated, "He certainly will not clear away (the impact/negative effects)." The words "guilty" and "unpunished" are not present in the Hebrew and the verb "clear" has only an implied object. Rather than focusing on punishing the guilty, it reveals God's relation to sinners in general. Even in the context of forgiveness, sin is sin. God gives forgiveness as a gift that does not obliterate "sinner" as a category of human existence. The Hebrew form is an emphatic negative verb, literally, "clearing, he will not clear" (*naqqeh loʾ yenaqqeh*, the *piʿel* infinitive + *piʿel* imperfect). In context, it could be paraphrased: "certainly not clearing the name/reputation or removing the ongoing negative impact of sin." Forgiveness does not remit all consequences (see also Plaut, *The Torah*, p. 663).

He punishes (*paqad*) the children and their children for the sin (*ʿawon*) of the fathers to the third and fourth generation. The NIV translation here has several problems that affect interpretation. First, the translation of the neutral word *paqad* as "he punishes" is not helpful in this context. The root means "he visits" (see comment of the meaning of *paqad* at 33:34). In addition, it is not an indicative verb but a participle. This expands the meaning of the previous phrase, "he does not clear away (the effects)," by using a participle ("visiting") and should not be taken as a separate statement. In certain circumstances, God did visit the people for their sins (*khattaʾah*) in a way that constituted an added punishment (e.g., 32:34–35). This is not, however, the point of this text. The third translation problem is related. The word that the NIV translates "sin" here is not *khattaʾah*, but rather the same as the word earlier translated "wickedness" (sin with ongoing impact, *ʿawon*). The word's meaning includes the enduring consequences of wicked actions.

The result of these translation issues is that this part of verse 7 is better translated, "visiting the wickedness (or 'impact/effects of the wickedness') of the fathers on the children and grandchildren to the third and fourth generation." This means that God does not add punishment but that the ongoing impact of wickedness will remain as a negative effect upon the family and the community.

34:8–9 / Moses bowed to the ground at once and worshiped. Moses immediately accepted the revelation and the offer of forgiveness. In worship, he repeated the Lord's promise as a petition. He did not doubt the Lord's offer to go with them (33:14–17). He repeated it as a confirmation. In the second part of his petition Moses used a word that the Lord had not included (*salakh*, **forgive** or "pardon"), a synonym for God's "forgive" (v. 7, *nasaʾ*, lit., "lift a burden"). Moses was saying, in effect, "Please apply your commitment to be a forgiving God in *this particular case* of the golden calf." As we shall see, the Lord's response is an implied, "Yes, I will."

Additional Notes §41

34:1 / "Write" (vv. 1, 27): in 21:1, the command, "These are the laws you are to set before them" is an oral formulation, but it was obviously also written down as the book of the covenant. In 24:4 the written words include the Ten Commandments and the whole book of the covenant (see comment on v. 27 in §42).

34:5 / Kohlenberger notes that the Jewish tradition identifies 13 attributes of God in this text. The first 4 (presence, salvation, provision, and constancy) are derived from the doubly spoken name and the context of the Exodus narrative. The other 9 occur in the list-like description of vv. 6–7 (Kohlenberger, "The Use of Exodus," pp. 111–23).

34:6 / In the midst of the destruction of Israel, Jeremiah quotes parts of v. 6 in Lam. 3:22–23: "the steadfast love of the Lord never ceases, his mercies never come to an end." After the defeat of the northern 10 tribes by Assyria, Hosea used the credo to comfort survivors and give Judah hope (Hos. 2:19–20). The Lord quotes the credo through the prophet Isaiah to the exiles in Babylon, to give them hope of restoration to their land (Isa. 54:9–10). The credo is also used in Num. 14:18; 2 Chr. 30:9; Ps. 111:4; Mic. 7:18; and Nah. 1:3. On the individual adjectives used in the name of the Lord, see Brueggemann, "Adjectives," pp. 213–28. On the relationship between "womb" and "compassion" see Trible, *God*, pp. 31–71.

34:6–7 / The word *khesed* ("love") in "abounding in love . . . maintaining love" is so multifaceted that several dissertations have been written to expound its meanings. See Glueck, *Hesed*; Sakenfeld, *Faithfulness*; Clark, *"Hesed."* The nearest equivalent word in the NT is the Greek word *agapē*, translated "unconditional love." The OT *khesed* and the NT *agapē* communicate God's unrelenting love for the creation and the people. "Full of grace and truth" is an Eng. translation of a Gk. version of *khesed* and *ʾemet* (John 1:14; see Hooker, "Johannine Prologue," also Belleville, "Tradition").

34:7 / Oddly, the phrase "love to thousands" is the only place the NIV does not include the word "generations," even though the Heb. is the same in 20:6 and Deut. 5:9–10. The grammar is also exactly the same for "to the third and fourth generation," which the NIV includes in v. 7. The NIV is partially following the LXX rather than the Heb. here (see the comments on 20:5–6). The NIV is correct in identifying the "guilty" as not unpunished. The difficult question is identifying "the guilty." Who else would be forgiven (v. 7a)? The NIV blurs this conflict by using two different Eng. words for the same Heb. word: "forgiving wickedness" (*ᶜawon*, v. 7a) and "punishes for the sin (*ᶜawon*) of the fathers." Are "the guilty" (*ᶜawon*) forgiven or punished? For a more common translation and interpretation of this passage (e.g., "punishment"), see Durham, *Exodus*, p. 450.

34:9 / The word *salakh*, "forgive," or "pardon," occurs only with God as the subject in the OT. It means to declare that the sin is forgiven.

§42 Crisis Resolved: Yahweh Renews the Covenant (Exod. 34:10–35)

34:10–28 / God responds to Moses' prayer of acceptance (vv. 9–10) by **making a covenant.** The content of the renewed covenant demonstrated the Lord's persistent intention to be present in the world in specific ways. These verses are an abbreviated summary of the book of the covenant (21:1–23:19) and the Ten Commandments (20:1–17). Detailed comments on each of the repeated laws may be found in the earlier texts listed here. The texts match in the following ways:

> Verses 11–13, 15–16 reiterate the warnings against idolatry from 23:20–33.
>
> Verse 14 reiterates the first commandment and God's jealousy from 20:3, 5.
>
> Verse 17 reiterates the second commandment against idols from 20:4.
>
> Verses 18–20 reiterate the Feast of Unleavened Bread from 23:14–15 and the law of firstborn redemption from 13:12–13.
>
> Verse 21 reiterates the fourth commandment of Sabbath rest from 20:8–10.
>
> Verses 22–26 reiterate the Festivals of Weeks and Ingathering from 23:16–19.

This summary of the book highlights the laws of worship, the need to love God exclusively, and the yearly calendar. In addition, the text mentions the Ten Commandments as a group (v. 28). These verses have been called the "ritual decalogue" since they integrate three of the ten with laws concerning worship practices and mention the new set of tablets. After the crisis of calf-worship, this text reiterates the most vital commands in the context of worship.

Verse 10 introduces the rest of the chapter. The Lord is the initiator and the promise maker once again: **"I am making a covenant . . . I will do wonders never before done."** The unique relationship between the Lord and Israel has a broader motivation:

"The people you live among will see how awesome is the work
that I, the LORD, will do for you." God persisted in the original intention for the world in remaking the covenant with Israel.

The previous book of the covenant and the tabernacle instructions remained as part of this covenant, but God had placed
them on a new foundation. God's forgiveness, faithfulness, and
promises would now secure the future of the people. Even in the
face of blatant disrespect, rebellion, and sin, the Lord would remain present.

Verses 11–17 raise the central question of God's lordship
again. The vitality of the renewed covenant with God depended
on the people's being loyal and telling the truth about the Creator
and redeemer. This meant that idolatry was the single greatest
threat. The Lord began by repeating the warnings against idolatry given at the end of the book of the covenant (23:20–33).
Poignantly, God had also given those warnings just before the
golden-calf idolatry. In this new context, God summarizes and repeats those same warnings (vv. 11–17).

The Lord begins by warning the people against making
treaties with the Amorites, Canaanites, and other groups. At the
center of the warning is the first commandment ("no other gods,"
v. 14). Following that is a reminder that the Lord, **"whose name is
Jealous** (*qanna*), **is a jealous God"** (*'el qanna*). God had made
them, delivered them from bondage, and forgiven them. God's
"jealousy" for the truth and the costly people had significant
grounds (see the comment on "jealous God" at 20:4–6).

God reminded them that their fidelity to the Lord was frag-
ile. They would ever be in danger of assimilation into an easier religion: **"they will invite you and you will eat their sacrifices,"**
your **sons** will marry and be persuaded by their **daughters** to
prostitute themselves to their gods. This special warning against
idolatry ends with the terse command, **"Do not make cast idols."**

These verses reiterate the three yearly festivals: the Feast of
Unleavened Bread (with Passover), the Feast of Weeks (harvest),
and the Feast of Ingathering (booths). The other repeated laws,
including **"Do not cook a young goat in its mother's milk,"** were
related to these festivals (see comment on 23:14–19; also Lev.
23:1–44; Deut. 16:1–17). In the midst of these reminders, God
gives the crucial Sabbath command again (v. 21; see also 16:23–30;
20:8–11; 21:2; 23:11–12; 31:13–17; 35:2–3). The law of firstborn redemption (vv. 19–20) repeats 13:12–13. The text here it included

because spring birthing of the livestock occurred at the same time as the Feast of Unleavened Bread.

The Lord commanded Moses once again to **"Write down these words, for in accordance with these words I have made a covenant with you and with Israel . . . And he wrote on the tablets the words of the covenant—the Ten Commandments."** The legacy of Sinai would be a written legacy. The rewriting of the commands on the tablets of stone is a consistent theme of this chapter, appearing at the beginning, middle, and end (vv. 1–4, 27–29, 32, 34; see comment on the written tablets at 24:12–18). The Lord promised to write the words in verse 1. The "he" in verse 28 is not any more specific in Hebrew than it is in English, but it seems to refer to Moses. Tradition has Moses writing "these words" of the book of the covenant given in verses 10–26 and the Lord rewriting the Ten Commandments in stone.

34:29–35 / The Israelites received the final part of their forgiveness in the unexpected gift of Moses' radiant face. It brought the glory of God back into Israel's midst in a human countenance. It was a visible sign of the Lord's forgiveness, presence, and restored communication with Israel through Moses. The accompanying sign of restoration God gave upon Moses' return from Mount Sinai was **the two tablets of the Testimony in his hands** (see comment on 31:18). In contrast to his previous descent after forty days, this time Moses did not encounter idolatry, burn with anger, or break the tablets (32:15, 19). Instead, the people were in awe, his face was radiant, and he gave them the commands (vv. 30–32).

At first the people **were afraid to come near him.** The last time they had seen Moses, he had failed to make atonement for them, the Lord had struck them with a plague and refused to go with them, and they had stripped off their ornaments (32:30–35; 33:3–6). Now they are afraid of even the reflection of the Lord on Moses' face. **But Moses called to them.** Restoration required this tenuous moment. **Aaron** led once again, but this time for the good. Then **all the leaders of the community** and **all the Israelites came near.**

The text mentions Moses' "radiant face" five times. He was not aware of it. It was not an "inner glow" but a result of being in the Lord's presence. The people were afraid, but they came near in spite of the Lord's reflected glory. Moses covered his face with **a veil** after speaking to the people. He uncovered his face when he spoke to the Lord (in the tent of meeting) and when he told the people what the Lord had said. The veil was not to hide the radiance of the Lord from the people. Moses would cover his face on ordinary days to keep his own words from being confused with the Lord's revelation.

Access to God was the import of Moses' radiant face. The unveiled radiant face in the people's presence demonstrated the Lord's acceptance and reestablished communication with the people. The friendship of God with Moses on the mountain continued in the midst of the camp through words and visible radiance. Later, in the wilderness, "The LORD make his face shine upon you" was the theme of the blessing given to Aaron to put upon the people (Num. 6:22–27). The psalmist used it as a refrain of salvation: "Restore us, O God; make your face shine upon us, that we may be saved" (Ps. 80:3, 7, 19).

Moses' transfiguration was the basis for understanding the transfiguration of Jesus. Jesus' face "shone like the sun" as he appeared with Moses (Matt. 17:2–5). They were also enveloped in a "bright cloud" from which God spoke. In this way the Lord revealed to the disciples that a new kind of "face to face" experience was possible in Jesus. The apostle Paul used the unveiled face of the resurrected Christ as a way to describe the source of the Christian's experience of God: "For God, who said, 'Let light shine out of darkness,' made his light shine in our hearts to give us the light of the knowledge of the glory of God in the face of Christ" (2 Cor. 4:6). This would be possible for anyone who turns to the Lord (2 Cor. 3:16, 18).

Additional Notes §42

34:10 / Source critics have attributed the commandments of Exod. 20 (J) and 34 (E) to separate sources. Lev. 19 (P) reiterates the Ten Commandments, also integrated with other laws. Deut. 5 (D) repeats them as a group.

34:29 / On being face to face with God, see comment on 33:11.

34:30 / Moses' "radiant" (*qaran*) or "shining" face was translated in the Latin Vulgate as "horned" (*cornuta*) because the similar Heb. term, *qeren* ("horn") is used once in the Bible to refer to rays (Hab 3:4). Michelangelo sculpted Moses with horns and anti-Semites started rumors that Jews had horns as a result of this translation choice. Rembrandt painted him with a radiant face.

34:33 / The veil has been compared to a "cultic mask" used by shamans. It has, however, exactly the opposite function. A shaman's mask is a window into the spirit world, while covering the human face. It is worn during cultic contact with spirits and during communication with the people. The Lord, by contrast, is present to Moses "face to face" without the veil. Moses also does not wear the veil when speaking the word of the Lord to the people. See the discussion in Durham, *Exodus,* p. 468. See also Davis, "Rebellion."

§43 Building Yahweh's Dwelling Place: Willing Hearts (Exod. 35:1–35)

Exodus 35 is remarkable for the dramatic reversal and transformation after a word of forgiveness from the Lord. The people prepared to build the tabernacle with full and willing hearts. The structure of the chapter illustrates the reversal by forming a mirror image of Exodus 31 (the last chapter before the golden-calf crisis), presenting similar material in reverse order. The last subject of Exodus 31 was the Sabbath, and the Sabbath command is now the first word after the golden calf crisis (35:1–3). The middle portions of both Exodus 31 and 35 list the components of the tabernacle to be built (31:7–11; 35:10–19). The first subject in Exodus 31 was Bezalel, "filled with the Spirit of God," which is the conclusion to Exodus 35 (vv. 30–35). The Lord's forgiveness had taken them back, to begin again. The remaining chapters of Exodus (36–40) will describe, again in detail, the building of the tabernacle. The first time these details occur in the text, the Lord was giving Moses instructions (chs. 25–31). Here, the text describes the people accomplishing the task in joy and voluntary obedience.

There is an abrupt change of style from the narrative of Exodus 32–34 to the Sabbath law and tabernacle lists of Exodus 35–39. In addition, the return to long detailed descriptions that the text of Exodus 25–31 has already provided is enough to end readers' (and scholars') attention to the last six chapters. In oral tradition, the abrupt change and redundancies performed an important theological function. They signaled a complete resolution to the crisis and a return to the harmony between the Lord's intention and the people's actions. In contrast to the worship of the golden calf and its ensuing chaos, the people participated in building an ordered sacred space according to the Lord's detailed instructions. The redundancy was a familiar comfort. We find the genuine newness in Exodus 35 in the refrain, "everyone who was willing and whose heart moved him came and brought an offering to the LORD for the work" (v. 21; see also vv. 5, 22, 26, 29).

35:1–3 / **Moses assembled the whole Israelite community.** Moses addressed the people about the Lord's ordering of time. He reiterated the pattern of working six days and resting on the seventh. This law focused as much on the necessity of working as on resting. It is a repetition of 31:13–17: **"For six days, work is to be done, but the seventh day shall be your holy day, a Sabbath of rest to the LORD."** God first gave the Sabbath law with the manna before Sinai (16:23–30) and repeated it in the Ten Commandments (20:8–11). The Lord added Sabbath details, including rest for debt slaves, land, and the animals, in the book of the covenant (21:2; 23:11–12) and after the golden calf crisis (34:12). This text also repeats the threat of **death** (see comment on 31:14–15). The prohibition against even lighting a cooking fire was probably related to cooking on the day before the Sabbath, when the Lord provided twice as much manna (16:23; see also Num. 15:32–36; Jer. 17:21; see the comments on Sabbath rest on 16:23–30; 20:8–11; 21:2; 23:11–12; 34:12).

35:4–19 / Moses, freed by the Lord's forgiveness of the people after the crisis, could now invite the people to participate in building the tabernacle. The text reminds us again that he spoke **to the whole Israelite community.** Moses began by taking **an offering** according to the list of materials that the Lord had provided; see the comments on the detailed list at 25:1–9).

"Everyone who is willing is to bring to the LORD an offering" (v. 5b). The fuller expression of this refrain is found in verses 21–22. This form is, literally, "everyone whose heart is moved." In verses 10–19 Moses repeated the Lord's request for skilled workers: **"All who are skilled among you are to come and make everything the LORD has commanded."** "Skilled" (*khakam leb*, "wise of heart") means "reflective and observant, integrating one's intelligence and passion." (See the commentary on the very similar list at 31:6b–10. On "skilled," see the comments on 26:1 and 31:1–11).

35:20–29 / The people responded with generous hearts. The response to the Lord's forgiveness and call for obedience was a triumph for the people and the Lord's work in the world. The travails of the whole book culminate in this offering. This was the voluntary response for which the Lord had originally hoped (25:2).

The people **withdrew** to go to their tents and gather their offerings. They presented the gold they brought, in contrast to the golden calf, for the specific purpose of participating in the Lord's work. They did not make a demand or make a god. Rather, they gave it to make a place and space for God in their midst. The **wave offering** was a way of visually presenting their gift to the Lord and using it according to God's instruction (see comment at 29:27).

The phrases **everyone who was willing** and **whose heart moved him** form an important refrain for this chapter (vv. 5, 21, 22, 26, 29; see also 36:2). The English translation "everyone who was willing" carries less impact than the Hebrew, which contains no indication of reticence or any implication that some were not willing. Its focus is on the movement of the hearts and spirits of the people. The translations "everyone whose heart lifted him" and "whose spirit moved him" may better communicate the Hebrew. This understanding is the fullest expression of the refrain "everyone whose heart moved him" (NIV **All who were willing**). The term **freewill offerings** is one Hebrew word (*nedabah*) from the same Hebrew root as "moved." Their own hearts urged them to give, and to give more than enough. The abundant offering was not over until after the work began (see 36:3–6).

A key word here is **everyone,** or **all,** from one word in Hebrew (*kol*). Describing the people, *kol* occurs eleven times in nine verses. Verse 25 especially notes the skill of **Every skilled woman** who could spin linen thread. **And all the women who were willing** (whose hearts lifted them) **and had the skill spun the goat hair** (v. 26). A comprehensive summary statement in verse 29 mentions the women again. The **leaders brought . . . gems,** that would be mounted on Aaron's **breastpiece.** Each leader had one stone representing their tribe (see the comments at 28:9–21). They also brought their tribes' contribution of **spices and olive oil** (see the comments at 30:22–38).

35:30–35 / Moses addressed the people concerning the overseers of the creation of the tabernacle (31:1–11). **Bezalel** was **filled . . . . with the Spirit of God.** God filled both Bezalel and **Oholiab . . . with skill, ability and knowledge.** God also gave them **the ability to teach others.** The last verse of the chapter refers to the others, who were taught. They, too, were **filled with skill** as **master craftsmen and designers,** in order to do all the work. The following verses also mention the skill of the men and women: verses 3, 6; 35:10, 25–26, 31, 35; see also 26:1, 31; 28:3, 6, 8 15; 29:5; 36:1–4, 8, 35; 39:3, 5, 8. (See the comments on these verses at 26:1 and especially at 31:1–11.)

Additional Notes §43

35:1 /   The last time the people "assembled" (*qahal*), in 32:1, they "gathered around" (lit., "assembled themselves") to build the golden calf. Some source critics consider Exod. 35–40 to be a secondary priestly addition, but there is no consensus. See Durham, *Exodus*, p. 473, for a discussion of alternate theories. In the Heb. text (Masoretic Text), Exod. 25–31 and 35–39 have extremely similar content. In the Greek text (LXX), however, these sets of chs. have significantly different content. For a comprehensive treatment of the differences in the LXX and a theory of composition, see Gooding, *The Account.*

35:35 /   Commentators often include 36:1 with Exod. 35 since Moses finishes his speech to the Israelites about Bezalel's commission from the Lord in that verse.

§44 Creating a Space for God: Overabundant Donations and Making the Tabernacle Tent (Exod. 36:1–38)

The work on the tabernacle began with a generous offering. Because verse 1 records the last sentence in Moses' speech about Bezalel's commission from the Lord, commentators often include this verse with the end of Exodus 35. In any case, this verse serves as a transition to the Israelite's overwhelming offering for beginning work on the tabernacle (vv. 2–6). The remainder of the chapter (vv. 7–38) and the three chapters that follow (37–39) repeat, almost verbatim, many of the detailed instructions that God gave to Moses in Exodus 25–31. The people, with an abundant offering and focused labor, now carried out these instructions.

36:1–7 / **Moses summoned Bezalel and Oholiab and and every skilled person.** (See the comments on these persons at 31:1–6; 35:30–35.) Moses presented them with the initial offerings of the people (v. 3a). The gifts included raw materials such as wood and precious metals, as well as items that the people had spun, woven, dyed, and tanned (see comment on 35:20–29).

An interesting problem arose, as the offering was **more than enough** (v. 5). Even after the offering had been received and presented, **the people continued to bring freewill offerings morning after morning.** This daily interruption of the craftsmen's work ironically prevented them from working on the tabernacle. They had to ask Moses to stop the people (v. 5) and he **gave an order** for the people to stop making materials. They **were restrained from bringing more . . . what they already had was more than enough** (v. 7). The gold the people had given for the golden calf had clearly been but a small token of their wealth. They added abundant precious metals to their offerings of time and labor for the tabernacle, pouring out expressions of gratitude for their renewed relationship with the Lord.

Several NT texts describe this kind of grateful giving among Christians. Brueggemann describes these texts as indicative of an "evangelical generosity" and the cost of discipleship (Matt. 10:8; Luke 14:28; 1 Cor. 3:9; 4:7; 2 Cor. 8:7). True faith in the Lord has an economic cost that followers bear gladly. In both the OT and the NT, forgiveness and reconciliation prompt giving. The gospel of the Lord moves people from selfishness to generosity (see Brueggemann, "Exodus," p. 963).

36:8–38 / The descriptions of the tabernacle construction are extremely similar to the Lord's instructions to Moses in Exodus 25–31, but the order differs. The construction, in this section, follows a more logical sequence. They built the tent of meeting before the ark so it would have a place. In Exodus 25, God had described the ark before the tent because of its preeminent importance.

They made the **tabernacle** first (vv. 8–19). They craftsmen sewed the four tent coverings from the materials that the people brought. They made the innermost covering of ten woven linen panels (NIV "curtains") first. First they made the panels of woven **linen,** then of woven **goat hair,** then of **ram** skin leather, and finally of dugong (sea cow) leather (see detailed comment on 26:1–14).

Then they constructed the tent **frames** of acacia wood (vv. 20–34; see comment on 26:15–30). They also made the veil shielding the holiest place (NIV **curtain;** a better translation, at 39:34, is "shielding curtain").

Then they made the entrance screen (NIV **curtain**) for entering the holy place, and also the tent in general (vv. 35–38; see comment at 26:31–37).

Additional Notes §44

36:1–2 / The text repeats that the people were **skilled** and **willing** (vv. 1–3). (See comments on these themes at 31:1–11 and 35:4–29.)

§45 Building: Ark, Table, Lampstand, Incense Altar, and Anointing Oil (Exod. 37:1–29)

After the people finished making the tent of meeting, they created the furnishings. The text continues to repeat, almost verbatim, the details of the instructions God gave to Moses in Exodus 25 and 30. The craftsman Bezalel, with focused labor, carries out the instructions using the generous materials that the people provided.

The text of Exodus 37 is a somewhat shorter form of Exodus 25 and 30. It omits some of the detail, as generally makes good sense for this kind of repeated list. The omissions are usually descriptions of the function of the furniture. The account of building the incense altar (vv. 25–28; 30:1–6) does not repeat the description of Aaron's regular burning of incense (30:7–10). The text here also omits the instructions about giving atonement money since it was not a necessary part of the construction (30:11–16). The text does not omit any of the necessary details for making things. They "did everything just as the LORD commanded Moses" (39:32).

37:1–9 / The **ark** was made of **acacia wood** and **gold** overlay. The Lord's instruction to "make *an* ark" became definite: "Bezalel made *the* ark." The ark was to stand in the holiest place of the tent of meeting (see the comments at 25:10–16). Then Bezalel made **the atonement cover of pure gold** for the ark, with the **two cherubim.** This is sometimes called "the mercy seat" (see the comments on 25:17–22).

The ark of pure gold was a paradigmatic alternative to the golden calf. The people could use gold as an idol or to honor the Lord. The ark cover was not an idol, but a symbol of the Lord's forgiveness of sin and presence with the people. When the Israelites built the Second Temple after the Babylonian exile they did not reconstruct the ark, partly out of concern for the temptation to worship the golden cherubim on the ark. In the First Temple, Solomon recast the cherubim in large form and stretched their wings from wall to wall, rather than simply over the atonement cover (1 Kgs. 6:23–24). He had them made ten cubits high with each wing five cubits long. The idolatry in the First Temple was part of the reason for the Lord's judgment, later brought through the Babylonians (Ezek. 10). So they avoided this in the Second Temple by not re-placing the images of the cherubim. In the NT, the idea of a place of meeting and covering of atonement describes Jesus' work in **covering** (*hilastērion*) the sins of humanity (Rom. 3:25).

37:10–16 / They made **the table** with **its plates and dishes and bowls and its pitchers.** The table, along with the lampstand and incense altar, were for the holy place. See the comments on 25:23–30.

37:17–24 / **They made the lampstand of pure gold** with its **flowerlike cups, buds and blossoms.** They also made its **seven lamps, as well as its wick trimmers and trays.** See the comments on 25:31–40.

37:25–29 / **They made the altar of incense** of **acacia wood** and **gold** overlay, with **horns with pure gold.** This altar, included here because it was part of the furnishing for the holy place, was not part of the sequence in Exodus 25. This has led some source critics to theorize that the altar of incense was not included in the earlier priestly list, but this is merely conjecture (see the discussion in Durham, *Exodus*, p. 483). The LXX does not mention the building of the incense altar. See the comments on the details of the incense altar at 30:1–10. A **perfumer** made the **sacred anointing oil and the pure, fragrant incense.** See the comments on 30:22–38.

§46 Building: Altar, Basin, and Courtyard (Exod. 38:1–31)

Again the text repeats, almost verbatim, the details of the work the craftsmen accomplished according to the instructions God gave Moses in Exodus 25–30. After completing the furnishings for the tent of meeting, they made the "altar of burnt offering" and the "bronze basin" for washing for the courtyard. They hung the "courtyard curtains" on their "posts." The chapter ends with some new information, a list of the amounts of gold, silver, and bronze used for the tabernacle.

38:1–8 / **They built the altar of burnt offering** with **acacia wood** and **overlaid . . . with bronze.** The skilled craftsmen also made **its pots, shovels, sprinkling bowls, meat forks and firepans** and its **grating.** (See the comments on the altar and its use at 27:1–8.) They also made the "bronze basin." (See the comments on the bronze basin at 30:17–21.)

Verse 8 briefly introduces new information: **They made the bronze basin and its bronze stand from the** (bronze) **mirrors of the women who served at the entrance to the Tent of Meeting** (lit., "the ministering women who ministered"). Who were the women ministers and how did they minister? The text does not describe their specific ministry. The Hebrew verb for "minister" (*tsaba*ʾ, NIV "served") occurs infrequently, usually referring to the Levites who were assigned to minister (*tsaba*ʾ) at the entrance to the tent of meeting (Num. 4:3, 23, 30, etc.). The women's "service" has been the object of wide speculation without evidence (from cleaning ladies to dancers; see Durham, *Exodus*, p. 487). The text simply says that they served and gave their bronze mirrors to make the bronze basin. This bronze is mentioned only here and is not in the list of materials in Exodus 35 or in 38:30–31.

The women served at the entrance to the tent of meeting. The bronze basin stood between the entrance and the altar in the courtyard. It was the most vital and active location in the tabernacle. The priests entered the tent daily to attend to the lamps in the holy place. They had to wash their hands and feet in the basin before entering (30:19–21). They prepared daily sacrifices at the entrance to the tent, at the basin, for burning on the altar. There they separated meat from the fat, cleaned it and, for many sacrifices, cut it for distribution. Whatever their "service" was, the women were in the midst of the active ministry between the altar, basin, and tent from the beginning.

38:9–20 / The final step in creating the tabernacle was enclosing the **courtyard** with its **posts,** hanging **curtains,** and entrance screen (NIV v. 18, **curtain for the entrance**). These verses include two brief comments concerning the entrance curtain for the first time. First, it was the same height as the hanging courtyard curtains (v. 18) and, second, its **posts** were capped with **silver** (v. 19; see the detailed comments at 27:9–19).

38:21–31 / This inventory of the gold, silver, and bronze used in the tabernacle serves as a preliminary conclusion to the construction. It supplements the general description of the offerings of the people in 35:20–29. The list expresses the generosity of the **wave offering** (vv. 24, 29; see the comments at 29:27; 35:22; 36:3–7). The gold and bronze represented the people's significant financial investment in the worship space. They had collected the silver as a census atonement tax for men over twenty years of age (see the comments at 30:11–16).

The expression **tabernacle of the Testimony** is unique in Exodus, referring to the testimony of the Ten Commandments in the ark (see comment at 31:18; see also Num. 1:50, 53; 10:11). This name communicates a primary purpose of the tabernacle. The commandments would be the *sine qua non* of their relationship with the Lord.

Verse 21 records that **Ithamar,** who was the fourth **son of Aaron,** was the accountant of the metals (see comment at 28:1; see also Num. 4:29–33; 7:8). These verses also mention **Bezalel** and **Oholiab** again as part of this summarizing statement (see comment at 31:1–6). Again the text says that Oholiab was a weaver of colors, known as a variegator (*not,* as in the NIV, **an embroiderer;** see comment at 26:36).

The total amount of the gold . . . was 29 talents and 730 shekels (approx. 2,210 pounds). They used the gold to make the furnishings for the tent of meeting. **The silver obtained . . . in the census was 100 talents and 1,775 shekels** (approx. 7,600 pounds).

They counted **a total of 603,550 men,** and each gave **half a shekel** (two-tenths of an ounce). They used the **silver** to make **the bases** for the wood frames for the tent of meeting and the entrance screen to the holiest place (**the sanctuary** and **the curtain**). See comment at 26:19–25. They used **one talent** (75 pounds) of silver **for each base.** They fashioned the silver **hooks, bands,** and post caps for the posts of the courtyard from the 1,775 shekels.

The bronze from the wave offering was 70 talents and 2,400 shekels (approx. 5,350 pounds). They used the bronze to make **the bases** for the posts to hold up the courtyard curtain, its entrance screen, and the entrance screen for the tent of meeting (see 26:37). Bronze was also necessary for making **the bronze altar, grating, its utensils,** and **all the tent pegs.** At the end of this formal accounting, the generous gifts of the people had provided everything for the tabernacle, down to the last tent peg.

Additional Notes §46

38:8 / The LXX (38:26) resolved the lack of information about the ministry of the women by saying that they "fasted" at the entrance on the day that the tent was set up. For an example of the corruption of the women's service under Eli's sons see 1 Sam. 2:22 (see also Deut. 23:17).

38:21 / The immense weight of the metals used in the tabernacle has generated discussion about the perspective of the final editor of Exodus (P). The issue is similar to the problem of 600,000 men (about 2 million people) walking through the Sinai (see comment on 12:37). While the burden of proof remains with the critic of the text, the numbers do reflect the time of Solomon. The quantity of these metals in comparison to quantities used in ancient Egypt are, in themselves, "not unrealistic" according to Durham (based on the research of A. Lucas on the use of metals in ancient Egypt; cited in Durham, *Exodus,* p. 490). Num. 7:2–8 describes the oxen and carts the tribal leaders provided for moving the very heavy tabernacle.

38:24 / Three thousand shekels = one talent. A talent in the OT is generally understood as approx. 35 kg./75 lbs. An OT shekel is approximately 11.4 g./.4 oz. If the "sanctuary shekel" was a smaller than the ordinary shekel, the weights would have been about 17% lighter.

After all the elements of the tabernacle and its furnishings had been made, but before it was erected, the artisans created the priestly garments. The first part of Exodus 39 repeats, almost verbatim, the commands the Lord gave Moses for the completion of the vestments for Aaron and his sons (vv. 1–31). The second part of the chapter provides a summary list of all the items Moses inspected when the people brought them to him (vv. 32–43).

39:1–31 / Just **as the LORD commanded Moses** is the sevenfold refrain that follows the successful completion of each part of the priestly clothing: woven garments (v. 1); ephod (v. 5); onyx memorial stones (v. 7); breastpiece (v. 21); robe (v. 26); other clothing (v. 29); and the engraved medallion (v. 31). The seven sections formed by this refrain each repeat material from 28:1–43 in a slightly compressed form. The refrain balances the Lord's repeated instructions to "make them just as I commanded you" (see also 25:9, 40; 26:30; 27:8; 31:11).

First they made the **woven garments** from the **blue, purple and scarlet** material (v. 1). The NIV adds **yarn,** but "thread" or "material" is better since the fabric was likely woven from fine linen thread (see the detailed comments on the material and colors at 25:1–9). Next they made Aaron's **ephod** (vv. 2–7; see the detailed comments on 28:6–8). Third, they made the **onyx memorial stones** for the ephod (vv. 6–7; see the comments on 28:9–17). Then they fashioned Aaron's **breastpiece** (vv. 8–21; see the comments on 28:15–30). Fifth, they created Aaron's **robe** (vv. 22–26; see the comments on 28:31–35). Sixth, they finished the other items of clothing **For Aaron and his sons** (vv. 27–31; see the comments on 28:39–43). Finally, they made the **engraved** medallion (NIV **plate**) for the crown (NIV **diadem**) on Aaron's **turban,** inscribed HOLY TO THE LORD (vv. 30–31; see the comments on 28:36–38).

39:32–43 / **So all the work on the tabernacle, the Tent of Meeting, was completed.** They had finished the labor on all the elements of the tabernacle. "The tabernacle, the Tent of Meeting" is, literally, "the tabernacle *of* the tent of meeting," so the Hebrew does not equate them. The construct ("of") is translated appositionally since, of course, it included the new tent of meeting. This may reflect the merging of the older tent of meeting tradition. (See the comments on 33:7–11.)

The list of the tabernacle's components is succinct and mirrors the list of all that the Lord asked the whole community to bring and to do in 35:10–19 (see the comments on 31:1–11; 35:10–19). Now they had completed these instructions, and the sevenfold refrain, **as the LORD had commanded,** is a threefold reprise for all the work done for the whole tabernacle. The refrain opens this section (v. 32) and is repeated twice for the conclusion (vv. 42–43).

Then they brought [the components of] **the tabernacle to Moses** for inspection. They **had done all the work** (*ʿabodah v.* 42) and Moses **inspected the work** (*melaʾkah*). There are two different Hebrew words translated "work" in verses 42–43. The first means "service" and is sometimes translated "worship" in other texts (*ʿabodah*, also in v. 32). The second means "workmanship" and refers to specialized work done as a vocation or calling (*melaʾkah*). It shares a root with the word for "angel," or "messenger," whose "work" is to deliver messages (*malʾak* from *laʾak*). So Moses inspected all the parts **and saw that they had done** [all the work] **just as the LORD had commanded. So Moses blessed them.** After the sevenfold format of the refrain, this blessing sounds like an echo of the creation account in Genesis 1–2:3 (see also Gen. 1:28; 2:3). Moses saw it was good (as the Lord had commanded) and blessed the people. They had done all they could do before they set up the tabernacle (40:1–33). After that, it was only the Lord who could add to their work and to Moses' blessing (40:34–38). They had completed their work (v. 32), but the Lord was not finished with them.

§48 The Presence of the Lord in the Midst of the Camp (Exod. 40:1–38)

In Exodus 40 (v. 34), "the glory of the LORD filled the tabernacle" for the first time. As Moses set up the tabernacle, in accordance with the Lord' instructions, God fulfilled the original intention to deliver and dwell with this chosen people. The outline of the chapter follows a chiastic structure:

A vv. 1–8: the Lord said to *set up* the tabernacle, in sevenfold detail

B vv. 9–16: the Lord said *to anoint; Moses did everything*

A′ vv. 17–33: Moses *set up* the tabernacle, in sevenfold detail

B′ vv. 34–38: the *glory of the Lord* filled the tabernacle

This structure sets a general pattern of the Lord's instruction (A) and Moses' response (A′). The order of the verses of (A) and (A′) matches exactly. The Lord specified the placement of an item in the tabernacle (A) and Moses placed it there (A′). Verse 16 functions as both the fulfillment of the Lord's instruction to anoint everything (B) as well as the foil of the pattern. A detailed description of Moses' anointing the tabernacle, Aaron, and his sons is conspicuously missing. Rather, the summary "Moses did everything" (v. 16) expresses the understated fulfillment. In the larger pattern, we might expect a long listing of all that Moses had anointed in (B′). We have in its place the climax of the narrative. "The cloud covered the Tent of Meeting, and the glory of the LORD filled the tabernacle." The Lord's presence was the true anointing of the tabernacle. It was the sign that God had fully forgiven and restored Israel. The Lord was present in their midst as never before.

40:1–8 / See (A) above. The Lord instructed Moses to set up the tabernacle on **the first day of the first month** in the second year after leaving Egypt (see v. 17). This was according to the new

calendar God had given them as they left Egypt (13:4; 23:15). They
had been at Mount Sinai for nine months. The first item Moses set
up was **the tabernacle, the Tent of Meeting.** "The tabernacle"
here refers to "the new tent of meeting." Exodus 39 and 40 intentionally merge the two terms. At the end of the chapter, the Lord's
glory fills the whole tabernacle, not just the tent (see vv. 6, 18–19,
21, 34–35).

God's second instruction was to **"Place the ark of the Testimony in it and shield the ark with the curtain."** The "ark of the
Testimony" is often called the "ark of the covenant" (see additional note on 25:22). Both "testimony" and "covenant" refer to
the commandments (see the comments at 25:10–22 and 37:1–9).
The entrance "curtain" (or veil) created the holiest place (see the
comments at 26:31–35 and 36:35–36).

Third, God instructed Moses to **"Bring in the table and set
out what belongs on it"** (v. 23, "the bread"; see the comments at
25:23–30 and 37:10–16). The fourth instruction was to **"bring in
the lampstand and set up"** the menorah/lamps. (See the comments at 25:31–40 and 37:17–24.)

God's fifth instruction was to **"Place the gold altar of incense in front of the ark of the Testimony,"** which were separated
by the veil/curtain that "shielded" the ark, and to hang **the curtain
at the entrance** to the tent. (See the comments on the incense altar
at 30:1–6 and 37:25–28 and on the entrance screen at 26:36–37 and
36:37–38.) The sixth instruction was to **"Place the altar of burnt offering in front of the entrance"** to the tent of meeting (see the
comments at 27:1–8 and 38:1–7).

The seventh instruction was to **"place the basin between
the Tent of Meeting and the altar and put water in it."** (See the
comments at 30:17–21 and 38:8.) God's final instruction was to
"Set up the courtyard ... [and its entrance] curtain." (See the comments on the courtyard at 27:9–19 and 38:9–7.) See 27:16 and
38:18–19 for a description of the courtyard's entrance curtain.

40:9–16 / See (B) above. The Lord gave instructions to
**"anoint the tabernacle and everything in it . . . Aaron and his
sons."** (See the comments on the anointing oil at 30:23–25 and
37:29.) **Holy** means "set aside for a special purpose." (See the comments on the **sacred garments** at 28:1–43 and 39:1–31.) See 29:1–35
for a detailed description of the instructions for Aaron's full ordination. They carried out the full ordination of the priests later (see
Lev. 8:1–36). Numbers 7:1–10 describes the day of the dedication

of the altar. A single verse in Exodus 40 describes what Moses did: **Moses did everything just as the LORD commanded him** (v. 16).

This sevenfold refrain, "just as the LORD commanded," refers to the creation of Aaron's vestments in Exodus 39 and occurs again here in this summary statement (v. 16). (See the comments at 39:1–31.) In the next section the same refrain occurs again in seven more specific ways (vv. 17–33).

40:17–33 / See (A′) above. Moses assembled the tabernacle and arranged its furnishings. As Moses set up the tabernacle, each act was declared done **just as the LORD commanded.** Moses completed them in the exact order of the Lord's instructions in verses 1–8. The text repeats this positive declaration seven times (vv. 19, 21, 23, 25, 27, 29, 32), over against the apostasy of the golden calf betrayal. The people proved their willingness to continue being formed as the people of God by carefully obeying the words of the Lord.

Verse 18 reflects the merging of the importance of the tent of meeting with the whole tabernacle. It says **tabernacle** but means the tent (see also vv. 6, 18–19, 21, 34–35 and comments on v. 1 and 39:32).

The text notes brief, but important, information as Moses carried out the Lord's instructions. In verses 20–21 he placed **the Testimony** (the Ten Commandments on the stone tablets) **in the ark.** Moses then **brought the ark into the tabernacle and hung the shielding curtain** (*paroket hamasak,* or "shielding veil") **and shielded** (*sakak*) **the ark of the Testimony.** (See the comments on the veil at 26:1.) Verse 27 reports that Moses **burned incense** on the gold incense altar for the first time. (See the comments on this ordinance at 30:7–10.) Verse 29 says that Moses offered the first **offerings** on **the altar of burnt offering.** (See the comments on daily offerings at 29:38–43.) Verse 31 reports that Moses, Aaron, and Aaron's sons washed **their hands and feet** for the first time in the bronze basin. (See the comments on the washing ordinance at 30:19–21.) **Moses finished the work** when he **set up the courtyard** and **put up the curtain at the entrance.**

40:34–38 / **The glory of the LORD filled the tabernacle.** See comment on (B′) above. Moses and the people had done all they could do. The resolution of the book of Exodus comes in these last verses as the Lord's presence is visible once again, for the first time after the golden calf, in the newly created tabernacle.

> **Then the cloud covered the Tent of Meeting**
> *and the glory of the* LORD *filled the tabernacle.*
> **Moses could not enter the Tent of Meeting**
> **because the cloud had settled upon it,**
> *and the glory of the* LORD *filled the tabernacle.* (40:34–35)

The cloud, first seen in Exodus 13 at the sea, and last seen by the people on top of Mount Sinai in Exodus 24, settled into the midst of the camp. The verb "settled" (*shakan*) is from the same root as "tabernacle" (*mishkan*) and means "dwell," "abide," or "settle down." God had come to live among them. These last five verses mention the cloud, a sign of the Lord's abiding presence, six times. It was the primary visible sign of the Lord's glory (13:21–22; 14:19–24; 16:7–10; 24:16–18; 33:9–10, 22; 34:5; see the detailed comments on the glory of the Lord at 16:7).

Building this home together best expressed the reconciliation between the people and the Lord. God designed it and directed the construction through Moses. The people made and gave everything. The long detail and labor of Exodus 35–40 are best explained as a fitting response to the betrayal and rift of the golden calf. By building the tabernacle they participated in the restoration of hope. These chapters tell the truth about the dependence of love and reconciliation on mutual labor and attention to detail. The Lord met the excellent work of the people with approval, "moving into" their camp to "tabernacle" in their midst.

Moses could not enter the Tent of Meeting. Moses had to wait for an invitation to enter and speak with the Lord, as on the mountain (24:15–16). God gives this invitation in the first verse of Leviticus: "The LORD called to Moses and spoke to him from the Tent of Meeting" (Lev. 1:1; Cassuto, *Exodus,* p. 484). The conclusion to Exodus is key to understanding the context of the books of Leviticus and Numbers. They set up the tabernacle in the first month of the second year (vv. 2, 17). The Lord's "call" to Moses from the tent, which comes promptly in Leviticus 1:1, is the beginning of further Sinaitic Levitical legislation. We find a narrative account of Aaron's ordination and the death of his older two sons by fire in Leviticus 8–10. Numbers 1:1 begins with Moses and the Lord in the tent of meeting one month later. The legislation continues for another twenty days until Israel's leaving Mount Sinai is taken up in a longer narrative, "The cloud lifted . . . [and they] set out from . . . Sinai" (Num. 10:11).

The book of Exodus ends as the exit from Egypt had begun, with the visible cloud of the Lord's presence leading, protecting, and providing. Yahweh had been present to them, calling them out of bondage. God had built their trust by providing for their daily wilderness needs. God had given them a new life based on teaching just laws. God had judged sin. God had called them to remember their deliverance, to worship, to sacrifice, and to celebrate as a community in the Lord's presence. God had revealed the goodness of the name of Yahweh. God had forgiven and restored the people, even in their rebellion. Finally, the Lord was present in the midst of their encampment.

The book ends, then, with a new beginning. The last three verses look forward to **the travels of the Israelites.** The primary function of the cloud of the Lord's glory would be to guide them through the wilderness (Numbers; esp. Num. 9:15–23). It would guide them to the edge of the land of promise, as Moses summarizes in the book of Deuteronomy. More is at stake, however, than guidance. The Lord had been guiding them since the exit from Egypt. The more significant denouement that transformed human history was that God had begun to dwell on earth in the midst of one people. Once God had begun to transform one people, other cultures would begin to know the reality of the enduring presence of God.

Additional Notes §48

40:2 / The first day of the first month is New Year's Day in the spring month of Abib. Traditionally, this is the day of God's creation of the world. The beginning of the Lord's presence in the tabernacle was a new act of creation. The created world cannot be the same after the Creator takes up residence among the people.

40:16 / Moses anointed Aaron and his sons. The full consecration and ordination service, described in ch. 29, takes place later, in Lev. 8.

40:38 / **"During all their travels."** After the people entered Canaan, for more than 300 years the tabernacle was the primary place to meet the Lord. Their first camp was at Gilgal (Josh. 5:10). The tabernacle was at Shiloh for a time (Josh. 18:1; 19:51; 1 Sam. 1:24; Ps. 74:60). During the time of Samuel, the Philistines stole the ark but returned it because of all the trouble it caused (1 Sam. 4:10–6:21). The people guarded it at Kiriath Jearim for 20 years (1 Sam. 7:1–2). During Saul's reign it was at Nob (1 Sam. 21:4–9). Later tradition has it at Gibeon (1 Chr. 16:39; 21:29; 2 Chr. 1:3–6, 13). David brought the ark (and everything else) to Jerusalem (2 Sam. 6:17; 7:5–7). Solomon brought the ark, the tent of meeting, and its furnishings into his newly built temple (1 Kgs. 8:1–11).

For Further Reading

Commentaries on Exodus

Brueggemann, W. "Exodus." Pages 675–981 in vol. 1 of *The New Interpreter's Bible*. Edited by L. Keck et al. Nashville: Abingdon, 1994.

Cassuto, U. *A Commentary on the Book of Exodus*. Jerusalem: Magnes, 1971.

Childs, B. *The Book of Exodus*. OTL. Philadelphia: Westminster, 1974.

Durham, J. *Exodus*. WBC. Waco: Word, 1987.

Enns, P. *Exodus*. New International Version Application Commentary. Grand Rapids: Zondervan, 2000.

Fretheim, T. *Exodus*. Interpretation. Louisville: John Knox, 1991.

Greenberg, M. *Understanding Exodus*. New York: Behrman House, 1969.

Houtman, C. *Exodus*. Translated by J. Rebel and S. Woudstra. 3 vols. Kampen: Kok Publishers, 1993–99.

Hyatt, J. *Exodus*. NCB. London: Oliphants, 1971.

Jacob, B. *The Second Book of the Bible: Exodus*. Translated by W. Jacob. Hoboken: KTAV, 1992.

Leibowitz, N. *Studies in Shemot: The Book of Exodus*. Translated by A. Newman. Jerusalem: World Zionist Organization, 1976.

Meyers, C. *Exodus*. CBC. Cambridge: Cambridge University Press, 2005.

Noth, M. *Exodus: A Commentary*. OTL. Philadelphia: Westminster, 1962.

Plaut, W. G. and B. Bamberger. *The Torah: A Modern Commentary*. New York: Union of American Hebrew Congregations, 1981.

Sarna, N. "Exodus." Pages 316–572 in *Etz Hayim: Torah and Commentary*. Edited by D. Lieber. New York: Jewish Publication Society, 2001.

———. *Exodus*. Philadelphia: Jewish Publication Society, 1991.

Other Works

Aharoni, Y. "The Horned Altar at Beersheba." *BA* 37 (1974), pp. 2–6.

Alt, A. "The Origins of Israelite Law." Pages 79–132 in *Essays on Old Testament History and Religion*. Oxford: Blackwell, 1966.

———. "The Settlement of the Israelites in Palestine." Pages 133–69 in *Essays on Old Testament History and Religion*. Oxford: Blackwell, 1966.

Anderson, C. "The Eighth Commandment: A Way to King's 'Beloved Community'?" Pages 275–89 in *The Ten Commandments: The Reciprocity of Faithfulness*. Edited by W. Brown. Louisville: Westminster John Knox, 2004.

Barton, J. "The Work of Human Hands: Idolatry in the Old Testament." *ExAud* 15 (1999), pp. 63–72.

Belleville, L. "Tradition or Creation? Paul's Use of Exodus 34 Tradition in 2 Corinthians 3:7–18." Pages 165–86 in *Paul and the Scriptures of Israel*. Edited by C. A. Evans and J. A. Sanders. Sheffield: Sheffield Academic Press, 1993.

Berlin, A. "Introduction to Hebrew Poetry." Pages 301–15 in vol. 4 of *The New Interpreter's Bible*. Edited by L. Keck et al. Nashville: Abingdon, 1996.

Biran, A. "An Israelite Horned Altar at Dan." *BA* 37 (1974), pp. 106–7.

Bosman, H. "Adultery, Prophetic Tradition and the Decalogue." Pages 266–74 in *The Ten Commandments: The Reciprocity of Faithfulness*. Edited by W. Brown. Louisville: Westminster John Knox, 2004.

Bruckner, J. "Ethics." Pages 224–40 in *Dictionary of the Pentateuch*. Edited by T. D. Alexander and D. W. Baker. Downers Grove: InterVarsity, 2003.

———. "A Theological Description of Human Wholeness in Deuteronomy 6." *ExAud* 21 (2005), pp. 1–19.

———. *Implied Law in the Abraham Narrative*. JSOTSup 335. Sheffield: Sheffield Academic Press, 2001.

———. "Law Before Sinai: Law and Liberty in Pre-Sinai Narratives and Romans 7." *ExAud* 11(1995), pp. 91–110.

———. "On the One Hand . . . on the Other Hand: The Twofold Meaning of the Law against Covetousness." Pages 97–118 in *To Hear and Obey: Essays in Honor of Fredrick Carlson Holmgren*. Edited by B. Bergfalk and P. Koptak. Chicago: Covenant Publications, 1997.

Brueggemann, W. "Adjectives: Yahweh with Characteristic Markings." Pages 213–28 in *Old Testament Theology*. Minneapolis: Augsburg Fortress, 1997.

Childs, B. *Introduction to the Old Testament as Scripture*. Philadelphia: Fortress, 1979.

Clark, G. *The Word "Hesed" in the Hebrew Bible*. JSOTSup 157. Sheffield: Sheffield Academic Press, 1993.

Cone, J. *God of the Oppressed*. Maryknoll, N.Y.: Orbis, 1997.

Craig, K. *A Poetics of Jonah: Art in the Service of Ideology*. Columbia: University of South Carolina Press, 1993.

Croatto, J. *Exodus: A Hermeneutics of Freedom*. Maryknoll, N.Y.: Orbis, 1981.

Crüsemann, F. *The Torah: Theology and Social History of Old Testament Law*. Translated by A. Mahnke. Minneapolis: Fortress, 1996.

Daube, D. *The Exodus Pattern in the Bible*. London: Faber & Faber, 1963.

Davies, G. I. *The Way of the Wilderness: A Geographical Study of the Wilderness Itineraries in the Old Testament*. Cambridge: Cambridge University Press, 1979.

Davis, D. "Rebellion, Presence, and Covenant: A Study in Exodus 32–34." *WTJ* 44 (1982), pp. 71–87.

Dykstra, L. *Set Them Free: The Other Side of Exodus*. Maryknoll, N.Y.: Orbis, 2002.

Eichrodt, W. *Theology of the Old Testament*. OTL. Philadelphia: Westminster, 1967.

Enns, P. "Exodus Route and Wilderness Wandering." Pages 272–80 in *Dictionary of the Pentateuch*. Edited by T. D. Alexander and D. W. Baker. Downers Grove: InterVarsity, 2003.

Exum, J. C. "'You shall let every daughter live': A Study of Exodus 1:8–2:10." *Semeia* 28 (1983), pp. 63–82.

Felder, C. H., ed. *Stony the Road We Trod: African American Biblical Interpretation*. Minneapolis: Fortress, 1991.

Finkelstein, J. *The Ox that Gored*. Philadelphia: American Philosophical Society, 1981.

Fokkelman, J. "Exodus." Pages 56–65 in *Literary Guide to the Bible*. Edited by R. Alter and F. Kermode. Cambridge, Mass.: Harvard University Press, 1987.

Ford, D. *Self and Salvation: Being Transformed*. Cambridge Studies in Christian Doctrine. Cambridge: Cambridge University Press, 1999.

Frazer, J. "Folklore in the Old Testament." Pages 263–78 in *Myth, Legend, and Custom in the Old Testament*. Edited by T. H. Gaster. New York: Harper & Row, 1969.

Fretheim, T. "Because the Whole Earth is Mine: Theme and Narrative in Exodus." *Int* 50 (1996), pp. 229–39.

———. "Book of Exodus." Pages 249–58 in *Dictionary of the Pentateuch*. Edited by T. D. Alexander and D. W. Baker. Downers Grove: InterVarsity, 2003.

———. *The Suffering of God: An Old Testament Perspective*. OBT. Philadelphia: Fortress, 1984.

———. "Law in the Service of Life: A Dynamic Understanding of Law in Deuteronomy." Pages 183–200 in *A God So Near: Essays on Old Testament Theology in Honor of Patrick D. Miller*. Edited by B. Strawn and N. Bowen. Winona Lake: Eisenbrauns, 2003.

———. "The Plagues as Ecological Signs of Historical Disaster." *JBL* 110 (1991), pp. 385–96.

———. "The Reclamation of Creation: Redemption and Law in Exodus." *Int* 45 (1991), pp. 354–65.

Gemser, B. "The *Rîb* or Controversy-Pattern in Hebrew Mentality." Pages 120–37 in *Wisdom in Israel and the Ancient Near East*. VTSup 3. Edited by M. Noth and D. W. Thomas. Leiden: E. J. Brill, 1955.

Gerstenberger, E. ". . . (He/They) Shall Be Put to Death: Life-Preserving Divine Threats in Old Testament Law." *ExAud* 11 (1995), pp. 43–61.

Glueck, N. *Hesed in the Bible*. New York: KTAV, 1968.

Goldin, J. *The Song at the Sea*. New Haven: Yale University Press, 1971.

Goldman, S. *The Ten Commandments*. Chicago: The University of Chicago Press, 1956.

Gooding, D. *The Account of the Tabernacle*. Cambridge: Cambridge University Press, 1959.

Gottwald, N. *Tribes of Yahweh*. Maryknoll, N.Y.: Orbis, 1979.

Gutierrez, G. *A Theology of Liberation: History, Politics and Salvation*. Maryknoll, N.Y.: Orbis, 1973.

Hanson, P. "The Theological Significance of Contradiction within the Book of the Covenant." Pages 110–31 in *Canon and Authority: Essays in Old Testament Religion and Theology.* Edited by G. Coats and B. Long. Philadelphia: Fortress, 1977.

Haran, M. "The Nature of the *'ohel mo'edh* in Pentateuch Sources." *JSS* 5 (1960), pp. 50–55.

———. *Temples and Temple-Service in Ancient Israel: An Inquiry into the Character of Cult Phenomena and the Historical Setting of the Priestly School.* Oxford: Clarendon, 1978.

Harrelson, W. *The Ten Commandments and Human Rights.* Philadelphia: Fortress, 1980.

Heschel, A. "A Palace in Time." Pages 13–24 in *The Sabbath: Its Meaning for Modern Man.* New York: Farrar, Straus & Young, 1951. Reprinted in *The Ten Commandments: The Reciprocity of Faithfulness.* Pages 214–22. Edited by W. Brown. Louisville: Westminster John Knox, 2004.

———. *The Prophets.* Vol. 1. New York: Harper & Row, 1962.

Hooker, M. "The Johannine Prologue and the Messianic Secret." *NTS* 21 (1974), pp. 40–55.

Hort, G. "The Plagues of Egypt." *ZAW* 69 (1957), pp. 84–103.

Iersel, B. van, and A. Weiler, eds. *Exodus: A Lasting Paradigm.* Edinburgh: T&T Clark, 1987.

Kitchen, K. "The Exodus." Pages 700–08 in vol. 2 of *ABD.* Edited by D. N. Freedman. 6 vols. New York: Doubleday, 1992.

———. "From the Brickfields of Egypt." *TynBul* 27 (1976), pp. 136–47.

Knight, G. *Theology as Narration: A Commentary on the Book of Exodus.* Grand Rapids: Eerdmans, 1976.

Kohlenberger, J. R., III "The Use of Exodus 34:6–7 in the Scriptures." Pages 111–23 in *Jonah and Nahum.* Chicago: Moody, 1984.

Koptak, P. *Proverbs.* New International Version Application Commentary Series. Grand Rapids: Zondervan, 2003.

Levenson, J. *Creation and the Persistence of Evil.* San Francisco: Harper & Row, 1988.

Lindblom, J. "Lot-Casting in the Old Testament." *VT* 12 (1962), pp. 164–78.

Luther, M. *The Smaller Catechism.* Minneapolis: Augsburg, 1797.

McCarter, P., Jr. "Exodus." Pages 119–44 in *HBC.* Edited by J. L. Mays. San Francisco: HarperCollins, 1988.

Mendenhall, G. E. "The Hebrew Conquest of Palestine." *BA* 25 (1962), pp. 66–87.

Milgrom, J. *Leviticus 1–16.* AB. New York: Doubleday, 1991.

Miller, P., Jr. "The Place of the Decalogue in the Old Testament and Its Law." *Int* 43 (1989), pp. 229–42.

———. "The Human Sabbath: A Study in Deuteronomic Theology." *PSB* 6 (1985), pp. 81–97.

Moberly, R. W. L. *At the Mountain of God: Story and Theology in Exodus 32–34.* JSOTSup 22. Sheffield: Sheffield Academic Press, 1983.

Muilenburg, J. "A Liturgy on the Triumphs of Yahweh." Pages 238–50 in *Studia Biblica et Semitica*. Festschrift for T. C. Vriezen. Wageningen: H. Veenman & Zonen, 1966.

———. "The Form and Structure of the Covenantal Formulation." *VT* 9 (1959), pp. 347–65.

Niebuhr, R. *Pious and Secular America*. New York: Scribner, 1958.

Olson, D. "The Jagged Cliffs of Mount Sinai: A Theological Reading of the Book of the Covenant (Exod. 20:22–23:19)." *Int* 50 (1996), pp. 251–63.

Osborne, N., and H. Hatton. *A Handbook on Exodus*. New York: United Bible Societies, 1999.

Paul, Shalom M. *Studies in the Book of the Covenant in the Light of Cuneiform and Biblical Law*. Leiden: E. J. Brill, 1970.

Poythress, V. *The Shadow of Christ in the Law of Moses*. Phillipsburg: Presbyterian and Reformed, 1991.

Pritchard, J., ed. *Ancient Near Eastern Texts Relating to the Old Testament*. 3d ed. Princeton: Princeton University Press, 1992.

Rad, G. von. *The Problem of the Hexateuch and Other Essays*. Translated by E. W. T. Dicken. New York: McGraw Hill, 1966.

Rendsburg, G. "The Internal Consistency and Historical Reliability of the Biblical Genealogies." *VT* 40 (1990), pp. 185–206.

Rendtorff, R. *The Problem of the Process of the Transmission of the Pentateuch*. Translated by J. Scullion. JSOTSup 89. Sheffield: Sheffield Academic Press, 1990.

Roberts, J. D. *A Black Political Theology*. Philadelphia: Westminster, 1974.

Sakenfeld, K. *Faithfulness in Action: Loyalty in Biblical Perspective*. OBT. Philadelphia: Fortress, 1985.

Sarna, N. "Book of Exodus." Pages 689–700 in vol. 2 of *ABD*. Edited by D. N. Freedman. 6 vols. New York: Doubleday, 1992.

Simpson, G. "Thou Shalt Not Kill"-The First Commandment of the Just War Tradition." Pages 248–65 in *The Ten Commandments: The Reciprocity of Faithfulness*. Edited by W. Brown. Louisville: Westminster John Knox, 2004.

Sprinkle, J. *The Book of the Covenant: A Literary Approach*. JSOTSup 174. Sheffield: Sheffield Academic Press, 1994.

———. "The Interpretation of Exodus 21:22–25 (*Lex Talonis*) and Abortion." *WTJ* 55 (1993), pp. 233–53.

Sugirtharajah, R., ed. *Voices from the Margins: Interpreting the Bible in the Third World*. Maryknoll, N.Y.: Orbis, 1991.

Tigay, J. "Exodus." Pages 102–202 in *The Jewish Study Bible*. Edited by A. Berlin and M. Brettler. Oxford: Oxford University Press, 2004.

Trible, P. *God and the Rhetoric of Sexuality*. OBT. Philadelphia: Fortress, 1978.

Van Seters, J. *A Law Book for the Diaspora: Revision in the Study of the Covenant Code*. Oxford: Oxford University Press, 2003.

Waltke, K. "Palestinian Artifactual Evidence Supporting the Early Date of the Exodus." *BSac* 129 (1972), pp. 33–47.

Walton, J. "Exodus." Pages 77–119 in *IVP Bible Background Commentary*. Edited by J. Walton et al. Downers Grove: InterVarsity, 2000.

———. "Date of Exodus." Pages 258–72 in *Dictionary of the Pentateuch*. Edited by T. D. Alexander and D. W. Baker. Downers Grove: InterVarsity, 2003.

Walzer, M. *Exodus and Revolution*. New York: Basic, 1985.

Warrior, R. "A Native American Perspective: Canaanites, Cowboys, and Indians." Pages 287–95 in *Voices from the Margin: Interpreting the Bible in the Third World*. Edited by R. Sugirtharajah. Maryknoll, N.Y.: Orbis, 1991.

Wenham, G. "Pentateuchal Studies Today." *Them* 22 (1996), pp. 3–13.

Whybray, R. *Introduction to the Pentateuch*. Grand Rapids: Eerdmans, 1995.

Williams, R. J. *Hebrew Syntax: An Outline*. 2d ed. Toronto: University of Toronto Press, 1976.

Wilson, R. "The Hardening of Pharaoh's Heart." *CBQ* 41 (1979), pp. 18–36.

Wright, C. J. H. *Deuteronomy*. NIBC. Peabody, Mass.: Hendrickson, 1996.

Younger, K. L., Jr. "Early Israel in Recent Biblical Scholarship." Pages 176–206 in *The Face of Old Testament Studies: A Survey of Contemporary Approaches*. Edited by D. Baker and B. Arnold. Grand Rapids: Baker, 1999.

Subject Index

Abihu, 6, 224, 256, 260
Abraham, 5, 6, 19–21, 38, 40, 42, 56, 62, 68, 220, 295
Aharoni, Y., 254
alien, 35–36, 38, 113, 120, 164, 185, 196, 198, 213, 217–18
Alt, A., 16, 196
altar of burnt offering, 236, 238, 242, 254, 265–66, 271, 322, 328–29
altar, incense, 236–38, 241–43, 254, 269, 272, 320–21, 329
Amalekites, 145, 156–57, 159–61, 165
Amram, 27, 29, 67
Anderson, C., 196
angel of the LORD, 39–41, 133, 136, 220–21, 295, 326
anger, 52, 56, 157–58, 283–84, 300–303
animals, 86–93, 106, 110–13, 124–25, 185–86, 205–6, 210–17, 262–64
anointing oil, 238, 269–72, 320–21
ark, 154, 232, 236–44, 248–49, 319–21, 328–31
atonement, 240, 244, 248–49, 262, 264, 266–67, 269–70, 272, 289, 320–21

banner, 160–62
Barton, J., 187
basin, bronze, 252, 254, 269–70, 322–23
Belleville, L., 307
Bezalel, 273–76, 314, 316, 320
Biran, A., 254
blood, 50–51, 70–78, 109–14, 225–28, 251–52, 262–68
boils, 86, 88, 93
book of life, 292
borrowing, 210–11
Bosman, H., 196
bread of presence, 241–43, 248–49
breastpiece, 238, 255–57, 260
Bruckner, J., 147, 169, 179, 195–96, 276
Brueggemann, W., 4–5, 9, 17, 107, 142, 163, 170–71, 178, 182, 280, 303, 307, 319

calendar, 109, 218–19, 309–11
calf, golden, 277–94, 300, 303–7
Canaan, 21–22, 42–43, 125, 218
capital punishment, 202
Cassuto, U., 330
census, 269–70, 323
cherubim, 232, 237, 239–41, 244–46, 248–49, 320–21
Childs, B., 12, 102, 126, 230–31, 280, 291, 298
circumcision, 54, 107, 110, 120
cities of refuge, 188, 200
Clark, G., 307
cloud, pillar of, 128, 133–34, 150–51, 174–76, 220, 294, 330–31
Cone, J., 11
consecration, 124, 174–75, 177, 228–29, 262–67, 271
courts, 166–68, 191
courtyard, 230, 245, 250–54, 270, 322–24
covenant, book of the, 191, 194, 197–202, 203–29, 309–11
covet, 181, 187, 192–93, 196
Craig, K., 291
creation, 4, 20, 81–82, 85, 96–97, 132–33, 154, 180, 222, 231–32, 291–92, 307, 331
creator, 4, 50, 70, 75, 89–90, 96–97, 183–84, 274, 202
credo, 301, 307
Croatto, J., 11
crossing the Sea, 16, 70, 74, 76, 127, 128–36, 194
Crüsemann, F., 201
cry, 36–38, 106, 215

damage to property, 209–12
dancing, 28–83, 286
darkness, 98–103, 110
Daube, D., 107
Davies, G. I., 16
debt slavery, 107, 120, 190–91, 199, 204, 210
deliverance, 7, 33–34, 65–66, 70, 114, 135, 138–39, 220, 282–83

desert/wilderness, 34, 39, 110, 125–26, 173–74, 178, 305, 331
Durham, J., 4, 37, 44–45, 56, 75, 78, 91–92, 99, 103, 116–19, 130, 139, 146, 154, 168–69, 178, 219, 228, 231, 253, 274, 286, 298, 307–8, 313, 317, 321–24
dwelling presence, 239
Dykstra, L., 11–12, 16

Eichrodt, W., 230–31
elders, 45–50, 56, 113–14, 136–38, 174, 224–27
Eleazar, 67–68, 256, 260
Eliezer, 53, 164
Elisheba, 68, 260
emerging people of God, 5, 13, 19, 227, 249, 267, 275
Enns, P., 16, 29–30, 37, 48, 254, 298
ephod, 238, 255–57, 259, 264, 325
exit from Egypt, 5, 6, 10–11, 16, 107, 114, 117–18, 125–26, 128, 330–31
Exum, J. C., 29

face: God's face, 40, 295–97, 298; radiant face of Moses, 280, 311–13
faith, 38, 139, 183, 195, 278–79, 284, 301–5, 319
fear of the LORD, 22, 92, 93, 193–94
feast of booths, 219, 310
feast of unleavened bread, 102–3, 112–15, 122–24, 218–19, 309–11
feast of weeks, 219, 310
Felder, C. H., 17
Finkelstein, J., 208
fire, 39–40, 94, 125–26, 133, 210
firstborn, 53–54, 56, 71–72, 104–9, 122–27, 214
firstfruits, 219
flies, 71–72, 77, 82–85, 87–88
Fokkelman, J., 6
Ford, D., 298
forgiveness, 241, 258–59, 262–64, 278–80, 287–89, 300–308, 310–11, 314–15
Frazer, J., 260
Fretheim, T., 4, 17, 28–30, 37, 48, 56, 62, 66, 79, 97, 102, 105, 127, 161–62, 169, 173, 178, 180–81, 187, 201, 231–32, 234, 291, 295, 298
frogs, 71, 77, 79–82, 87–88

Gemser, B., 161
Gershom, 35–36, 53, 164
Gerstenberger, E., 202

glory of the LORD, 97, 150–51, 153, 154, 260, 301, 329–30
Glueck, N., 307
golden calf. *See* calf
Goldin, J., 140
Goldman, S., 187
Gooding, D., 317
Goshen, 24–25, 83, 85, 91
Gottwald, N., 16
Greenberg, M., 24

hail, 47, 60, 72, 77, 86–87, 89–94
Hanson, P., 201
Haran, M., 231, 244
hard heart, 4, 53, 73, 76, 89, 95–102, 107
Harrelson, W., 187
Heschel, A., 187, 215
Hittites, 42, 200–201, 220
Hivites, 42, 220
holiest place, 230, 236, 241–44, 248
holiness, 124, 153, 177, 179, 214, 239, 260–61, 268, 273–74
holy place, 236, 239–44, 246–49, 321
Hooker, M., 233, 307
hope, 6–7, 11–12, 16
Horeb, 39, 141, 158, 169, 178. *See also* Sinai
horns, 175, 251, 254, 264, 312–13
Hort, G., 78, 88
Houtman, C., 22, 30, 48, 56, 102, 201, 207
Hur, 159–60, 227
Hyatt, J., 121

idolatry, 182–83, 187, 283, 287, 290, 309–11, 320–21
Iersel, B. van, 17
images, 137–41, 182
incarnation of God, 14, 40, 56, 97, 226–27, 232–35, 241, 295
incense. *See* altar
Ithamar, 256, 260, 323

Jacob, B., 37, 110, 115, 235, 244, 250
Jebusites, 42, 220
Jesus, 14, 35, 38, 56, 103, 114–15, 179, 195, 228, 232–33, 259, 263, 268, 312
Jethro, 34, 37–38, 52, 163–69
Jochebed, 15, 26–27, 29
Joseph, 6, 19–21, 55, 99, 125, 126–27
Joshua, 16, 156, 159–61, 222–23, 227, 285

Kenites, 168–69
killing, 32–33, 37, 186–89
Kitchen, K., 15–16
Knight, G., 130
Kohlenberger, J. R., III, 307
Koptak, P., 196
Korah, 67–69

lampstand, 230, 236–38, 241–44, 249, 321
land, 19–20, 22, 42–43, 85, 123, 186, 220–23; of milk and honey, 42, 46, 123, 293
law, 5, 146–47, 169, 190–91, 195–23
Leibowitz, N., 32, 37
lending, 213–14
Levenson, J., 232
Levites, 27, 66–68, 124–25, 288–91
lice, 33, 81
life, 14, 78, 87–90, 106–7, 189, 204–6, 226, 270
Lindblom, J., 260
livestock, 86–88, 93, 310–11
locusts, 77, 92, 95, 97–102, 305
LORD. See name of God
love, 97, 183, 284, 301–5, 307
Luther, M., 179, 183, 185, 240

magic, 76–77, 80, 82, 212, 219
manna, 148, 150–54, 276, 315
manslaughter, 32, 188, 200. See also murder
Marah, 145–46, 150, 221
Massah and Meribah, 156–59
materials for the tabernacle, 232, 234, 236–39, 244, 318
McCarter, P., Jr., 78, 102
meat, 110, 114–16, 148, 150–51, 206–7, 222, 251–52, 254, 264–66, 268
Mendenhall, G. E., 16, 272
mercy seat. See atonement
messenger. See angel of the LORD
Midian, 26, 34–37, 52–53, 163–64
midwives, 22–23, 25, 93
Milgrom, J., 268
Miller, P., Jr., 183, 187
Miriam, 26–28, 137–38, 141–42
miracle, 47, 56, 87, 101, 105, 111, 132–34
Moberly, R. W. L., 280, 290
Muilenburg, J., 142, 171
murder, 31–32, 188, 195, 200, 204–7
music. See Song at the Sea

Nadab, 68, 224, 256, 260
name of God, 14, 44–45, 64–65, 68, 184–85, 297–98, 307
negligence, 188, 207, 209–12
neighbor, 47, 109, 191–93, 209–11
Niebuhr, R., 215
Nile, 23–24, 51, 76–78
Noth, M., 15

Oholiab, 249, 273–75, 316, 323
oil, lamp, 238, 253. See also anointing oil
Olson, D., 198, 201
Osborne, N., 260
ox, goring, 201, 206–8

parents, 181, 186–87, 204
Passover, 66, 68–69, 102–3, 108–16, 117, 119–21, 122–24, 127, 218–19
Paul, S. M., 201, 205
Pharaoh's daughter, 28–30
pillar of cloud. See cloud
pillar of fire. See fire
plagues. See blood, frogs, lice, flies, livestock, boils, hail, locusts, darkness, or firstborn
Plaut, W. G., 180, 243, 244, 250, 306
plunder, 104–5, 118, 282
pomegranate, 232, 257–58
poor, 11, 191–93, 196, 215, 216–18, 222
Poythress, V., 230
priesthood, 168–69, 179, 259, 260
Pritchard, J., 15
Puah. See midwives

Quail, 151, 154, 174
Quarrel, 156–58, 161, 166

Rad, G. von, 230–31
Rameses, 10, 21, 22, 24–25, 36, 118, 121, 125
Reed Sea/Red Sea, 100–101, 125, 127, 223
Rendsburg, G., 69
Rendtorff, R., 16
repentance, 280, 285, 287–88, 293–94, 297
Rephidim, 156, 166, 169
Reuel. See Jethro
robe, 255–60
Roberts, J. D., 11
rock, 156, 158, 169, 299
rod. See staff

Sabbath, 152–55, 185–87, 218, 273–76, 314–15
Sacrifice, 83–84, 114–15, 165–66, 262–63, 266–67
Sakenfeld, K., 307
Sarna, N., 7–8, 15, 68–69, 85, 115–16, 119, 141, 145, 162, 203, 207, 254, 265
seraphim, 133, 241
shining face of Moses. *See* face
Shiphrah. *See* midwives
signs, 49–51, 56, 74, 95–97, 126
Simpson, G., 195
sin, 148, 154, 178
Sinai, 10, 16, 39, 56, 144–81, 227–29, 301
skill of workers, 238, 246, 249, 273–74, 316
slavery, 12, 44, 121, 197–99, 281
Song at the Sea, 137–42
spices, 232, 238, 270–71
Sprinkle, J., 201, 203, 207–08, 214–17
staff, 49–53, 74–78, 132–34, 158
stealing, 181, 190–92, 196
stones, 230, 238, 255–57, 260
Sugirtharajah, R., 16–17
Sukkoth. *See* feast of booths
Sword, 58, 61, 133–34, 139

tabernacle, 227–41, 244, 245–50, 269–82, 314–19, 322–31
Ten Commandments, 180–96, 225, 227, 241, 275, 285–86, 309, 311–12
Tent of Meeting, 230, 233, 236–37, 244, 245–54, 294, 322–26, 328–31

theophany, 40–41, 136, 171, 295, 298
Tigay, J., 127, 216, 243, 299, 305
Trible, P., 307
tunic, 195, 255
turban, 255, 258, 261

Urim and Thummim, 255–57, 260

Van Seters, J., 201–2
violence, 22, 31–34, 203–5, 208

Waltke, K., 16
Walton, J., 16, 85
Walzer, M., 16
warrior, R., 12, 48, 222
water from the rock, 156–59
Wenham, G., 16
Whybray, R., 16
wilderness. *See* desert
Williams, D., 12
Williams, R. J., 178, 237
Wilson, R., 102
witness, 138–39, 163–65, 191–92
women at door of Tent of Meeting, 323–24
wood, 232, 238–40, 247–49
worship, 43–44, 71–72, 84, 89, 103, 170–72, 221, 254, 265, 309
Wright, C. J. H., 181–82, 186–87, 195–96

YHWH. *See* name of God
Younger, K. L., Jr., 16

Zipporah, 26, 35, 37, 52–56, 164

Scripture Index

OLD TESTAMENT

Genesis **1**, 6, 88, 132, 231–32; **1–2**, 231, 263; **1–2:3**, 326; **1:1**, 83; **1:2**, 77, 101, 132, 142, 231, 273, 276; **1:6**, 142; **1:7**, 132, 231; **1:9**, 132, 142; **1:16**, 231; **1:21**, 24, 75; **1:24**, 88; **1:25**, 231; **1:26**, 231; **1:28**, 6, 20, 326; **1:31**, 231, 302; **2–3**, 40; **2:1–2**, 273; **2:1–3**, 6; **2:2–3**, 155; **2:3**, 326; **2:3–4**, 231; **2:7**, 81; **2:15**, 22; **2:18**, 231; **2:19**, 301; **2:19b**, 250; **3**, 14–15, 92, 263, 289; **3:5–6**, 177; **3:6**, 192, 289; **3:12–13**, 289; **3:19**, 81; **3:21**, 231; **3:24**, 241; **4**, 251; **4:10–12**, 189; **6:14**, 27; **6:17**, 135–36; **7**, 20; **7:7**, 27; **8:17**, 24; **9:1**, 20; **9:6**, 189; **9:9**, 135–36; **12:3**, 173; **12:7**, 160–61; **12:17**, 104; **13:18**, 160–61; **15:2**, 64; **15:5**, 284; **15:13**, 6, 10, 21, 119; **15:14**, 47; **16:13**, 36–37, 295; **17**, 6; **17:1**, 64; **17:1–14**, 54; **17:2**, 20; **17:10–27**, 120; **18:1**, 64; **18:2**, 133, 295; **18:10**, 295; **18:13**, 295; **18:18**, 20; **18:18–19**, 191; **18:22**, 133; **18:23–24**, 94; **19:1**, 133, 295; **20:11**, 23; **22:11**, 40; **22:17**, 284; **22:18**, 173; **23:4**, 38; **25:2–4**, 34, 163; **25:21**, 64; **26:4**, 284; **26:8**, 290; **26:25**, 160–61; **26:28–30**, 226; **28:3**, 64; **28:14**, 20; **28:16**, 64; **28:16–22**, 223; **32:10**, 303; **32:28**, 19–20, 24; **32:31**, 295; **34:25–31**, 29; **34:30**, 67; **35:1**, 160–61; **35:9–15**, 20; **35:11**, 64; **35:11–12**, 21–22; **35:17**, 160–61; **35:23–26**, 20; **35:27**, 38; **36:16**, 159; **37–50**, 20; **39:9**, 189; **41:38**, 276; **41:42**, 238; **41:53–57**, 99; **43:32**, 84; **46:8**, 19; **46:8–27**, 20; **46:27**, 20; **46:28–34**, 83; **46:34**, 84; **47:5–6**, 8; **47:6**, 83; **47:11**, 8; **48:4**, 20; **49:5**, 67; **50:4–14**, 21; **50:24**, 19; **50:24–25**, 126; **50:25**, 6, 126; **50:26**, 21, 239

Exodus **1:1**, 6; **1:1–22**, 19–25; **1:6**, 6; **1:7**, 6; **1:11**, 10; **1:12**, 6; **1:14**, 8; **1:17**, 93; **1:20**, 6; **1:21**, 93; **2:1–10**, 22, 26–30; **2:11–25**, 31–38; **2:16**, 163; **2:18**, 39, 163; **2:24**, 6, 45, 74; **3:1**, 163; **3:1–22**, 39–48; **3:6**, 45, 74, 295; **3:7**, 4; **3:8**, 42, 123, 223; **3:12**, 56; **3:14**, 13, 14, 298; **3:15**, 45, 74, 123; **3:16**, 62, 127; **3:17**, 42, 223; **3:18**, 5; **3:20**, 56; **4:1–31**, 49–56; **4:5**, 45, 74; **4:22**, 5, 107, 140; **4:24**, 5, 22; **4:25**, 120; **4:31**, 48, 127; **5:1**, 5, 12, 48, 105; **5:1–6:1**, 57–63; **5:6**, 22; **5:7**, 8, 191; **5:13**, 8; **5:14**, 22, 58; **5:15**, 191; **6:1**, 103; **6:2**, 12, 63, 67; **6:2–30**, 64–69; **6:3**, 45, 74; **6:4**, 6; **6:6**, 5; **6:8**, 6, 45, 74; **6:23**, 260; **7:1–25**, 70–78; **7:3**, 56, 93; **7:7**, 27; **7:9**, 56; **7:14**, 93; **7:16**, 12; **7:17**, 4, 105; **7:19**, 8; **8:1**, 12, 105; **8:1–32**, 79–85; **8:10**, 4; **8:17**, 93; **8:19**, 56; **8:20**, 12, 105; **8:22**, 4; **8:23**, 6; **9:1**, 12, 105; **9:1–35**, 86–94; **9:7**, 93; **9:13**, 12, 105; **9:14**, 4, 165; **9:16**, 4, 13, 70; **9:20**, 135, 136; **9:29**, 4, 165; **10:1**, 56, 73, 93; **10:1–29**, 95–103; **10:2**, 4, 93; **10:3**, 12, 105; **10:9**, 103; **10:21**, 6; **10:29**, 105; **11:1**, 103; **11:1–10**, 104–7; **11:2**, 47, 107, 118; **11:4**, 105; **11:7**, 4; **11:9**, 56; **12:1–27**, 108–16; **12:13**, 56; **12:14**, 103; **12:27**, 93; **12:28–51**, 117–21; **12:37**, 10, 291, 324; **12:39**, 103; **12:40**, 6, 10, 21; **12:41**, 103; **12:43**, 6; **12:48**, 38; **13:1–22**, 122–27; **13:5**, 42, 223; **13:6**, 103; **13:8**, 93; **13:11**, 42, 223; **13:12**, 310; **13:18**, 10, 121, 129; **13:21**, 5, 6, 330; **14:1–31**, 6, 128–36; **14:4**, 4, 118; **14:16**, 142; **14:18**, 4; **14:19**, 6, 330; **14:20**, 101; **14:24**, 221; **14:31**, 93; **15–18**, 1; **15:1**, 5; **15:1–21**, 76, 128, 135, 137–43; **15:11**, 56; **15:16**, 184; **15:18**, 138; **15:20**, 5, 27; **15:22–27**, 144–47; **15:23**, 10; **16:1–36**, 148–55; **16:7**, 97, 296, 330; **16:23**, 276, 310, 315; **16:33**, 244; **17:1–16**, 156–62; **17:4**, 228; **17:6**, 169; **17:14**, 8; **18:1–27**, 163–69; **18:10**, 34; **18:12**, 169, 226, 242; **18:21**, 93; **19–24**, 1; **19:1**, 103; **19:1–25**, 170–79; **19:2**, 10, 169; **19:4**, 5, 13, 171; **19:6**, 179, 214, 228; **19:10**,

5; **19:12**, 276; **19:16**, 94; **19:18**, 94; **19:21**, 295; **20**, 276, 312; **20–23**, 71; **20:1**, 9, 13–14, 171; **20:1–12**, 180–87; **20:2**, 5; **20:4**, 310; **20:5**, 127, 307; **20:6**, 307; **20:7**, 44; **20:8**, 6, 155, 276, 310, 315; **20:10**, 202; **20:13–26**, 188–96; **20:17**, 202; **20:20**, 93, 136; **20:24**, 225; **20:26**, 259; **21:1–17**, 197–202; **21:2**, 155, 276, 310, 315; **21:12**, 32, 276; **21:14**, 276; **21:16**, 196; **21:17**, 212, 214, 276; **21:18–36**, 203–8; **21:20**, 202; **21:26**, 202; **21:28**, 201; **21:29**, 276; **21:32**, 202; **21:33**, 209; **22:1–31**, 209–15; **22:19**, 276; **22:20**, 291; **22:21**, 11, 15; **22:25**, 192–93; **23:1**, 192, 196, 215; **23:1–33**, 216–23; **23:2**, 161; **23:4**, 219; **23:6**, 196; **23:9**, 38; **23:10**, 215, 226; **23:11**, 155, 219, 276, 310, 315; **23:13**, 183; **23:14**, 310; **23:15**, 103, 109; **23:16**, 109; **23:23**, 12, 42, 223; **23:28**, 42, 223; **24–31**, 71; **24:1**, 260; **24:1–18**, 224–29; **24:4**, 8, 161, 228, 307; **24:9**, 56, 169, 260; **24:10**, 295; **24:11**, 169, 242, 295; **24:12**, 161, 311; **24:16**, 296, 330; **25**, 2, 14, 295; **25–31**, 2, 317; **25–40**, 17, 230–35; **25:1**, 276, 315, 325; **25:1–40**, 236–44; **25:2**, 234; **25:4**, 245, 257; **25:5**, 251; **25:8**, 231; **25:9**, 233; **25:10**, 320, 328; **25:17**, 320; **25:22**, 233, 328; **25:23**, 321, 328; **25:31**, 321, 328; **25:40**, 233; **26:1**, 315, 316, 319, 329; **26:1–37**, 245–50, 254; **26:15**, 319; **26:19**, 324; **26:31**, 316, 319, 328; **26:36**, 253, 259, 323, 328; **26:37**, 324; **27:1**, 322, 328; **27:1–21**, 251–54; **27:9**, 323, 328; **27:16**, 328; **27:20**, 244; **28:1**, 179, 225, 323; **28:1–43**, 68, 255–61, 328; **28:3**, 316; **28:6**, 255, 316, 325; **28:8**, 316; **28:9**, 316, 325; **28:15**, 325; **28:31**, 325; **28:36**, 271, 291, 325; **28:39**, 325; **29:1**, 328; **29:1–46**, 262–68, 291; **29:5**, 316; **29:10**, 254; **29:23**, 242; **29:27**, 316, 323; **29:38**, 254, 329; **29:42**, 233; **29:46**, 4; **30:1**, 244, 254, 321, 328; **30:1–38**, 269–72; **30:6**, 233; **30:7**, 329; **30:11**, 276, 323; **30:12**, 127; **30:17**, 276, 322, 328; **30:18**, 254; **30:19**, 329; **30:22**, 276, 316, 321; **30:23**, 328; **30:28**, 254; **30:34**, 276; **30:36**, 233; **31:1**, 231, 242, 276, 315, 316, 318, 319, 323, 326; **31:1–18**, 273–76; **31:12**, 6, 231, 276; **31:13**, 155, 176, 310, 315; **31:14**, 276, 315; **31:18**, 311, 323; **32–34**, 2, 69, 71, 228–

29, 233, 277–80; **32:1**, 317; **32:1–35**, 69, 136, 281–92; **32:4**, 233; **32:9**, 293; **32:10**, 298; **32:13**, 45, 74; **32:15**, 228, 311; **32:16**, 161; **32:22**, 289; **32:30**, 311; **32:32**, 161; **32:34**, 127; **33–34**, 62; **33:1**, 45, 74, 176; **33:1–23**, 293–99; **33:2**, 223; **33:3**, 42, 290, 311; **33:5**, 290; **33:7**, 236, 250, 326; **33:9**, 330; **33:11**, 40, 56, 176, 226; **33:12**, 302; **33:19**, 45; **33:20**, 226; **33:22**, 330; **33:34**, 306; **34**, 298, 312; **34:1**, 161; **34:1–9**, 300–308; **34:5**, 297, 330; **34:6**, 2, 4, 14, 183, 287, 289, 296, 298; **34:7**, 279; **34:9**, 290; **34:10**, 47, 56; **34:10–35**, 309–13; **34:11**, 42, 223; **34:12**, 315; **34:14**, 187; **34:17**, 183; **34:18**, 109; **34:21**, 155, 229; **34:22**, 109; **34:27**, 8, 161, 228; **35–39**, 317; **35–40**, 2, 71, 233, 300, 317; **35:1**, 6; **35:1–35**, 314–17; **35:2**, 155, 276, 310; **35:4**, 319; **35:10**, 326; **35:20**, 318; **35:22**, 323; **35:30**, 318; **35:31**, 276; **36:1**, 316, 317; **36:1–38**, 318–19; **36:2**, 316; **36:3**, 323; **36:3b**, 229; **36:8**, 316; **36:35**, 316, 328; **36:37**, 328; **37:1**, 328; **37:1–29**, 20–21; **37:10**, 328; **37:17**, 328; **37:25**, 328; **37:29**, 328; **38:1**, 328; **38:1–31**, 322–24; **38:8**, 328; **38:9**, 328; **38:18**, 328; **38:26**, 324; **39:1**, 328, 329; **39:1–43**, 325–26; **39:3**, 316; **39:30**, 291; **39:32**, 329; **40:1–38**, 229, 327–31; **40:2**, 231; **40:17**, 231

Leviticus **1:1**, 254, 330; **1:8**, 254; **1:11**, 254; **1:15**, 254; **3:1**, 165–66; **4:3–21**, 264; **4:27–35**, 264; **5:7–13**, 270; **6:3–5**, 184; **6:24–29**, 264; **7:11–17**, 114; **7:15**, 160–61; **7:28–36**, 265–66; **8**, 331; **8–9**, 259, 262; **8–10**, 260, 330; **8:1–36**, 328; **8:10–11**, 271; **8:30**, 228; **9:4–6**, 267; **9:23–24**, 267; **10:1–2**, 68, 260, 270; **10:3**, 291; **10:16–20**, 291; **13–14**, 50; **13:47–52**, 250; **15:16–18**, 175; **16**, 239, 244, 264; **16:11**, 240; **16:16**, 269; **17**, 189; **17:10–16**, 251; **17:11**, 189, 226; **17:14**, 226; **17:15**, 214; **18:1–30**, 190; **18:3–30**, 221; **18:20**, 189; **18:24–27**, 220–21; **19**, 189, 312; **19:3**, 186; **19:4**, 183; **19:11**, 192, 216; **19:11–12**, 191; **19:11–13**, 192; **19:12**, 184; **19:13–14**, 193; **19:15**, 189, 196; **19:15–16**, 191; **19:15–18**, 216; **19:16**, 192, 216; **19:16b–18**, 189; **19:26**, 183; **19:30**,

273; **19:33**, 38; **20:1–5**, 183; **20:6**, 183; **20:8**, 239, 261, 274; **20:9**, 186; **20:10**, 189; **20:10–23**, 190; **20:15–16**, 213; **20:27**, 183, 212; **20:31**, 183; **21:8**, 239, 261, 274; **21:15**, 274; **21:23**, 274; **22:9**, 261, 274; **22:16**, 261, 274; **22:27–28**, 219; **22:32**, 239, 261, 274; **23:1–44**, 218, 310; **23:3**, 186; **23:5–6**, 115; **23:16–20**, 219; **23:39**, 103; **23:42–43**, 219; **24:2–4**, 243, 253; **24:5–9**, 242; **24:6**, 242; **24:16**, 214; **24:17–22**, 205; **24:26**, 223; **25:1–7**, 186, 218; **25:2–7**, 222; **25:8–55**, 186; **25:9–10**, 175; **25:20–22**, 218; **25:23**, 222; **25:35**, 38; **25:35–38**, 213; **25:36–37**, 192–93; **25:39–55**, 199; **25:47–49**, 65; **25:53–55**, 199; **26:1**, 183; **26:2**, 186

Numbers **1:1**, 330; **1:2–3**, 270; **1:16**, 118–19; **1:50**, 323; **1:53**, 323; **3**, 68; **3:4**, 260; **3:11–13**, 124–25; **3:21–26**, 68; **3:32**, 68; **3:40–51**, 124–25; **4:3**, 322; **4:5**, 244; **4:7**, 242; **4:22**, 322; **4:29–33**, 323; **4:30**, 322; **5:16–22**, 286; **6:22–27**, 312; **7:1–10**, 328; **7:2–8**, 324; **7:8**, 323; **7:89**, 244; **9**, 114; **9:14**, 38; **9:15–23**, 331; **9:22**, 240; **10–11**, 6–7; **10–36**, 156; **10:11**, 6–7, 323, 330; **10:29**, 34, 37; **10:33**, 244; **11:7–8**, 153; **11:9**, 151; **11:12**, 140; **11:16–17**, 225; **11:24–25**, 225; **12**, 51; **12:2**, 141; **12:5**, 236; **12:7–8**, 295; **12:8**, 295, 299; **13:16**, 161; **13:23**, 258; **13:29**, 159; **14**, 34; **14:6**, 161; **14:18**, 7, 307; **14:18–23**, 305; **14:21**, 97; **14:30**, 161; **14:38**, 161; **14:44**, 244; **14:45**, 161; **15:32–36**, 186, 274, 315; **16**, 34, 68, 69, 134; **17:1–11**, 244; **17:8–10**, 78; **18:16**, 127; **19:17–22**, 228; **19:19**, 146–47; **20**, 156; **20:5**, 258; **20:11**, 37; **21:1**, 161; **21:4–9**, 70; **21:14**, 161; **21:23**, 161; **21:26**, 161; **21:33**, 161; **22:3**, 140; **24:2**, 276; **25**, 68; **25:1–8**, 70; **26:11**, 69; **26:59**, 26, 27; **27:18**, 161; **28:16–17**, 115; **28:26**, 219; **29:12–39**, 219; **31:5**, 126; **32:21**, 126; **32:27**, 126; **32:29–32**, 126; **35:10–15**, 200; **35:21**, 202; **35:22–28**, 200; **35:30–31**, 204; **35:30–34**, 188; **35:31**, 189, 207; **35:31–32**, 200; **35:33–34**, 189

Deuteronomy **1:9–18**, 168, 225; **1:30**, 138; **1:38**, 161; **3:18**, 126; **3:22**, 138;

4:9–12, 183; **4:13**, 181; **4:16**, 183; **4:23**, 183; **4:24**, 187; **4:25**, 183; **4:35**, 181; **4:37**, 181; **4:41–42**, 188; **4:41–43**, 200; **5**, 312; **5:7**, 181; **5:8–10**, 183; **5:9**, 187; **5:9–10**, 307; **5:11**, 184; **5:12–15**, 185; **5:15**, 7; **5:16**, 186; **5:17**, 188; **5:18**, 189; **5:19**, 190; **5:21**, 192; **5:20**, 191; **5:22**, 181; **5:23–28**, 194; **6:8**, 124; **6:13**, 184; **6:15**, 187; **6:20–25**, 180; **7:6**, 178, 260–61; **7:12–26**, 221; **7:15**, 146; **9:4–6**, 260–61; **9:10**, 181; **9:20**, 287; **9:26–29**, 284; **10:4–5**, 181; **10:8**, 244; **10:16**, 290; **10:18**, 38; **10:20**, 184; **11:18**, 124; **12:2–5**, 183; **12:3–4**, 221; **12:23**, 226; **12:27**, 165–66; **12:31**, 183, 221; **13**, 183; **13:1–18**, 182; **13:6–11**, 196; **14:2**, 178, 260–61; **14:21**, 219; **15:1–11**, 222; **15:1–18**, 186; **15:11–18**, 121, 199; **15:12–15**, 104–105, 118; **15:12–18**, 202, 222; **15:13**, 47; **15:15**, 7, 107; **16:1–8**, 115; **16:1–17**, 218, 310; **16:3**, 115; **16:7**, 115; **16:10**, 219; **16:11**, 218; **16:12**, 7; **16:14**, 218; **16:19**, 217; **16:22**, 223; **17:6**, 202; **18:1–8**, 291; **18:4**, 214; **18:9–12**, 221; **18:9–14**, 212; **18:10**, 183, 212; **18:15–22**, 194; **19:1–13**, 188; **19:8–10**, 200; **19:11–13**, 188; **19:15**, 202; **19:15–21**, 216; **19:16–21**, 191; **19:21**, 205; **20:1–18**, 188; **20:4**, 138; **21:1–9**, 189; **21:18–21**, 186, 201; **22:6–7**, 219; **22:11**, 250; **22:13–21**, 190; **22:22**, 189; **22:23–27**, 212; **22:23–29**, 190; **23:10–11**, 175; **23:17**, 324; **23:19–20**, 213; **24:7**, 196; **24:10–13**, 213; **24:12–13**, 214; **24:17**, 38; **24:18**, 7; **24:22**, 7; **25:17–18**, 160, 162; **26:1–11**, 219; **26:2**, 214; **26:5–9**, 7; **26:18–19**, 178; **26:19**, 260–61; **27:1–8**, 226; **27:5–6**, 195; **27:7**, 165–66; **27:15**, 183; **27:16**, 186; **27:20**, 186; **27:21**, 213; **27:25**, 217; **28:1–14**, 221; **31:9**, 244; **31:14–15**, 236; **31:25–26**, 244; **31:27**, 290; **32:10**, 178; **32:10b–11**, 172; **32:33**, 75–76; **32:39**, 146; **34:10**, 295

Joshua **2:9–11**, 140; **3:3**, 244; **4:16**, 244; **4:19**, 110; **5:8–11**, 110; **5:10**, 331; **5:12**, 154; **5:15**, 255; **8:30–31**, 195; **10:10–11**, 221; **10:14**, 138; **10:42**, 138; **18:1**, 331; **19:51**, 331; **20:3**, 188; **20:6**, 200; **22:1–34**, 68; **23:3**, 138; **23:10**, 138;

24:5–8, 7; **24:12**, 223; **24:14**, 7; **24:19**, 187; **24:25–27**, 226

Judges **4:4**, 141; **4:11**, 34; **5**, 142; **5:4–45**, 134; **5:20–21**, 134; **5:30**, 201; **6:13**, 47; **6:15**, 118–19; **6:22–23**, 226, 295; **6:24**, 194–95; **6:25–32**, 221; **11:34**, 142; **13:22**, 295; **21:19**, 103

1 Samuel **1:24**, 331; **2:22**, 324; **3:10**, 40; **4:4**, 241; **4:10–6:21**, 331; **7:1–2**, 331; **7:10**, 134, 221; **7:12**, 164; **10:10**, 276; **11:6**, 276; **14:15**, 221; **14:32–35**, 252; **14:35**, 194–95; **18:6**, 142; **19:20**, 276; **19:23**, 276; **21:3–6**, 242; **21:4–9**, 331; **23:6–12**, 257

2 Samuel **6:15**, 175; **6:17**, 331; **7:5–7**, 331; **7:14**, 104; **22:26–28**, 283; **24:1–2**, 270

1 Kings **1:50**, 200; **2:28**, 200; **6:1**, 16; **6:7**, 195; **6:23–24**, 320–21; **7:18–20**, 258; **7:48**, 242; **7:49**, 244; **8:1–11**, 331; **8:11**, 150; **12:26–33**, 290

2 Kings **5:2**, 201; **5:22–27**, 51; **12:10**, 239; **17:21**, 291; **22:14**, 141; **23:2**, 226; **25:17**, 258

1 Chronicles **4:43**, 160; **6:1–48**, 69; **16:39**, 331; **21:1–15**, 270; **21:29**, 331

2 Chronicles **1:3–6**, 331; **1:13**, 331; **2:17–18**, 270; **13:11**, 242; **15:1**, 276; **24:20**, 276; **26:16–21**, 51; **29:18**, 242; **30:8–9**, 7, 301–302; **30:9**, 307

Ezra **2:63**, 260

Nehemiah **2:1**, 109; **6:4**, 141; **7:65**, 260; **8:5–9**, 226; **9:9–21**, 7; **9:17**, 7, 302; **9:31**, 7, 302

Esther **2:5**, 62–63; **3:7**, 109

Job **7:12**, 75; **13:5**, 131; **26:12–13**, 143; **31:16–40**, 191; **33:4**, 276; **40:23**, 115

Psalms **5:8–10**, 192; **11:4**, 241; **14:1–2**, 283; **15:2–3**, 192; **17:15**, 299; **18:7**, 176; **18:9–13**, 126; **18:9–14**, 134; **18:10**, 241; **18:13**, 176; **19:1**, 154; **20:1**, 44;

20:5, 44; **22:1–5**, 106; **24**, 92; **25:10**, 303; **26:3**, 303; **27:1**, 90–91; **27:12–14**, 192; **29**, 154; **29:3–5**, 176; **34:20**, 121; **42**, 69; **44–49**, 69; **44:20**, 44; **46:1**, 164; **47:5**, 175; **50**, 192; **50:16–18**, 190; **50:19–22**, 192; **53:1–2**, 283; **60:4**, 161; **68:8**, 176; **69:28**, 292; **74:13**, 75; **74:13–14**, 143; **74:60**, 331; **77:16**, 143; **77:16–20**, 7; **77:19–20**, 143; **78**, 97, 102; **78:4**, 47; **78:9–16**, 7; **78:11**, 47; **78:24–25**, 153; **78:38–39**, 302; **80:1**, 241; **80:3**, 213; **80:7**, 312; **80:19**, 312; **81:1–16**, 7; **81:9–10**, 182; **84–85**, 69; **84:4**, 142; **86:5**, 7, 301; **86:15**, 7, 301; **87–88**, 69; **89:9–10**, 143; **89:14**, 241; **91:13**, 75–76; **93:2**, 241; **95:1–11**, 7; **95:7b–8**, 159; **97**, 154; **99:1**, 241; **103:8**, 7, 301, 303; **103:12**, 7, 301; **103:19**, 241; **104:1–4**, 231; **104:3**, 134; **104:25–26**, 143; **105**, 97, 102; **105:23–45**, 7; **106:6–33**, 7; **106:22**, 47; **106:30–31**, 68; **108:5**, 154; **111:2–9**, 45; **111:4**, 7, 307; **112:1–9**, 191; **114:1–7**, 143; **114:1–8**, 7; **115:1**, 303; **118:27**, 254; **119**, 303; **119:142**, 303; **119:151**, 303; **119:160**, 303; **123:1**, 241; **135:4**, 178; **136**, 303; **136:10–16**, 7; **145**, 301; **145:8–13**, 7, 301; **145:8–17**, 154; **148:7**, 75

Proverbs **4:1–27**, 187; **5:1–23**, 190; **6:23–35**, 190; **7:7–27**, 190; **10:1**, 187; **13:1**, 187; **15:5**, 187; **17:23**, 217; **19:18**, 187; **24:17**, 111; **25:21–22**, 217; **29:24**, 190; **30:9**, 190

Isaiah **1:2**, 305; **1:10–23**, 190; **1:11–17**, 184–85; **1:17**, 215; **1:28**, 305; **2:1–15**, 11; **5:23**, 217; **5:23–24**, 191; **6:1**, 241; **6:2**, 133, 241; **6:3b**, 154; **6:5**, 295; **8:22**, 101; **10:1–12**, 191; **11:15–16**, 11; **14:1**, 120; **16:5**, 303; **19:19**, 223; **24:17–20**, 221; **27:1**, 75; **28:2**, 94; **28:17**, 94; **30:7**, 143; **30:30–31**, 94; **31:5**, 112; **35:1–2**, 154; **35:1–10**, 11; **35:6–7**, 174; **40:3**, 11; **40:11**, 11; **41:17–18**, 174; **41:17–20**, 11; **42:8–17**, 184; **42:10–11**, 11; **43:1–3**, 7, 11; **43:9–10**, 7, 11; **43:16–21**, 7, 11; **43:19–21**, 174; **44:8–22**, 183; **44:9–20**, 290; **48:20–21**, 11; **48:21**, 174; **49:7–12**, 11; **49:22**, 161; **50:2**, 143; **51:9**, 75; **51:9–10**, 11, 143; **52:7–12**, 7, 11; **52:12**, 115; **53:4**, 305;

53:12, 305; **54:9–10**, 307; **55**, 32; **55:12–13**, 11; **56:3–8**, 120; **59:15b–16a**, 32; **61:4–7**, 179; **62:10–12**, 174; **63:11–16**, 11

Jeremiah **5:1**, 191; **5:26–28**, 191; **7:4**, 182; **7:5**, 215; **7:5–10**, 191; **7:8–11**, 182; **7:26**, 290; **17:21**, 274, 315; **17:23**, 290; **19:15**, 290; **22:3**, 215; **23:7–8**, 11; **23:10**, 190; **31:31–34**, 11; **46:7–8**, 142; **48:44**, 221; **51:34**, 75; **52:22–23**, 258

Lamentations **3:18**, 7; **3:22–23**, 307

Ezekiel **1:26–28**, 295; **8:12**, 283; **9:9**, 283; **10**, 240–41, 321; **10:14**, 240–41; **11:24**, 276; **13:11–13**, 94; **16:4–6**, 178; **18:10–13**, 190; **20:33–42**, 7; **27:7**, 238; **29:3**, 75–77, 142; **30:24**, 36; **32:2**, 75–76, 142; **38:22–23**, 94; **41:18–19**, 240–41

Hosea **1:10**, 75; **2:19–20**, 7, 307; **2:23**, 75; **4:1–3**, 191; **4:2**, 190; **8:1**, 305; **9:5**, 103; **11:1–9**, 278

Joel **2:2**, 101; **2:13**, 7, 302

Amos **2:8**, 214; **5:10–15**, 191; **5:21–24**, 185

Jonah **4:2**, 7, 302

Micah **4:1–5**, 11; **7:15**, 47; **7:18**, 7, 307

Nahum **1:2**, 187; **1:3**, 7, 307; **1:7**, 90–91

Habakkuk **3:4**, 312

Zephaniah **1:15**, 101

Haggai **2:17**, 94

Zechariah **1:14–16**, 184; **5:3–4**, 190; **8:23**, 179; **14:16–21**, 219

Malachi **2:16**, 190; **3:5**, 190; **3:16–18**, 292; **3:17**, 178

NEW TESTAMENT

Matthew **2**, 26; **3:16**, 276; **5:21–26**, 189; **5:27–32**, 190; **5:38–47**, 189; **5:39**, 208; **5:43–45**, 217; **10:8**, 319; **10:16**, 136; **11:12**, 177; **12:1–13**, 186; **14:22–34**, 143; **17:2–5**, 312; **19:3–9**, 190; **19:8**, 199; **25:32–46**, 191; **25:33–34**, 97; **25:41**, 97; **25:43–46**, 298; **26:17–19**, 114; **26:28**, 226; **28:20**, 136

Mark **1:5**, 8; **1:41**, 302; **2:23–3:5**, 186; **10:5**, 199; **10:17–22**, 193; **12:19**, 8; **14:12–16**, 114; **14:24**, 226

Luke **2:40**, 303; **4:1–13**, 161; **6:1–10**, 186; **6:27–38**, 217; **14:28**, 319; **20:28**, 8; **22:7–13**, 114; **24:49**, 136

John **1:14**, 14, 154, 233, 299, 307; **1:14–15a**, 233; **1:14–17**, 303; **1:14–18**, 232–33; **1:16**, 299; **1:18**, 233; **8:1–11**, 190; **8:58**, 14; **9**, 186; **19:14**, 114; **19:31–33**, 114; **19:36**, 121; **19:42**, 114

Acts **5:1–11**, 54–55; **7:17–44**, 17; **7:18**, 24; **7:23**, 31; **7:25**, 32; **13:47**, 179; **15:14–18**, 179; **15:28**, 168

Romans **2:5–8**, 303; **3:24**, 303; **3:25**, 321; **3:25–26**, 240; **3:31**, 195; **4:7–8**, 240; **4:16**, 303; **5:15–17**, 303; **6:4**, 134, 154; **6:10**, 263; **8:21–23**, 174; **8:22–23**, 176; **11:17–20**, 93; **13:14**, 240; **15:8–12**, 179

1 Corinthians **3:9**, 319; **4:7**, 319; **10:3–6**, 159; **10:26**, 92; **11:7**, 154; **11:25**, 226; **15:24–26**, 132; **15:39–45**, 154

2 Corinthians **3:16**, 312; **3:18**, 154, 312; **4:6**, 298–99, 312; **5:10**, 97; **8:7**, 319

Galatians **3:8–9**, 179; **3:27**, 240

Ephesians **2:19**, 38; **6:1–4**, 187

Philippians **1:6**, 285; **2:10–11**, 132; **4:3**, 292

Colossians **1:15–20**, 285; **2:12**, 134; **3:20–21**, 187

348

Exodus

Hebrews **2:17**, 259; **4:1–11**, 186; **4:15**, 259; **7–11**, 17; **7:27**, 263; **8:2–5**, 233; **9:4**, 78; **9:7**, 228; **9:11**, 233; **9:12**, 228, 263; **9:13–15**, 228; **9:19–22a**, 228; **9:26**, 263; **10:1–22**, 114–15; **10:10**, 263; **10:19**, 228; **10:22**, 228; **11:13**, 38; **13:11–12**, 228, 268

James **3:1–18**, 192; **4:11–12**, 192

1 Peter **2:5–9**, 179; **2:11–12**, 38; **3:10**, 192; **3:18**, 263

Revelation **3:5**, 292; **7:15**, 233; **19:11–16**, 290; **20:12–15**, 292; **21:3**, 233; **21:27**, 292